Muslim Preacher in the Modern World

Muslim Preacher in the Modern World

A Jordanian Case Study in Comparative Perspective

R I C H A R D   T .   A N T O U N

Princeton University Press
Princeton, New Jersey

Library of Congress Cataloging-in-Publication Data
Antoun, Richard T.
Muslim preacher in the modern world : a Jordanian
case study in comparative perspective / Richard T. Antoun.
p. cm. Bibliography: p. Includes index.
ISBN 0-691-09441-1 (alk. paper) ISBN 0-691-02847-8 (pbk.)
1. Preaching, Islamic. 2. Islam—Jordan.
3. Jordan—Religious life and customs. 4. Islamic sermons.
I. Title. BP184.25.A5 1989 297'.65—dc19 88-21482 CIP

Contents

v

Illustrations

Tables and Figures

ix

Key to Transliteration of Arabic Letters and Symbols

CONSONANTS

ا	a	د	d	ط	ṭ	م	m
ب	b	ذ	dh	ظ	TH	ن	n
ت	t	ر	r	ع	ʽ	ه	h
ث	th	ز	z	غ	gh	و	w
ج	j	س	s	ف	f	ى	y
ح	ḥ	ش	sh	ق	q		
خ	kh	ص	ṣ	ك	k		
		ض	ḍ	ل	l		

VOWELS

	short	long
◌َ	a	ā
◌ِ	i	ī
◌ُ	u	ū

OTHER SYMBOLS

◌ْ	indicated by the doubling of the letter
◌ّ	indicated by the doubling of the letter followed by a vowel
ء	indicated by '

The voiced velar stop characteristic of Transjordanian (but not classical) Arabic and pronounced as the "g" in the English word "goat" will be transliterated by the letter "g".

Key Arabic words frequently repeated in the course of the text will not be italicized and their long vowel marks will not be transliterated after first mention. Place names will be spelled according to the most common usage found on maps.

Preface

My interest in the Islamic sermon and the Muslim preacher began in November 1959 when I moved to the village of Kufr al-Ma, Jordan to undertake an ethnographic study that was to be the basis of my Ph.D. dissertation in anthropology for Harvard University. I became friends with the preacher, Shaykh Luqman,* a young man of thirty-two at the time, and subsequently listened to the sermons he delivered at the village mosque every Friday for a full year. In addition I met with him once a week to read the Quran. On six subsequent field work trips in 1965, 1966, 1967, 1979, 1984, and 1986, I listened to his sermons and observed his wider role in the community. I was fortunate that Luqman wrote out his sermons in longhand and delivered them from a text from which he departed occasionally to make extemporaneous remarks. When the subject of the sermon piqued my interest I was able, later in the week, to go to his home where he read the sermon for me as I typed up a transliterated version.

The Friday congregational sermon or *khutba* is a formal oral presentation delivered and subdivided according to set rules and interspersed with well-known prayer formulas, Quranic verses, and Traditions of the Prophet. But it is also an opportunity for selection and choice—selection of subject, and weighting of interpretive categories (theology, ethics, politics, and religious history). Perhaps more important, it is an opportunity for the preacher to articulate the formal religious message of Islam with the needs of the community, its problems, and its weltanschaung.

The author's modus operandi was to allow the content of each sermon to lead him in the direction of the analysis: for example, a sermon on kinship (chapter 4) to investigate the symbolic meaning of kin-based social relations and their articulation with other symbolic arenas in the community; sermons on work, magic, and education (chapter 5) to reflect on the potentiality of the Islamic sermon for modernization; sermons on the Meccan Pilgrimage (chapter 6) to pursue the meaning of pilgrimage multivocally within the Islamic tradition as well as cross-culturally; sermons, "lessons," and remarks about "factions" and "parties" to investigate a Muslim view of political parties and politics (chapter 7); and various sermons on the night journey and ascent of the Prophet,

---

* This name is a pseudonym, as are the names of many other villagers in this book.

Muhammad, to explore the possibilities of diverse interpretations of Muslim theology by different preachers (chapter 8).

The separate chapters of this book, then, are discrete essays that compose, if one may use a mixed but nevertheless appropriate metaphor, the single Muslim string of prayer beads. They unite in their variable presentation persistent themes regarding worship, social relations, ritual, style of life, kinship, and the changing modern world. While, therefore, most readers will probably feel more comfortable proceeding from the first chapter to the last in order (the first three essays are in some sense preparatory ethnographically and analytically for the others), they should feel free to examine each bead on the string in their own fashion and order, depending on personal interest and inclination.

More and more, as I continued to reflect upon this collection of sermons and upon other sermons that came to my attention, it became clear that they cross-cut the entire range of human concern from the most mundane (e.g., sexual intercourse, child-rearing, eating, entering a house, defecating, sitting down, walking, picking the teeth, working) to the most sublime (e.g., honor, death, learning, compassion, salvation). In what follows I have been able to describe only a small part of that panoramic concern, perhaps enough to disturb the stereotypes currently being trumpeted from the most elevated platforms by many Americans who see in Islam only violence and power or, contrarily, fatalism, and in any case not a genuine religion at all.

I would be very much remiss at this point if I did not thank all those individuals, institutions, and foundations who have helped and encouraged me in my research, though they are in no way responsible for my conclusions. A joint grant from the Department of Anthropology and the Middle East Center of Harvard University enabled me to undertake my initial research in Jordan, and a later grant from the Milton Fund allowed me to remain in the field for a full year. Later, a grant from the International Affairs Center at Indiana University covered my transportation costs to and from Jordan, and a grant from the Joint Committee on the Near and Middle East of the Social Science Research Council covered the expenses of field research. During part of this second period of research I served as Visiting Lecturer in the Department of Sociology and Anthropology and the Department of Cultural Studies of the American University of Beirut. The chairmen of these departments, Samir Khalaf and James Peet, extended to me their full cooperation in arranging my academic schedule so as to make my research trips possible. Still later a grant from the American Council of Learned Societies that supplemented two grants from the State University of New York Research Foundation enabled me to conduct comparative research in Iran.

Many of the sermons analyzed in this book were first discussed in a graduate seminar on the Social Organization of Tradition in Islam co-taught with my colleague, Akbar Muhammad, at the State University of New York at Binghamton in 1976. I wish to thank Professor Muhammad for affording me his insights on Islamic preaching traditions and for helping in the translation of some difficult passages. I also wish to thank Sohair Muhammad for transcribing and typing tapes of sermons. In 1977 I had the opportunity of presenting and discussing the sermons in an informal seminar on Islamic institutions held by Victor Turner at the University of Chicago. I wish to thank him and the students at both Binghamton and Chicago for their contributions. Although he has not read or specifically commented on this manuscript, I also wish to thank my friend and colleague, Fuad Khuri of the American University of Beirut, for the insights he has provided on Islamic institutions in our many conversations over the years. I also wish to thank Ralph Crow of the same university for calling to my attention the disparate content of urban and rural sermons.

Specific thanks is due to my friends and colleagues, those at other universities as well as those at the State University of New York at Binghamton for taking time out of busy schedules to read parts of the manuscript and to offer helpful comments and criticisms. In particular I wish to thank Jon Anderson, Bruce Borthwick, Jane Collins, John Esposito, James Fernandez, Michael Fischer, Patrick Gaffney, Catherine Lutz, Mary Hegland, Michael Horowitz, Jane McAuliffe, Michael Meeker, Alan Morinis, Henry Munson, Jr., Muneera Murdock, Judith Nagata, Manning Nash, David Powers, Khalil Semaan, James Toth, and Saral Waldorf. Dale Eickelman, Bruce Lawrence, Helen Rivlin, and Abd al-Aziz Sachedina read and commented on the entire manuscript and made many helpful suggestions about style and organization as well as analysis. I wish also to thank my brother-in-law, David Miller, for reading and commenting on chapter 3. All of the above helped to improve the manuscript but are not responsible for my interpretations and conclusions. I also wish to recognize the efforts of Peg Roe in typing numerous drafts of this manuscript, Stan Kauffman for preparation of figures, and Essa Al Sadi for photographs taken in Kufr al-Ma in 1987. I am also grateful to Gail Ullman, social science editor at Princeton University Press, and Maria Bulgarello, copy editor of this manuscript, for their guidance in improving it.

Finally, I wish to thank the Jordanians, too numerous to mention, particularly the people of Kufr al-Ma, who have received me with warmth and hospitality over these many years and all those who have tolerated with patience my interminable questioning and prying into every nook and cranny of their affairs. Special thanks are due to Shaykh Luqman

whose sermons inform this book. He received me warmly on every visit
and shared with me his understanding of Islam in an open and straightforward manner and without expectation of return. My debt to him and
his family cannot be repaid unless it be by the small contribution this
book might make to a better understanding of Islam.

Muslim Preacher in the Modern World

Introduction

This is a book about the Islamic sermon and the Muslim preacher, a book that explores the potentiality and diversity of the Muslim preaching tradition. It is also a book about the process by which religious beliefs, ritual norms, and ethics are transmitted selectively by knowledgeable religious specialists or culture brokers to the people of their communities. Such a study is as much concerned with the symbolic message of the sermon as it is with the articulation of that message with society, whether with kinship group, village community, State, or community of believers.

The aim of the study is threefold. The first aim is to document what scholars have referred to as "normative Islam," or "normal Islam."[1] Normative Islam refers to how Muslims are expected to, or ought to act and think. That is, it refers to prescriptions for believers in the areas of worship, social relations, daily transactions, and politics. This study examines the diversity of normative Islam with respect to a single preacher's sermons but also, to a lesser extent, between the sermons of different preachers in the same area. The first goal, then, is documentation and exemplification.

Documentation and exemplification are crucial at this stage in the relationship of Western, particularly North American and European, societies with the Muslim societies of Asia and Africa. Over the last fifteen years discussion of "Islamic revival," "Islamic resurgence," and "Islamic fundamentalism" has preoccupied scholars and diplomats, businessmen and journalists, military strategists and ordinary citizens. Unfortunately, the entire discussion within and outside academia has taken place, for the most part, in the absence of most of the vital evidence: the message of Islam as it is rendered every Friday in mosques throughout the Muslim world in milieus as varied as peasant villages, urban bidonvilles, prosperous suburbs, and Sufi convents. One cannot discuss intelligibly the resurgence of Islam toward the end of the century (or any other time, for that matter) unless one has some prior idea of the themes that have been propounded by the mainline carriers of religious tradition before that time. This book documents and exemplifies that tradition in one peasant village in Jordan in the 1960s, some time before the presumed Islamic resur-

---

1. See the discussion of "normal Islam" in relation to Abdul Hamid al Zein's "Beyond Ideology and Theology: The Search for the Anthropology of Islam" in the next chapter.

3

gence, in order to give interested parties some sense of what it is that is "resurgent."

Beginning with Geertz's classic *Religion of Java* (1960), many excellent studies of the Islamic religious tradition in its local environment have been written by anthropologists including, among others, *Saints of the Atlas* (Gellner 1969), *The Rope of God* (Siegel 1969), *The Hamadsha: A Study in Moroccan Ethnopsychiatry* (Crapanzano 1973), *Saint and Sufi in Modern Egypt* (Gilsenan 1973), *Moroccan Islam, Tradition and Society in Pilgrimage Center* (Eickelman 1976), *Iran from Religious Dispute to Revolution* (Fischer 1980), *Recognizing Islam* (Gilsenan 1982), *The House of Si Abd Allah* (Munson 1984), *Knowledge and Power in Morocco* (Eickelman 1985), and *Hindu Javanese: Tengger Tradition and Islam* (Hefner 1985). These authors have provided the interpretation of Islamic tradition in a wide variety of contexts including urban Sufi orders, legal and theological shrine centers, small market towns, mountain villages, coastal entrepots, and remote hinterlands. And they have dealt with a number of interesting themes: the psychological functions of shamanism, the adaptation of a mystic order in the bureaucratized environment of a centralized state, the study of religious discourse in a formal educational as opposed to a popular everyday context, the role of such discourse in revolution, the impact of historical change on religious roles, symbols, and ideologies, the reinterpretation of hinterland religious traditions against the background of a changing (money) economy, and the juxtaposition of Muslim world views taking into account differences of age, sex, education, occupation, and style of life. However, none of these studies has documented and exemplified the message of the single most important institution/role for the propagation of Islam historically and contemporaneously: the congregational sermon delivered in the Friday mosque by the Muslim preacher. That documentation and exemplification is the first goal of this book.

The second and related aim is processual and analytical—to analyze the process by which the Islamic message is handed down and interpreted by the culture broker (here the rural Muslim preacher) in his particular environment, the Jordanian village, and—to afford perspective—to compare that process, however briefly, with similar processes outside both Jordan and the Muslim world. That process is "the social organization of tradition" and involves the necessary selection from and interpretation of tradition. In several chapters, therefore, the focus will alternate between the Muslim preacher in Jordan and other culture brokers within and outside the Islamic tradition who must confront the same general problem: interpreting a message for a particular clientele (who interpret the message themselves as well as receive it) at the same time that they deal with overarching political and religious hierarchies whose norms and aims often differ from those of both the culture broker and his audience.

The study of the social organization of tradition or, as I prefer to call it, the accommodation of traditions, can be pursued from five perspectives: (1) from the perspective of the beliefs themselves or the text (here, the sermon); (2) from the perspective of the linker and interpreter (here, the preacher); (3) from the perspective of a cognitive system; (4) from the perspective of the social structure; and (5) from the perspective of the folk. The first perspective involves sorting out the elements in the text, noting the mix of little and great tradition elements, and analyzing the attempt to deal with behavioral and cognitive diversity through social processes such as accommodation, toleration, universalization, compartmentalization, and juxtaposition of elements.[2] It is obvious that for the scholar interested in the actor (preacher) as well as the cultural product (the sermon), the two perspectives blend in the analysis. Therefore, in a previous essay (Antoun 1968c), I focused on both perspectives, that of the linker and the text, in analyzing a sermon on violations of modesty by women and noted that such violations were classified as reprehensible (*munkarāt*) by the preacher who invoked Islamic law and ethics and vigorously and uncompromisingly condemned them.[3] Taking the text (sermon) as a point of departure as do many of the chapters in this book, involves simultaneously a third perspective, that of a cognitive system, broadly construed (in the instance mentioned above, modesty as the logic of protection and control). This third perspective, which involves the perspective of argument cumulatively pursued metaphorically and metonymically, is taken most explicitly in discussing kinship (chapter 4) although its parameters are introduced in analyzing the role of the preacher (chapter 3) and pursued again in a more analytical vein in comparing five sermons on the Prophet's night journey and ascent (chapter 8). The fourth perspective is that of the social structure in which beliefs, rituals, or eco-

2. The emphasis here is on dealing with and accommodating diversity and not on identifying and tracing the origins of cultural elements. Anthropologists such as Marriott have made some interesting attempts in this latter direction (see Marriott 1955). The present author is less sanguine than Marriott about the possibilities of tracing the particular origins of elements in traditions with a capital or small *t*.

3. At the same time, many violations of modesty were tolerated by him and by others on a day-to-day basis. The tacit assumption was that as long as the most elevated interpretation of law and ethics prevailed at the cognitive level, toleration of deviance at the behavioral level was permitted. This is in accordance with a view of the world as a laboratory in which the Islamic ethic in institutionalized settings (such as mosques, religious courts, and mystic orders) would constantly reduce the scope of unbelief and wrong action. See Richard T. Antoun, "On the Modesty of Women in Arab Muslim Villages: A Study in the Accommodation of Traditions," *American Anthropologist*, Vol. 70, No. 4, 1968c for details of this argument.

nomic dispositions are analyzed in relation to such contextual variables as age, sex, status, and kinship differences as well as implications for social control and politics. This perspective, although not the dominant one in the book, is important and recurring; it is taken up at the end of chapter 2 with respect to the peasant predicament, in chapter 4 with respect to kinship, in chapter 5 for economic activity, and in chapter 7 for politics and social control. The fifth perspective is the perspective of the folk, the perspective from the bottom up. Those who listen to the preacher are, after all, not simply passive receivers of a dogma as one scholar has suggested.[4] They themselves interpret, if only by giving more or less weight to various parts of the message, but also interpret by sometimes rejecting outright certain interpretations in favor of others. All five perspectives, then, are utilized in varying degrees in each chapter to study the process of the social organization of tradition.

If the first aim of this study is documentary and the second is analytical, the third aim is humanistic and experiential. The sermons recorded in this book are not only examples of guiding norms for Muslims in worship, social relations, and everyday transactions. They do not simply provide information for Muslims about prayer, fasting, and pilgrimage on the one hand and how to treat your neighbor, kinsman, and co-religionist on the other. These sermons also provide meaning at the deepest experiential level from the side of both intellect and emotions. The Quranic verses, Traditions of the Prophet, and prayer formulae that lace the sermons together "are" the ultimate reality for both the preacher and his listeners. As William A. Graham has pointed out (1985), the recited Quran (not its written form) is the closest approximation to the divine for the believing Muslim. Its character as the verbatim speech of God sets it apart: "Whereas the divine presence is manifest for Jews in the Law and for Christians in the person of Christ, it is in the Quran that Muslims directly encounter God."[5]

Quranic verses were meant to be recited aloud as attested to by the introduction of three hundred passages in the Quran by the word *Qul* ("recite"). Graham states that "to read the bare text one had to (already)

4. Gilles Kepel, in an otherwise rare and perceptive analysis of a sermon by the popular "free" (see chapter 3) preacher of Egypt, Shaykh Kishk, has taken this view. Shaykh Kishk's audience, as that of any other Muslim or non-Muslim preacher, has been regarded as passive and uninterpreting only because that audience has been ignored by scholars who failed to treat it with the same serious intent as the religious specialist. See Gilles Kepel, *Muslim Extremism in Egypt: The Prophet and the Pharaoh* (University of California Press, Berkeley, 1986), esp. 186.

5. Graham "*Qur'an* as Spoken Word: An Islamic Contribution to the Understanding of Scripture," in *Approaches to Islam in Religious Studies*, Richard C. Martin, editor (University of Arizona Press, Tucson, 1985), 29.

know it by heart."[6] Hodgson (1974 :367) has said that the Quran "was never designed to be read for information or even for inspiration, but to be recited as an act of commitment in worship" and Nelson (1985) has stressed that the professional Quranic reciters themselves aim to engage the heart to produce the various emotions that facilitate understanding and reflection upon particular Quranic verses.[7]

The Quran is recited outside the mosque in taxis, shops, homes, Sufi convents, and Husayniyyahs. It is recited on the occasions of mourning, burial, the birthday of the Prophet, and daily during the fast month of Ramadan. In addition, Quranic phrases accompany and often introduce or terminate the daily activities of eating, entering a house, leave-taking, sneezing, and undertaking a journey.

But the most regular and significant recitation of the Quran is on the occasion of the Friday congregational prayer service. Recitation precedes the Friday sermon and follows it, and the preacher punctuates his sermon with appropriate verses as does the worshiper in the culminating Friday congregational prayer. This experiential dimension of Quranic recitation in which, as Hodgson states (1974: 367), "the event of revelation was renewed" on every occasion of worship permeates the preacher's Friday sermon and has been therefore rendered in **boldface** type to bring it to the attention of the reader.

The sermon delivered and heard has a power rendered pale and second-hand in read sermon texts such as those included in this book. When the preacher describes the "womb" (kinship) in terms of "The Compassion-ate" in Traditions of the Prophet and his companions, when he declares that the heavens do not rain down gold and silver (and therefore that the believer must work for his daily bread), when he retraces the steps of Muhammad on his last pilgrimage to Mecca, the holy, and when he de-scribes the Prophet's night journey to Jerusalem and ascent through the seven heavens, he is affirming an ultimate reality, a faith-driven society, and a personal commitment.

Since the personal experiential component of Islam is conveyed in Tra-ditions of the Prophet (*hadith*) as well as the Quran, such Traditions are italicized in the sermon texts and excerpts. Despite the wide cultural gap between the reader of these sermon texts and the Muslim believer in the worship setting it is to be hoped that they convey, in however incomplete a manner, the feeling of Muslim preaching as well as its intellectual and ethical message, which are, in any event, inextricably tied together.

The stress on the experiential dimension of this study along with the

6. Ibid., 32, 34.
7. See Kristina Nelson *The Art of Reciting the Qur'an* (University of Texas Press, Austin, 1985), 87ff.

analytical may offend the social scientifically oriented reader. How utterly romantic, obtuse, and muddleheaded can a scholar be—suggesting that he can represent the experience of one's religion! Of course, faithful representation is impossible. In the discipline of anthropology, however, attempts to give some sense of the flesh-and-blood nature of other cultures has a solid basis in the work of one of its pioneers, Bronislaw Malinowski. Moreover, anthropologists have recently begun to recognize more clearly, reinforcing the tendencies in the work of Clifford Geertz and Victor Turner, the necessity of enriching normative, model, and system-oriented work with the texture of human experience. Lila Abu Lughod's discussion of the relationship of the existential situation of Bedouin women to their composition of poetry, Robert Hefner's attention to the impact of individual culture brokers and their distinctive family traditions of learning on the transmission of old and new intellectual technologies in Java, and Henry Munson, Jr.'s intimate study of the contrasting world views of a young modern Muslim woman and her first cousin, a middle-aged Muslim fundamentalist, all emphasize the necessity of taking account of individual experience (and not just the individual as an analytical category) in order to understand the complicated process of the interpretation and transmission of tradition.[8] Pierre Bourdieu has addressed the problem of the gap between analysis and experience from the analytical side, insisting on the complication of the analytical concepts with experience-oriented insights (e.g., distinguishing between "ordinary" and "extraordinary" marriages, "first-order" and "second-order" strategies, and calendars as opposed to "practical [islands of] time").[9]

The discussion and analysis of Shaykh Luqman's sermons (chapters 3, 4, 5, 6, 8) stand in their own right as an exemplification of one version of the Islamic preaching corpus and as an indication of its diversity and potentiality. But this study also aims to deal with *Luqman's* human situation as examined in the "peasant predicament" and the "social structural (village) predicament" (chapter 2), as well as his idiosyncratic life history (chapter 3). At the same time, the study calls attention to the cross-cultural character of the culture broker's predicament across a variety of religious traditions and locales (chapter 1). In so doing this study fulfills one of its primary aims: to describe a process analytically without dispensing with the individual and human dimensions that give it substance.[10]

8. See Abu Lughod 1986; Hefner 1985; and Munson 1984 for details.

9. See Bourdieu, *Outline of a Theory of Practice*, Richard Nice, translator (Cambridge University Press, Cambridge, 1982) for details of this argument.

10. Because of the humanistic and cross-cultural implications of this study and the hope that it will have value to more than a strictly academic audience I have, with rare exceptions, not italicized frequently mentioned foreign (mainly Arabic) terms after first mention.

I will now outline the particular circumstances which led to the present study. In 1959–1960 I began conducting research in the Jordanian village of Kufr al-Ma, a peasant community with a population of about two thousand Muslims. In view of the paucity of data on peasant societies in the Middle East, I determined to carry out an ethnographic study of the village. Part of that study involved the translation of sermons delivered by the village preacher every Friday as part of the congregational prayer service. I listened to well over sixty such sermons during that and subsequent field trips in 1965, 1966, and 1967, and recorded and translated twenty-seven. I found the preacher and the sermons extraordinary in a number of respects. The preacher had achieved his vocational status at the age of twenty-four only after a struggle with both his father and the village community, this in a thoroughly "Muslim" community; the preacher never had any formal training in Islamic law or ethics, but had learned Islam from a number of peripatetic preachers some of whom were hardly noted for their sophistication—this was, after all, an economic backwater of Transjordan. Yet when I left the village in 1967, the preacher had gathered a considerable library, including four commentaries of the Quran and the most sophisticated works of al-Ghazzali (the Muslim Aquinas).

The sermons, always effective and delivered in an evangelical style to a large congregation, ranged over a variety of topics, including ritual (the obligations of worship, such as prayer, fasting, and pilgrimage), theology (the meaning of judgment day), and religious history (e.g., Muhammad's prophetic career). But the great majority of sermons were ethical in intent—for example, how to treat one's wife, one's children, one's neighbors, one's kinsmen, and how to divide one's inheritance. The great majority of sermons were apolitical unlike the sermons given in large towns and cities where, for instance, pan-Arabism, the struggle for Palestine, and the struggle for Algeria loomed large. I have waited twenty years for the publication of comparative data so that I might place this particular preacher and his sermons in perspective. It has not been forthcoming. The reasons are not too difficult to infer. Muslims, no matter how educated or how secularized, find it difficult to describe and analyze what still has a powerful emotional appeal. Indeed, how many of us would be able to walk into our own church or synagogue and do so? And Westerners find it difficult to master the classical Arabic in which sermons are invariably delivered.

The in-depth study of the content of Islamic sermons and the role of the culture broker, the preacher, in selecting themes from the vast corpus of Islamic law and ethics—and he must select—will help fill a gap in the literature and at least form the beginning point for the study of process and constitute a baseline for comparative work in both time and space.

The study of the Islamic sermon is particularly instructive for the study of comparative religion and comparative social structure. Islam, unlike Christianity, has a focus on orthopraxy rather than orthodoxy. That is, Muslim law and ethics have direct and detailed applications for the minutiae of personal relations, and the orientation of religion is toward society rather than toward theology on the one hand or the State on the other. This conclusion is attested to by a number of facts. The Muslim calendar begins not with the birth of Muhammad, or the revelations of the divine message, but with the foundation of the Muslim community in Madina in 622. The term of reference for the religion is "Islam," referring to the society stamped by religion as well as to the religion itself. There is no word for orthodoxy in Islam, but orthopraxy (*sunna*), Muhammad's deeds and words, is a leading source of Islamic law and ethics, and its opposite, innovation (*bid'a*), is abhorred. Of the five so-called "pillars of the faith"—profession of faith, prayer, fasting, the giving of alms, and pilgrimage—only the first refers to belief; all the others refer to actions. The main charge of the Muslim ruler is to protect the law and to safeguard its implementation; otherwise, basically a laissez-faire view of the state is taken. The Quran, in fact, propounds ethics rather than law. Very few penalities for misdeeds are found in the Quran while there are many specific exhortations toward right conduct. Of the sermons I heard during the Friday congregational prayer service each week over the course of a year, two-thirds related to ethics. Finally, orthopraxy is institutionalized in the Friday sermon, the mystic brotherhood, and the Muslim court. The point is that the khuṭba in Islam is not a "sermon" as we understand it. Historically, from the beginning, the mosque was a community center in which a whole range of political, economic, and social problems were addressed, disputes mediated, advice sought, and vital information passed. That is, the sermon with all its symbolic richness as an exemplar of Muslim culture and history—Muhammad was the first Muslim preacher—cannot be considered apart from its social structural context and the vital changes stimulating or besetting the community.

Certain social scientists (e.g., Borthwick 1965) have argued that although the sermon has significance for such traditional themes as the propagation of nationalism, it has limited significance for the propagation of modernization. Other social scientists (e.g., Bloch 1975) have argued that as language becomes more formal and "restricted" it loses its capacity to deal with special problems. The Islamic sermon, to some extent, approximates such "restricted codes" and therefore can be used as a rough test of the hypothesis. The study of the Islamic sermon, then, will be significant for resolving some important questions currently being posed in some of the social and cultural sciences.

However, the main contribution of this study will be to provide documentation of the nature of the Islamic corpus, its degree of diversity, its flexibility with respect to current social issues and specific social structures or, given a more Machiavellian view, its capacity for manipulation, that is, its significance for social process. Given this general orientation, I follow the implications of each sermon selected, in the various directions indicated by its content (e.g., the rhetoric of religion, modernization, family ethics, education, attitude toward political parties or individual salvation). In the final chapter the processes of Islamization, Islamic resurgence, and reinterpretation of tradition will be discussed generally in terms of their significance for the modern world.

Although the bulk of the data included in this book is from my own field research in Jordan, it is my intention, as indicated by the first chapter, to be cross-cultural in perspective, drawing on examples from within as well as outside the Islamic world. This cross-cultural perspective is evident whether the focus is on a process (cultural brokerage), an institution (pilgrimage), a role (the preacher), or a broad interest area (politics). I have introduced data on culture brokers from Latin America and the Philippines, on preachers from the United States and England, on fundamentalism from Iran and West Virginia, and on pilgrimage from India and Iran. The aim in each instance is not to carry out a cross-cultural study in any formal sense but to illuminate by way of contrast the distinctive character of the institution or process being analyzed in its Muslim and/or Jordanian and/or peasant context. But a second and equally important aim is to remind the reader of the universal aspects of the process or interest area being discussed and the variety of responses/patterns possible.

At a number of points, particularly in chapters 1, 3, 4, 5, 7, and 9, questions are posed about the reinterpretation of tradition in relation to the transformation of society. It is no secret that the revolution in the oil-pricing system in 1973 had and has a powerful impact not only on the oil-producing countries of the Middle East but also on nonoil producers like Jordan, who sent large numbers of migrants, both white-collar and blue-collar, to work in the Arabian peninsula. Although we have raised questions along the way, particularly in chapters 4, 6, 7, and 9, concerning the relationship between socioeconomic change and cultural change, here religious change, few answers to such questions have been given in this book. This is by intent. The author has recently (1986) gathered considerable data on the impact of international migration and the pursuit of higher education abroad on this now substantially postpeasant community, and he intends to analyze that impact on the religious institution in a sequel to the present study. To read back these startling changes into the sermons of the 1960s, however, would be a major error of analysis. Although Jordan had undergone a variety of political and economic vicissitudes by the 1960s and Kufr al-Ma had been touched by most of them (see chapter 2), the moral economy of the village still reflected to a large degree a peasant and tribal culture with a focus on kinship and the guest house arena, and the sermons of the preacher reflected this fact (see chapter 4). The problem of the reinterpretation of tradition against the background of international migration and the transformation of rural society, a transformation which posed a challenge to a way of life based upon kinship and community ties, is quite another story still to be told.

The Social Organization of Tradition

In modern times Robert Redfield, M. N. Srinivas, and McKim Marriot were the first to write analytically about the process of "the social organization of tradition."[1] The social organization of tradition is the process of constant interchange of cultural materials necessarily involving choice and interpretation between the self-styled "learned" (but also so styled by the common people) men and women of a society and the great majority of people whom Redfield designated as "folk" in earlier works and "peasants" in later works.[2] This process usually involves some kind of accommodation between what the learned men ("literati" or "intelligensia" as Redfield called them[3]) would like to see done or believed and what the

1. See Redfield's *The Folk Culture of Yucatan* (1941); *The Primitive World and Its Transformations* (1953); and *Peasant Society and Culture* (1956); Srinivas's *Religion and Society Among the Coorgs of South India* (1952); and Marriot's "Little Communities in an Indigenous Civilization" (1955).

2. These two terms are sometimes used as synonyms in Redfield's works, and at other times they convey quite different meanings. Singer (1974) argues that Redfield's contrast of "folk" and "urban" in the *Folk Culture of Yucatan* relates to "structures of conventionalized meanings" in which "folk" cultures "are transformed by contact and communication with urban kinds of cultures." Redfield's central interest was "whether cultures differ as to degree to which the quality of organization is present and as to the nature of the connections among the elements." "Folk culture" is an "ideal type towards which a well organized culture tends." According to Singer, Redfield's folk-urban continuum concept was not a theory about borrowing or diffusion of discrete cultural traits. Rather, Redfield was concerned about the transformation of meaning structures and the acculturation of elements. See Singer, "Robert Redfield's Development of a Social Anthropology of Civilizations," in *American Anthropology, The Early Years*, John V. Murra, editor (West Publishing, Boston, 1974), esp. 224–29.

3. By "literati" Redfield meant that part of the elite in a complex society (i.e., after the urban revolution) who "are official carriers of the classical written tradition which provides the social system with a sophisticated and elaborate justification for its existence and continued survival" (Redfield 1956: 29). The literati consciously reflected upon and refined cultural materials having their origin in the traditional "folk" tradition, and they usually did so in an institutionalized setting (e.g., school, temple, cloister, guild). The "intelligensia" for Redfield were also culture brokers, intermediaries between local life and the wider life, sophisticates and interpreters who represented the powerful rather than the weak. But they were a modern version of such brokers, operating now as intermediaries for a "national" state, "national" church, and "national" school system (e.g., as mayors, doctors, school teachers, and engineers). Moreover, the cultures for which they mediated and on which they reflected were "heterogenetic" and intrusive rather than traditional and folk; they reflected the breakdown of local traditions and the development of mass culture through changes inspired by science, technology, free general education, mass production and organized consumption, and the mass media.

13

great majority of people regarded as proper in deed and word. Redfield argued specifically that peasants were men of the countryside rooted in villages who had to take account of the city—its power, its marketplace, its beliefs, its style of life—and the kind of people it produced, gentry or townsmen. Redfield, perhaps unfortunately, stressed acceptance on the part of the folk at least at a normative level[4] of a more "sophisticated" way of life and neglected investigating the numerous options and kinds of accommodation available to peasants including sheer juxtaposition of beliefs, revival, dissimulation, and outright defiance. Still, like most pioneers, Redfield's broadest formulations allowed and even pointed to the way for future analysis.

Although Redfield had designated the formalized, literate, and institutionalized views of the learned as the "great" tradition and the views of the folk as the "little" tradition, he defined the process of the social organization of tradition as a two-way flow of ideas. Srinivas and Marriot analyzed this two-way flow in terms of "parochialization" (by which ideas flowed from urban centers and were accepted and fixed in many "parochial" milieus [villages]) and "universalization,"[5] a flow of ideas from the villages and tribal encampments to the urban intellectual centers by which folk concepts were given the imprimatur of the sophisticates. Redfield's designations of the options of the folk, whether in terms of belief or action, resulted from his view that the transformation of "folk"[6] society was caused by the urban revolution which had marked the turning point of the human career and the development of "civilization"—with which peasants had to come to terms intellectually as well as politically and economically. The city and its elite exercised moral guidance as well as political domination.

If Redfield emphasized the gap between the great and little traditions—and, therefore, the necessity of the social organization of tradition and

4. A norm is a statement that can be elicited from an informant as to what behavior "ought" to be (or is expected to be) in any particular situation and in relation to any particular person. A normative level of analysis, therefore, stresses the ethical implications of action rather than cognitive, expressive, or statistical (incidence) aspects.

5. Actually, the terms *parochialization* and *universalization* were first used by Srinivas in 1952 and later elaborated and refined in an important essay by Marriott (1955).

6. For Redfield "folk" clearly did not mean "peasant," but rather prepeasant mainly tribal tradition. Redfield has been much criticized for his delineation of a folk-urban continuum, particularly in his 1941 work; for its evolutionary implications ("folk" are assumed at some point to become "urban"); for its implicit devaluation of folk tradition; and for its ahistorical view, particularly as applied to Latin America with its long colonial tradition. The weakness of Redfield's framework, although recognized and commented on in the last section of this chapter, is not the proper focus of this chapter or this book. Rather, it is its potentiality and refinement that is the focus. I have especially profited from discussions of Redfield's early Latin American work with my colleague, Jane Collins.

the accommodation of traditions[7]—he also emphasized (to the continuing good fortune of social anthropology and social anthropologists) the necessity of studying civilization from the bottom up. His interest in the "the little community" (1955) stemmed from his recognition of the importance of the study of simpler social units to facilitate the later study of the more complex; his recognition that most of the world still lived in peasant communities; and his view that the proper study of civilization—peasant villages were implicated in civilization as "part-societies" and "part-cultures"—was *in vivo*. That is, beliefs and actions ought to be analyzed in the flesh-and-blood context of family, work, neighborhood, and ceremonial life.[8]

Redfield's focus on the organization of "tradition" presumed a structure of tradition, what might perhaps be described today as "culture structure" (i.e., persisting forms of ideas and cultural products together with arrangements for transmitting them). By "culture" he meant an organized body of conventional understandings or, phrased another way, learned, historically derived behavior.

The "social organization of tradition" directly implied a focus on linking institutions and roles, on linking between the great and little traditions—schools, temples, mystic orders, dramatic companies, mandarins, priests, mayors, traders, preachers, dons, and singers. Redfield did not in fact carry out a detailed study of such linking institutions and seemed to be more interested in the products of culture—the beliefs and the particular patterns of their accommodation and incorporation—than in the culture brokers themselves and their exercise of choice in the social organization of tradition. Anthropologists who followed Redfield did focus on linking institutions as well as patterns of belief and considered a variety of interest areas, such as J. Bennett's *Northern Plainsmen* (commerce and agriculture), J. Peacock's *Rites of Modernization* (drama), and, most important, M. Singer's *When a Great Tradition Modernizes* (religion and industry).

There is no question that the linker must exercise choice or, from another perspective, management, or from still another, manipulation, in choosing which aspects from the vast corpus of a particular great tradition to emphasize. For instance, in the Islamic case in dealing with mar-

7. The phrase *accommodation of traditions* is my own characterization of the process and is used to stress the necessity to come to terms intellectually and/or by action with the discrepancy between traditions.

8. I wish to acknowledge insights gained by reading Singer's "Robert Redfield's Development of a Social Anthropology of Civilizations," in *American Anthropology, The Early Years* (1974). Singer was one of Redfield's students and later collaborators, and probably the most productive in carrying on the exploration of Redfield's ideas, particularly in *When a Great Tradition Modernizes* (1972).

riage the preacher can emphasize either the first or the second clause in the key Quranic phrase on polygyny:

Marry of the women who seem good to you, two or three or four; and if ye fear that ye cannot do justice (to so many) **then one** (only). (Surah 4, Verse 3, *P*)[9]

Emphasis on the first clause emphasizes permissiveness as to plural marriage; emphasis on the second stresses restriction and, by implication, supports monogamy.

The linker must also interpret local custom and take some stance with respect to its particular components. For instance, what attitude does a Muslim preacher take to the home-town magician and his magic—simple acceptance and juxtaposition with Islamic ethics, or toleration with condescension or reinterpretation and integration into that ethic, or outright condemnation?

A satisfactory study of the social organization of tradition must have a dual emphasis, then: an emphasis on the cultural product—the art form, the set of religious beliefs, the dramatic presentation, the sermon text, the implicit attitudes governing marketplace behavior—as well as on the interpreter of that cultural product—the linker, keeper of the culture, or culture broker as he is variously termed. The following study of the Islamic sermon and the Muslim preacher pursues this dual perspective throughout with various emphases in particular chapters. It differs somewhat from the above-mentioned works in probing into the social organization of tradition in an in-depth case study of a single linker in a particular village milieu in one country. Although this restricted canvas precludes the systematic generalizations that might be gained from a controlled comparison or a cross-cultural investigation, it illuminates the working out of the process in a more detailed manner than a strictly comparative study would have allowed.

Although it may seem strange to say so, three decades after Redfield's work, we still know very little about the process by which the great religious traditions are passed on to believers in their respective communities. Studies of church organization, sectarian and theological differences, and religious law and ethics are numerous, but studies about the relation-

---

9. In translating passages from the Quran, the author has referred to the following English translations: Arberry 1974; Pickthall 1959; Rodwell 1957; Sale 1888; and Yusuf Ali 1973. In each case the author has chosen the translation of the passage that he considers closest to the original Quranic passage in Arabic. The Arabic Quran used as reference and for numbering of all verses was published in Cairo under the supervision of Al-Aznar University in 1926. After each designation of Quranic sura (chapter) and verse, a capitalized letter appears standing for the translation used: *A* for Arberry, *P* for Pickthall, *R* for Rodwell, *S* for Sale, and *YA* for Yusuf Ali.

ship of popular religion to the religion of the specialists—priests, rabbis, ministers, and 'ulemā—are few. Although we know much about Christianity, Islam, and Judaism, we know relatively little about Christianization, Islamization, and Judaization. That relationship is mediated at the local level by a few key culture brokers such as parish priests, teachers, and jurisconsults. It is these figures who must accept, reject, reinterpret, or accommodate the diversity of local custom with the ordinances of religion, be they ritual, ethical, legal, or theological. How they do so remains obscure. Nowhere is this more the case than in the study of Islam.

The problem and the process is of wide scope in both time and space. Indeed, the social organization of tradition is a universal process found among all societies at all times once particular hinterland communities become linked to overarching political, economic, and religious structures and implicated in the concommitant processes of debt, politics, social control, and the quest for salvation. Therefore, the discussion that follows of culture brokers, the process of interpretation of tradition, and the constraints on that process exacted by the people of local communities, the state, and various hierarchies, will range cross-culturally and include examples from both the East and the West.

THE ACCOMMODATION OF TRADITIONS: PERSPECTIVES OF THE FOLK AND THE CULTURE BROKER

Although the accommodation of traditions involves a constant and two-way interchange of cultural materials, the process has to contend with the often wide gap between popular and elite (even hinterland-rooted local elite) beliefs and styles of life. For instance, when I asked the prayer leader and preacher of Kufr al-Ma what the justifications/inducements for polygynous marriage were, he stated that there were three: lack of male heirs (from the first wife), barrenness and menopause, and disease and constant sickliness of the first wife. When I asked the same question of peasants from the same village they gave four answers: the need for labor power, conspicuous display (horses and women constituted a man's pride and joy), the desire for progeny, and hedonism or, as they put it, "the love of buttocks." The preacher and the peasants shared only one inducement/justification, the desire for progeny.

Four examples, three from the United States and one from Jordan, illuminate the problem of the gap between great and little traditions and the necessity but also the difficulty of culture brokers bridging that gap. In the United States, discussion of religious or political great traditions or of religious little traditions and their relations with the political great tradition (that of the central government) must occur within the framework of a gradually developing pluralistic society in the nineteenth and twen-

tieth centuries, a society in which pluralism is mediated by law and con-
stitutionally mandated in provisions for sectarian tolerance/separation of
church and state. Such a society managed the gap between traditions and
perhaps narrowed that gap somewhat in the process of assimilation, but
it nowhere abolished it. Indeed, daily newspaper reports in all parts of the
country in the last quarter of the twentieth century document the existence of that gap.

Sometimes the gap between great and little traditions may have a quite
explicit spatial dimension. In Minneapolis it was reported that Roman
Catholic opposition to adding an abortion clinic in the administrative offices of the Planned Parenthood Association of Minnesota had aroused
vigorous protests. The newspaper report (*New York Times*, November
1976) stated that the plan to add a clinic "to terminate pregnancies in the
first trimester" instigated picketing, stone-throwing, and graffiti on the
walls of the administrative center. The protesters argued that residents
have the right to decide how land in their neighborhood should be used.
Said one protester, "I wouldn't care if it were in another section. I
wouldn't picket there. We don't want the clinic in our neighborhood
where our children will be exposed to it."[10] Here, the gap between the
national political and legal tradition (supporting abortion) and another
great tradition, Roman Catholicism, is expressed in the demand for local
spatial autonomy, that is, as a demand for the respect of a "little" tradition.

In 1969, another and perhaps more clear-cut instance of the gap between the state political and here, specifically administrative tradition,
and a little religious tradition is the case of the Old Order Amish in southern Indiana.[11] Indiana state law required the display of a triangular, red
and orange emblem on all slow-moving vehicles. This law was applied to
the buggies and wagons of the Old Order Amish. Many of them construed the red and orange reflector as a violation of their religious principles (the living of a simple life as Jesus Christ had led) and as representing the "mark of the beast" or "the sign of the devil" as maintained in the
Book of Revelation (displaying the sign was interpreted as worshiping the
devil and leading to damnation). In September of that year eight men
were arrested for refusing to display the sign, and sixteen families were
considering moving to another state such as Ohio where their religious
beliefs would not conflict with state law. Over several months the Amish
always chose imprisonment for twenty days rather than payment of the
fine since they construed the latter as admission of guilt. Early in Decem-

10. As reported in the *New York Times*, November 15, 1976.
11. The following references are from newspaper reports in the *Louisville Courier Journal*
for September 28 and December 3, 6, and 9, 1969, and from the *New York Times*, July 3,
1984.

ber, two Amish families left for Tennessee by boxcar. Their neighbors said that they were sorry to see them go since they were good farmers and provided employment for the non-Amish population in the district. A year before, fifty-one Amish had boarded a flight at Louisville for South America where they planned to resettle.

The former governor, Roger Branagin, who had introduced the emblem law had relaxed its enforcement, but the new governor, Edgar Whitcomb, proceeded to enforce it in July 1969. The Amish had indicated they would be willing to display an alternate (gray and white) emblem such as one used in Ohio. The American Civil Liberties Union suggested that the impasse could be resolved by an administrative ruling allowing an alternate emblem to be used. On December 6 Governor Whitcomb indicated he would support a change in the application of the emblem law that would alter the sign to make it acceptable to the Amish. The Indiana General Assembly had legislated the use of an emblem but left its shape and color to be determined by the Director of the Office of Traffic Safety. The Amish case illustrates the option of defiance by members of a local community; those who refused to compromise their religious principles went to jail or migrated. It also illustrated a possible accommodation when state law conflicts with religious beliefs—the exercise of adminstrative judgment to reconcile the two.

That this conflict between a religious little tradition and a political great tradition is not ephemeral is attested to by the fact that in July of 1984 Old Order Amish of New York were arrested for refusing to display the emblem for slow-moving vehicles. This time an administrative accommodation was worked out to deal with both the violation and the jail sentence. The Amish agreed to use gray, not orange, reflector tape, to hug the right side of the road, to stay off the roads at night and, if that was not possible, to mount a kerosene lantern with a red lens on the rear of their buggies. An ingenious administrative accommodation was worked out to deal with the jail sentence (of five days):

> The sheriff brought the Amish to jail shortly before midnight on a Thursday. All prisoners are automatically granted two days off their sentence for good behavior. And since prisoners who are to be released on weekends must be freed on the Friday before a weekend, the sheriff released the Amish in the early hours Friday morning. A five-day jail sentence was thus collapsed into but a few hours.[12]

The contrast between the long conflict between the Amish and the State of Indiana and the "short and sweet" conflict between the Amish and the State of New York reflects, among other things, a different capacity in the critical skill of culture brokerage.

12. *New York Times*, July 3, 1984.

A more dramatic example of defiance by the upholders of a little tradition against a great cultural tradition and its political allies is the West Virginia textbook case. According to a correspondent for the *New York Times* (October 1974), the opposition of parents in Kanawha County, West Virginia in the heart of the Appalachian coal fields to the introduction of certain textbooks by various school boards (actually, 325 books out of 96,000 volumes paid for by the school boards) took on such forms as prayer rallies, picketing, cursing from the pulpit of school board members, beating of newsmen, and attempted dynamiting of schools.[13] This reaction indicated that something much more important than the introduction of textbooks was at stake. The city editor of one Charleston newspaper stated that "the books were only a symbol that many of the protesters are demonstrating against a changing world: short skirts, long hair, civil rights, nudity, dirty movies."[14]

Of course, the gap here is not between an illiterate peasantry and an urban intelligensia since the parents who protested presented a fundamentalist bill of particulars against the textbooks; they were part of a fundamentalist tradition and were led by fully literate Protestant ministers and, to some extent, by professionals. Nevertheless, the gap of sophistication and power, as viewed from the local elite's perspective, remained and is probably responsible for the fact that the people who objected to the books were brushed aside. The six minority members of an eighteen-member citizens' panel set up to examine the books, quit, complaining of "pressures and ridicule" from the majority on the panel. Moreover, the opposition often took the form of community opposition to the cultural domination by a local elite (the school board) whose values were regarded as alien. Posters such as "Out with the Books," "Out with the Devil," "We're as smart as you are," and "Reds run our schools," appeared among the demonstrators. One textbook asked students to consider six theories on the origin of language, one of which was that a universal language was a "divine gift" to Adam and Eve as asserted in Genesis, and that God later withdrew the gift at the Tower of Babel, punishing man by creating many different tongues. A computer executive who was one of the antitextbook book reviewers and who quit the citizens' panel stated, "Any student of the seventh grade level would have to find that the divine gift theory comes off as just one of several ideas, and on very shaky ground."[15] Many of the textbooks struck directly at the

---

13. The following references are from the report of *New York Times* correspondent, Ben A. Franklin, entitled "Textbook Dispute Has Many Causes," *New York Times*, October 14, 1974.

14. Ibid.

15. Ibid.

literal interpretation of the Bible—a basic belief of the conservative Pentacostal churches of Appalachia.

But the cultural gap was not strictly a religious one. In this overwhelmingly white area parents were disturbed that textbooks depicted nearly as many black children as whites in illustrations—and they were living next door and playing together; excerpts from violent antiwhite writing by black revolutionaries such as George Jackson, Eldridge Cleaver, and Malcolm X in high school texts were condemned. Perhaps the strongest objections were to writings questioning patriotic values, in particular, antiwar poems ridiculing loyalty to the nation and endorsing draft-card burning and draft evasion—this in West Virginia "which has consistently sent the highest number of enlistees into combat in every war since World War I and has suffered more casualities than any other state in proportion to its population."[16] In a part of the state where war resistance and draft-card burning were taboo, the following poem appeared in a textbook:

> I did not want to go.
> They inducted me.
> I did not want to die.
> They called me yellow.
> I tried to run away.
> They court-martialed me.
> I did not shoot.
> They said I had no guts.
> They ordered the attack.
> A shrapnel tore my guts.
>
> . . . .
>
> They crossed out my name and buried me under a cross.
> They made a speech in my home town.
> I was unable to call them liars.
> They said I gave my life.
> I had struggled to keep it.

The antitextbook protesters, then, were protesting against a range of beliefs, values, and life-styles that violated their own: civil rights (construed as "nigger rule"), a multi-ethnic society, immodesty in dress, personal conduct, and popular entertainment, the ridicule of patriotism, the belief in evolution, and, as the symbol of all the above, the scornful laughter that greeted their own views by the elites that ran their schools. That the gap was wide was attested to by the views of the majorities in the school boards who consistently out-voted (and ignored) the minority. They found the disputed books, as one member put it, "delightful, delect-

16. Ibid.

able, delicious," and "the best reading I've done in years." Although other options were available to both sides, such as acceptance of the rules but manipulation of them, juxtaposition of elements, dissimulation, compartmentalization, and reinterpretation, at this point in the history of Kanawha County the accommodation of traditions and the emergence of culture brokers to manage it was conspicuously absent.

To place the last three examples of the social organization of tradition, or more accurately, examples of difficulty in organizing such a tradition, in context, one has to remember that the dominant U.S. religious tradition of the nineteenth century has broken down. Henry F. May has characterized this tradition as "Progressive, Patriotic, Protestantism."[17] This tradition was not defined denominationally, that is, it was not defined wholly or perhaps mainly by what went on in the churches. However, it did include religious elements of revivalism—evangelism (an intense emotional response to the religious message), millennialism (belief in the end of the world and a following reign of peace), and perfectionism (a belief that the soul after conversion can grow in grace till free from sin). In including such elements, this tradition developed a theodicy, a vindication of God's justice. But these elements and this theodicy were projected onto a secular, national, and political stage.

Belief in secular progress was wedded to the view that it was America's God-given manifest destiny to expand territorially and grow demographically and economically. Peculiar American institutions such as the free school, the Christian mission, and representative government were established by divine providence. Protestantism's salvation by faith and belief in the open Bible and the priesthood of all believers found an extension and parallel in the belief that American democracy was capable of perfection and, indeed, part of the divine plan. May argues convincingly that the dominant preachers of this national faith were statesmen such as Theodore Roosevelt and Woodrow Wilson (the son of a minister) and not ministers in the churches.[18]

With the failure to make the world safe for democracy, the disaggregation of the national religion proceeded apace, such that the reaction to the depression of the 1930s, the New Deal, May notes, was "the most secular movement of reform in American history."[19] Thereafter, Catholics and Jews "refused, any longer, to accept associate membership in American national religion," liberals regarded it as racially, religiously, and nationally arrogant, and the working classes were drawn to personal

17. See May's perceptive essay, "The Religion of the Republic," in *Ideas, Faiths and Feelings: Essays in American Intellectual and Religious History* (Oxford University Press, Oxford, 1983).
18. Ibid., 177–80.
19. Ibid., 180.

piety in either ecstatic (e.g., Pentecostal) or fundamentalist forms.[20] The anti-abortion movement in Minneapolis, the administrative constraints applied against the Indiana Amish, and the West Virginia textbook protest are all indicators that "Progressive Patriotic Protestantism" has broken down as a national religion and furthermore, that other claimants are in the field, some powerful, but none of which has yet given any clear indication of asserting dominance. Of course, one of these claimants, the religious and political right (popularly known as the "Moral Majority") espouses a religion basically quite different in its view of theodicy than Progressive Patriotic Protestantism: "America, instead of leading the world in an inevitable march toward a better future, must hold the line against powerful and evil forces. Instead of spreading the message of progress it must reassert ancient values [such as retaliation] which have been widely forgotten."[21]

The social organization of tradition in a society where national consensus over important elements of world view and ethos have dissolved clearly places extraordinary pressures on the capacity of culture brokers to ply their profession.

The social organization of tradition in Jordan, unlike the United States, occurs in a society where religious consensus continues to exist among the great majority of people. However, Jordan is also a complex society where bureaucrats, religious and secular, are posted in local communities where peasant and tribal traditions continue to engage a substantial part of the population to some degree or another. The culture broker is on the spot there too, even when it comes to the necessity of interpreting basic life cycle rituals that one might assume are standard and set (such as the rituals surrounding death). Early in my field work I noted a certain discrepancy between the way the preacher and religious leader of the village viewed funeral processions and burial rites and the way most peasants viewed them. The village preacher or *shaykh*, chastised the peasants for their behavior during the simple village funeral processions. He said that in the procession to the burial ground men should not utter various ritual formulas; they should not chant the *burda*, a special collection of formulas from the Prophet's biography; they should not use incense. They should proceed in silence to the cemetery so that each one can better reflect on death and fear God more. If they had to chant something they should chant only the profession of faith's first phrase or *tahlil*, "There is no god but God," and that under their breath. He also stated that the traditional meal invitations extended to the deceased's family from various unrelated households in the village should not go on more than three

20. Ibid., 180ff.
21. Ibid., 182.

days as they were wont to do. All mourning after three days was reprehensible. He also told villagers that any close partrilineal kinsmen could
perform the ritual ablutions for the dead to prepare the body for burial;
it was not a special duty reserved for the preacher. He also told them any
Muslim could read a Quranic verse and a burial prayer when the deceased
was interred in the cemetery.

The shaykh viewed his role as a twofold one: "To organize relations of
people with their Lord and to organize the relations of people with one
another in all matters." Most of his time was spent on this second mission, inculcating social relational norms regarding the proper behavior of
wives, husbands, children, parents, neighbors, kinsmen, and fellow Muslims, and ranking them in order of importance. Typical of this effort, for
instance, is the following Tradition of the Prophet (hadith) related by the
shaykh:[22]

> *The obligations/rights of a Muslim to his fellow Muslims are six: if
> you meet him you should greet him—the greeting and the shaking of
> hands cause joy in the heart; if a joyous occasion overtakes him (your
> fellow-Muslim) you should congratulate him—"May you be blessed,
> brother"; if despair afflicts him, you should console him; if he dies,
> you should join in his funeral procession; and if he invites you to his
> house or asks a favor of you, you should accommodate him.*

But many peasants view religion otherwise. An adjoining village invited
the preacher of Kufr al-Ma to leave his own village and become their
preacher. They had none and were chagrined over the fact. As one peasant summed it up: "The reason we need a preacher—the main reason—
is the shame of people dying and there being no one in the village to wash
them and pray for them. We have to go to the next village (to get a
preacher); and the shame of not knowing (the proper time of) the five
prayers."

For the peasants, then, the main function of the preacher was life-crisis

22. Traditions of the Prophet, Muhammad, are, after the Quran, the main source of Islamic law and ethics. Strictly speaking, the sayings and doings of Muhammad during his
lifetime or sunna are the "Traditions." But the authenticity of such sayings and doings had
to be vouched for. Therefore, they were collected, each with a text and accompanying chain
of authority that vouched for their authority by tracing a lineage of oral transmission back
to a companion of the Prophet. These formal Traditions or hadith have been the subject of
a science of scholarship and have been collected in a few famous collections such as those
of Muslim and Bukhari. When "Tradition" is capitalized, unless the context indicates otherwise, the reference is to one of these formalized Traditions found in an established collection. It should be noted that as a matter of style Arabic words will be transliterated and
italized on first mention with appropriate long vowel marks, but not thereafter. Traditions
of the Prophet will be italicized in the text because of their core position in Muslim religious
experience. See introduction for details.

ritual management and their main concern was soteriological rather than ethical. A key part of the burial rite is the "instruction" or *talqīn*, that is, the instruction on how to answer the angels when they question the dead risen from their graves, and the prayer asking forgiveness of sins or *duʿā*. For the peasants the presence of the preacher is the key to salvation and preservation from the fire. This is clear from the "instruction" to the deceased on the burial ground as recited by the preacher:

> Know oh servant of God and daughter of my father's brother (woman) that two merciful angels will descend upon you; they are held responsible for you and those like you of the community of Muhammad, in its entirety. So when they come to you and sit beside you and ask you, "Who is your Lord" and "Who is your Prophet?" and "What is your religion?" and "Who is your *imām* (leader)?" and "What is your direction of prayer (*qibla*)?" and "Who are your brothers?" Say to them in an unequivocal way and without fear— since they are the children of God: "God is my Lord" and "Muhammad is his Prophet" and "The Quran is my imam" and "The *Kaʿbah* is my direction of prayer" and "Prayer, fasting, almsgiving and pilgrimage is my obligation" and "Muslim men are my brothers" and "Muslim women are my sisters" and "I lived and I died with the words, 'I testify that there is no god but God' and 'I testify that Muhammad is the Messenger of God.' "

The shaykh then continues:

> Know, servant of God, that death is authentic.
> And that the descent over the grave is authentic.
> And that the questions of the angels are authentic.
> And that the Hidden (God) is authentic.
> And that Accounting is authentic.
> And that the Scales (of Judgment Day) are authentic.
> And that the Bridge (over hell) is authentic.
> And that Paradise is authentic.
> And that the Fire (hell) is authentic.
> And that God resurrects those who are in their graves
> (And sends them to the place of judgment).

The chagrin of these peasants over not having a preacher was a recognition of their own incompleteness, religiously, morally, and intellectually compared to the sophisticated (from their own point of view) tradition the preacher represented. The peasants of Kufr al-Ma were, then, from their own perspective, rightfully disturbed when the representative of that tradition refused to make accessible to them its benefits (e.g., chanting the burda during the funeral procession or washing the bodies of the dead in the prescribed manner).

The representatives of the great Islamic tradition, on their side, reinforce the view of their own superiority over a substantially illiterate peasantry with various Traditions of the Prophet and proverbs. One religious judge in the subdistrict who tried cases involving peasants told me, "The dweller in villages is like the dweller in the graves (in respect to piety)" that is, he is dead to religion. And another judge was disturbed that I might be recording the wrong things about Islam in the village, specifically about death. He said, "Many preachers address the deceased on the burial ground and give him directions—as if the dead can reply!" He quoted a hadith to the opposite effect and then said that a knowledge of Arabic grammar clearly demonstrates what is meant by the Quranic phrase, *Instruct your dead*. "It means give advice to the living, that is, those on the point of death, not to the dead, for how can a dead man receive advice?"

The gap between the peasant interpretation of "instruction" and the judge's is obvious, wide, and uncompromising. It dramatizes the critical role and power of the culture broker, here the preacher (he is the spokesman of God and at the same time a spokesman of his community), his social structural weakness (he is caught between the expectations of the bureaucracy in that he is the lowest figure on the bureaucratic totem pole), and the expectations of the community of which he is a member.[23]

CULTURE BROKERS IN RELIGIOUS INSTITUTIONS

Most of the cases discussed in the last section involve problematic cultural brokerage between "local-level" religious and political groups across a substantial cultural gap. However, sometimes the problem of the accommodation of traditions pits the top hierarchy of one great tradition (e.g., religious) against the top hierarchy of another (e.g., political), thereby increasing the tension and escalating the conflict. For instance, Roman Catholic Archbishop Camara of Brazil, operating from his seat in Bahia, has opposed guerilla warfare against the Brazilian government, but he has given political and legal advice to peasants and workers, helping to organize labor and peasant unions; aided in the organization of eighty thousand self-help congregations; and denounced the torture and killing of the country's political prisoners by the government. The Brazilian government has condemned his activities and forbidden Brazilian newspapers to

23. During the 1960s the preachers in Jordan were supervised by the local judge (*qadi*) of the religious court. Today (1986) they are supervised separately by the local office of the Department of Religious Endowments (*awqāf*).

conduct interviews with him or to mention his name in any communication.[24] In Chile Cardinal Enriquez and Archbishop Fresno have urged priests to denounce arrests, disappearances, and cases of abuse and torture by police; they support the publication of a biweekly magazine, *Solidarity*, for years the only organ of dissent in Chile; in Chilean shantytowns priests have converted their churches into meeting places for social activists and have opened many day-care centers, schools, and soup kitchens.[25] After three policemen set upon and severely beat three bishops who had been outspoken social activists, the Chilean church hierarchy excommunicated the policemen.[26] In June 1983 American Catholic bishops produced, voted upon, and approved a pastoral letter on war and peace, holding it immoral to start a nuclear war.[27] This letter clashed with U.S. government policy which allows and justifies a first-strike nuclear option.

In the above-mentioned cases the problem of the accommodation of traditions by the local-level culture broker (the parish priest) is reduced. Although the gap at the top between the two hierarchies is wide, the cultural gap between the priest and his own bishops is small; if the gap between the priest and his parish is wide, he has the support of his own hierarchy in interpreting the new policies to his congregation.

What happens, however, when the linker is asked to implement edicts of his own religious hierarchy that he himself opposes or edicts of the State that he opposes but that the upper echelons of his own hierarchy support openly or tacitly? The possibilities of accommodation, juxtaposition, defiance, and reinterpretation are numerous here.

Let us take the case of the French worker priests who doffed their clerical uniforms and went to work in French factories, joined labor unions, and participated in worker demonstrations after World War II as a way of affirming Christian concern for the laboring man. In 1954 Pope Pius XII issued an edict recalling all priests who worked in factories and had joined the Marxist General Confederation of Labor. "The Pope stated that Marxism bred atheism and that there was too much risk that priests might lose their faith. The worker priests retorted that siding with the poor was in the spirit of the New Testament."[28] French worker priests reacted to the pope's edict in a number of ways. Some went along with the edict and withdrew from their work, returning to standard priestly duties; others quit full-time jobs and union membership but remained in

---

24. As reported by correspondent Jonathan Kendall, *New York Times*, August 28, 1976.

25. Reported in the *New York Times*, November 20, 1983.

26. Kendall, *New York Times*, August 28, 1976.

27. As reported in the *Saturday Press*, Binghamton, New York, November 12, 1983.

28. As quoted in an article by *New York Times* correspondent Andreas Freund, *New York Times*, May 27, 1979.

part-time jobs as male nurses, bus conductors, and lab assistants still in contact with workers; still others quit the priesthood.[29]

Or let us take the case of the 1973 Rabbinical Assembly of the National Conservative branch of Judaism which passed a resolution allowing women to be counted in the *minyan*, the required quorum of ten for Jewish public worship. Rabbis in one city in upper New York State proceeded to accommodate, reinterpret, and juxtapose (qualify) the ruling in various ways.[30] One conservative rabbi said he would support the resolution, but that it would have little practical effect. Another said that he would hesitate to call on a woman to fill the minyan since it "let men off the hook"; that is, Jewish law placed the obligation of attendance on men and absolved women. These two interpretations suggested support for the policy change introduced by the corporate religious body without any intention of seeking implementation. The latter interpretation justified nonimplementation among the core religious category—adult men. An Orthodox rabbi of a Conservative congregation stated that small congregations do not change their customs as quickly as large ones; he opposed the resolution, saying that the ruling was not mandatory even for Conservative rabbis; according to him, the rabbi of a congregation is the final authority on Jewish law. In explaining and justifying his opposition this rabbi stressed congregational autonomy and rabbinical independence. Furthermore, he noted the necessity to accommodate to the cultural gap between his congregation and what he implicitly construed as an excessive religious avant garde dominating the assembly.[31]

The difficulties of the culture broker in dealing with policies propounded by his own hierarchy, and the cultural gap between laity and the upper echelon of the religious hierarchy is illustrated dramatically by the wide variety of responses among parish priests to the Roman Catholic Church's opposition to the divorce law in Italy. In 1974 the patriarch of Venice sent individual letters to more than twenty of his priests warning them about participating in prodivorce rallies.[32] Stating that their support for the divorce law was causing "scandal and confusion," he threatened to forbid them from saying mass if they persisted. Many of these priests had been crusading for the Catholic's right to vote against repeal of the

29. Ibid.

30. The following accounts were reported in the *Binghamton Evening Press*, September 12, 1973.

31. Of course, the necessity of a rabbi to accommodate to a formal religious hierarchy as in the Roman Catholic examples cited above and below, is quite absent in Judaism. Nevertheless, the rabbi, even the orthodox rabbi, had to take account of the Conservative assembly's decision and explain his own position (i.e., he had to interpret and accommodate).

32. The following accounts were reported in the *New York Times* by correspondent Paul Hofmann, May 5, 1974.

three-year-old divorce statute in a national referendum in May 1974. The range from accommodation through defiance on the part of parish priests was wide. Some priests made known the bishop's pastoral letter asking Catholics to vote against divorce but asked a layman to do the reading; some priests ignored the divorce issue completely in sermons, sensing the critical mood of their parishioners; other priests supported a Catholic's right to vote against repeal of the divorce legislation currently existing, citing Vatican II's emphasis on the paramount role of individual conscience; and some priests continued to participate in prodivorce rallies and were ousted from particular religious orders and/or had their clerical functions suspended.

The potential for conflict and violence is greatest when the cultural gap between the lower-echelon culture brokers and their congregations is narrow and the gap between the upper-echelon political hierarchy and the religious hierarchy is wide; or, alternatively, the gap between the upper-echelon and lower-echelon religious hierarchy is wide. An instance of the first type is the well-publicized Iranian Revolution of 1979. The Shah had banished Ayatollah Khomeini from the country, arrested other religious leaders, assaulted the religious seminary at Qum, secularized the system of education, seized the religious endowments of the religious elite, and drafted young mullahs into the army.[33] All of this occurred in a country where the great majority of the peasantry and urban working class and a large part of the traditional commercial class were deeply religious and interacted intimately in thousands of mosques and *husayniyyas* (halls of mourning and religious education) with thousands of local-level (as well as some upper-echelon) preachers and religious chanters. Iran is a country, moreover, where these local-level religious specialists and their more learned and renowned urban counterparts were supported at the grassroots level by substantial monetary contributions made on an annual basis. The result, unforeseen but comprehensible, was the Iranian Revolution.

An example of the second type of gap—little publicized, but equally instructive—is the Philippines, where several groups of diocesan priests were engaged in printing and distributing antigovernment propaganda, collecting funds for underground organizations, and disseminating propaganda from the pulpit.[34] In the prerevolution period (1986) many of these priests broke with their own bishops who still blessed or at least tolerated President Marcos. At the parish priest level, the social organization of tradition involves a range of defiance: some Filipino priests con-

33. See Akhavi 1980 for an account of the clash between the Pahlavi dynasty and the Shiite clergy in Iran.
34. The following accounts are from a report of correspondent Robert Whipmany of the *Manchester Guardian*, appearing in the *Binghamton Evening Press*, January 22, 1974.

fined themselves to reading a message in favor of "an inspiring figure (Father Luis Jalandoni) whose love for the poor and oppressed and whose courage in defending their rights against the powerful and privileged few . . . cannot but rally our sympathy and support"[35]; others propagandized sugar workers and farmers into an awareness of their basic rights; others helped workers form free unions and join picket lines; and others joined guerilla groups composed of left-wing peasants, students, and workers. Among the latter is Father Luis Jalandoni, the son of a rich landowner, who pleaded with the landowners of his own class to pay minimum wages; having sold his estate, he kept strikers alive for months with the proceeds. He disappeared two days after martial law was declared in 1973. He had become convinced that only armed struggle could bring the changes he had failed to achieve by legal means; most of the seventy cases of land-grabbing by landowners which Jalandoni had been fighting for dispossessed tenants were after years of litigation still in the courts. Jalondoni reemerged as a guerilla priest in the new People's Army, the military wing of the Communist party. In 1974 he and other priests and nuns were arrested for subversion. The cultural gap between these priests and their own hierarchy is as complete as their intimacy with the peasants. Soon after Bishop Fortich of Barcolod disassociated himself from Jalondoni, congregations in a number of churches dwindled and collections shrank. The Provisional Commander of the Philippine Constabulary warned priests against "using the pulpit to denounce the Philippine Constabulary and to picture Jalondoni as a hero and martyr."[36]

These last two cases—the clash of great political and religious traditions (the Iranian) and the alienation between upper and lower levels of the religious hierarchy (the Filipino)—are, admittedly, extreme cases of the social organization of tradition stressing defiance, but they are still accompanied by necessary interpretations or, in Jalondoni's case, consecutive reinterpretations of the priest's role: from student in Rome, to head of the social action committee of Barcolod Diocese, to labor organizer, to guerilla priest.

Perhaps a more typical example of the parish priest as culture broker can be found in the United States. Although the Roman Catholic Church has facilitated to some degree the procedure by which married members of the church may obtain an annulment, the grounds for obtaining an annulment are still relatively narrow. Consequently, thousands of Catholic couples who are estranged and still married in the eyes of the church are cut off from the sacraments of the church. Some priests in the United States have begun to give communion to divorced (by secular law) and

35. Ibid.
36. Ibid.

remarried couples without going through the process of gaining an annulment. The reinterpretation or accommodation of traditions is through
an institution known as the "internal forum," a private and personal conversation between priest and couple in a second marriage to see if they
have made a lasting permanent commitment and are desirous of raising
their children as Catholics.[37] American priests who have innovated in this
way are obviously basing their action on Vatican II's elevation of individual conscience as a determining factor in the decision to refuse or offer
the church's most valuable resource—its sacraments. It has been argued
that the Catholic Church's increasing tendency to grant annulment
through the marriage tribunal process (700 in 1967, 7000 in 1972,
15,000 in 1976) and to grant them on the grounds of "psychological
readiness" is also an accommodation to the twentieth century's acceptance of depth psychology.[38]

All the cases discussed in the last two sections illustrate two points.
First, the social organization of tradition in a variety of circumstances
involving a variety of closely or loosely knit hierarchies, a variety of culture brokers, and a variety of folk, and cutting across many different cultural or subcultural traditions, is a critical and necessary process in all
complex societies. Second, the precise form of the accommodation (passive acceptance, disassociation [from the message] after communication,
ignoring the message, simple juxtaposition, dissimulation, reinterpretation, compartmentalization, defiance, or some consecutive combination
thereof), its content, and its success vary widely with the situation, the
social structural context, and the genius of the culture broker. In the next
section some of these concepts will be spelled out and their strengths and
weaknesses as analytical tools will be examined.

The Problem of the Global Nature of Tradition (Processes)

Earlier, "universalization" and "parochialization" were described as two
of the main processes characterizing the social organization of tradition;
the first focuses on the flow upward of ideas and customs from various
peripheral folk and their eventual incorporation as part of an embracive
philosophical or religious tradition emanating from urban centers; the
second focuses on the process by which various ideas and customs flow
downward, often through culture brokers, and are eventually accepted or
accommodated by various peripheral folk. There are three problems with

37. The preceding account is based on a February 14, 1977 report of the religion editor
of the *Chicago Tribune*, James Robison.
38. Ibid.

all such concepts—including the concept of the social organization of tradition itself. It is not that such concepts are false or irrelevant, but rather
that they are all "global," that is, unitary, comprehensive, and general.
Furthermore, they fail to relate the processes described to the flow of time
and to the different reactions of separate generations. Finally, the processes described by the concepts are uncontextualized.

For instance, Ernestine Friedl's useful and provocative concept of "lagging emulation" can be considered a form of parochialization.[39] Peasants
and postpeasants accept ideas and customs emanating from urban centers—but only long after urbanites have held them and usually only after
urbanites have discarded them (e.g., in Jordan peasants gone-to-town traditionally adopted the veil at the same time that many of their urban up-
per-middle-class sisters were discarding it for Western dress, and this long
before the so-called Islamic resurgence of the 1970s). But so defined
Friedl's concept leaves much of the complexity of the process uncompre-
hended and uncontextualized. Lagging emulation assumes the existence
of another process of "synchronic" emulation which immediately raises
the question of what kinds of beliefs and customs—in what situations and
social structural, economic, and political contexts—are quickly accepted
or reinterpreted or accommodated by the generation of the receivers as
opposed to the generation following the receivers or by a later generation
or never. Lagging emulation as a form of parochialization may occur and
not occur at the same time. That is, many Jordanian peasants who have
condemned tribalism and outmoded religious beliefs continue to eat,
dress, marry, and recreate in a traditional fashion or vice versa. The
preacher of Kufr al-Ma, who is the subject of this case study, condemned
what he considered the evils of modernization and Westernization but he
was the first to invest in a water meter to bring piped water to his house,
and he was the only person in the village who upheld the right of a person
holding an indefensible view (according to the great majority) to express
it in a public meeting. And the magician of the village who had built up a
sizable clientele based on his belief in preternatural spirits (*jinn*) had
bought the saint's tree in the village, chopped it up, and sold it for firewood in the village shop he had opened. He had also purchased a tractor,
when almost no one in the village had one. The point is that lagging emulation can take place in style of life but not in belief (or vice versa) or
both or neither. To complicate the matter further, emulation can be self-
sought or vicarious. Many Jordanian peasants never realize their dream
of a religious or a professional education but spend their lives scrimping
and saving so that their sons may do so.

39. See Friedl, "Lagging Emulation in a Post-Peasant Society," *American Anthropologist*,
Vol. 66, No. 3, June 1964.

I have spoken above of juxtaposition as one option in the social organization of tradition. That is, intrusive beliefs or customs are simply tolerated without reinterpretation or even conscious acceptance along with the old. But juxtaposition cannot usually take place simply in this manner since human action takes place in time and space. For instance, in Jordan, committing murder, theft, or adultery ostensibly involves at least three legal/political institutions and jurisdictions: the tribal court, the Islamic court, and the civil court or district officer. Therefore, three culture brokers are involved. But in fact a practical order of relevance that is also temporal prevails. In rural areas after a murder the modern political great tradition immediately intervenes in the person of the police and the subdistrict officer; the tribal tradition (of law) is recognized by the great political tradition (subdistrict officer) but in a selective and circumscribed manner, that is, in terms of genealogical recognition of patrilineal kinsmen to be banished and in the establishment of a truce and the taking of truce money, ʿatwa, and finally and much later in the precise etiquette of peace-making, sulha. But police intervention (at the behest of the subdistrict officer) absolutely prohibits the occurrence of the traditional tribal three-day period of "the boiling of the blood" in which the victims may wreak with impunity destruction upon the kinsmen of the killer and their property. Islamic law, although potentially applicable, is not applied but Islamic ethics become pertinent in the establishment of the truce and in subsequent peacemaking since compensation and forgiveness are religiously commendable, and religious leaders such as preachers and religious judges are present at most attempts at conciliation. Moreover, Islamic law enters by the "back" or tribal door since the size of the traditional tribal compensation (diyya) for the murder of a man stated in camels and converted into Jordanian dinars is in fact precisely based on a Quranic verse stipulating the appropriate diyya in case of murder.[40]

"Compartmentalization" is a process in the social organization of tradition referred to by a number of anthropologists including Redfield, Spicer, Dozier, Linton, and particularly Singer.[41] Compartmentalization is

a phase in the contact between different cultures in which elements from another culture have entered and coexist with traditional elements of a host culture without close interdependence or incompatibility among the elements. The phase is considered transitional to other phases of cultural change in which the novel elements are eliminated or are interpreted and incorporated into the traditional culture. Compartmentalization, then, is an adaptive process reducing

40. See M.J.L. Hardy, *Blood Feuds and the Payment of Blood Money in the Middle East* (Beirut, 1963).

41. See Dozier 1961; Linton 1936; Redfield 1941; Singer 1972; and Spicer 1954.

conflicts between new and old traits by keeping separate and gaining time for internal adjustments, reinterpretation and elective incorporation.[42]

Redfield originally used the term to describe, among other things, the coexistence of the Spanish Catholic Cult of Saints with the Mayan Cult of the Beehive. For him, compartmentalized ideas or customs are not inconsistent with one another; they are simply separate and connotatively as well as denotatively unconnected. Ralph Linton introduced the concept of a set of "alternatives" or "elements" known to every adult or to all members of a socially recognized group but among which the individuals may exercise choice.[43] Linton regarded these alternatives as a kind of "trial and error zone" in which full acceptance never occurs before a period of mutual competition.[44]

In *When a Great Tradition Modernizes*, Singer used the term *compartmentalization* to analyze the relationship between local custom and the great Sanskritic Hindu tradition on the one hand and the demands placed on businessmen and workers by modern factories and bureaucracies on the other. Indian businessmen carefully followed the prescribed rules of ritual behavior appropriate to the Hindu great tradition in their homes but departed from them substantially without major social disjunction or psychological stress in the work sphere, the factory—ignoring there, for example, the rules forbidding the social and commensal mixing of members of different castes. For Singer, compartmentalization implied the separation of activities in physical space on a day-to-day basis with the individual also applying separate and often contrasting norms of behavior in each space. One might almost argue that compartmentalization as viewed by the anthropologists mentioned above is a form of "nonaccommodation" in that separation is implied psychologically, spatially, normatively, cognitively, and perhaps temporally as well.[45]

But here again a "global" term disguises many possibilities. Compartmentalization may involve separation spatially or temporally; or concealment visually and symbolically as when the Pueblo Indians of the American Southwest worship indigenous Indian gods under the label of Catholic saints; or actual dissimulation, *taqiyya*, by which, for instance, Druze or Shi'a Muslims (or historically the Jews of Mallorca) deny their own religious identity in order to survive in a hostile social and/or politi-

42. Singer *American Anthropology*, 233.
43. Linton as quoted in Singer *American Anthropology*, 233.
44. Ibid., 234.
45. For examples of compartmentalization or nonaccommodation in a Middle Eastern context see Richard T. Antoun, "The Islamic Court, the Islamic Judge, and the Accommodation of Traditions: A Jordanian Case Study," *International Journal of Middle East Studies*, Vol. 12, No. 4, December 1980.

cal environment; or acceptance of peripheral cultural elements—those which do not alter the main orientation of the culture (e.g., governors, wheat, and the saint's cult for Pueblo Indians)—as opposed to core cultural elements in order to resist an intrusive colonial power as suggested by Spicer; or the resuscitation of traditional elements of culture to disguise the defense of economic and political interests as in Abner Cohen's "retribalization."[46] That is, compartmentalization may involve transformation at many different levels in the long run, and, with respect to human action produce many particular combinations of cultural elements in the short run. The particular strategies of compartmentalization pursued in many different situations are so varied and contrasting that the application of the concept in any single context carries with it a halo of ambiguity.

The depiction of the social organization of tradition must also be complicated with respect to sequencing. A number of the processes described above occur in the same milieu with the same group of actors but in consecutive fashion. For instance, the Bori Cult, an indigenous religious institution of West Africa involving spirits which can possess men, was juxtaposed for some time with intrusive Islamic beliefs; but at some point it was reinterpreted by culture brokers of the Tijaniyya Order to accommodate to the politically and increasingly socially dominant Islamic tradition: the Bori spirits became jinn, creatures of God mentioned in the Quran.[47] Or, for instance, acceptance may be followed by condescending toleration followed by parochialization as with magic in a village in Jordan. Magic, which was traditionally recognized there by the *fellahīn* as a legitimate option, is now more commonly regarded as suitable only for women, and still more recently was denounced by the culture broker (preacher) of the great Islamic tradition.[48]

The problem of the global nature of the social organization of tradition goes back to the conceptualization of the traditions themselves, that is, treating them as "Great Traditions" and "Little Traditions" as if they were one in content and form and as if that content and form was embracive in its scope. Although this problem may be more obvious on the "Great Tradition" side because we commonly assign uniform content and form to such religious traditions as Islam, Christianity, or Buddhism, in fact it also exists on the Little Tradition side as well. Each of these "Traditions" must be broken up on either side of the part-culture divide.

Let me illustrate by a Middle Eastern case, the Jordanian one. Viewed from the bottom, that is, from the side of the peasantry, the "Great Tra-

46. For a discussion of "retribalization," see Cohen, *Custom and Politics in Urban Africa*, (University of California Press, Berkeley, 1969).

47. Ibid., 58, 163–64.

48. See chapter 5 for details.

dition" is by no means unitary. One tradition with which the villager must deal is the Islamic tradition. The Sunni Muslim Hanafite version is common in Jordan. ("Hanafite" refers to one of the four accepted major law school traditions.) But the peasant must in fact deal with two very different representatives of this tradition, the home-town preacher to whom I have alluded above and the religious judge (qadi) who is always a stranger and almost always an urbanite. Although the preacher is usually cognizant of the little tradition of peasant custom and is sometimes empathetic if not sympathetic to it, the qadi is quite often not so empathetic as attested to by the above-mentioned qadi's remark about the "religion of villages." Even the strictly legal application of the Islamic tradition is not clear-cut. Although Hanafi law was applied by the Ottoman Empire, and Jordan as a successor state continued to apply that law, the formulation of new law codes in Jordan as in many other Muslim countries took account of all four law school traditions. Maliki, Shafi'i, and Hanbali law are also applied in Jordan to the degree that particular items from their traditions were incorporated in the new law codes.[49] But the matter is still more complex since the traditional school of Islamic law applied in Transjordan by the older generation of religious teachers is Shafi'i law, taught by itinerant preachers before the introduction of central government and localized Islamic law courts. Therefore, a father and a son, performing their prayers in the mosque, may do so in a somewhat different manner since one learned his Islam from itinerant preachers and the other from courses on religion in government schools.

Entirely apart from the Islamic tradition in many areas of the Middle East is another "great" tradition, the tribal tradition. Such a tradition does not fit easily into Redfield's dichotomy since it is not urban-based and does not reflect the result of systematic reflection by a group of intelligensia or literati. It is nevertheless "great" in its ancient origin, its wide application over many Arabic-speaking nomadic and rural areas, and, most important, its detailed though often unwritten codes for social life and legal violations. The tribes, moreover, have their own well-recognized judges or perhaps more accurately, arbitrators. The peasants of Kufr al-Ma come to terms directly with this tradition through the figure of the pasha.[50] It is the pasha to whom they often resort (and not the civil court or the subdistrict officer) for advice and, if needed, arbitration about a whole variety of matters including murder, elopement, and assault but also more mundane matters such as crop destruction, animal incursion, and acting as go-between in the contraction of marriage and

49. The Ottoman legal reform known as the Majallah had already resulted in selection from, and arrangement of, Islamic legal norms of personal status (marriage, divorce, inheritance) but the reform was guided by the principles elucidated by the Hanafi school of law.

50. See chapter 2 for details.

divorce (though this latter matter, as the pasha is quick to recognize, is under the jurisdiction of the Islamic court).

A third great tradition with which the peasant in the Middle East and in Jordan must contend is that of the State—the secular, urban interpolated elite also represented variously in Kufr al-Ma by the subdistrict officer, the civil court judge, the land registry officer, the agricultural inspector, and the forest ranger, all living in the adjacent village of Deir Abu Said. Though these officials are not ignorant of either Islamic law and ethics or tribal law and ethics and though they may not be unsympathetic with such traditions or certain elements of them, they clearly regard them as irrelevant for most of their work, which is guided by state laws and administrative rulings. If peasants wish to sell land, register it, settle a boundary problem, plant trees, fetch firewood, build a new school in the village, or obtain drinking water for that village in a drought, these are the brokers they must consult.

It might be argued that there is a fourth tradition, perhaps not "great" in the same way or to the same extent—the merchant tradition. This tradition is town- but not necessarily city-oriented and is often composed of villagers gone-to-town who have opened up small retail shops.

If it has become evident by now that the "great" tradition is not unitary or global, it may not be so evident that the "little" or peasant tradition is likewise complicated and broken up but it is. In Kufr al-Ma one of the mayors and the schoolmaster, a native villager, are "traditional modernizers"—pious men who recognize the rightful application of tribal norms in cases of honor and in day-to-day conflict resolution; but they are also committed to "progress" in terms of material modernization and education—afforestation, tractors where feasible, new schools, paved roads, piped water, electricity, high school education for daughters, and higher education abroad for sons. Other men of the elder generation are village traditionalists proud of their tribal traditions ("We are Arabs! Arabs!" they said), staunch in their religious beliefs and maintaining a strict application of tribal and religious norms. They gather frequently in guest houses where they exchange hospitality, enjoy the camaraderie of mutual visitation, arrange marriages, and arbitrate disputes. They oppose the payment of taxes, the establishment of a village council, the establishment of a municipality, the taking of usury (i.e., the borrowing of money from banks), and a relaxation of the modesty code to permit the education of girls; they are termed by villagers as "the coinage of Abd al-Hamid" (Abd al-Hamid was an Ottoman sultan noted for his reactionary policies). Other villagers can be described as Horatio Algers, often villagers-gone-to-town who become successful operators of retail shops or small restaurants. Many of these men are quite atypical of the peasant's life history (as is the village preacher discussed in chapter 3), even at an early age.

One villager recounted that he had never shepherded his father's sheep, a common apprenticeship for peasants in their early teens. Once during the celebration of a religious festival his father had asked him to take the sheep out to pasture; he had refused whereupon his father stripped him and made him lie down on thorns; then he fled and his father repented and ran after him, bringing his clothes and crying. This villager had never ploughed his father's lands either, as was expected of sons on reaching the age of fifteen. He had read the Quran for four years with a home-town Quran teacher and then had gone on to Haifa in Palestine where he worked in a restaurant for two years; he saved a little money and eventually opened a small restaurant in Beisan across the Jordan Valley where he remained until 1948 and the first Arab-Israeli War. Upon returning to Transjordan he opened a small beanery in the nearest market town, Irbid, where he remains to this day. In my conversation with him it became clear that he knew, and had read, a good deal more about Islam than the fellow-villagers he had left many years before. He said that Muslims were allowed to take Christian girls in marriage because Muslims believed in all the Christian and Hebrew Prophets but would not give them girls in marriage because they (Christians and Jews) had altered, that is, garbled or falsified the holy books they had received and, more important, because they committed the one unforgivable sin—polytheism (referring here to the Christian belief in the Trinity). Jesus, he said, was "a breath of God" (*nafakhat allah*) like all the other prophets; he was created just as Adam from the earth. "How could Jesus be God," he asked, "when he was created? God has no sons or daughters or wife, and we can't even imagine that."

Only one villager in Kufr al-Ma can be designated a radical modernizer, and in that respect in the village setting, deviant. He scoffed at his fellow-villagers who grew wheat and barley; he had borrowed money from a town cooperative—no one else had done so at the time—and had purchased two hundred chickens which he was raising "scientifically." He did not visit other villagers including his own brother and they did not visit him which almost made him a social pariah since mutual visiting among neighbors and kinsmen was a village norm. Moreover, in his later thirties he was unmarried. He had been arrested twice by the Jordanian authorities for engaging in prohibited political party activities and speaking against the king. After some time in prison he was released on the condition that he stay in the area of his home village and not venture into the large towns. I had been warned about seeing or interviewing him; even his own brother said he would not talk to me or even offer me tea. But he did so and inquired about my work in the village. He told me that he had read widely, in prison, and asked me what I thought about Pareto's concept of the "circulation of the elite"!

So far we have spoken as if these little traditions or dispositions for change are unique to particular individuals. But this is not the case. Abu Fayid quickly comes to mind.[51] Abu Fayid lives with his wife and family in the village. He is employed in the adjoining subdistrict center as a lower-echelon civil court clerk. His eldest son, whom he sent to medical school in Turkey, now works as a doctor in Saudi Arabia. Another son is a professor of linguistics at Yarmuk University in Irbid, Jordan. He is one of the few men in the village who buys a daily newspaper. He is one of the few men in the village who has spoken in favor of the Palestinian cause. He fought in the Arab-Israeli War of 1948. He wears a Western suit, a white shirt and tie, and shiny black shoes at his office in the civil court. When he returns to the village, however, he wears a long flowing wide-sleeved gown, prepares Bedawin-style coffee, and entertains anyone who happens to come to his guest room (*madāfa*) in the evening. He is called upon to arbitrate disputes. A recent case of honor involved the killing of several men of his own clan who then had to seek tribal protection (*dakhl*) from a tribal shaykh in the Jordan Valley. This shaykh had given his protection to the clan and, thereby, to the village, after many others had refused. Abu Fayid was out urging villagers to vote for this shaykh—he was running in the parliamentary elections of March 1984— even against a candidate from the Muslim Brotherhood with whom many if not most villagers sympathized. What "Tradition" does Abu Fayid represent? The great secular political and administrative tradition? He is and has been a bureaucrat for over forty years and dresses accordingly. The radical modernizing tradition? Both of his sons are professionals, and he is a patriot and a supporter of Palestinian nationalism. The great tribal tradition? He prepares coffee in his guest house, arbitrates disputes, and lobbies for a tribal candidate in parliamentary elections. He represents all and none of these traditions. He is an accommodator of traditions and it is precisely the mix of traditions and the peculiar set of circumstances accompanying it that constitutes the study of the social organization of tradition.

I do not wish to indicate that the village of Kufr al-Ma or any other village in Jordan is filled with Horatio Algers or radical modernizers though the economic revolution of the 1970s has made the former more common. What I want to indicate is that the "little" tradition about which Redfield spoke—even in a single village—is not unified. Therefore, when we speak about the social organization of tradition we must speak about many different versions of tradition with a small *t* on both sides of the part-society, part-culture divide, and perhaps not about a divide at all, but rather about a culture and power gap of greater or lesser degree

51. Many of the proper names for villagers in this book are pseudonyms.

that can be accommodated more or less easily in the same or different spaces over a short or long period of time.

John Bennett's analysis of the farmers of the Great Plains of Canada is helpful here.[52] Bennett studied three groups of farmers, growing crops and raising cattle, exploiting external resources such as agricultural credit, dealing with government regulations (e.g., on owning, leasing, and inheriting land), and operating within an international market of prices and costs and a particular national political climate. Bennett assumed that unlike the peasants studied by Redfield and those anthropologists departing from his work, these agrarians generally desired closer relations with the national urban society whether they were cattle-grain farmers on relatively small land areas or cattle ranchers on very large tracts. These two groups and a third, the Hutterian Brethren, a religious group settled in six close-knit colonies in the region, used the same roads and service centers and were "attuned to the processes of market economy."[53] At the same time Bennett discovered a discrepant pattern of involvement in the great secular, political, and economic tradition. This discrepant pattern was a result of different strategies developed by the three groups for acquiring access to needed resources and for controlling external agencies—a "farming strategy," a "ranching strategy," and a "Hutterite strategy."

> Farmers saw the game with the government and the market as a condition of doing agriculture in a modern world. Ranchers were more inclined to externalize and resent the factors and forces—these were *impositions*, not simply conditions. Whereas the farmer has been trained in the world of marketing pools and political action, the rancher has consistently avoided such interlinked systems. He adheres to views that stress the isolation of the local community. . . . He resists methods of sale where the animals are shipped out and impersonally evaluated, as they would be in a pooled marketing system or in "rail grading." . . . The farmer is willing to play the game by making the required moves in a known sequence; the rancher resists being "told" how to do things—he prefers his own rules. The farmer writes letters and arranges appointments with government officials in order to get what he wants; the rancher may do likewise, but not as often and usually with reluctance—he prefers to remain aloof, to play the game at a distance or with minimal investment. He

---

52. See Bennett's "Further Remarks on Foster's Image of the Limited Good," *American Anthropologist*, Vol. 68, No. 1, February 1966; "Microcosm-Macrocosm Relationships in North American Agrarian Society," *American Anthropologist*, Vol. 69, No. 5, October 1967; and *Adaptive Strategy and Agrarian Life* (Aldine, Chicago, 1969).

53. Bennett "Microcosm-Macrocosm Relationships," 422.

wants all he can get, but he will sometimes take less in order to maintain what he defines as his autonomy.[54]

While farmers utilize the local culture brokers, here politicoeconomic brokers (the local agricultural extension agent and the social conservation men), to the fullest, ranchers usually avoid them and deal with cattle buyers who come to them at their own ranch, a matter of some pride for independent cattlemen. Bennett continues:

> Hutterites never pull strings or exert pressure, partly because they do not have to, owing to their relative prosperity. However, they do require information and they are indefatigable information-seekers, hanging around the government agencies and places of business, picking up the latest word on policy, bargains or available resources. They seek to compete with local operators and to "get there first," but they are barred by their beliefs from entering into "deals" and local interactional networks that influence resource allocation. They are also uninvolved in the complex influence-channeling from the local community to the government bureaus in the capital, partly because they are legally barred from sharing in many of the benefits and partly because this type of action involves politics, which are barred by their religious beliefs. As noted, their relative success is due to in the main to their efficient and large-scale economic operation, which makes them excellent risks and can cushion losses they might sustain owing to their inability to "get in on the ground floor."[55]

In terms of our previous discussion this case brings out clearly the impossibility of studying the social organization of tradition, here a great political and economic tradition, in a generalized or global manner. That is, although the farmers were fully participant in the political, economic, and cultural great traditions of the Canadian Northwest—involving themselves in politics and the political struggle for natural resources, applying technological improvements to agriculture, and stressing literacy and higher education for their children—the ranchers, freely participant in applying technological improvements, avoided politics and the political struggle, and desired a secular education but not to the same degree as the farmers. The Hutterites, on the other hand, excelled in technological modernization and fully exploited the informational function of administrative agencies; but they did not enter politics and they rejected the culture and style of life of their neighbors on the Canadian Great Plains for a culture and style of life ordered to their fundamentalist "Protestant"

54. Ibid., 449–50.
55. Ibid.

(of the culture of the majority) religious tradition. If one were to speak of parochialization or the interchange of cultural materials between three local agrarian traditions and their several great traditions—this being wholly appropriate since it is clear that a distinctive ethos impels each of the strategies of the three groups—one could not generalize over the separate interest areas and one would have to treat politics, economics and technology, and style of life quite separately in the analysis.

Dale F. Eickelman has recently argued that there is no "Islamic essence" either in religious texts, ritual, or particular religious experience,[56] and that Islam is a rich and varied tradition that differs with the historical period, the spatial situation, and the different conceptions being propounded. Edward Said on a broader canvas has attacked "Orientalism," the Western tradition of scholarship for the study of the Middle East in modern times, for seeking to identify and capture an essence, of which Islam is one part, and to use it to describe a generic "East" for the purposes of denigration and exploitation.[57] What are the implications of such views for the study of the social organization of tradition?

Abdul Hamid el-Zein in a provocative essay has discussed the problem of describing a great tradition, specifically the Islamic tradition. The elite formulation of that tradition by the ulema, the learned men of Islam, although it may be more reflective, is less related to the sense experience of the individual Muslim and to social action.[58] In this respect el-Zein's views are close to those expressed by Eickelman (1976) and Geertz (1968) in previous case studies of Islamic tradition.[59] El-Zein goes on to argue that this problem is compounded by the nature of social anthropological study close to the daily lives of particular Muslims in specific local environments where the meaning of Islam is always contextualized and fluid. El-Zein rejects the attempts of Crapanzano (1973) to locate the essence of Islam or its unity at the psychological level or the attempts of Bujra (1971) and Gilsenan (1973) to reduce it to its social structural and political context.[60] Moreover, he argues against the view that elite Islam or "normal Islam"—the Islam of the literati or ulema—is more reflective in comparison to folk Islam, as a long line of anthropologists including Red-

56. Eickelman, *The Middle East: An Anthropological Approach* (Prentice-Hall, Englewood Cliffs, 1981), 202–4.

57. See Edward Said, *Orientalism* (Vintage Books, New York, 1979).

58. El-Zein, "Beyond Ideology and Theology: The Search for the Anthropology of Islam," *Annual Review of Anthropology*, Vol. 6, 1977.

59. See Clifford Geertz, *Islam Observed* and Dale Eickelman, *Moroccan Islam: Tradition and Society in a Pilgrimage Center.*

60. See Abdullah Bujra, *The Politics of Stratification: A Study of Political Change in a South Arabian Town*; Vincent Crapanzano, *The Hamadsha: A Study in Moroccan Ethnopsychiatry*; and Michael Gilsenan, *Saint and Sufi in Modern Egypt: An Essay in the Sociology of Religion.*

field, Geertz, and Eickelman have argued. El-Zein argues that it is the anthropologist who has made a "scientific" distinction between folk and elite Islam, and that in fact folk theology rivals formal theology in degree of abstraction, systematization, and cosmological implications.[61] He argues further that "the traditions of the ulema developed historically out of already established principles of the nature of spiritual reality entwined with the life of the Islamic community."[62] He concludes that "the dichotomy of folk Islam and elite Islam" or in our terms, the little and great traditions, is "infertile and fruitless."[63]

This indictment seems to strike at the heart of the conceptual framework introduced in this chapter: great and little traditions, the culture gap and the accommodation of traditions by a series of mediating institutions and culture brokers. But, in fact, it does not. Indeed, Redfield spoke of a two-way flow of cultural materials, universalization as well as parochialization. That is, Redfield assumed that great traditions were built up out of little ones and Marriott and Singer, among others, have documented instances of such a process in the study of Hindu society and culture in India.[64] Evidence for the Middle East has not yet emerged but the recent research of R. Loeffler and E. Loeffler on Iran and F. Khuri on sects in the Arab World has begun to document the same kind of process for Christian, Druze, and Muslim communities in the Middle East.[65]

What is infertile is not the dichotomization of traditions as such, as long as scholars remember that accommodation occurs over a culture gap of greater or lesser distance and not over an unbridgable divide; and as long as they remember that the "traditions" are not global, general, and unified but varied and contextualized.

What is infertile and, indeed, dangerous, as El-Zein suggests is that superiority be assigned by the "scientist," here the anthropologist, the sociologist, the political scientist, the geographer, and the historian—that superiority be assigned to the elite tradition in any of its renditions and inferiority to the tradition of the folk. "Great Tradition" in this book is used to refer to beliefs, rituals, and actions that are formalized, institutionalized, and central and embracive in space. It does not indicate superiority either in moral elevation or even necessarily in detailed elaboration over those labelled "little" or "folk" or "peasant."

This book will focus on the process of parochialization and will document the great diversity of "normal" Islam in one peasant village in Jordan; but it does not deny the critical role of universalization or the cul-

61. El-Zein, "Beyond Ideology and Theology," 246.
62. Ibid., 248.
63. Ibid., 252.
64. See Marriott 1955; and Singer 1972.
65. See Loeffler 1987; and Khuri 1988.

tural contribution of peasant cultures to civilization. It will become clear with each subsequent chapter and the analysis of each sermon how complex the process of the social organization of tradition is, and how necessary it is for the cultural broker to have a firm handle on the tradition of the peasant as well as the tradition of the ulema. Indeed, when the culture broker is a son of the village, this is inevitable.

Islam in Its Local Environment: The Village, Its Constituent Units, and the Peasant Predicament

Kufr al-Ma is an Arab village located in the denuded eastern foothills of the Jordan Valley. It is one of two hundred cereal-growing villages of the Ajlun district of northwestern Transjordan. Its population of two thousand is composed entirely of Sunni Muslims. Approaching the village along a dirt road from its eastern side, one sees that only a few ancient olive trees soften the unrelieved bleakness of the stone-strewn soil.[1] Nothing in the outer aspect of the village itself suggests that it differs from the hill settlements which surround it—neither its close-jammed, brown, clay-covered houses, its dusty paths, nor its gardens and orchards.

Unless the traveler passed through the rolling foothills in the late spring or early summer when the verdure of the winter crops covers the landscape, he would never suspect that peasants could eke out a living in these surroundings. No streams exist to resuscitate crops from the summer heat and the blasts of desert wind. Although a number of ravines and gullies dissect the landscape, no springs provide water for wells from which men or animals might drink. Each family in the village has dug a cistern to catch the precious winter rains. In July, when these cisterns run dry, the peasants of Kufr al-Ma must trudge to the nearest spring in the adjoining village of Deir Abu Said (see map). There they purchase water from the

---

1. The description of the village that follows is timebound. It pertains to the period 1959–1967, the time when I collected the great bulk of my data on village social structure and culture, and more specifically on the Islamic sermon and the role of the preacher. Astonishing changes have occurred in the life of the village since then—some of which are briefly reported in the next chapter. For instance, the population of the village has more than doubled and now (1987) stands at about 4800. The village has been electrified, and piped water reaches the houses of all villagers. Thousands of olive trees have been planted in the region in a major afforestation effort. And, perhaps most significant, hundreds of sons of the village work and study outside it, many of them in foreign countries, earning incomes quadruple those that prevailed in the early 1960s. That is, there has been a revolution in the occupational structure of the village. However, as significant as these changes are for all aspects of life, to dwell on them in this work would be inappropriate since the sermons that provide the focus of this work were delivered at a time when the village had not yet undergone the radical economic and social changes that occurred after 1973 with the rapid rise in oil prices and the subsequent economic boom on the Arabian Peninsula. The village social structure described in this chapter, though changing in certain pronounced directions (see Antoun 1972 for details) still constituted the framework for religious belief and ritual, as well as interpersonal relations and local-level politics.

45

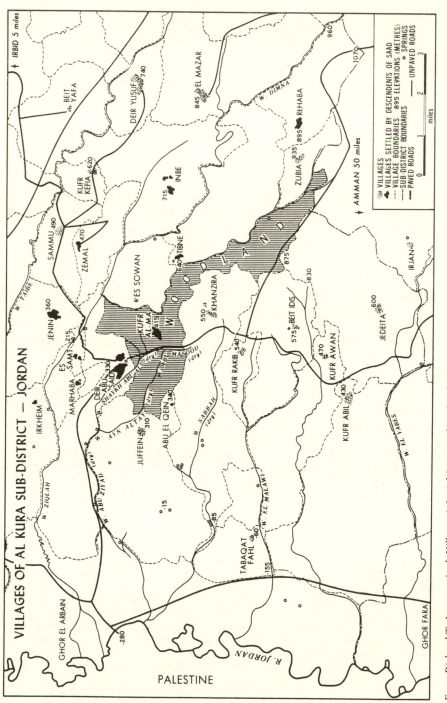

VILLAGES OF AL KURA SUB-DISTRICT — JORDAN

↑ IRBID 5 miles

PALESTINE

BEIT YAFA

DEIR YUSUF ₄740

845 EL MAZAR

KUFR KEFA ₄620

REHABA ₄895

INBE
715 ₄

ZUBIA ₄935

SAMMU ₄490

ZEMAL ₄470

W ES SOWAN

TIBNE
640

₄875

W. DIMNA

960

1070

JENIN ₄360

ES SAMT ₄215

KHANZIRA ₄550

₄830

IRJAN ₄

MARHABA

DEIR ABU SAID ₄530

KUFR AL MA ₄415

W. SHAYKH ABU ALI (dry)

EL MASOOD (dry)

BEIT IDIS ₄575

KUFR AWAN ₄470

JEDEITA ₄600

IRKHEIM

W. ZIQLAH

W. TAIBE (dry)

JUFFEIN ₄310

ABU EL QEIN ₄340

W. SABBAH (dry)

KUFR RAKIB ₄540

KUFR ABIL ₄430

GHOR EL ARBAIN

W. ABU ZIYAD (dry)

W. AYN ALTA (dry)

₄15

₄85

W. EL MALAWI

W. EL YABES

TABAQAT FAHL ₄601

₄155

₄280

R. JORDAN

GHOR FARA

W O O D L A N D

LEGEND

- 🝑 VILLAGES
- ◆ VILLAGES SETTLED BY DESCENDENTS OF SAAD
- --- VILLAGE BOUNDARIES   895 ELEVATIONS (METRES)
- ─── SUB-DISTRICT BOUNDARIES   ○ SPRINGS
- ━━━ PAVED ROADS   UNPAVED ROADS

→ AMMAN 50 miles

miles
0   1   2   3

From Richard T. Antoun, *Arab Village: A Social Structural Study of a Transjordan Peasant Community* (Indiana University Press, Bloomington, 1972), 3.

residents, load it on their donkeys, and return along the dusty track to their village.

However barren its outer aspect, Kufr al-Ma lies in the center of a populated cereal-growing region. Located in the northwestern corner of the Transjordanian plateau, its sedentary subsistence agriculture is apparently of some antiquity as evidenced by the ancient ruins of towns such as Jerash and Pella. An estimate of the population per square mile of cultivated area is about 780, making the northwestern corner of Transjordan one of the most densely settled areas in the Middle East.

The Transjordanian plateau is the center of Jordan's grain production. In the 1960s the bulk of Transjordan's population lived in some 226 towns and villages of the Ajlun District and were engaged in cultivating most of the million acres devoted to rain-fed cereals. Wheat, barley, and legumes (for fodder) are the chief winter crops and maize and sesame seed are the chief summer crops.

In Kufr al-Ma and adjoining villages these cereals are grown for subsistence.[2] Only the straw from the winter crops and the sesame seed are sold. Trucks pick up these commodities in the village and transport them to Palestine for sale. In a bumper year some peasants will harvest much more grain than they can consume. This surplus is used to pay off their previous debts at the village shops, is stored against future purchases, and is expended for marriage payments. The leguminous crops are mainly vetches, kersenneh, chickpeas, and lentils. All of these crops are grown in Kufr al-Ma, but only kersenneh takes up substantial acreage. In the hills of southern Ajlun, where rainfall is greatest, vineyards produce grapes and raisins. Tobacco is also grown for home consumption.

The peasants[3] of Kufr al-Ma are engaged in what geographers have termed "dry land farming"—"crop production under conditions of deficient rainfall."[4] In Jordan, dry farming is associated not only with low

2. Today (1987) Jordan imports most of its grain and in Kufr al-Ma cultivation of cereals is a minor endeavor. Agriculture has declined sharply in the Al-Kura region since 1960 with the exception of olive-growing, which has expanded at an astonishing rate.

3. Following native usage I am using the word *peasant* (fellah) to designate a man who is primarily engaged in subsistence farming, who owns and tills his land, or who sharecrops land for one-half of the crop. The critical distinction between a peasant and other men who till the soil is the amount of capital (land, seeds, animals) contributed to the enterprise rather than land ownership. These economic distinctions are reflected in the occupational terminology used by the inhabitants themselves (see discussion above). Many of the men considered peasants, plowmen, or agricultural laborers spend a considerable part of their time working as nonagricultural laborers, particularly in years of drought. This definition of peasant is not meant to rule out a broader definition of peasant based upon cultural criteria. For certain purposes of analysis such a definition is more useful than the economic definition given above (see, for instance, Richard T. Antoun, "The Social Significance of Ramadan in an Arab Village," *The Muslim World* Vol. 58, January 1968; see also chapters 1 and 3).

4. *The Proceedings of the Conference on Middle East Agricultural Development*, Report No. 6, 23.

rainfall, but also with uneven falls of rain, long intervals between rains, scorching winds, and daily oscillations in temperature. Since water is the overall limiting factor in crop production, efforts are centered around the conservation of moisture. Ploughing, fallowing, and weeding are three aspects of this conservation effort.

UNDER THE SHADOW OF THE CORPORATE VILLAGE

Until 1939, when the lands of the village were individually registered, Kufr al-Ma held the greater part of its cultivated lands under an unofficial category of land tenure known as *mushāʿ*. Under this system village crop-lands were regarded as belonging to the village community with individual cultivators owning only shares in land without ownership of any fixed plots. The fields were redistributed periodically (every one or two years) among the members of the community. Alienation of land from the village was hardly possible since co-villagers had prior rights to purchase the shares of any land to be sold. Under mushaʿ villagewide cooperation in the coordination of planting, the protection of crops (by hiring a watchman), and the consecutive harvesting of crops and pasturing of animals was necessary.[5]

Today, Kufr al-Ma cannot be regarded in any sense as a corporate village with control over economic resources. Land may be sold—even to nonvillagers. However, the village has not yet passed from under the shadow of its corporate history despite the formal revolution in land tenure (the registration of land to individual owners in 1939). After 1939 little land was alienated to nonvillagers. Owners of adjacent land plots are still usually granted the privilege of prior purchase before a sale is made. (Villagers have sometimes failed to exercise this privilege, however.) Most sales are to neighbors on the land or to lineage mates and clansmen (often the two are synonymous). A comparison of the distribution of land plots in terms of lineage and clan affiliation in 1939 and in 1960 shows very little change. Owners of abutting land plots tend to be affiliated with the same clans and lineages (though they may not be the same individuals) as in the earlier period.

The two most important events affecting the social structure of the village in the first half of the twentieth century were the breakdown of the district political structure with the bombing of Tibne in 1922 and the termination of the communal system of land tenure and cultivation in 1939.[6] The registration of land destroyed the corporate nature of the vil-

5. For a fuller description of the musha' system of land tenure see Richard T. Antoun, *Arab Village: A Social Structural Study of a Transjordanian Peasant Community* (Indiana University Press, Bloomington, 1972).

6. For a more detailed description of the breakdown of the district political structure, see Antoun, *Arab Village.*

lage, at least in its economic aspect and, in a sense, freed individual house-holds for enterprise within and mobility outside it. The remarkable fact is that despite the revolution in land tenure and the increase of occupa-tional mobility, so little change occurred in the village up to 1967, whether in the actual alienation of land outside it or the agglomeration of land within it. Its religious life remained strongly Islamic and its pro-cess of social control egalitarian and traditional. Despite considerable economic differentiation, social status differences remained minimal.

Land tenure relationships are reflected in terminology and to a consid-erable extent determine the social status of the individual. The term *Fellah* refers to a man who owns land and derives his main income from it whether he tills it or not and provided he lives in the village; it also refers to a sharecropper who works land as an equal partner contributing capi-tal along with the owner, that is, his plough animals and one-half the seeds for a one-half share in the harvest. The sharecropper for a one-fourth share, however, is termed *ḥarrāth* (ploughman). He has no plough animals to contribute and offers only his labor; moreover, he often lives in a room in his employer's house if he comes from another village, and eats with his employer's family; he has additional duties such as feeding and watering the animals and running errands for his employer's house-hold. The daily agricultural laborer or *ʿāmil* works for a daily wage and his employment may be summarily ended by his employer. Finally, there is the agricultural piece-worker or *qatrūz*. He is usually a young man who is hired as sort of apprentice ploughman. The owner contracts to give him a certain number of sacks of grain at the end of the season in return for his labor on the land. A man without land and who has other permanent nonagricultual employment (army, shopkeeping, low-echelon govern-ment position) is rather invidiously termed *landless one (fellawti)*. Each of the terms mentioned refers to one category of land tenure relationship with the exception of the term *fellah*, which includes men who own and till their own land and also sharecroppers working for one-half the crop. This discrepancy may be explained by the fact that the important factor involved from the peasant's point of view is not simply the ownership of land or the lack of it. Kufr al-Ma is, after all, a village of very small land-holdings with 61 percent of all landowners holding twelve acres or less. In 1960, the largest landowner owned only one hundred acres. The im-portant factor is the investment of capital in land and the sharing of prof-its and losses. The sharecropper for half the crops shares these risks. He contributes animals and seeds and shares with the owner the costs of pay-ment of wages to the blacksmith and agricultural laborers hired in the course of the season.

Among these land-tilling villages, land tenure relationships not only determine their economic status but also, to a large degree, their social status. The leaders of the village, the elders who assemble in the guest houses of the village to decide upon policy of kin or village affairs belong, in the main, to the category *fellah*. One landless villager, a stonecutter, was nominated by his descent group to serve on a planning committee for village improvement. He refused to serve, saying, "I have no time for such things. Besides, you know that we are landless ones (fellawti)." And the mukhtar of one of the landed descent groups belittled the claim of another descent group to equal membership on a village committee. "Who are the Beni Dumi?" he asked. "They are nothing but landless ones." He then proceeded to tick off on his fingers the names of the few landowning families of that particular descent group, as if to confirm his evaluation.

The Occupational Structure

Up until the end of World War I the land of Kufr al-Ma, like that of its sister villages, was given away to men who would settle on it, till it, and defend it. In 1960, forty years later, the land of Kufr al-Ma was in such short supply that one-half of the families in the village were landless and the remainder (with the exception of nineteen) had to seek alternative part-time employment to eke out a living.

The reduction of land holding has occurred as a result of the pressure of increasing population on a fixed amount of cultivable land. In the absence of irrigation and with the creation of the woodland preserve, all possible land in the village has been brought under cultivation. The population of Kufr al-Ma has increased considerably since 1940 while the amount of cultivable land has actually decreased. With the registration of village lands in 1930, 1037 acres were withdrawn from use either as pasture or crop land. This land (about one-third of the total possible cultivable land in Kufr al-Ma) was claimed by the government as woodland preserve (see map). At the same time, the population has been expanding steadily. Although no previous population figures were available for the village by 1960, eighty-seven new houses had been built outside the boundaries of the village settlement since 1940. All of the old houses, in the meanwhile, have remained occupied. It is this relationship of expanding population to shrinking land resources that explains why Kufr al-Ma, in appearance a typical peasant village, counts only 39 percent of its employed men as cultivators of the soil.

Typical of the contraction of land holdings in successive generations is the case of the mukhtar of Kufr al-Ma, Muflih al-Hakim. In 1960, Muflih possessed four acres in Kufr al-Ma. He owned one plough horse, two geese, and a few chickens. His father and his two brothers possessed twenty-two acres in Kufr al-Ma, Rehaba, and the Jordan Valley as well as 250 sheep, seventy goats, one team of oxen, three donkeys, two milch cows, and one purebred horse. The division of land of these three brothers among their ten sons has reduced the share of each to such an extent that seven of the ten have left the village to seek employment elsewhere.

The consequences of such land shortage are seen in the occupational structure of Kufr al-Ma. In 1960, less than 40 percent of the employed men covered by my census were engaged in subsistence agriculture. Of 369 men, 39 percent or 147 were engaged in agricultural occupations; 30 percent or 114 were engaged in nonagricultural occupations, and 29 percent or 108 were engaged in military occupations. Beni Yasin, the descent group with the most land, had only 46 percent of its employed men engaged in agriculture while the independent families (not associated with the three main descent groups) had only 27 percent so engaged.

Even in 1960 the consequences of such an occupational structure for mobility were plain. A certain number of men found employment in the village as shopkeepers, artisans, and stonecutters (34); others worked out of the village but in the locality as builders, peddlers, and local laborers (39); the remainder (141) found employment as soldiers, government clerks, and laborers in distant towns, in army camps, and in the capital, Amman. In addition, many peasants, particularly sharecroppers, were forced to hire out their labor in surrounding villages or in the Jordan Valley due to the shortage of land in Kufr al-Ma.

The occupational mobility characteristic of Kufr al-Ma, while perhaps more pronounced, is not unusual for villages of the area. Of the twenty-five villages in Al Kura subdistrict, only five have more than the 2700 acres of privately owned cultivable land which Kufr al-Ma claims as its own. Land shortage, population growth, and occupational mobility characterize all the villages of the subdistrict.

In addition to the ties created by the movement of sharecroppers, builders, and peddlers into the surrounding villages (where they may reside for part of the season), numerous kinship and marriage ties link Kufr al-Ma with other villages in the area (see Figure 2.1). These extravillage local ties are related not only to shortage of land and population pressure but also to the district political organization which once linked the villages of Tibne. Figure 2.1 dramatizes the multiplicity of extravillage links into the immediately surrounding area as well as their diverse nature, cutting across several distinct interest areas including agriculture, construction, marriage, and descent.

THE SOCIAL STRUCTURAL BACKGROUND

The single most important fact about the occupational structure of the village is not its dominance by those employed in agriculture. On the contrary, less than 40 percent of the employed men are engaged in subsis-

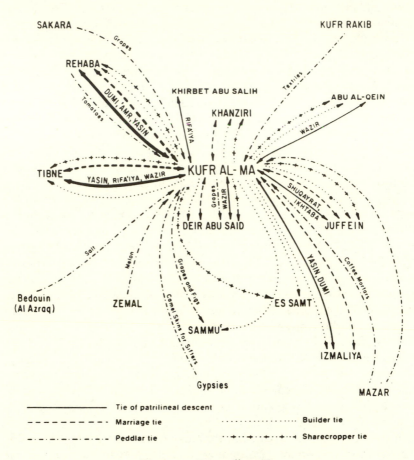

Figure 2.1 Extravillage Ties

From Richard T. Antoun, *Arab Village: A Social Structural Study of a Transjordian Community* (Indiana University Press, Bloomington, 1972), 29.

tence agriculture, and a substantial number have had to seek employment outside the village.[7] Kufr al-Ma has been characterized by long-distance mobility since the establishment of the British Mandate in Palestine (1920). A large majority of the villagers worked in Palestine on three or more separate occasions. Many used to leave after the harvest or during drought seasons to spend three or more months in Haifa or Tel Aviv

7. The percentage engaged in subsistence agriculture is probably smaller and the percentage engaged in nonagricultural occupations outside of the village is probably higher, since many falling in the latter category were not present in the village during my stay and therefore were not recorded in the occupational census.

where they worked as fishermen, construction laborers, factory hands, gardeners, and harvesters.

With the end of the Palestinian War in 1949 and the closing of the western border of Jordan, the towns that had provided an outlet for such migration—Haifa, Akka, Jaffa, and Tel Aviv—were suddenly cut off. Long-distance migration now, to some degree at least, turned toward the north (Damascus and Beirut) and the east (Amman). But this remained a trickle as compared with the former migrant flow to Palestine.

The expansion of the Jordanian army during and following the first Arab-Israeli war counterbalanced the economic opportunities lost by the securing partition of Palestine. Indeed, the new opportunities were so much better than the old that bribery was often the only sure means of securing enlistment into the Jordanian army. Yet only forty years earlier men had given away their lands in order to avoid service in the Turkish army!

The labor migration to Palestine had been largely sporadic. Men would leave the village after the harvest, only to return two or three months later. They might not go again for several years if agricultural production proved sufficient. The monetary returns varied, but they were, in general, small. After three months a man might return to the village with the equivalent of twelve dollars saved, at most twenty-five. Since most migrants turned to fishing, where a day's wage depended on the catch, returns were unpredictable—from nothing to about three dollars. As political disturbances increased, the better paid jobs within the Jewish section of the economy disappeared, particularly after the Jewish Agency in Zurich decided in 1929 to exclude Arab labor from all Jewish enterprises.

Employment in the Jordanian army, on the other hand, guaranteed a young recruit a monthly salary. For every child the soldier received an additional stipend. Of fourteen lineages examined in Kufr al-Ma, seven had a soldier as the highest salaried man, while in four, the highest salaried man worked as a government employee outside the village. The seven army men who led their respective groups in salary had annual incomes in pound sterling as follows: 170, 192, 310, 312, 428, 444, and 580. The four government employees had incomes of 420, 480, 600, and 695. Three of these four men lived outside the village in the town where they worked, but all had land or houses in the village or wives and children living there. In only three of the fourteen lineages did cultivators receive the highest income. Their incomes in 1960 were £186, £190, and £225, respectively. The richest farmers in Kufr al-Ma were not able to match the income of the salaried employees; in general a gap of £100 or more separates them. The same gap exists between prosperous village grocers (who earn about as much as wealthy cultivators) and salaried employees.

After World War II another change occurred that drew Kufr al-Ma po-

litically, economically, and ideologically into a larger world. The region
of Al-Kura was elevated to the status of a subdistrict or *qaḍā'*. Deir Abu
Said, a neighboring village, became the administrative center, and access
to government offices became easier for the peasants of Kufr al-Ma. A
subdistrict office in charge of government wheat distributions, water al-
locations, and school improvements resided in Deir Abu Said. The chief
forest ranger, who guarded the woodlands from depredation by peasants
searching for firewood and from foraging animals, established his office
there, as did the inspectors of agriculture and health. A civil court which
heard all cases regarding crop damage, a land registry office which han-
dled all cases involving land title and sale, a dispensary, and a tax office
were established there. Finally in 1953, a religious court was set up in
Deir Abu Said to hear cases involving marriage, inheritance, divorce, and
endowments.

There are, then, two economic sectors within the village. The first, the
agricultural, is strongly affected by contingent environmental conditions
that have placed a ceiling on economic differentiation and supported an
egalitarian ethic rooted in religious belief. Within this sector land is the
key to economic and social status. The second and larger sector, the nonagricultural, seeks its income largely outside the village. Within this sector
economic differentiation is considerable (a poor peasant may find his
closest kinsman, a brother or a cousin, earning a salary four times his
own) and the household unit tends to be small (conjugal rather than extended families).

SIGNIFICANT SOCIAL UNITS

Of the twenty-five villages of Al Kura subdistrict, a majority of the inhabitants of ten (see darkened village settlements in map, p. 46) including
Kufr Al-Ma claim to be descended from a common ancestor variously
named Ahmed, Saʿad, or Hammad. Peake's account of the origin of Al
Hammad corresponds fairly well with the account given to me by the
villagers of Tibne.[8]

> The tribe claims descent from Khalid ibn al Welid, but have nothing
> to support such a claim. It is said that they are descended from a man
> called Hammad, who with two brothers, Shafi and Nafi, came to
> Tibna some 500 years ago from the Wadi Hammad of Kerak Dis-

8. Peake's book has been translated into Arabic and at least one copy was available in
Kufr al-Ma. This copy was probably passed around from hand to hand, as is the villagers'
habit with interesting reading material. The possibility certainly exists that the villagers were
merely recounting what was read to them in Peake's book. But the fact remains that Peake
originally elicited the information from the heads of the descent groups in the area.

trict. Nafi went to Jerusalem and his descendants are said to be the Khalidi family. Shafi went to Safed and his descendants are said to be the Shahin family of Nabulus and the Qaddura family of Safed.

Of the three large local descent groups in Kufr al-Ma only one, Beni Yasin, claims direct descent from Hammad. Beni Yasin is, however, the largest of the local descent groups in the village, comprising about 40 percent of the population and owning over 60 percent of the land. Moreover, the other two local descent groups—Beni Dumi and Beni ʿAmr— claim to be "of the peoples of Tibne," having resided there before the division of land at the turn of the century. This division scattered the residents to daughter villages such as Kufr al-Ma. The term *the peoples of Tibne*, then, refers to people who identify themselves by a common historical experience in a certain locale and, for the great majority, by a claimed common descent from a named patrilineal ancestor.

Although the common ideology of propinquity *cum* descent has not provided economic privileges or advantages of status, for certain clans it has been associated historically with political cooperation at the subdistrict level. In 1921 the seven villages which remained loyal to Kleb Wazir were mainly populated by the peoples of Tibne. Moreover, the peoples of Tibne still held certain norms of political action.[9] Among these norms is one still important for social control—the peoples of Tibne must cooperate in cases of honor involving violations of their women by men of other groups. The significant social units in Kufr al-Ma are stipulated in table 2.1. In order of size from smallest to largest we find the household, the close consultation group, the lineage, the clan, the village, and that part of the subdistict identified by the phrase *the peoples of Tibne*.[10]

The basic social group of the village is the household. The smallest permanent economic unit in the village, it is defined by the possession of a common purse to which all members contribute. Approximately 74 percent of all households censused were nuclear families, while only 23 percent were extended families. Household size ranged from one to twenty-two persons with the modal number being seven. The close consultation group contains a number of households—those which must be consulted in matters relating to land, marriage, and local politics. It is usually composed of several brothers and their families or of first partrilateral cousins and their families, but it may also include matrilateral relatives or affines. Quite often in the previous generation the group lived as one household

9. "A norm . . . is an idea in the minds of the members of a group, an idea that can be put in the form of a statement specifying what the members or other men should do, ought to do, are expected to do, under given circumstances" (Homans 1950: 123).

10. For a fuller description of the social structure of Kufr al-Ma, including a discussion of the household, marriage, and social control, see Antoun, *Arab Village*.

TABLE 2.1
Significant Social Units in Kufr al-Ma, 1960

Local Groups	Size or Number of Units	General Term of Reference for the Group	Ideology	Principle of Recruitment
Part of Sub-district	9 Villages	The Clans of Tibne (*'ashā'ir tibne*)	"The people of Tibne" (*ahāli tibne*)	Common Historical Origin and/or Patrilineal Descent
Village	2000	The Village (*al-balad*)	"Son of the Village" (*ibn al-balad*)	All Residents Linked in Multiplex Relationships
Clan	3 clans: largest 786 smallest 359	The Clan (*al-'ashīra*)	Patrilineal Descent	Patrilineal Descent
Lineage	28 Lineages	The Branch (*al-fandi*)	Patrilineal Descent	Patrilineal Descent
Close Consultation Group		Name of Group or ["Must" (Group)] (*luzum*)	Patrilineal Descent	Patrilineal Descent, Matrilaterality, and Affinity
Household	ca. 250: largest 22 smallest 1	Family or House (*'ayla*) or *dār*)	Both Patrilineal and Bilateral	Patrilineal Descent

Source: From Richard T. Antoun, *Low-Key Politics: Local-Level Leadership and Change in the Middle East* (State University of New York Press, Albany, 1979), 27.

under their grandfather or uncle in one big house. The close consultation group may be named or unnamed, is usually characterized by propinquity of land and houses, and often holds land undivided among its members. Members are legally responsible for paying "truce money" in cases of honor.

The lineage includes patrilineally related men, their wives, and their children. Its size ranges from 12 to 304. Almost invariably it has a name and is usually characterized by spatial agglomeration of houses and land.[11] The lineage claims its own women in marriage, though it does not always enforce such claims. It aligns in disputes and expects representation on ad hoc village committees.

11. For the precise spatial relations of the lineages of the village, including the few exceptions to the pattern stipulated, see the map in Antoun, *Arab Village*, facing p. 90.

There are three clans in Kufr al-Ma. They are defined ideologically on a sliding scale by patrilineal descent. The largest (Beni Yasin) numbers 786 members and the smallest (Ben ʿAmr) numbers 359. Like the lineage and the close consultation group, the clan is characterized, with some exceptions, by spatial agglomeration of houses and land.[12] This agglomeration is remarkable in view of the fact that more than twenty years of a free market in land has prevailed, with land held in individual ownership and the buying and selling of land legally permissible to outsiders as well as nonclansmen within the village.[13] As is true of the close consultation group and the lineage, visiting is much more frequent between clan members than between them and other villagers. The clan, moreover, plays a key role in social control. Prominent clan elders act as self-appointed admonishers of clansmen who have violated fundamental norms of behavior, such as respect for the aged or modesty, and they help resolve disputes within the village so that resort to government agents is avoided. The clan also acts as a prestige unit, since villagers not of the clan may call in its elders to mediate a dispute. In addition the clan is an important political unit, for it can be represented by a formally recognized leader. This leader is the mayor (mukhtar), who is selected by his clansmen and confirmed by the government as their functionary in the village.[14] Local administrative policy allows one mayor for every thousand residents of a village, so Kufr al-Ma has two mayors. This means that one clan will not have direct representation through a mayor, although all villagers, willy-nilly, relate politically to one mayor or the other.

The Village as Community

Like other Jordanian villages, Kufr al-Ma can be distinguished by certain formal criteria: it is a nucleated village with its population clustered in a

12. For the precise spatial relations of the clans of the village, including the few exceptions to the pattern stipulated, see Antoun, *Arab Village*, map facing p. 74.

13. For the distribution of land according to descent groups in 1960, together with land sales since 1939, see Antoun, *Arab Village*, map facing p. 24.

14. The translation "mayor" for mukhtar is not entirely appropriate, since, unlike his U.S. counterpart, he does not represent a legal corporation (municipality), but an administrative unit. Moreover, he is not this unit's sole representative—in Kufr al-Ma there is a second mayor. He is not elected, nor is he subject to renomination and reelection in order to continue his tenure; he is chosen by a consensus of clansmen and confirmed by the central government. His tenure ends only when that consensus changes or when the district officer declares him no longer able or willing to discharge his duties fairly. Despite these differences, it would even be more misleading to translate mukhtar as "headman," since he performs few of the tasks performed by a headman in the literature of sub-Saharan African ethnography (whether ritual, economic, or social). Moreover he is not necessarily or even usually a first among equals in terms of power or influence; other clan elders often exert more influence in clan and villagewide policy making.

close-packed living area and surrounded by the cultivated lands that mark it off as a discrete unit, spatially separate from other villages; it is an administrative entity, the basis of government plans, estimates, and handouts and represented by an officially confirmed mayor or mayors. In some respects it is regarded as a legal corporation, for it is held responsible for damages done to government woodland in its area. The village is also a locus of kinship.

Certain functions also distinguish the village and set it off from other villages. It is a credit area in which debt can accumulate at village shops, usually for a year, without demand for payment. Kufr al-Ma is a framework for political competition—this in spite of the fact that it has no single political leader and no single political center. That is, members of clans and lineages vie for control of the prizes (e.g., land, jobs, money) made available within the village and not within some other unit. Moreover it is the village that is consciously regarded as the framework of status differentiation. Thus a former mayor belonging to the Beni ʿAmr, a clan no longer represented by a mukhtar, commented on the plight of his clan by saying, "We have no name in this village!" Certain men are singled out as curtaining the village, that is, enhancing its prestige by offering hospitality on a regular basis in their own guest house. Men from other villages know that strangers passing through are always assured of finding food, lodgings, coffee, and good company. Above all, the village is a unit of social control, that is, a common area of living where limits must be placed on the show of hostility and where men can be made to subordinate their own desires and interests to those of the larger unit.

Membership in a village "community" does not proceed automatically from residence within it or from formal connection to a representative of external authority (the mayor). It comes about by the gradual accumulation of interests, each constituting an additional strand to a relationship that becomes increasingly "multiplex."[15] Thus any individual who moves into a quarter of the village necessarily becomes involved with his neighbors in the giving and receiving of hospitality. The activities of planting, harvesting, building, and providing adequate drinking water for his family and his animals soon bring him into a relationship of day-to-day economic cooperation with many villagers. If he has nubile daughters, he marries them within the village either to kinsmen with whom he already has patrilineal ties or to other villagers, thereby establishing a tie of affinity to complement those already formed on the basis of neighborship and economic cooperation. In order to receive formal authorization for a

15. A multiplex relationship is one that serves many interests (e.g., economic, political, religious, recreational). See Max Gluckman, *The Judicial Process Among the Barotse of Northern Rhodesia* (Manchester: University of Manchester Press, 1955), 18 for a discussion of this concept.

marriage, he must solicit from a mayor of the village an official document that certifies the identities of the bride and bridegroom, their ages, and the lack of legal impediments to the marriage. The villager, whether he belongs to the mayor's clan or not, has now established a political connection in the village. The final stages of absorption into the community are marked by claiming to be a member of a particular patrilineal descent group, usually a clan, and finally, the actual representation of this claim on a genealogy. This last action is important because full-fledged community membership can only occur through the establishment of ties with a patrilineal descent group, and these ties are always described in a kinship idiom of descent ("my father's brothers," *ʿamāmi*), matrilaterality ("my mother's brothers," *akhwāli*), or marriage ("my affine," *nasībi*).

There is an extended sense in which a significant part of the subdistrict, that part identified as "the peoples of Tibne," is also a community (see table 2.1 for attributes of the peoples of Tibne). The ancestors of many Kufr al-Ma residents and those of other villages identified as the peoples of Tibne once lived together in Tibne, coming down seasonally to till the surrounding lands and to harvest them. Thus the ideology of subdistrict unity ("the peoples of Tibne") carries with it the ideology of common villageship. In this sense all "the peoples of Tibne" are "sons of the village." They say of themselves, "our ancestor is one, our attack is one, our genealogical tree is one" and they claim to have a common call of distress. But the solidarity of the peoples of Tibne has more than ideological significance. Collections of money are occasionally made from those so-designated in matters of common interest (e.g., to influence government officials to return land appropriated and set aside as a woodland preserve). More important, the peoples of Tibne still seek to coordinate actions in outstanding cases of honor. In 1960 they refused to give "protection" (dakhl) to some men (not of Tibne) who had impugned the honor of the group by taking sexual advantage of its women. In cases where an individual of the peoples of Tibne impugns the honor of other groups, the peoples of Tibne contribute to the compensation necessary for reconciliation and peacemaking (sulha). To be sure, they do not contribute the same amount as the culprit's immediate patrilineal relatives, but however small, a sum is always expected and nearly always forthcoming. In addition the peoples of Tibne "rush to succor" (*yifzaʿu*) one another by a bodily and occasionally armed presence when they are threatened by others. Again, patrilineal kinsmen compose the core of the armed delegation dispatched, but it may include others. Finally, there is a sense in which the peoples of Tibne offer one another "moral succor" (*fazʿa maʿnawiya*). That is, they counsel and restrain one another and push each other toward reconciliation when that is clearly the reasonable and just solution.

In cases of honor, social control can extend beyond the peoples of Tibne, although the ethical obligation is much weaker. Village members have been known to go as far as Kerak, a distance of one hundred miles, soliciting monetary contributions to provide the necessary compensation in a case of honor. This sort of obligation represents the furthest stretch of village involvement in social control and reveals the underlying reality of the phrase always heard among Transjordanians—"We are the children of tribes and clans" (*ihna awlād gabā'il wa 'ashā'ir*).

Cases of honor have additional significance for the village as a community. The obligation of social control cuts across political divisions. That is, a villager contributes to compensation solicited by a co-villager regardless of the political faction to which that villager belongs. In like manner, members of one clan call upon elders of other, politically opposed clans for counsel in mediating disputes. Since a significant percentage of marriages are out of the clan entirely, most villagers have affines who are members of clans and lineages opposed politically at any given moment. Thus numerous social ties cut across the ties of political factionalism and reinforce the solidarity of the village.

THE PEASANT PREDICAMENT

This review of the various environmental, economic, historical, social structural, political, and cultural aspects of the village's and subdistrict's life has been necessary to describe what might be designated as the "peasant predicament" and the "social structural predicament." That, is, residents of Kufr al-Ma are faced with certain constraints, pressures, and choices that shape their existential situation. These pressures emerge as a result of the individual's participation in a dry cereal-farming regime or, alternatively, in migrant labor or village shopkeeping, in a tribal legal structure, a former subdistrict political organization, a national administrative system, and a village community and descent structure which stress propinquity and kinship. As a result of participation in these institutions and the multiplexity and cross-cutting ties[16] they imply, the indi-

16. Multiplex ties are those that serve many interests. That is, when two villagers from Kufr al-Ma interact they are interacting according to a number of roles simultaneously. They may own adjacent plots of agricultural land. They may meet in the same village guest house in the evening. They may be affines or men tied by membership in a descent group. Any particular interaction between the two men assumes not one line but many possible lines of interest—economic, religious, political, consanguineous, or recreational. Because they are many-sided, these relationships become tinged with moral and ethical meaning. They remain moral and ethical even after the occurrence of occupational mobility and economic differentiation. Cross-cutting ties are social relationships in which men united by one set of interests or affiliations are divided by another set. Clanmates within the village may be united by patrilineal descent and perhaps spatial propinquity but divided (and thereby united to other villagers) by clan exogamy and economic differentiation.

vidual is involved in a network of rights and obligations with their accompanying values: achievement of status through hospitality, generosity and arbitral excellence, prior loyalty to kinsmen, good fellowship, harmony at the expense of individual expression, group consensus and mutual aid, and the right to be one's brother's keeper.

The peasant predicament is aggravated first of all by peasant poverty in a modern world which requires change and material and educational modernization.[17] A man, for instance, must often choose between expending hospitality on his kinsmen, friends, and neighbors and gaining the respected status of elder (shaykh) in his old age or sending his son on for further education—first, through high school in the nearest market town and then to a university, most likely abroad—and achieving a reputation for miserliness. Part of the peasant predicament is that a short-handed cultivator must choose between sending his daughters out to the woodland to collect wood or out to the fields to harvest with unrelated men, thereby violating the deep-rooted norms of modesty, or refusing to do so, maintaining his reputation for honor at the cost of critical agricultural production.[18]

A part of the peasant predicament is to choose whether to accept or at least tolerate the peasant tradition of magic (for instance, to treat barrenness—see chapter 5) or to condemn it as both urban intelligensia and the local religious leader demand. Part of the peasant predicament is to determine whether and to what degree in a period of inflation one should search for marriageable mates of lower social status for one's sons, thereby paying a manageable marriage payment (mahr) or searching for a mate of equal status, paying a much higher mahr, thereby gaining status but plunging into debt.

One aspect of the peasant predicament is the social structural predicament. That is, every individual is classified in certain social relational categories and, therefore, has certain rights and suffers certain disabilities as a result. For instance, in Jordan, state inheritance rules for land stipulate that agricultural land should be equally divided between all children regardless of sex. Yet the demographic composition of the households of siblings is almost always unequal—some siblings marry early and have large households and many mouths to feed, while others marry late and have no or few children. The father, then, may attempt to avoid the egalitarianism of the law and apply a "fairness doctrine" in terms of demo-

17. As mentioned above, the economic status of the community has changed quite radically since 1973, and Kufr al-Ma can no longer be designed as a poor peasant community. The description of social and economic status in this chapter pertains to the period 1960–1967. The author hopes to analyze the impact of recent economic changes on the community in a future study.

18. This peasant predicament is analyzed in detail in Antoun, "On the Modesty of Women."

graphic realities. Co-wives are expected to be treated equally in all amen-
ities and in terms of sexual access according to Islamic law, yet husbands
tend to neglect wives who do not bear children. Moreover, Quranic verses
although permissive of polygyny make it conditional upon equal treatment of spouses and suggest that such treatment is impossible.[19] Should
a fellah who wishes to marry a second wife because his first has not borne
him heirs or because he needs more working hands on the land refrain
from doing so?

The social structural predicament involves the young and the old. Most
households in Kufr al-Ma are two-generation "conjugal" rather than
three-generation "extended" families; that is, most are composed of husband, wife, and unmarried children and not husband, wife, and married
sons with their wives and children. The predicament of conjugal families
has been accentuated by sons joining the army or leaving the village for
nonagricultural work; when they marry, since they are earning their own
salary and not receiving it from their father as a reward for a contribution
to a joint cultivating enterprise, they set up independent households. Parents now frequently complain about sons not contributing to their support. This noncontribution is particularly painful in view of the norms of
filial piety and the traditional economic dependence of sons on fathers.
Many mothers have gone to the religious court to raise cases against their
sons for noncontribution toward a living allowance (*nafaqa*). The opposite has occurred in the past—the domination of the old over the young.
Fathers have traditionally "eaten" the mahr of daughters. The marriage
payment, given by the husband to his wife and required by Islamic law,
has been used in the past by the fathers for their own purposes, most often
in the case of poor peasants to buy flour to secure the year's bread supply.
To do so is a substantive though not technical violation of Islamic law.
Daughters, abetted by their husbands, have begun to raise cases in the
Islamic court, demanding that their fathers turn over the mahr, quite
often a substantial sum—a year's income for a peasant—to them. Fathers,
on the other hand, have defended their actions in court as quite justified
by peasant tradition. Their daughters, whom they reared, were now to go
to other men for whom they would work and bear children, bearing their
husbands' names. Did they not have the right to be compensated (by the
mahr)?[20]

19. The pertinent Quranic verses are as follows:

And if ye fear that ye will not deal fairly by the orphans, marry of the women who seem
good to you, two or three or four and if ye fear that ye cannot do justice (to so many)
then one (only) or (the captives) that your right hands possess. Thus it is more likely
that you will not do injustice. (Surah 4, Verse 3).

Ye will not be able to deal equally with your wives." (Surah 4, Verse 129)

20. I have analyzed aspects of the peasant and more specifically social structural predic-

One aspect of the social structural predicament is the "community predicament." That is, in a cheek-by-jowl, multiplex, nucleated community of peasants where face-to-face relations prevail friction is bound to bring estrangement, and relations that were cordial and face-to-face become back-to-back with the practice of mutual avoidance. Visiting relations between close kinsmen and neighbors are neglected and gossip which usually prevails in any case through the use of invidious nicknames (e.g., "Father of Cabbages" for a man who loves to eat them, "Dripping-nose," "The Cripple," "Walrus" for a man of gross proportions with a mustache) becomes slander. Such behavior is specifically condemned by Islamic ethics in the Quranic verse, "**Do not revile one another with nicknames**" (49: 11). The elders of the community cannot allow such estrangement to continue indefinitely because it is disruptive to social, economic, and political relations in a close-knit community.[21] Usually after some time has elapsed a delegation of respected elders pounce on one of the estranged men, usually the younger or the one presumed to be at fault, and ask him to respect their honor by reconciling with his opponent. It is very difficult to refuse such a delegation; to do so will alienate them as well, when the goal of much community behavior is to capture their praise. Often the delegates will refuse to drink the man's tea or eat his food—and also refuse to go home—until their host has agreed to reconciliation. No matter what, estrangement should end after a year's time when at the end of the fast of Ramadan all adult men are supposed to buss one another on leaving the mosque. Not to do so would not only violate village norms but also religious ones. Once having bussed a man publically, ending the estrangement on a substantive basis after a decent interval is easier.

The community predicament involves the necessity of maintaining harmony among neighbors and kinsmen on whom one has been dependent in the past and will be dependent in the future: one may need to ask for water from a cistern or help in the harvest or the hand of a daughter in marriage for one's son. But the preservation of harmony often conflicts with what one may construe as justice. Late one night one of the mayors of the village, an elder of the largest clan in the village and a respected arbitrator and patriot, got word that a bogus magician was in the house of a villager at the edge of a settlement. He was treating women for bar-

---

ament as it relates to the work of the Islamic court in Jordan in "The Islamic Court, the Islamic Judge, and the Accommodation of Traditions: A Jordanian Case Study," *International Journal of Middle East Studies*, Vol. 12, No. 4, December 1980, as well as in "The Impact of the Islamic Court on Peasant Families in Jordan," in *Law and Islam in the Middle East*, Daisy Dwyer, editor (Bergin and Garvey, in press).

21. For an analysis of the significance of names, including nicknames in Kufr al-Ma, see Antoun, 1968b. "On the Social Significance of Names in an Arab Village," *Ethnology*.

renness—and in private.[22] This mayor, though quite religious, was a man of the world, having served with the British army in World War II and worked under Jews as a construction laborer in Palestine. He regarded men such as this magician as hypocrites who exploited the superstitious among the villagers. Moreover, the magician's seeing women in private was a gross violation of modesty. He immediately went to the house of the other mayor and got him out of bed, telling him that they should go at once to the house where the bogus magician was and drive him out of town. The younger mayor got up reluctantly and set off with his indignant co-mayor, but managed to get away and return home. The older mayor and his son confronted the magician alone. The mayor berated the native villager who was hosting the magician and told the latter to leave town immediately. When the host and the magician objected, the mayor and his son pummeled both. Next day, a story appeared in the newspaper of the adjacent subdistrict center stating that a bogus magician treating women in private had been apprehended in Kufr al-Ma. This piece scandalized the village, for now the honor of many men was called into question: how could they have let their wives go alone to consult a strange magician?[23] The villagers upbraided the older mayor and implicitly praised the younger mayor for his circumspect behavior—he had not scandalized the village. One mayor had valued harmony over justice and the other had not.

The preacher of the village must deal with these predicaments and weigh the constraints and options they represent since most important village events and conflicts are reflections of them.

But the matter goes further than this. The preacher of Kufr al-Ma is directly involved in these predicaments since he is a son of the village, born and raised in it. As the following chapter will indicate, the status of the hometown village preacher is not always enviable. He does not receive the respect given to a preacher who is a stranger since his foibles and his life history are well known. More important, his co-villagers do not always honor the contract stipulating conditions of employment. On the other hand, the home-towner or *ibn al-balad* ("son of the town") as he is called, has the advantage of knowing his community inside-out and being able to address its most intimate problems. He also has a comfortable and set position in a particular lineage and clan of his village, though this, too, may pose problems when his own kinsmen become involved in disputes.

We are dealing with a continuum of intimacy, from the priest of the

22. See chapter 5 for the implications of this incident for the social organization of tradition and, specifically, the village preacher's interpretation of the relationship (or nonrelationship) between magic and religion.

23. For an analysis of the critical importance of modesty as a value among Arab Muslim peasants see Antoun, "On the Modesty of Women."

Greek Orthodox village of Munsif in Lebanon studied by John Gulick in which the priest and the local church were identified with the village and not with an outside hierarchy, where the priest was a village member chosen by other village members, where the priest was married into the village and working its land;[24] to the Methodist chapel of Staithes, England where "ministers were, and are, frequently perceived as interfering 'foreigners' who, unacquainted with local conditions and attitudes, attempt to assert their will over that of the village populace."[25] One member of this Methodist chapel stated, as if to sum up the parishioners' attitudes: "The old men always used to say to us, 'Don't take any notice of ministers, don't let them get a whip hand over you, because they're only ships that pass in the night.' "[26] Doubtless this view of Methodist ministers was related to Methodist circuit policy which assigned ministers or "circuit-riders" to a number of churches on a circuit without being attached to any one. Even today with a modification of the above practice, it is understood that ministers will change parishes after five years.

The culture broker who is a stranger, then, also has to deal with the problem of intimacy. Quite often, culture brokers realize their weakness in this respect and seek to become more intimate with the folk for whom they must interpret. As indicated in chapter 1, following World War II French worker priests enrolled in labor unions, engaged in political protests, went to work in the factories, and often went unrecognized as priests by their co-workers.[27] In the Philippines, Father Jalondoni, the activist priest who joined workers and peasants against landlords stated the problem clearly: "We (priests) need to feel their hunger and share the harassment and intimidation which is their lot."[28] In both these cases, for the culture broker the path to intimacy is regarded as proceeding through cultural assimilation and political activism. In each case such behavior brought the priests into conflict with their own church hierarchies and with the State. In becoming so intimate with their parishioners they became estranged with their own bishops who lived in a different experiential world.

Recently (1984), pressure has mounted, including some by members of the U.S. Congress, to establish a "civilian" chaplain program supervised by particular church bodies for the U.S. armed forces to replace "military" chaplains. Military men, including the army chaplains themselves, have defended the present program largely in terms of the problem of

24. See Gulick, *Social Structure and Culture in a Lebanese Village*.
25. See David Clark, *Between Pulpit and Pew Folk Religion in a North Yorkshire Fishing Village* (Cambridge University Press, Cambridge, 1982), 78ff.
26. Ibid.
27. Andreas Freund, *New York Times*, May 27, 1979.
28. Robert Whymany, *Binghamton Evening Press*, January 22, 1974.

intimacy. At present army chaplains are members of the regular army; they jump out of planes like parachute trainees and sleep outside with infantrymen. The chaplains when explaining their activity (which is on a voluntary basis) say, "Ours is a ministry of presence."[29] One regular army officer said, "You might have trouble recruiting civilian chaplains to join my four-mile run at five in the morning." Unlike the cases mentioned above, the (military) hierarchy is quite supportive of the regular recruitment of chaplains as a way through the predicament of intimacy; "military" chaplains, it is said, understand the army and are trusted by both officers and enlisted men and women.[30]

In Kufr al-Ma the culture broker (preacher) is very much a part of his congregation, lives in a stone and adobe house[31] in a quarter of the village, eats its food, was brought up in its public ways and schools, and married one of its daughters. He even has an invidious nickname, referring to his spindly-legged boyhood: "Young billy-goat" (*jiddī*). His status as a "son of the village" involves its own peculiar predicament.

29. *New York Times*, March 4, 1984.
30. Ibid.
31. That is, until 1984 when he moved to an attractive concrete and smooth-cut stone two-storied house with modern bathroom facilities. But this is another story—the story of the economic revolution that began in 1973 with the oil boom on the Arabian peninsula.

3

The Role of the Preacher,
the Content of the Sermon: The Case of Luqman

For Muslims the first and model preacher (*khaṭīb*) was the Prophet, Muhammad. Muhammad injected into this role a specific moral and sociopolitical content that had hitherto been absent since the Quran had been sent to provide guidance in the darkness of this world and to impel men to take action to propagate and fulfill its message. However, in Arabia before Islam a number of speaking roles existed: the poet (*shāʿir*), the chief (*sayyid*)—who was often said to be the possessor of special spiritual gifts—and the soothsayer (*kāhin*), who delivered oracles in rhymed prose, blessed followers, cursed enemies, and acted as faith healer.[1] Indeed, Muhammad, since he performed some of the same functions and since the Quran was articulated in rhymed prose (*saja'*) was accused by his enemies of being a soothsayer.[2] The word *qur'an* is derived from the Arabic root, *qara'a* ("to recite") and means "reading aloud," "chanting," or "recitation." Muhammad was commanded by the angel, Gabriel, to **Proclaim!** (or Read) **in the name of thy Lord and Cherisher, who created—created man, out of a** (mere) **clot of congealed blood** (96: 1–2, *YA*).[3] The verses of the Quran not only moved to tears the hearers of Muhammed's own day; it also served as a model for future generations of Muslim preachers. For the enemies who aimed to discredit him, however, Muhammad's recitation in rhymed prose (rather than the verse of the poets) strengthened their charge of soothsaying, particularly in view of the Quran's declaration (69: 41) that he was no poet!

The role of preacher existed, then, in the pre-Islamic period, but with a different ethical and sociopolitical significance. He was a brave warrior as well as a public spokesman for his tribe. His insignia were the lance,

1. See the article on khatib in *The Encylopaedia of Islam*, rev. ed., 1109–11.
2. Of course, Muhammad also explicitly denied the accusation.
3. I have sought to find in the case of each Quranic verse the English translation that most accurately represents the verse in Arabic. As a secondary consideration in the selection of the English translation I have considered literary form. After each of the Quranic verses, I have placed the capitalized first letter of the English translator's name as follows: A for Arberry's *The Koran Interpreted*; P for Pickthall's *The Meaning of the Glorious Koran*; R for Rodwell's *The Koran*; S for Sale's *The Koran*; and YA for Yusuf Ali's *The Glorious Kur'an*. In those instances where none of the translations closely rendered the literal meaning, I used my own translation, indicated by a lower-case a following the verse number. Numbering of the Quranic verses was standardized according to a Cairene, Arabic copy of the Quran put out under the supervision of al-Azhar University in 1926.

staff, or bow, indicators of the military honor of the tribe.[4] In the public arena of verbal competition along with the poet he heaped glory on his own tribe and opprobrium on its opponents, comparing deeds, origins, and noble (ignoble) qualities.

In the early Islamic period the khatib retained many of his earlier attributes, but now the role took on a primarily religious significance inasmuch as Muhammad's preaching was to Muslims, and boasting about tribal valor was devalued in the new Islamic ethos in which "**the noblest among you in the sight of God is the most godfearing**" (49: 13, A). To say that the role of the khatib assumed a primarily religious character in the Islamic period has to be qualified in an important way. Islamic society from the very beginning was an "organic" society.[5] Religion tended to permeate all institutions rather than to be differentiated and/or autonomous. The mosque from the beginning of the *umma* or Islamic community in Medina was a multifunctional institution. It was a place of asylum, a place to discuss important public matters including preparations for collective defense, a school, a resting place for travelers, and a place of worship. The *minbar* or elevated seat of honor in the mosque represented religiopolitical authority. Not only was the Islamic Friday sermon delivered by the preacher from its base, but important public pronouncements were also made from it, including the Quranic prohibition of wine. In later times the appointed representatives of the Muslim rulers (caliphs), the governors of provinces or their representatives, sat on it and delivered the Friday sermon, whose content was often more political and social than ritual or theological.

The interpenetration of religion and family life, ritual and ethics, and eschatology and property are clearly demonstrated in Muhammad's famous sermon (khutba) delivered on the Plain of Arafat from the back of a camel during the Prophet's farewell pilgrimage. This sermon is recorded in Ibn Ishaq's *Sirat Rasul Allah* (1967).[6] In it Muhammad combines exhortations against usury, dishonesty, and the continuation of blood revenge, with warnings of Judgment Day, admonitions to keep the sacred months holy, and exhortations against adultery and excessive severity in the treatment of wives by husbands. The sermon ends with the affirmation of the Quran and the practice of the Prophet as the unfailing guide for Muslims in the future.

The interpenetration of religion and society is also reflected in another fact. What were often sociopolitical messages delivered from the minbar possessed extraordinary religious and even ritual legitimacy since the

4. *Encyclopaedia of Islam*, rev. ed., 1110.

5. Donald Smith's *Religion and Political Development* (1970) has one of the best discussions of the different implications of religion in organic and differentiated societies.

6. See p. 651.

minbar, along with the *mihrāb* or prayer niche, was located in the most sanctified area of the mosque regarded by some as the source of special blessing.[7]

From the prophetic period through the Umayyad dynasty the khatib's role was closely associated with his symbolic position as the representative of the Prophet and his successors (*khulafā'*) in a religiopolitical sense. Indeed, it was not until the Abbasid period that the caliph left it to the religious judges to deliver the Friday sermon.[8] The khatib always spoke on behalf of the community,[9] even after every Friday mosque possessed a minbar and the khatib no longer was caliph, governor, qadi or, indeed, possessed any title other than "preacher."

The khatib, however, was not the only Islamic preacher. A variety of others going by the name of *wā'iz*, *mudhakkir*, and *qāṣṣ* were quite active. Indeed, in the early Islamic period during the rule of the four "rightly guided" caliphs the precise reference of all these terms was somewhat ambiguous and overlapping. The mudhakkir or "reminder" (of Judgment Day), the wa'iz or "admonisher" (to follow the right path stipulated in the Quran), and the qass or "teller" of (edifying religious) stories were all preachers and, in that sense, like the khatib. But they were free preachers not usually associated with a particular Friday mosque; they did not deliver the official Friday sermon in its formal classical style in the main mosques of the city or town, and they did not have the associated insignia of the khatib's dignity—the minbar or staff.[10] Many of these free preachers were criticized not only for their own somewhat wild behavior in the pulpit but also for the exaggerated emotional reactions they elicited from large public gatherings as a result of the fear they inspired in their warnings of Judgment Day.[11]

In a well-known book on free preachers partly addressed to them, Ibn al-Jawzi, a famous Islamic scholar and preacher of twelfth-century Baghdad, warned against their excesses: they (the preachers) sang the Quran

---

7. See the *Shorter Encyclopaedia of Islam*'s article on *masdjid*, 344–45.

8. See ibid., 1110. The ruler's use of the mosque for making political pronouncements has not ended, however. In fact, during the 1970s and 1980s it is not rare (e.g., Anwar Sadat, president of Egypt, talked to the congregation from the Al-Azhar mosque after the Friday sermon and congregational prayers, taking the occasion to address the incoming Christian president of Lebanon, Elias Sarkis, in 1976 regarding the necessity of interreligious respect and cooperation).

9. See Johannes Pedersen, "The Criticism of the Islamic Preacher," *Die Welt des Islams*, Vol. 2, 1949–1950, 216; and *Shorter Encyclopaedia of Islam*, article on masdjid.

10. See Pedersen, "Islamic Preacher," 235; and *Encyclopaedia of Islam*, article on khatib. It is worthy of note that after the Iranian Revolution of 1979 many Iranian mullahs in Teheran were photographed delivering khutbas holding rifles with the butt resting on the floor in their right hand.

11. Pedersen, "Islamic Preacher."

(rather than chanted it);[12] they draped the minbar with multicolored garments; they feigned weeping to advance a reputation for piety; they rent their garments at the pulpit to give the impression of mystical experience; and they applied oil and cumin to their faces in order to look pale.[13] He went on to admonish the listeners of these free preachers for their behavior—violent bodily movements, striking the head and face, swooning when the Quran is read, crying out for help, and the crowding of unrelated men and women together.[14]

Ibn al-Jawzi was a preacher at the other end of the sociopolitical and cultural spectrum—very much associated with the rulers rather than the ruled. It is reported that he took over four pulpits of his major professor in Baghdad, preaching at the age of fifteen. Ibn al-Jawzi was hired by the caliph to preach "orthodox" (Sunni) Islam to the masses and, thereby, to support the claims of the caliph against the ruling sultan. He was a professor at five different Islamic law colleges, and it is reported that he addressed crowds of one to two hundred thousand. On Thursdays he spoke at the caliph's palace.[15] Here, then, we find an Islamic scholar (ʿālim) combining the roles of free preacher, waʿiz, professor, ustadh, and de facto government minister (wazīr). To prosecute the caliph's antiheresy campaign he was given the power to search and raze houses, humiliate heretics in public, and imprison them.[16]

From these brief historical references to preachers of various kinds in various periods the following inferences can be drawn. First, from the beginning the Muslim preacher has been oriented toward both this world and the next. Muhammad was both prophet and statesman, and his message was both soteriological and social. Second, the original undifferentiated politicoreligious role of the khatib began to differentiate separate religious functions with certain roles such as qass and waʿiz (free preacher), oriented more toward soteriological concerns, usually outside the mosque on weekdays and directed toward the conversion of nonbelievers to Islam. Other roles, such as khatib and imam; were oriented toward more formal classical (with respect to language and style) religious concerns inside the mosque on Fridays. They sought to educate believers in Islamic law and ethics and to consolidate the Islamic community in conjunction with a particular rule. Third, the religious institution dif-

---

12. Singing the Quran was to allow emotion to carry the believer away from meditation on its meaning. See Kristina Nelson, *The Art of Reciting the Qur'an* (University of Texas Press, Austin, 1985) for a discussion of this point in a modern Cairene context.

13. See Ibn al-Jawzi, *Kitāb al-Quṣṣāṣ wa'l-Mudhakkarīn*, Merlin S. Swartz, annotator and translator (Dar el-Mashreq, Beirut, 1971), 170.

14. Ibid., 179.

15. Ibid., 26ff.

16. Ibid., 34.

ferentiates along class lines. Most free preachers are associated with the ruled, while qadis, law professors, and appointed or co-opted officials such as Ibn al-Jawzi are associated with the rulers.

Although the present-day Islamic preachers in peasant communities, particularly at the local level, have in many Middle Eastern countries lost their close association with the State (in many countries they repudiate that association), they continue to play a sociopolitical role in four respects: (1) in most cases they articulate the bureaucracies of their own states through departments such as religious endowments (*waqf*); (2) they continue to express in their sermons a concern for the problems and policies of their fellow-Muslims in the Islamic community; (3) symbolically, they continue as khatibs, particularly in the Friday sermon, to represent the Islamic community in each local context; and (4) preachers continue to act as "prayer leaders," "warners," "reminders," "admonishers," and "edifying story-tellers" in the quest for salvation.

What of the khutba itself? The Friday congregational sermon is encased in a formal ritual framework of individual prayers, calls to prayer, congregational prayer, and numerous prayer formulae that punctuate the worship and the sermon. An early Shafi'i scholar described the rules of the khutba in the following manner:

> Regarding the sermon itself, three are obligatory: the *hamdala* ["Praise be to God"], the *salat* on the Prophet ["May God bless him and greet him with peace"], admonitions to piety in both *khutba*s, prayer [*du'ā'*] on behalf of the faithful, and recitation of a part of the Kur'an in the first *khutba* or, according to some doctors, in both. It is commendable [*sunna*] for the *khatib* to be on a pulpit or an elevated place; to salute the audience when directing himself towards them; to sit down till the *adhān* is pronounced by the mu'adhdhin; to lean on a bow, a sword or a staff; to direct himself straightway to his audience; to pray [*du'ā'*] on behalf of the Muslims.[17]

In the prayer on behalf of the faithful (*du'ā' al-mu'minīn*) that precedes the congregational prayer it became customary in many areas to mention the name of the ruler. Scholars, partially drawing on the formalized traditions of the Prophet (hadith), prescribed a number of other norms for the organization and the delivery of the khutba:

> The *khutba*s of Muhammad usually begin with the formula *amma ba'du* ["Now then"]. . . . Side by side with the *hamdala* . . . the *shahāda* ["I bear witness that there is no god but God and I bear witness that Muhammad is the Messenger of God"] occurs. . . . "A *khutba* without the *shahāda* is like a mutilated hand" [from Ahmad ibn

17. *Encyclopaedia of Islam*, article on *khutba*, 74.

Hanbal]. In a large number of traditions it is stated that Muhammad used to recite passages from the Quran. . . . The *khutba* must be short, in accord with Muhammad's saying: "Make your *salāt* [prayer] long and your *khutba* short."[18]

The two successive sermons delivered by the standing preacher, who sits down on the minbar between them, is also based on Muhammad's practice. The longer initial khutba has usually been called the "warning sermon" or the "sermon of exhortation" (*khutba al-waʿziyya*) and the much shorter second sermon which usually includes a benedictory prayer addressed to God, the Prophet, his family, and the believers, has been called the "descriptive" or "qualifying sermon" (*khutba al-naʿtiyya*).[19]

THE FRIDAY WORSHIP

The *adhān* or call to prayer punctuates the Friday congregational worship three times: the first prayer occurs before worship, the second initiates individual prayers, and the third occurs between the first and second khutbas when the preacher is sitting on the minbar. The adhan, composed of seven formulae, is as follows:

> God is most great.
> I testify that there is no god besides God.
> I testify that Muhammad is the Messenger of God.
> Come to prayer.
> Come to salvation.
> God is most great.
> There is no god besides God.[20]

In Kufr al-Ma the khutba is customarily preceded by the "lesson" (*dars*). About half an hour before the first call to prayer the preacher enters the mosque and sits in front of the prayer niche (*mihrāb*) with legs folded under him facing the members of the congregation who enter the mosque and seat themselves in a semicircle around the shaykh, as the preacher is referred to and addressed by all who know him. During the dars the preacher, usually quoting from the Quran or hadith, briefly examines some matter of Islamic law and ethics. Some members of the congregation have brought their own Qurans and use the preprayer period

18. Ibid., 75.

19. I wish to thank my colleague, Akbar Muhammad, for information on the scholarly norms for the delivery of khutbas, in his lecture at the State University of New York at Binghamton, fall 1976.

20. The adhan of the Shiites adds an eighth formula between the fifth and the sixth: "Come to the best work."

to read from them. Often, the seated believers raise questions regarding the shaykh's interpretations of such matters as obligations of prayer, fasting, pilgrimage, alms-tax, marriage payment, inheritance, treatment of wives or children, or ritual ablution—and the shaykh replies. After about twenty minutes, just before the lesson has ended, the *mu'adhdhin* is sent to the roof of the mosque where he gives the second call to prayer. Every time the mu'adhdhin states, "Muhammad is the Messenger of God." The congregation responds, "I bear witness that there is no god besides God."

The preacher then stands facing the prayer niche and in his role as prayer leader (imam) leads the congregation in prayer, though the prayers at this point are individual and not always in unison since latecomers constantly enter the mosque to join in worship. After the prostrations have been completed and while the imam is still facing the prayer niche, a member of the congregation with a particularly mellow voice stands and chants a few verses of the Quran. The preacher then turns and mounts the first step of the minbar, whispering a prayer as he does so. On reaching the top, he faces the congregation and greets them, saying, "Peace be upon you and the mercy of God and his blessings." He then proceeds to deliver the first khutba. The beginning of the first khutba follows a set pattern with praise to God, the Prophet, his family, and his companions. Some examples of the preacher's introductory statements follow:

> Praise be to God who raised up justice as the standard of his sovereignty and confirmed by it the foundations of his divine law. He favored the just over all [other] creatures. He blessed for them their dwellings, their wealth and their lives and he bestowed upon them bounty. Testify that there is no God but him. There is no escaping revenge for the wrongdoers whether in this fleeting world or in the world to come. **Think not that God doth not heed the deeds of those who do wrong. He but giveth them respite against a Day when the eyes will fixedly stare in horror** (14: 42, YA).[21] I testify that Muhammad is his servant and his messenger who rendered justice (*'adāla*) among his people. May the blessings of God be upon him and his family and his companions and those who followed their footsteps from among just rulers (*muqsitīn*) and judges (*munṣifīn*).
>
> Now then, God, most high, said in his book, and he is the most truthful of sayers: **O believers, be you securers of justice (*qist*), witnesses for God. Let not detestation for a people move you not to be equitable; be equitable—that is nearer to godfearing** (5: 8, A). (Sermon delivered July 8, 1960—14 Muharram—Kufr al-Ma, Jordan)

21. Citations in parentheses refer to chapter and verse in the Quran.

Praise be to God who instructed in script. He taught man what he did not know. The praise of the thankful praises him and the thanks of the penitent thank him, submissive to his will. I pray and confer salutations on the choicest of his creation and the best of his prophets and his true friends, our master and imam, Muhammad, the one who was sent as a mercy to the world and a faithful guide to the straight path, and on his family and his companions, the good ones, the pure ones—the sincere callers to religion, the fighters in the path of God. May the pleasure of God be upon them and those who followed their guidance to the day of judgement.

Now then, God, most high, and he is the truest of sayers, said: **God will raise up in rank those of you who believe and have been given knowledge** (58: 11, A). Oh people, knowledge(*ilm*) is the basis of all virtues and the source of light and wisdom. (Sermon delivered April 22, 1960—27 Shawwal—Kufr al-Ma, Jordan)

Praise be to God who joined the hearts of the true believers and made them loving brothers. He reminded them of the bounty he had given them and he, may his state be glorified, said: **and remember with gratitude God's favour on you; for ye were enemies and he joined your hearts in love, so that by His Grace, ye became brethren** (3: 103, YA). And testify that there is no god but God who has warned us against dispute (*tanāfar*) and contention (*shiqāq*). God, most high, said: **Do not contend; you will fail and your strength will dissipate. Be patient. Verily, God is with the patient** (8: 46, a). And testify that Muhammad is his servant and Messenger and the chosen one of his creation and his beloved who connects hearts with affection and ties the true believers with brotherhood. He joins them with purity and harmony. Oh, God, may your prayers and salutations and blessings be on him and his family and his companions and his followers (*tābi'īn*).

Now then [God] the exalted, said: **The Believers are but a single Brotherhood. So make peace and reconciliation between your two** [contending] **brothers and fear God that ye may receive Mercy** (49: 10, YA). (Sermon delivered August 19, 1966—Kufr al-Ma, Jordan)

Each of the introductory sermon extracts includes the praise to God (ḥamdala), the profession of faith (shahāda), and the praise and blessings on the Prophet and his family and companions (taṣliya). After this set introduction each sermon goes on to introduce the theme after the phrase *Now, then*. The first sermon concerns justice; the second sermon is on the value of education (the village improvement officer had come to the village that day to discuss the possibility of raising money for the purpose of building a new school); and the third sermon is about the obligation of peacemaking and the reconciliation of estranged co-villagers and co-believers.

After finishing the first khutba the preacher sits down on the minbar and after several seconds rises to deliver the shorter second khutba. Following the second khutba he utters a quiet prayer, chants from the Quran, and finally descends and takes his place in front of the prayer niche to lead the congregation in the special Friday congregational prayer.

In Kufr al-Ma the Friday congregational prayer and sermon usually take one hour with an added half-hour for the preceding lesson. Preachers are urged in prayer manuals, both classical and modern, to make the sermon short. With this brief introduction to the khatib and the khutba it is now necessary to focus more sharply on the role of the preacher in his local environment, the village of Kufr al-Ma. The following capsule life history is drawn from my field notes and seeks to reflect as far as good literary form allows the account related to me in the preacher's own words.

A Capsule Life History

Shaykh Luqman[22] is the second son of Hajj Muhammad, a fairly large landowner and the head of a large polygynous family composed of two wives, six sons, two daughters, and numerous grandchildren. He is a member of the largest clan in the village, Beni Yasin, and a member of one of its two most influential patrilineages, which numbered one of the two village mayors, a prominent local bureaucrat, and a number of prominent elders.[23] However, his own clan and lineage also included some of the poorest community members. At the time of the initial research (1960), Luqman was thirty-two years of age. From age eight to age eleven he studied and completed the Quran with two teachers, one a hometowner (with whom he was later to compete for the position of village preacher) and the other a peripatetic teacher. In 1939 he entered the secular primary school in the next village (there was none in Kufr al-Ma at the time) where religion was one of the regular subjects. At the end of the third grade his father told him that it was time for him to join his older brother behind the plough. Without his father's knowledge Luqman went by himself on the first day of school and registered for the fourth grade. His father found out, went to the school, and told the teacher that he

22. Many of the proper names in this study are pseudonyms.

23. See table 2.1 for a skeleton outline of the social structure of the village. For more information about these leaders, see chapter 7 in Richard T. Antoun, *Low-Key Politics: Local-Level Leadership and Change in the Middle East* (State University of New York Press, Albany, 1979).

needed Luqman to work the land since he already had two (younger) sons in school. The schoolmaster replied, "No, you cannot have him. He is our son now."[24] Luqman remained in school for three more years, finishing his primary education in 1945 at the age of sixteen. He asked his father to allow him to continue his schooling—he was first in his class in all subjects—but his father refused. For the next three years Luqman grudgingly worked as ploughman on the family land, but took every opportunity to absent himself from the village (or to sneak out) to study with the preacher and marriage officer in the next village, Deir Abu Said, which was also the subdistrict center. The preacher, Shaykh Ahmed, had pursued Islamic studies for six years in Damascus. When the fast month of Ramadan arrived, Luqman was always the first in the mosque, preceding Shaykh Ahmed.[25]

Finally, after three years of friction between father and son, Shaykh Ahmed came to Luqman's father and told him that if he gave permission, the shaykh wished to hire Luqman as assistant instructor and drill-master for three and one half sacks of wheat a year. Every student used to give Ahmed two measures of grain as payment, and Ahmed gave them private lessons in history, geography, and religious studies in the subdistrict center. Luqman's father agreed provided that Luqman continued to work every harvest time.

For the next three years Luqman taught students for Shaykh Ahmed and at the same time pursued religious studies with him. Often, when he was sitting in his father's guest house—all village men were expected to attend a guest house, converse, and drink coffee in the evening—and someone addressed him, he did not reply, being sunk in silent recitation of the Quran or meditation or study of the books he brought back from Ahmed's. His father became angry at this breach of guest house etiquette and told Shaykh Ahmed that if Luqman brought any more books into the house he would burn them, and he forbade Ahmed to continue to instruct his son. Luqman's father thought that his son was on the verge of insanity. Thereafter, Luqman never brought any books home, but spent whole nights at Shaykh Ahmed's reading there.

24. Beginning in the 1940s, the central government began following a policy of compulsory primary education for boys, and this policy was enforced in the subdistrict of Al-Kura despite attempts by some peasants, such as Luqman's father, to avoid it.

25. The rewards of arriving early at the mosque have been detailed in many Traditions of the Prophet. In particular, the rewards of early arrival at the mosque for the Friday congregational prayer service have been mentioned in hadiths. For instance, al-Ghazzali in his *Revivification of the Religious Sciences* states: "In Tradition it is said, 'When it is Friday the angels sit on the doors of the mosque with leaves in their hands and pens of gold, writing the first [in the mosque] as the first, according to their orders.' " And again, al-Ghazzali says, "It is said, 'Men will be near, when they look upon the Face of Allah, in proportion to the earliness of their going to the Friday Observance' " (al-Ghazzali, 155).

At this point in his quest for religious knowledge, Luqman's behavior became decidedly mystical. He recounted to Ahmed that often when he slept in the summer and awoke, he thought he was covered by a tent, white like the sun. Ahmed replied that knowledge was like that.[26]

When Ahmed declined to teach him further, Luqman threatened to cease teaching his students. Ahmed continued teaching Luqman without the knowledge of his father. The final breach with his father occurred in the summer of 1949. The Hajj demanded that Luqman go down to the Jordan Valley and harvest along with his brothers. Luqman declined because that year the harvest coincided with the holy fast month of Ramadan, and Luqman had vowed to fast. The Hajj charged Ahmed with discouraging Luqman from fulfilling his harvest obligation. Ahmed prevailed on Luqman to join his brothers in the Jordan Valley for the harvest. Luqman went, but continued to fast during the harvest. His brothers excused him and told him they could get along without him. On Fridays during the month he returned to the village to attend the Friday congregational prayer. On one occasion he was late getting back to the threshing grounds. His father grew even more angry and raised his arm to hit him. For a week Luqman did not see or talk to his father, sleeping in the mosque by night and working on the threshing ground by day, all

26. On occasion Luqman spoke to me about Islamic mysticism (Sufism). In 1960 he told me that the Shari'a had clamped down on the Sufi orders (the use of snakes, fire, drums, and banners) but not on the *dhikr*, repetitive mention of God itself. He said that in his childhood the Sufis formed circles and performed the dhikr. They brought the drum and cymbals; then they shook and threw themselves into the fire. Shaykh Luqman witnessed the ritual of a Sufi order in Beisan (Palestine). He said that the Rabab'a of Kufr Rakib, an adjoining village, belong to the Qadiriya order and the Mustirihiyya of Jenin, another nearby village, were a branch of the Qadiriya. He said they had not performed for fifteen years. Luqman said the *tariqa*s (Islamic mystic orders) are distinguished by the following: the avoidance of all prohibited food (*akl ḥarām*); the avoidance of men who do not give the alms-due and all who resort to "eating wealth under suspicion" (*akl mal bi shubha*); the refusal to eat in the house of one of these individuals; the avoidance of all bureaucrats (*muwaTHTHafīn*) and refusal of income from the government (e.g., land tax money, money from permits, and customs tax money—all money that is taken by government employees by force and is, therefore, taboo [*ḥarām*]); prayer, fasting, and recitation of the names of God (e.g., "Oh, Forgiving One" [*ya ghāfūr*]); and the reading of regular supererogatory private prayer (*awrād*) sections of the Quran recited privately. He (the Sufi) says, "Oh, God, Oh God, Oh Gentle One, Oh Gentle One" (*ya laṭīf, ya laṭīf*). Luqman said of the dhikr, the central ritual recitation of Islamic mystics: "He who mentions the names of God (repeatedly) finds such delight—as if he were swimming in a lake." He said that the aim of the dhikr meeting is to become a saint (*wali*). Luqman said that in Irbid, the nearby market town, there were dhikrs every Monday and Friday nights. Regarding the common recitation of the names of God by Sufis, every one of the (ninety-nine) names of God has its delight and its own joy, especially God (*allah*). This word has hidden letters (*ḥurūf bāṭiniyya*). Luqman said that he used to recite the *wird*, a section of the Quran, himself in Kufr al-Ma. He used to recite it till he saw nothing and felt that his heart was a burning light.

the while fasting. He and his father were temporarily reconciled by a relative and village elder—Ramadan was the time when all estranged believers should be reconciled. But Hajj Muhammad's patience had been exhausted. He told Luqman that as soon as the harvest was over he was to move his belongings out of the house. On hearing this Luqman's mother said, "If he goes, I go too." In the summer of 1949 at the age of twenty-one Luqman, his mother, and his full brother moved out of the Hajj's house.[27] The Hajj gave Luqman's mother and brother their fair share of the harvest but gave Luqman nothing. Luqman's full brother started ploughing as a sharecropper and Luqman continued his studies, now as a full-time teaching assistant to Ahmed; they split all proceeds equally. These were hard years but the mother and her two sons at first rented a house from a relative and then, in 1951, managed to buy a small two-room house in the village. To add insult to injury, Luqman's father used the proceeds of the harvest to obtain a wife for Luqman's younger half-brother, a violation of village norms which respect the order of age among siblings in marriage. The same year Luqman suffered another blow when his mentor, teacher, and friend, Shaykh Ahmed, moved to a village in another area, ending their four-year working relationship.

In the meantime, in 1951, the preachership of the mosque in Kufr al-Ma became vacant. It had always been occupied by peripatetic preachers who generally stayed a year or more and then moved on. A preacher from Syria who passed through the village was hired as village preacher, and Luqman became the prayer leader at the mosque. At this time another itinerant preacher came to stay in the village. He was an Egyptian who had been trained at the famous religious university of Al-Azhar in Egypt. He was sustained by the community and in turn taught the Quran and gave occasional Friday sermons. In addition, for a year he gave Luqman intensive training in Arabic and religious studies. After this shaykh left, the village was without a preacher for four months. Mustafa Basboos, an elderly villager and self-styled preacher (he wore the white turban of the learned man) with a smattering of religious learning picked up in Egypt where he had been interned during World War I as a prisoner in the Ottoman army, began delivering the Friday sermon. Luqman thought he was better qualified, but most considered him too young.

One Friday morning, against the advice of many of his friends and to the amazement of the assembled worshipers, he strode up to the minbar from one side and Mustafa Basboos strode up from the other and both

27. In polygynous households in the rural areas of the Middle East it is quite common with the advancing age of the older mother and her adult sons, for her to move in with the latter and live out her remaining years with them. She continues to be married, and her husband continues to contribute to her support although the domiciles are separate.

proceeded to deliver the sermon at the same time.[28] With his evangelical delivery and surer sense of learning Luqman apparently drowned out his rival and proceeded to give a sermon on hypocrisy. After the sermon those who had opposed him recognized his talent and congratulated him. For two months he continued to deliver the Friday sermon but without remuneration or any formal designation by the village. He finally said to several village elders, "I have been offered the preachership at Tibne" (a smaller and more remote village in the vicinity). "If you want me you must hire me as imam." The elders said, "Go write up a contract; we will hire both you and Mustafa Basboos at ten sacks of grain (annually) each." Luqman agreed and drew up such a contract. At this time there were two village mayors (mukhtars) from the two largest clans, Beni Yasin and Beni Dumi, respectively. Luqman was a member of Yasin and Mustafa Basboos was a member of Dumi, and so the arrangement seemed acceptable. But when presented with the contract, the mayor of Dumi said, "No, we want only Luqman. Mustafa Basboos can't perform the duties. He's a dunderhead.[29] Draw up another contract for yourself and all of Beni Dumi will sign it." In August 1952 at the age of twenty-four Luqman was hired as imam of the village at a salary of twenty sacks of wheat to be paid in proportion by each household at harvest time. A year later Luqman married a woman from his own clan.

That same year he applied to become marriage officer (*ma'dhūn*) but no vacancy was available. In 1956 after passing an examination administered by the Religious Court system he was given a certificate (*ijāza*) and was officially appointed imam by the central government. This appointment carried with it a stipend of nine dollars a month. Perhaps more important, after passing this examination Luqman began wearing the red fez and white turban, the symbols of certified religious knowledge. It was the status, man of knowledge, rather than ritual specialist, marriage officer, or pilgrim guide—all subsequently achieved roles—that was most important to Luqman and constituted the basis of his own self-image. And it was the role of preacher that allowed him to elaborate that status in the fullest and most satisfactory manner.[30]

28. Of course, this unlikely occurrence was possible since Islam has no official priesthood and any Muslim deemed knowledgeable can deliver the khutba.

29. Actually, this is an overstatement. Mustafa Basboos did have some knowledge of Islamic law and ethics. But he had not paid the marriage payment (mahr) to his wife to which she was entitled (it was a sister-exchange marriage). On returning from Egypt he was quick to do so, recognizing that Islamic law and ethics required it.

30. Practically all the nonpreaching roles Luqman performed, however, involved imparting knowledge, beginning with his role of student drill-master and including the role of marriage official and, by definition, pilgrim guide.

THE LIFE HISTORY ANALYZED

It would be a mistake to characterize Luqman's struggle to pursue the preacher's career as heroic in proportion. He had the support of the great Islamic tradition, mediated by his mentor Shaykh Ahmed. In addition, he was supported by his mother and full brother. Nevertheless, his case illustrates the possibility of a genuine struggle for identity within the framework of traditional village life and values.[31] Village youth do suffer constraints, but they also have choices. The career choice Luqman made was one of rebellion against community and family, and although he did not aim at displacing his father from his lands or his household leadership his career objective could only be fulfilled by challenging his father's authority and eventually separating from his father's household.

It is important to note that Luqman was an unusually sensitive and reflective individual, particularly about his own life. He regarded his life as eventful and problematic, involving struggle against his own father and the community. Only one other villager ever volunteered his life history to me, unsolicited. Generally, villagers are quite unreflective about their lives, and in many cases were even unable to supply an occupational history in any detail when I questioned them.

It is also important to understand the social status implications of this case. Luqman was the son of a peasant with ample land in a land-short village. Half of the employable men in his own clan were landless. To have a father who had land available for sons to plough, crops to harvest, and, thereby, to have marriage possibilities—since marriage required substantial marriage payment, usually six hundred dollars in a village where that sum constituted the entire annual income for the majority—was considered a stroke of good fortune. In addition, Luqman's father though illiterate, was a well-off peasant able to extend hospitality in his own guest house; he had the essential qualification (in the early 1950s) to serve as mayor of the village. The vocation of village preacher, on the other hand, was not considered prestigious. In a climate with a dry cereal-farming regime in which rainfall and crops might be cut by half in any given season compared to the previous year, the lot of the village preacher (who was paid in kind by each household on the threshing ground) was not a happy one. A village proverb sums up the situation: "There are three things unseen to the eye—the legs of the snake, the eyes of the scorpion and the bread of the preacher" (*fi thalatha la yura bil ʿayn, rijlay al-ḥayya, ʿuyūn al-ʿaqrab wa khibz al-khatīb*). In a drought year the preacher would often have to make the rounds himself, collecting his due

31. See Richard T. Antoun, "Social Organization and the Life Cycle in an Arab Village," *Ethnology*, Vol. 6, No. 3, July 1967 for a brief analysis of Luqman's early career in terms of the problems of succession and identity.

share when the households begrudged surrendering it. This was considered tantamount to begging. Indeed, early in his career (1960) Luqman considered going to preach in another village because of what he regarded as the niggardliness of his fellow-villagers. Such "begging" was particularly inappropriate for the son of a well-to-do peasant who could have been making an adequate living ploughing the land. Other tasks usually performed by the village preacher such as the ritual washing of the dead and drumming in the middle of the night during the month of Ramadan to wake up the believers for the before-dawn meal of *suhūr*, were also considered demeaning. Luqman often made it a point to tell his fellow-villagers that these tasks were appropriate for any true believer (*mu'min*) and not especially for the preacher, since there was no priesthood in Islam or, to put it another way, a priesthood of all believers.

In speaking of the niggardliness of his fellow-villagers the mayor, Abu Yasin, reminisced about the treatment of preachers in the past. Once an itinerant preacher had come to the village from Syria. He was given a house by the villagers. He demanded water (not all houses had water cisterns); he was given water. He asked for wood; wood was collected for him. He asked for grain to tide him over until the next harvest (when he would be paid by the households of the village); grain was provided for him. Then he said he wanted to return to Syria. A handsome measure of grain was collected for him, and he never came back.[32] The mayor said that Shaykh Luqman provided everything himself—his house, his water, and his wood.

In 1960 the village paid Luqman 150 bushels (*mudd*) of wheat or approximately 25 sacks annually. This total was levied on the approximately 300 males above the age of 15 residing in the village, each male in a household paying 7/8 of a mudd or 7 *ratl*s, approximately 35 pounds. In fact, by mutual agreement, Luqman collected from 172 villagers, and the 2 watchmen, who were also paid annually by the village, collected their own salaries from the remaining households. Since 1960 was a drought year Luqman collected from only about half the households on his roll; some paid him in olive oil instead. This situation contrasted with the neighboring comparatively land-rich village of Khansiri, where the preacher received 200 bushels of wheat plus vegetables annually.

When, therefore, in 1960 another village in the district requested Luqman to come as preacher (most villages in the subdistrict had no preacher at that time) he insisted on the following conditions: (1) either 10 dinars ($28) a month or 200 bushels of wheat; (2) a house with an enclosed courtyard, for the privacy/modesty of his wife, at a reasonable rent; (3)

32. The villagers' generous treatment of this Syrian preacher was, of course, before World War II when land was plentiful, whereas Shaykh Luqman lived in a land-short village.

he refused to act as "drummer" during Ramadan to awaken fasters in the middle of the night for the predawn meal but would hire someone at his own expense; (4) he objected to washing the dead; (5) the grain had to be brought to his house—he would not "beg" for it; and (6) he consented to act as mu'adhdh'in and give the call to prayer. Nothing came of these negotiations since the village in question was also short of land and could not afford to pay 200 bushels. Moreover, Luqman's family preferred to stay in their own village, among their own relatives. And so Luqman remained a somewhat status-conscious hometown preacher with all the comforts of the position as well as its disabilities. The discrepancy between the rather low socioeconomic status of the village preacher and the rather high socioeconomic status of his father's household was less important to Luqman than the realization of his goal, religious learning, and the recognition of that learning by the community in the official position of prayer leader, imam, and preacher.

Luqman's decision to remain in his own village as prayer leader and preacher for the length of his career (as of 1988) is quite significant for his own self-image and aspirations. He sought status and approval from his own community rather than from another village community or from some wider regional community of believers—despite his past struggles within it. His limited formal education probably precluded the latter possibility.

It is important to understand at this point the multiple functions attached to the role of village preacher and his position in the community. Luqman is intimately associated with and knowledgeable about the daily life of the village, particularly since he was born and reared there. His daily round and his various activities as village preacher and prayer leader are as follows. At approximately 4:30 A.M. he arrives at the mosque to lead morning prayers; he leaves around 5:30. In the 1960s between eight and twenty persons usually attended the morning prayers in the mosque, most praying at home instead.

After breakfast he studies. In 1960 Luqman had a modest library in his home, but by 1984 he had in addition two other collections of books, one in the Quranic Study Center and the other in the new mosque. Occasionally, women come to him at his home asking for advice or requesting that he write out a Quranic amulet (*ḥijāb*). He writes such amulets for practical problems as well as for psychological and physical ailments: some encouraging mutual love and reconciliation; some against headaches and possession; some preventing destructive acts, such as birds snatching chickens. Occasionally, in the course of the day the shaykh records property transactions (*ḥujja*s) when they do not involve agricultural land (recorded by the land registry officer). Occasionally he calculates shares in the division of inheritances according to Islamic inheritance rules, preparatory to legitimation by the Islamic court. He also prepares requests for marriage contracts to be taken to the Islamic court in the next village, Deir Abu Said, for registration. Quite often around 10:00 A.M. he attends sessions of the subdistrict Islamic court (*maḥkama shar'iyya*) and stays till early afternoon, acting as a friend of the court, particularly when parties or witnesses are from Kufr al-Ma. He might be asked by the judge to verify the statements of witnesses, testify as to the economic status of the parties to maintenance cases and verify ages. After the mid-afternoon *'asr* prayer he occasionally gives a short lesson in the village mosque. He always gives such a lesson at that time during Ramadan. He leads prayers in the mosque five times a day: early morning, noon, mid-afternoon, sunset, and evening (though in his absence any believer can do so). Since he is one of the most learned and trustworthy men in the village he is often called on to write bills of sale for villagers. He also writes and witnesses land tenure contracts for sharecroppers.

Villagers often come to him asking for instruction on points of ethics, law, or ritual. For instance, an old woman came to him asking if it was all right for her to eat the meat of a goat she herself had slaughtered. She said that some villagers had told her that meat slaughtered by a woman was forbidden. He told her it was not true, and that a woman could slaughter animals as well as a man. Another woman came to him and complained that she had not had a bowel movement; he suggested that she go out to the fields and pick some special herbs. A man came to the preacher with a hypothetical question: In a polygynous family if the father died could the son marry the father's widow (i.e., not his own mother)? The preacher was appalled at the question and told him absolutely not.

The khatib is reluctant to perform ritual ablutions for the dead (see chapter 1), but he accompanies the body to the burial ground, recites the prayer for the dead, and reads a verse from the Quran; then he supervises the proper Islamic burial. The preacher is sometimes called on to help in the mediation of disputes. Though he does not take an active role in such mediation, leaving it to the accomplished elders and arbitrators of the village, his presence as the religious leader of the village lends moral support to the arbitrators' efforts and helps set the proper atmosphere for reconciliation—a significant theme of many sermons. The shaykh enters every house in the village at one time or another in the performance of these various tasks and is quickly aware of both petty and major violations of village norms as a number of his sermons indicate. Although he never mentions names in his sermons, most villagers know the specific events that triggered the sermon.

Luqman never performed all of these activities on any given day or even most of them, but most of these activities would likely occur during a fortnight's passage. The astonishingly varied roles he played in the life of the village—scribal, ritual, legal, medical, arbitral, psychoanalytic, magical, scholarly—demonstrate the "organic" character of religious life in Kufr al-Ma. Religious activity is not differentiated institutionally from other interest areas (e.g., political, legal, economic, or kinship), and religious practitioners are not organized in formally autonomous corporate units. (See chapter 7 for a more detailed discussion of "organic religion.")

An important factor to be considered in evaluating the careers of village preachers is that Islamic religious organization in Jordan and many other Islamic countries is congregational rather than episcopal. Although a village mosque, or any other mosque, does not constitute a "parish" in the sense of a formally defined discrete corporate religious unit, it is the village community and not some other social unit that sets the terms of a preacher's service, and that contract is open to renegotiation on an annual basis. Both the preacher and the village are free to terminate the contract at the end of each harvest season. It was precisely the local and achieved character of his status as preacher that allowed Luqman to struggle for and win the position. Moreover, it is within the village community that influence is gained and status recognized. In the past and to a large extent still today an overarching religious authority does not effectively monitor or control events at the village level. Were such a hierarchy to have existed the process by which Luqman became the preacher of the village—an open competition in the pulpit—would have been unthinkable. There is, however, an increasing tendency to seek to influence the course of events at the village level. For instance, the Department of Religious Endowments now conducts a two-year training school for preachers in Amman, and the graduates of this school are placed in various villages that request a preacher. The junior preacher of Kufr al-Ma is a graduate of this training school. In 1983 he was officially moved from the neighboring village to Kufr al-Ma, probably at his own request, when the second mosque was built in the village. The Department of Religious Endowments has always certified preachers such as Luqman who are not graduates of formal courses of instruction, by giving them examinations (which Luqman took and passed in 1962). At the present time the Council of the Islamic Organization of the Islamic World sends examiners to test children in the Quranic Study Center (*dar al-qur'an*) three times a year.

Nevertheless, in terms of hierarchical control, religious organization still remains essentially congregational rather than episcopal.[33] It must be

33. It should be noted that even in the Christian Protestant tradition membership in a parish's congregation is not always indexed by church attendance on Sunday. Clark points out that in the Methodist chapel in Staithes, England, affiliation with the chapel was indicated mainly by three events: baptism of children in the chapel, attendance at the annual harvest festival, and burial in the chapel's cemetery (see Clark 1982).

remembered, moreover, that in the 1960s the shortage of preachers placed Luqman in a somewhat favorable bargaining position vis-à-vis his own congregation. As the government trained more preachers this position was somewhat weakened, but this weakening was offset by Luqman's increasing incorporation in the salary structure of the religious endowments department, which by the 1970s granted him a degree of economic independence from the village.

Luqman's appointment as village preacher in 1952 was a milestone in his early occupational life history which had proceeded from student (six years), to cultivator (three years), to student-apprentice-teacher (four years). It was also the beginning of a career trajectory that within modest limits brought increasing economic and social status: the achievement of the certificate of learning in 1956; the official appointment by the government as khatib in 1958 with its accompanying stipend of 3 dinars monthly, and then the appointment as marriage official (*ma'dhūn*) for a number of villages in the subdistrict in 1961; in 1971 he was appointed guide (*murshid*) for Jordanian pilgrims going to Mecca. The cumulative acquisition of these religious roles has increased his annual income substantially. In 1979 he received 10 Jordanian dinars a month from the village council; 73 dinars a month from the Department of Religious Endowments (*waqf*); 60 dinars a year for his services as marriage officer; and 150 dinars a year for his services as pilgrim guide, for a total of 1206 dinars. In addition, he received 60 dinars a year from 25 dunums of agricultural land for a grand total of 1272 dinars or well over $3000. In 1966 his annual income was just over $800 whereas in 1960 it had been just over $300.

Although in 1984 he was still a "village" preacher, the village itself had changed quite substantially since 1952 when he had assumed its religious leadership, and the significance of the preachership had changed accordingly. The village's population had more than doubled to over 4800 persons. Moreover, it had more the aspect of a town with new houses of smooth-cut stone rather than rough-hewn rock plastered with adobe, piped water to all homes, and electricity. By 1979 there were eighty-five automobiles and trucks in the village (there was one vehicle in 1967). The village had an increasing number of young men engaged in middle-class professions: army officers, doctors, teachers, and engineers, practically all of whom worked outside the village and the majority outside the country. Yet practically all those maintained ties with the village, either through resident family members, lands, or holiday visits.

Perhaps the most important symbolic change for the community was the construction of the resplendent green dome for the mosque in 1971, which up till then had looked from the outside like any other house in the village. In 1971 the Philanthropic Society of Kufr al-Ma (*jam'iyyat kufr al-ma al-khayriyya*) was founded with Luqman as its president. Its activities included weaving and maintaining a kindergarten. It has future plans to include a program for the disabled, a children's center with provision of free milk, and a center for the supervision of pregnant women; it plans to hire a permanent staff nurse and trained midwife. In 1977 Luqman initiated the Quran Study Center. The students, ten to fifteen years of age, meet three times a week after supper for two hours and memorize four out of thirty parts of the Quran and about twenty Traditions (hadith) of the Prophet. Examinations are given three times a year and books are awarded as prizes. In 1978, twenty-five students graduated. In 1983, a second mosque was built initially funded by a charitable donation of five thousand dinars by a villager, and ten thousand dinars from the village at large; later, a contribution of three thousand dinars from the government of Abu Dhabi allowed the mosque to be completed. This mosque is adjacent to the boys' school at the entrance to the village and was built to facilitate daily prayer by the students. The Quran study classes are held inside it. With the building of the second mosque the Department of Religious Endowments established Luqman as the preacher in the new mosque and appointed another man as the preacher in the older central mosque.

All of these changes—economic, social structural, and religious—have important implications for the life of the village, the region, and the nation—implications that are beyond the scope of this study. It is important to remember, however, that when Luqman delivered the sermons analyzed in the following chapters in the years 1960–1967, most of the changes outlined above had not taken place, indeed, could not be and were not foreseen or predicted. The sermons, therefore, relate to a relatively stable period in the village's life. It was not an uneventful period by any means for Jordan had been in the process of weathering the establishment of the Amirate of Transjordan, the consequences of the British Mandate in Palestine, two Arab-Israeli wars, and the steady attempts of the central government to introduce material modernization, decentralization, and local participation.[34] Relative to the changes that followed, however, the period 1960–1967 was stable in terms of degrees of social mobility, occupational change, emigration, educational opportunity, and standard of living.

The social psychological implications of Luqman's early career struggle deserve comment. It is clear that his career goal could only be realized through a social structural crisis: the flaunting of parental authority and

34. For details on material modernization and the attempt by the Jordanian government to introduce decentralization and local government, see Antoun, *Low-Key Politics*, particularly chapters 5 and 6.

village opinion. The selection of a religious vocation may often involve such a crisis both in sober Muslim peasant communities and in lower middle-class industrial communities in the West.[35] On the other hand Luqman did not suffer a religious crisis, that is, a shaking of faith leading to a sudden conversion or reaffirmation of belief. Although he seemed to verge on mystical activity early in his career, there is no evidence for a "sudden calling" to religion. His career trajectory is steady and cumulative whether as student, teacher, prayer leader, preacher, or marriage officer. Moreover, his sermons, although evangelical in style and fervor, were hand-crafted rather then ecstatic and extemporaneous in the tradition of the American folk preacher.[36] Indeed, what seemed to be extraordinary about his sermons was that every one was carefully prepared, written out in longhand, and delivered on the basis of the text, though he sometimes extemporized from it. One might argue that Luqman's careful preparation of his sermon reflected his self-made status. Not having the assurance provided by a formal religious education in an established university or law college, he felt obliged to prepare his sermons.[37] Many of his sermons were, then, constructed and filled with the traditional repetitive phrases drawn from the Quran and the Traditions rather than developed as an unfolding idea. But this repetition, for the believer, was perhaps the critical element in the sermon since what was being conveyed was meaning and (certainty) rather than information (the particular topic addressed).[38] Occasionally, however, the preacher developed an idea with power and turned it into an art form, converting repetition into shades of difference and insight (see the sermon on *raḥm*—"kinship, compassion, womb"—in chapter 4 below).

Whether or not he suffered a religious crisis, the career struggle that Luqman waged against his own family and the consensus of his own community quite probably strengthened his unusually strong commitment to religion—and possibly his commitment to education, the subject of some

35. In an unpublished manuscript on English preachers in the London area, Saral Waldorf has pointed out that parents were quite often severely disappointed when their children chose the ministry as a vocation after completing a secular education that promised to afford upward mobility. See also David Clark, *Between Pulpit and Pew: Folk Religion in a North Yorkshire Fishing Village* (Cambridge University Press, Cambridge, 1982) on this point.

36. See Bruce A. Rosenberg, *The Art of the American Folk Preacher* (Oxford University Press, New York, 1970) for an extended discussion of the style of American folk preachers who lived their sermons in a progression of prose, chant, and song framed in a call-and-response pattern.

37. I wish to thank my colleague, Fuad I. Khuri, for pointing out this possible interpretation.

38. See the discussion of information and meaning in the section below on the impact of the audience.

of his strongest sermons. This struggle may also have given him a certain independence of mind. When I asked twenty villagers of different occupations and ages the question, "If you were in a public meeting and a citizen arose to defend a point of view that you and the majority of the assembled considered contrary to the interests of the country and the people, do you believe that he has the right to be heard?" Luqman was the only one who answered in the affirmative. The career achievement pattern, then, and its social structural and social psychological concomitants may leave an impact not only on the character of the leader but also on certain ideological positions he may hold.

It cannot be argued that Luqman was "born to be a preacher" since he came from no preaching lineage. Indeed, the extraordinary fact about the subdistrict of Al-Kura in the 1950s and 1960s was that it had very few preachers; only four of the twenty-five villages had a preacher in 1959. Luqman can be said to have been "called" in the sense of experiencing a summons to a religious vocation, provided one understands that the experience was not sudden and ecstatic but rather gradual and reinforced over a period of more than ten years. The techniques of persuasion (rhetoric) used by him in preaching the Friday congregational sermon were set by a long and established preaching tradition referred to above: call to prayer, prayer formulae, individual set prayers, the profession of faith, the long and the short sermon, and the congregational prayer. Numerous prayer manuals, classic and modern, are available to preachers for guidance in composing sermons. For instance, Al-Ghazzali, a renowned jurist, religious scholar, mystic, and law professor of eleventh-century Baghdad, gave the following advice on the aims and contents of the sermon: Its aim was to help man realize his religion and to revive and animate the indifferent; the sermon should draw on verses of the Quran, authentic Traditions of the Prophet, and edifying tales of the prophets and saints of past; the sermon might even include recitation of poetry and weeping, but it should not arouse false hopes (of salvation).

Although it may be considered "evangelical" in its fervor and its devotion to spreading an authentic religious message, this tradition of preaching is quite different than, say, the "evangelical" tradition of the American folk preacher in which "apostles" are not instructed to school themselves or attend seminary but rather to " 'tarry' until the Spirit comes to them."[39] That is, in this version of the American Christian tradition truth will come directly from God and will emerge in the course of the sermon. American folk preachers are urged to "live" their sermons, that is, not to prepare written sermons. That fact does not mean that the sermon lacks structure. On the contrary, it has an "oral formulaic" in which

39. Rosenberg, *Art of the American Folk Preacher*, 23.

certain traditional themes (e.g., "You shall know truth and it shall set you free") are elaborated in a diverse manner by the preacher but always in a given progression which begins in conversational speech, moves to non-rhythmical oral delivery, switches into chanting, and finally, quite often, particularly in the case of the black preacher in the American South, bursts into song.[40] This "lived" sermon is dependent on the call-and-response pattern of the congregation for its success. Such a sermon at one and the same time represents community solidarity and allows for ritual freedom in the rhetoric of the preacher who may resort to idiosyncratic behaviors such as unbuttoning the collar, staring silently at the congregation, and popping suspenders.[41]

All this is in distinct contrast to the Muslim preacher in Kufr al-Ma who dresses in the traditional red fez, white turban, and long, dark flowing gown characteristic of religious scholars, follows a set pulpit style, delivers his sermon in classical Arabic, and generally aims at inculcation of ethics.[42] Although Shaykh Luqman's sermons always impart the "glad tidings" of the coming of the Islamic message of salvation and although they are framed in the prayer formulae that adumbrate, denote, and enunciate that message, their construction often makes the climax of the sermon coincidental with asking for particular works of righteousness.

The American folk preacher by contrast usually digresses and operates through a chain of associations, making the climax of the sermon dependent on the spiritual experience that must occur during the sermon in tandem with the call-and-response participation of the congregation.

The Friday Sermon (Khutba)

We have spoken at length about the preacher, his peculiar role as a "son of the village," his life history, his economic status, the social psychological implications of his career struggle, and the style and ethos of his preaching. But what of the sermon, khutba, itself? In the course of four field work periods in the years 1959, 1960, 1966, and 1967, I listened to over sixty-five Friday congregational sermons delivered by Shaykh Luqman and transliterated and translated twenty-six (see table 3.1).[43] In each

40. Ibid., and Eugene Genovese, *Roll, Jordan, Roll: The World the Slaves Made* (Vintage Books, New York, 1976), 268.

41. See Rosenberg, *Art of the American Folk Preacher*, chapters 4 and 5.

42. It is interesting to note that the young preacher trained at the teaching institute in Amman and now preaching in the central mosque in the village does not choose to wear such formal dress, rather dressing in shirt, khaki pants, and the traditional shawl and headband characteristic of Transjordanian peasants, nomads, and many urbanites.

43. After listening to each sermon in the mosque, I assessed its significance in terms of highlighting important religious themes or important events in the village or nation. Then, I went to the khatib's house the following week, and the preacher read the prepared text

TABLE 3.1
Friday Congregational Sermon Topics in Kufr al-Ma, 1959, 1960, and 1966

Islamic Date	Subject of Sermon	Circumstances	Western Date
13 Muharram	JUSTICE		July 8, 1960
17 Rabi' al-Awwal	MUHAMMAD	Friday before the Prophet's birthday	September 9, 1960
3 Rabi' al-Thani	MARRIAGE AND MARRIAGE PAYMENT (*mahr*)		July 22, 1966
15 Rabi' al-Thani	DEATH	After a death in the village	October 7, 1960
2 Jamadi al-Awwal	THE INDIVIDUAL OBLIGATION OF RECONCILIATION		August 19, 1966
16 Jamadi al-Awwal	THE OBLIGATIONS OF KINSHIP (*rahm*)	After a woman came to him and complained of relatives who did not help	September 2, 1966
21 Jamadi al-Awwal	ON GOOD TREATMENT OF PARENTS		November 11, 1960
3 Jamadi al-Thani	EQUALITY		December 4, 1959
16 Rajab	WORK AND ITS VALUE		January 15, 1960
19 Rajab	THE NECESSITY OF MUTUAL AID AND PHILANTHROPY AND THE ORGANIC VIEW OF SOCIETY		January 8, 1960
23 Rajab	PALESTINE	Three days before the commemoration of Muhammad's night journey and ascent, *isra' wa al-mi'raj*	January 22, 1960
7 Sha'ban	FEARING GOD (*taqwa*)		February 5, 1960
28 Sha'ban	RAMADAN: ITS INTERDEPENDENT ETHICORITUAL NATURE		February 26, 1960

TABLE 3.1 (*cont.*)
Friday Congregational Sermon Topics in Kufr al-Ma, 1959, 1960, and 1966

Islamic Date	Subject of Sermon	Circumstances	Western Date
(probably Sha'ban)	THE NIGHT JOURNEY AND ASCENT		(probably February 1960)
6 Ramadan	THE SOTERIO-LOGICAL AND ETHICAL SIG-NIFICANCE OF RAMADAN		March 4, 1960
13 Ramadan	THE GLORIES OF QURAN		March 11, 1960
22 Ramadan	THE NIGHT OF THE DIVINE DE-GREE (*laylat al-qadr*)	Beginning of the last week of Ramadan	January 14, 1966
Last Friday in Ramadan	THE DOING OF GOOD DEEDS (*iḥsān*): ALMS-GIVING (*ṣadaqat al-fiṭr*), PRAYER AND THE ASK-ING FOR FOR-GIVENESS		March 25, 1960
29 Ramadan	THE NIGHT OF THE DIVINE DECREE: ITS SOTERIOLOGI-CAL SIGNIFI-CANCE		January 21, 1966
18 Shawwal	PILGRIMAGE: ITS SOTER-IOLOGICAL-ETHICAL SIGNIFICANCE		April 15, 1960
25 Shawwal	EDUCATION	Village improve-ment Officer had just been in the village talking about the possibil-ity of obtaining a government loan for the building of a new village school	April 22, 1960

TABLE 3.1 (*cont.*)
Friday Congregational Sermon Topics in Kufr al-Ma, 1959, 1960, and 1966

Islamic Date	Subject of Sermon	Circumstances	Western Date
3 Dhu al-Qa'da	THE PILGRIM-AGE: THE RELI-GIOUS HISTORY OF MUHAM-MAD'S STRUG-GLE		April 29, 1960
10 Dhu al-Hijja	THE MEANING OF THE DAY OF ARAFAT, DAY OF THE PROPHET'S FAREWELL SER-MON	The day before the Festival of the Sacrifice, '*īd al-adha*	April 1, 1966
15 Dhu al-Hijja	WOMEN'S IMMODESTY, MEN'S HONOR	Several days after a killing resulting from a case of honor	June 10, 1960
21 Dhu al-Hijja	MAGIC AND WIZ-ARDRY (*sihr*)	14 days after an incident involving the unmasking of a bogus magician	April 23, 1965
22 Dhu al-Hijja	THE ALMS TAX (*zakāt*)	At harvest time	June 17, 1960

instance I have assigned a title to the sermon based on its content and recorded specific contextual circumstances when they were known. The sermons are listed according to the annual Islamic ritual calendar.

THE FOCUS ON ORTHOPRAXY

It is clear that the timing and contents of Luqman's sermons relate to six factors: the ritual calendar, the calendar of religious history, the calendar of political history, the agricultural calendar, day-to-day village events, and current themes being prosecuted by the national government. For instance, sermons on fasting and pilgrimage are always given during the months when those rituals become obligatory; a sermon on Muhammad's prophetic career is customary on the Prophet's birthday and a sermon commemorating his night journey and ascent occurs at the end of

---

which I typed in the transliterated form. The selection of sermons to be translated represents just under half of those heard. I have no reason to believe that the half selected are atypical either in terms of content, style, or context for the corpus of this preacher.

Rajab; a sermon on Palestine is usually given to commemorate (denigrate) the Balfour Declaration; a sermon on the obligation of giving the alms-due (*zakāt*), is given before harvest time, just before peasants calculate the tithe on their crops (but also at the end of Ramadan when shopkeepers usually inventory their shops to calculate the 2.5 percent alms-due on capital).

Many sermon subjects relate to more than one calendar and might be given at different times of the year. For instance, a khutba on Palestine relates to the religious historical calendar and is usually given during Rajab to commemorate the night journey and ascent of the Prophet to Jerusalem, but it is also given in November in relation to the secular political historical calendar (the date of the Balfour Declaration). A sermon on zakat and supererogatory alms (*şadaqa*) is appropriate to the ritual calendar (Ramadan), as indicated above, but it is also appropriate at any time of the year in relation to day-to-day events in the village (e.g., in relation to the miserliness of particular individuals on particular occasions during the year when generosity is called for). It is important to note as well that the general subject of a khutba is no necessary indication of the content of the sermon. For instance, on both April 15 and April 29, 1960, the preacher gave a khutba on pilgrimage; the first focused on the ethical obligations of the pilgrim (before he left, after he returned) and on his heavenly rewards, while the second was almost entirely devoted to the vicissitudes of the prophetic career of Muhammad (see chapter 6 for the content of these sermons).

A number of sermons are closely related to events that have occurred in the village in the previous week or shortly before (e.g., those of April 22, 1960, June 10, 1960, October 7, 1960, April 23, 1965, and September 2, 1966, relate respectively to the visit of the Village Improvement Officer to investigate the villagers' willingness to contribute to the building of a new school, the killing of a young woman in the village in a case of honor, the death of an elderly villager, the unmasking of a bogus magician, and the complaint of a woman to the preacher that her relatives refused to help her). Each of these sermons, capitalizing on the hometown preacher's intimate knowledge of his community, established and reaffirmed ethical standards in the fields of education, kinship, modesty, and folk healing and magic.

It might be argued that many sermon topics were chosen to correspond to themes being pursued by the central government through the Ministry of Religious Endowments. However, the evidence on this score is not convincing. The sermons chosen in 1959 and 1960 were Luqman's own choice. By 1965 the Department of Religious Endowments had begun to send out a newsletter suggesting topics for sermons without specifying appropriate times. Luqman denied that his selection of sermon topics in the 1965–1966 period differed substantially from those selected in 1959–1960. My own comparison of the sermon topics for these years revealed no significant differences. By the 1970s the Department of Religious Endowments sent out a handsomely illustrated monthly journal to preachers. Each issue included an exemplary sermon. Luqman continued to compose his own sermons. Sometime in the 1970s Luqman began to collect the taped sermons of Shaykh Kishk, the popular, highly critical anti-establishment "free" Egyptian preacher. If there were any models to be followed they were as apt to be of this type as those distributed through the Department of Religious Endowments. I classified the content of the twenty-six sermons listed above in terms of their dominant themes and noted their incidence as follows: political (1); life cycle crisis (1); religious history (6); ritual (6); theological (7); and ethical (15). This classification is not wholly satisfactory inasmuch as a number of the sermons had to be classified under two rubrics. For example, the sermon of 28 Sha'ban was both ritual and ethical in content and that of 6 Ramadan was both theological and ethical, stressing both the heavenly rewards of the completed fast and the high standard of right conduct demanded during the month, e.g., not simply fasting but also refraining from slander and idle gossip. Nevertheless, the weighting is clear and significant. One sermon concerned a life cycle crisis, death. Overtly political matters are given little weight; the single sermon on Palestine being the regular exception. Luqman told me that in the past he had also delivered a sermon on Algeria during the anticolonial struggle against the French. This underweighting contrasts with the highly political content of sermons delivered in large urban mosques in Jordan, Syria, Lebanon, and Egypt.[44] Ritual, theology, and religious history all received some attention with sermons stressing the importance of the ritual pillars of the faith (prayer, fasting, and pilgrimage), key theological events such as the night journey and ascent, the night of the divine decree (when the Quran was revealed), and Judgment Day, and key events in religious history such as the birth of Muhammad, the Prophet's mission and its vicissitudes, and the farewell pilgrimage.

But by far the strongest emphasis throughout is on ethics: justice, equality, the obligation to kinsmen and family members, alms-giving, asking for forgiveness, the obligation to work, guarding against immodesty, forbidding magic, moderation of the size of marriage payments, reconciliation of estranged friends and neighbors, and respect for one's par-

44. These urban sermons reflected a militant Islam, reformist in rejecting nonreligious ethics and law, generally pan-Arabist and politically active in calling for staunch—including armed—opposition to colonialism and neocolonialism. For an analysis of the sermons in the large urban mosques of Syria, Lebanon, Jordan, and Egypt see Bruce M. Borthwick's "The Islamic Sermon as a Channel of Political Communication" (Ph.D. diss., University of Michigan, 1965).

ents. Even when the topic of the sermon is overtly ritual (Ramadan, the month of the fast or pilgrimage) or theological (the night journey and ascent of the Prophet), an intertwined theme is always ethical (e.g., the pilgrim who leaves on the pilgrimage without paying his debts will not have his pilgrimage accepted by God, and the faster of Ramadan who slanders his neighbor has thereby broken the fast.

THE SOURCES OF SERMONS

An examination of the sources on which the preacher draws for the construction of sermons sheds more light on the content of the khutba and both its logic and its ethos.[45] In 1960 when I first queried Luqman on the books he consulted frequently in preparing sermons he listed nine. In 1966 after the lapse of six years I asked Luqman the same question and he listed seven (see table 3.2). I have characterized in parentheses after each source, when known, the genre of religious literature it represents.[46]

The primary source in both 1960 and 1966 is, of course, the Quran and the secondary source is the Traditions of the Prophet, hadith, formalized in texts and chains of authority and gathered in well-known collections. Luqman's khutbas were punctuated by references to Quranic verses which often formed the proof-text of the sermon, and hadith were quoted frequently (see chapter 4). The third important source is books on preaching, and the fourth is Quranic commentaries. It is notable that aside from the Quran, the books on the second list do not replicate the first, indicating a growing library. The second list also indicates a greater sophistication in religious learning in the fact that two advanced commentaries of the Quran are added as well as a commentary on the Traditions of the Prophet. Already in 1960, however, a number of very sophisticated books are found: the classical commentary on the hadith by Al-Bukhari, the great work on Islamics (including traditions, theology, law, and philosophy) by Al-Ghazzali, the then recent biography of Muhammad by Husayn Haykal, and the recent work on the reform of preaching by Al-Khuli. It might be argued that many village preachers might amass libraries of sophisticated books, as indeed Luqman had done, to enhance

---

45. By "ethos" is meant, following John J. Honigmann, *Culture and Personaity* (Harper & Brothers, New York, 1954), 42–43, "the emotional quality of socially patterned behavior reflect[ing] the motivational state of the actor" and, more broadly, following Clifford Geertz, "Ethos, World-View and the Analysis of Sacred Symbols," *Antioch Review*, Vol. 17, No. 4, December 1957, 421, "the tone, character and quality of their [a people's] life, its moral and aesthetic style, and mood; it is the underlying attitude toward themselves and their world that life reflects."

46. I wish to thank my collegue, Akbar Muhammad, for helping me to characterize these works.

TABLE 3.2
Sources of Sermons in Kufr al-Ma, 1960 and 1966

1960

The verses of the *Quran*	(QURAN)
Commentary on the Verses (of the *Quran*) *for* (the purpose of) *Remembering Wisdom* by Khazin	(QURANIC COMMENTARY)
The Revivication of the Religious Sciences by Al-Ghazzali	(TRADITIONS OF THE PROPHET, THEOLOGY, PHILOSOPHY, LAW)
The Instruction of Worshippers in the Best Way of Right Conduct by Zayn al-Din Abd al-Aziz	
The Excursion of the Observers by Taqi al-Din ibn Abd al-Malik	
The Sahih of Al-Bukhari with a Commentary by Qatlani	(CLASSICAL COLLECTION OF TRADITIONS OF THE PROPHET)
The Life of Muhammad by Husayn Haykal	(BIOGRAPHY OF THE PROPHET)
Reform of the Religious Sermon by Abd al-Aziz al-Khuli	(PREACHING)
Preaching by Mahmoud Ali Ahmed	(PREACHING)

1966

The noble *Quran*	(QURAN)
What Muslim Added to What Bukhari and Muslim Agreed Upon	(CLASSICAL COLLECTION OF TRADITIONS OF THE PROPHET)
The Guide for the Successful (Those Who Achieve Salvation) in the *Commentary: The Training of the Righteous* by Nawwawi	(COMMENTARY ON THE TRADITIONS OF THE PROPHET)
The Key to Oratory and Admonition	(PREACHING)
Incitement of Fear and Awakening of Desire	(THEOLOGY)
Commentary of the Quran by Ibn Kathir	(QURANIC COMMENTARY)
Commentary by Wadih	(QURANIC COMMENTARY)

their status among their more learned contemporaries—the judges, religious officials, and teachers in the secular schools with whom they came into contact. Books, like furniture, can be used to impress the members of one's reference group. This motive might have grown, unconsciously, as Luqman's horizon widened, with his travels to the Arabian Peninsula as a pilgrim guide in the 1970s and with his son's attendance at the Islamic University in Medina in the early 1980s. On the other hand, there is no doubt that in his contact with these more learned contemporaries, beginning with his mentor, Shaykh Ahmed, in his early days, he had acquired greater sophistication in interpreting religious law and ethics. Beginning in the 1970s with his frequent trips to Mecca as pilgrim guide he collected many of these books gratis from various religious institutions and universities. Perhaps, more to the point, he had sent his son to receive his education, as mentioned, in the Islamic University at Medina, an education that he himself lacked. By 1984 his son had completed five years of study and returned to the village. The son had vicariously realized his father's ambitions. The constant interaction between father and son must have deepened Luqman's understanding.

With respect to the third source of sermon compositions, the books on preaching, I specifically asked Luqman in 1979 whether he consulted old collections of sermons when composing his own. He replied that he did not use old collections of sermons because they did not deal with contemporary problems. He stressed again that he used commentaries on the Quran and collections of the Traditions. He said that he selected the appropriate hadiths from the books dealing with various subjects. He likened the preacher to a doctor. When a man comes to the doctor he must examine him and treat him. The preacher must treat the prevalent sicknesses. He stated that the monthly journals sent by the Waqf Department did not stipulate subjects for sermons, and that he did not keep his sermons on file.

Three inferences regarding Luqman's sermons may be made from this examination of their sources. First, his basic sources are the Quran and the Traditions of the Prophet. Consequently, his sermons are crafted with an entirely familiar traditional content at once religious, historical, ethical, and soteriological. But, second, the addition of sophisticated Quranic commentaries, interaction with his son, interaction over the years with the religious officials of his own district, and the collection of books and taped sermons by such antiestablishment figures as Sayyid al-Qutb, Khalid Muhammad al-Khalid, and Shaykh Kishk injected into his preaching a message that is both fundamentalist and radical, both practical and devoted to the everyday life of his own village as well as otherworldly and directed to salvation.

The three above-mentioned scholars are all Egyptians. Luqman was influenced early on by an Egyptian shaykh, an Azharite, who settled as preacher in the adjoining subdistrict center of Deir Abu Said. Several times over a period of many years this shaykh came to live in Luqman's (father's) house and stayed there for two-month periods, teaching him Islamic law, the Unity of God (*tawḥīd*), Quranic commentary (*tafsīr*), Arabic language, and Quranic recitation (*tajwīd*). While Shaykh Ahmed taught Luqman Islamic law according to the Shafi'i school only, the Egyptian shaykh taught him Islamic law according to all four accepted law schools. This intimate, multiplex (involving domicile and commensality as well as learning) tutorial relationship (between older teacher and younger student) which Luqman shared with both Shaykh Ahmed and the Egyptian shaykh has been recognized as a traditional mode of Islamic learning by scholars in many different parts of the Muslim world.[47]

Third, in that Luqman did indeed study Islamic law, perhaps the most significant fact about the sources of his sermons are those that are not mentioned. Luqman failed to include in his list of sources the fifth potential source, books elaborating principles and rules of the four Sunni Muslim law schools (*fiqh*). Luqman possessed many of these books in his library which I inventoried in 1979. The books are listed by date and order of accession in table 3.3.

The absence of books on Islamic law as a designated primary source for sermons is as significant as the prominence of references on the Quran.[48] Luqman said in 1960 when I queried him about the matter that he consulted books on law when he gave the lesson that preceded the khutba. For instance, he would consult these books when he wished to give instruction on the proper rules for ritual ablution (*wuḍū'*) or discuss penalties for violation of Islamic mores, as for instance when he quoted the following hadith on adultery:

> Five men committed adultery with a woman; the first was killed; the second was stoned; the third was whipped; the fourth suffered half the penalty; the fifth was exonerated from all penalty. Who were these five (men)? The first was an unbeliever and had to be killed; the second was a free married Muslim and had to be stoned; the third was unmarried and had to be whipped a hundred lashes; the fourth was a slave and incumbent on him was half the penalty (of the freeman); and the fifth was insane. Stoning involves public scorn, *taʿzīr*, and many people are gathered to watch the stoning.

Although Luqman's sermons are primarily ethical in intent, they are not legal in content or ethos and do not include discussions of the kind quoted above. That is, they are not concerned with legal questions such as the division of inheritances or the rules governing a proper marriage or

47. See Bulliet 1972 on Iran, Eickelman 1985 on Morocco, and Hussein 1948 on Egypt for other examples of traditional learning.

48. The term *fiqh* (lit. intelligence or knowledge) refers to jurisprudence in Islam, covering all aspects of civil, political, and religious life including laws of inheritance, property, contract (including marriage), and ritual obligations. It also refers in a narrower sense to the application of the independent exercise of the intelligence to decide legal points. See the article on fiqh in the *Encyclopaedia of Islam* for details.

TABLE 3.3
Shaykh Luqman's Personal Library, December 1979

Tafsīr jalalayn	?
Tafsīr al-baydāwi (Quranic commentary)	1950
Al-futuḥāt al-wahība by al-Shabb Rakhti (hadith)	1950
Kitab nuzhat al-nāthirīn by Shaykh Taqi al-Din ibn abd al-Malik (hadith)	1955
Al-fiqh ʿala al-mathāhib al-arbaʿa, 5 volumes (fiqh)	1958
Al-tāj al-jāmiʿ; lil usul fi aḥādīth al-rusūl (hadith and fiqh) by Mansur Ali Nasir, 5 volumes	1960
Tafsīr al-wādiḥ (Quranic commentary) by Muhammad Mahmoud Hijazi, 3 volumes	1960
Dalīl al-fāliḥīn by Abd al-Rahman Hamad ibn 'Allan al-Siddiq al-Shafi'i al-Ash'ari, 4 volumes (hadith)	1960
Iḥyā ʿulum al-dīn by Al-Ghazzali (hadith and fiqh)	1965
Al-ʿaqīda al-islamiyya wa usasuha by Abd al-Rahman Habanaka ('aqida or tawhid)	1968
Al-nutham al-islāmiyya by Shubhi al-Salih (social structural, political and economic principles of Islam)	1968
Jund allah by Sa'id Hawwa (Islamic culture)	1969
Allah by Sa'id Hawwa (Islamic culture)	1969
Al-islām by Sa'id Hawwa (Islamic culture)	1969
Al-rasūl by Sa'id Hawwa (Islamic culture)	1969
Layl al-awtār by Al-Imam Muhammad ibn abu al-Shawkani, 4 volumes	1970
Fatāwi al-kubra by Ibn Taymiyya, 5 volumes (fiqh, questions and answers)	1970
Iʿanat al-ṭālibīn by Al-Sayyid al-Bakri, 4 volumes (fiqh)	1970
Kitāb al-māli by Yahya ibn Husayn al-Shirazi, 2 parts (hadith)	1970
Fatḥ al-mubīn li sharḥ al-arbaʿīn by Ibn Hajam al-Haytham (hadith)	1974
Kitāb al-umm by Imam al-Shafi'i, 5 volumes (fiqh)	1974
Al-muhaththab by Imam al-Shirazi, 2 volumes (fiqh)	1974
ʿIlam al-muwaqqaʿīn by Ibn al Qayyim al-Jawzi, 4 volumes (fiqh)	1974
Al-ghuniyya by Abd al-Qadir al-Jilani, 2 parts (fiqh)	1975
Fatḥ al-bāri by al-Bukhari (hadith)	1976
Sharḥ saḥīḥ al-bukhāri (commentary on hadith)	1976

TABLE 3.3 *(cont.)*
Shaykh Luqman's Personal Library, December 1979

Taysīr al-'allām sharḥ 'umdat al-aḥkām by Abdullah ibn Abd al-Rahman Abi Bassam, 2 volumes (commentary on hadith)	1976
Muqtasir sīrat al-rasūl by Muhammad ibn Abd al-Wahhab (biography)	1977
Mawārid al-thamān fi durūs al-zamān by Abd al-Aziz Muhammad al-Sulayman, 2 volumes (preaching)	1977
Adhwā al-bayān by Muhammad Amin ibn Muhammad al-Shanqiti, 9 volumes (commentary on the Quran)	1977
Fatḥ al-qādir by Muhammad ibn Ali al-Shawkuri, 5 volumes (Quranic commentary)	1978
Tafsīr al-nasafi by Al-Imam al-Nasafi (Quranic commentary)	1979
Majmū'āt al-tawḥīd by Muhammad ibn Abd al-Wahhab (tawhid)	1979
Tafsīr al-tabari by Al-Tabari, 38 parts and 12 volumes (Quranic commentary)	1979
Saḥīḥ al-muslim by Al-Muslim, 18 parts and 9 volumes (hadith)	1979
Al-mughni by Abi Muhammad Abdullah ibn Qudama al-Makdisi, 9 volumes	1965(?)
Al-mughni by Abi Muhammad Abdullah ibn Qudama al-Makdisi, 9 volumes	1965(?)
Tafsīr ibn kathīr by Ibn Kathir (Quranic commentary)	undated accession
Marāqi al-fallāḥ by Shaykh Ahmed Tahtawi (fiqh)	undated accession

* Books from his son's university collection—Al Jāmi'a al Islamiyya, al-Medina al-Munawwara

divorce or the ritual-legal norms of prayer. In so far as khutbas do touch on these matters, they are concerned with the religio-ethical principles that underly them. For example, his sermon of July 1966 on marriage and marriage payment (*mahr*) emphasized the "religious" nature of the contract and the dominance of religious rather than economic or social structural (pedigree) considerations in selecting a partner. Mahr was a "gift," freely given and received and not a payment for services rendered or expected. He capped the sermon with a Tradition of the Prophet: "*Go seek* (her hand in marriage) *even with an iron ring*"; poverty was not to be a bar to marriage between co-believers. Or, for instance, when Luqman gave a sermon on the obligation of kinship when he might have mentioned the rights of patrilineal kinsmen to inheritance, he emphasized instead the compassionate nature of kinship on the model of God's compassion for man (see chapter 4). Luqman clearly separated out the legal implications of religion and treated them in the preliminary lesson (dars). The khutba, the centerpiece of the Friday congregational prayer service, was the proper focus of the central religious message which was simultaneously ethical and soteriological in intent and not legal or political.[49]

THE IMPACT OF THE AUDIENCE

To this point although much has been said about the role of the khatib and the content of the khutba, nothing has been said about the audience. It is necessary to shift briefly to the khatib's audience and examine the sermon from its perspective. But to appreciate the role of the audience one must, however briefly, place the preacher and the audience in a comparative perspective. Preaching styles and audience responses vary on a continuum from the highly formal to the highly informal with respect to vocabulary, syntactic forms, loudness and intonation patterns, use of printed materials, and content of illustrations used in the sermon (see chapter 8 for a fuller discussion and analysis of formalized speech acts in the khutba). These styles also vary in the emotional involvement of both preacher and audience and the mutual implication of preacher and audience in the sermon's development and tone. At the end of the continuum are sermons delivered, for instance, in the "mainline" Protestant churches in the United States. There, a didactic message is conveyed with the preacher acting mainly as teacher, to a rather sedate audience which has a printed order of worship handed out at the beginning of the service to guide and regulate the ritual. The audience's involvement in the sermon is minimal—it is its passive recipient.

On the other hand, the call-and-response pattern of the American folk preacher accentuates the role of the audience in the sermon. Indeed, the quality of the congregation's performance has a considerable impact on the folk sermon, and if the congregation is not moved, the sermon might be considered a failure. The preacher's intimate relationship with the audience is often conveyed in direct questions such as, "Do you know what

49. In a personal communication (1985) Ira Lapidus has suggested alternative explanations to the lack of emphasis on law in Luqman's preparation of sermon bibliographies: "It is possible that it (law) is simply not central to the role of the preacher. It is also possible that the practical application of law is declining, as it is in many other parts of the Muslim world. Finally it is possible that Luqman is being influenced by reformist movements (*tajdīd* or *iṣlāḥ*) which stress the primacy of the Quran and hadith and the secondary importance of the law. All of the movements which Fazlur Rahman calls neo-Sufi movements take this line. While the Shari'a is in principle a touchstone of a Muslim life, the actual interest in fiqh is, at least in many other Muslim regions, in decline."

I'm talking about?" which require an answer.[50] The congregation punctuates the folk preacher's chant and marks its progress by saying,
"Amen" and "Oh, yes!" They sing or hum along with the sermon. The
chant and song has its own rhythm which carries it along. American folk
sermons generally become unintelligible as they progress; the words and
their denotations are lost. Rosenberg argues that in the American folk
sermon "the medium is the message."[51] The preacher and the congregation combine in a reciprocal and at times mutual relationship to enjoy/
suffer a religious experience in which, though not much information is
disseminated, much meaning is imparted. Both Mitchell, in describing
black preaching in the United States in the last half of the twentieth century, and Genovese, in describing black preaching in the antebellum
South, accentuate the experience-centered nature of such preaching.[52]
With the chanting, moaning, and whooping of the congregation and the
tendency for everything to be sung, with much of the singing improvisa-
tional and without a printed order of service, a free flow of religious emotion wells from the pulpit out to the congregation and back to provide
both an ecstatic and cathartic experience.

The Islamic khutba in Kufr al-Ma by contrast constrains ecstatic and
cathartic responses on the part of the audience though not to the same
degree as the mainline Protestant sermon just characterized. It does so
through its set (though unprinted) Friday worship ritual: its initial "lesson," its three predictable calls to prayer, its two sermons specified in style
and length, and its individual and, finally, congregational prayers. If
American folk preaching and black preaching allow for a certain "ritual
freedom" on the part of the audience, the Islamic khutba in Kufr al-Ma
stands for "ritual order," as befitting a sermon whose main thrust is orthopraxy (i.e., norms governing day-to-day interpersonal relations between family members, kin, neighbors, and co-religionists, and including
norms against community and societal factionalism [see chapter 7]).

One must be quick to add, however, that the Islamic sermon in Kufr al-
Ma does not simply convey "information" on right conduct to the audience. It also conveys "meaning," that is, ultimate understanding that has
an affective as well as cognitive aspect. This meaning is conveyed in the
many religious prayer formulae that punctuate the sermon, such as "I
bear witness that there is no god but God"; "God, may he be exalted";
"Muhammad, May God bless and grant him salvation"; "Moses, on him
be peace"; "I take refuge with God from the accursed Satan." Such for-

50. Rosenberg, *Art of the American Folk Preacher*, 54ff.
51. Ibid.
52. See Henry M. Mitchell, *Black Preaching* (J. B. Lippincott, New York, 1970), and
Genovese, *Roll, Jordan, Roll*, 255ff.

mulae proclaim the Islamic world view and provide the certainty that frames any discussion of problems in this world.

The preacher's communication with his audience in a community and societal context is critical here. Does the preacher speak to the audience's contemporary needs and, further, even if he does, does the audience understand his message?[53] In the latter part of the twentieth century black preachers, beginning with Martin Luther King, Jr. and continuing to Jesse Jackson, have declared the gospel in the language and culture of the people, and they have attempted to articulate contemporary needs from the pulpit. But the khutba in Kufr al-Ma, as elsewhere in the Arab world, is delivered in classical Arabic rather than in any colloquial form of Arabic.[54] Since classical Arabic is to a great extent the language of the Quran—a sacred language—its use confirms the sermon's meaning and not only legitimizes but also sacralizes its message of salvation. For the Islamic sermon, too, to a large extent the medium is also the message.

But the use of classical Arabic also poses the problems of audience comprehension. Although the congregation at the Friday worship service certainly understands the "meaning" of the sermon, that is, the fundamentals of the Islamic world view and ethos, the degree to which it understands specific messages is problematic. In the 1960s a substantial portion of the congregation in Kufr al-Ma was illiterate. To what degree did and do they decipher the rich metaphorical, metonymical, and allegorical "informational" messages of the khatib? These metaphors are steeped in a sophisticated scholarly tradition of over a thousand years. To what degree can peasants steeped in the metaphors of their own "little traditions" (metaphors of earthly wisdom) and in the metaphors of a "great" but unsophisticated tribal tradition of law and ethics penetrate the Islamic metaphors expressed in the classical language?

With increasing educational opportunities, occupational differentiation, and occupational mobility an equally important question is, How does a variously situated (spatially, economically, and culturally) congregation made up of engineers, teachers, students, clerks, army officers, soldiers, auto mechanics, truck drivers, construction workers, carpenters, stonecutters, shopkeepers, and cultivators interpret Luqman's sermons?

53. Raymond Firth in "Problem and Assumption in an Anthropological Study of Religion," *Essays on Social Organization and Values* (Athlone Press, London, 1964) has posed the general problem of the audience's variable understanding of any ritual or dramatic performance and, from the other side, the possibilities of innovation on the part of the performer. See particularly pp. 247–48ff.

54. Although classical Arabic is the dominant speech form used in the sermon, Luqman occasionally lapses into colloquial Arabic to emphasize a point. Some free preachers like Shaykh Kishk commonly do so (see Kepel 1986, chapter 6). Khatibs in official mosques sometimes stop to explain an obscure point in colloquial Arabic.

Or, to put the question differently, to what degree is the audience composed of worldly-wise "militant Muslims,"[55] "Islamic Marxists,"[56] and sober, hard-working peasants? To what degree does the interpretation of old men differ from that of the increasingly large numbers of young men? Do the men of the generation of Luqman's son view his message as genuine and moving or do they regard it as old-fashioned and somewhat irrelevant? How do women—who do not hear the sermon since by local peasant custom they are not allowed in the mosque—understand the sermon when they hear it from the men? Luqman urges the men of the congregation to impart the Islamic "informational" message to the women of their households when he often interpolates in the middle of a sermon, "Go tell your women. . . ." (He bemoans the fact that there are no loudspeakers in the village to broadcast the Friday sermon so all women can hear it.) How do the "sober peasants" in his audience, who may have been a majority in the 1960s but are certainly a minority in the 1980s, reconcile an increasingly influential religious message with the demands of a tribal ethos? Indeed, this is a problem for nearly all residents of Kufr al-Ma regardless of their degree of education or occupation since in Jordan tribal norms are not cancelled by education, mobility, or occupational differentiation. These are important specific questions relating to the universal problem of the social organization of tradition and its reinterpretation (not simply by specialists but also by common men) in rapidly modernizing societies for which, as yet, we have few answers.[57] Occasionally, however, the problem is dramatized and clarified in a critical event.

In February 1984 on the occasion of a brief visit to Kufr al-Ma I noted the difficulty with which villagers were coming to terms with Islam in the modern world of election campaigns. The first elections for parliament to be held in Jordan since 1968 were about to take place. Election banners, posters, and graffiti were readily visible in the towns and in the village. A

55. For G. H. Jansen (1979) the mark of the "militant Muslim" is: (1) his view that Islam must be central to every aspect of life, especially politics; (2) his concern with how to come to terms with the Western way of life; (3) his attempt to remodel his public and private life according to the precepts of his faith in a way to make Islam relevant to the special needs of the day; and (4) his staunch anticolonialism. Jansen argues that "militant Islam" is no new thing and has existed for at least two hundred years.

56. This is a phrase first used to describe many of the left-oriented opposition elements to Muhammad Reza Shah in the 1970s in Iran. It has been construed to include Muslims who wish to combine elements of Islam and elements of socialism.

57. Among the best attempts to answer some of these questions and elucidate the processes of interpretation and transformation involved is Hefner's (1985) study, *Hindu Javanese.* I hope to answer some of these questions in the Jordanian context in a future study on the basis of my recent (1986) research on the impact of international migration and higher education abroad on postpeasant society in Jordan.

candidate associated with the Muslim Brotherhood was running from the district, and villagers were clearly in sympathy with his views and the ethos they represented. On the other hand, a tribal Shaykh from the Jordan Valley was also running for the same seat. This Shaykh had offered protection (dakhl) in a complicated case of honor in which several men from a nearby village had been killed by men from Kufr al-Ma. Many other tribal groups had refused to provide "protection" for the clan of the perpetrators—this would have left their crops and their homes open to depredation by the victim's clan and their personal safety jeopardized. Finally, after much pleading, the Shaykh offered the protection of his tribe and thereby guaranteed the security of the clan and a large part of the village of Kufr al-Ma since the clan in question constituted more than one-third of the village's population.

The question being deliberated by villagers, young and old, literate and illiterate, cultivator and professional, was: Who should they vote for, the tribal Shaykh who had come to their aid in a crisis or the Muslim Brother who also represented their world view and ethos? And they did not know the answer!

How did and does this audience interpret and respond when Luqman gives a sermon on kinship and balances the obligations of "specific kinship" (i.e., obligations of members of patrilineages and patriclans to one another) with those of "general kinship" (i.e., the obligations to "Muslim" brothers)? And how do they respond to Luqman's exhortation, "Help your brother, oppressor be he or oppressed" when he interprets the exhortation as meaning that if one's brother is the oppressor one helps him by restraining him from oppression?

The fact is, the study of the audience's understanding, interpretation of, and response to religious messages of the kind given by Luqman is a subject about which we know almost nothing. And until we do, the study of Islamic sermons or any others, for that matter, will be incomplete.

4
The Rhetoric of Religion:
An Analysis of Rahm (Womb, Kinship, Compassion)

The Islamic sermon is a rhetorical form, that is, an argument whose elements are linked images and symbols composed in such a way as to express an underlying message through the organizing metaphor of kinship. This chapter explores both the metaphor and the modes of articulation of that sermon within its social and cultural context. In the course of this exploration several questions will be examined: Is the Islamic sermon an example of formal speech? If so, does that formal speech, as Bloch (1975) argues, preclude the handling of specific issues? If not, what is the nature of the articulation of formal speech with its social structural context? If the Islamic sermon is regarded as a particular speech code among a multiplicity of codes, what is the mode of accommodation of those codes to one another? If there is a division of labor among symbols, is it possible to categorize that division in terms of a system of positions?[1] Since the mosque is but one of three symbolic arenas for community interaction and meaning, the guest house and the bureaucrat's office being the others, one must avoid analyzing the mosque/sermon in isolation and investigate the articulation of the three symbolic codes that accompany each arena. This exploration compares, then, for each arena the following attributes: central actors, modes of power, legitimation, ethos, ritual focus, age, gender and speech and clothing patterns.

The sermon to be analyzed was delivered by Shaykh Luqman in the mosque of Kufr al-Ma on Friday, September 2, 1966 (16 Jamadi al-Awwal).

THE SERMON AND ITS ANALYSIS

[1]* Praise be to God who has exalted [he] who has said: **And give the kinsman (dhi al-qurba) his rights and the needy, and the traveler; and never**

---

1. The description and analysis that follow have been stimulated by the work of James Fernandez (1975), David Parkin (1975), Ronald Grimes (1976), Kenneth Burke (1961), and Victor Turner (1962, 1967). Although Fernandez distinguishes between symbolic analysis and the analysis of metaphor (which he labels "pronominalism"), it is clear from his analysis of Christian ritual, particularly in the identification of "secondary associations," that he is involved in tracing the multivocality of symbols. The study of "images" and the study of "symbols," therefore, are mutually implied although a difference of weighting may occur.

* Bracketed numbers in margins indicate the paragraph number in the sermon for ease of reference in following the analysis later in the chapter.

squander (17: 26, A).[2] And witness that there is no god but God who has made the link of rahm (kinship, the womb, blood kindred) among the best of relationships (qarābāt). He has sanctioned (confirmed) it with the greatest acts of forgiveness (matūbāt) and made it the key to good, the lock to evil. And witness that our master, Muhammad, the Messenger of God, bestowed upon people rahma (compassion, pity, human understanding, sympathy, kindness, mercy) and fortified them with its free gift. Thus, the Messenger said: Khayr (blessing, good thing, wealth, benefit, advantage, charity) *hurries as a reward* [after] *righteousness* (birr) *and the link of rahm* (blood kindred, kinship, compassion), *and wickedness hurries as punishment* [after] *the oppressor and the cutter of rahm.* God pray and bless our master, Muhammad and his family and companions who were with their arhām (blood kindred, blood kinswomen, wombs) always in touch and with their Lord always trusting.

[2] Now then: God, may he be exalted, said: **Would you, then, if you were put in authority sow corruption on earth and cut to pieces your blood kindred** (arham, wombs, maternal relatives). **Those** [are the ones] **whom God has cursed and made deaf and blind** (47: 22–23, a). Worshipers of God, the generous (noble) Quran has promised the cutter of kinship (blood kindred, wombs, rahm) painful torture and has introduced him amongst those upon whom the curse of God (the Lord of worlds) has fallen. He was deaf and blind, not listening to what was for his right guidance [the keeping up of kinship ties] and not seeing what was for his good interest.

[3] Al-rahma (compassion, pity, mercy) is the distinguishing characteristic of the true believer and the sign of the obedient and in it there is [the] favor of the Lord of the worlds. Verily, God, may he be exalted, has placed among people different kinds of ties (silāt) by which they may express pity (compassion, understanding, sympathy) amongst themselves and aid one another in repelling harm and bringing benefits in its place. The strongest of these ties is the tie of kinship (qarāba) which close kinship (the womb—rahm) concentrates (amasses), and agnation (nasab) and affinity (musāhara) confirm (reinforce). Because of this, religion has ordained [their adhering to] their tie [of kinship] (silatihim) and has incited caring for them (female relatives, wombs, blood kindred—arham). Muhammad said: *"The cutter of blood kindred* (kinship—rahm) *will not enter paradise" and he said also: "Who resolves to increase his wealth and immortalize his deeds, let him persist in keeping the tie of kinship* (blood kindred, the womb—rahm)." The tie of blood kinship consists in demonstrating affection for relatives (aqārib) and meeting their needs—in

---

2. In the body of the sermon text, parentheses are used to indicate the Arabic equivalent of a term or to indicate alternative meanings. Brackets are used to indicate words or phrases that are understood, or added to render an accurate meaning but are not part of the literal Arabic text.

wealth and high rank and sickness and lightening their burdens in tragedy
and joining in the celebration of their joys and their sorrows and laying
bare their anxieties and executing their requirements. And Abu Hurayra[3]
said: *I heard the Messenger of God say, "Learn your* [patrilineal] *pedigrees (ansāb) in order to know your blood kindred (arham), for verily,
the tie of kinship (wombs)* [brings] *affection among kinsmen (ahl), opu-
lence among riches and preservation of traditions."* These Traditions of
the Prophet and others confirm the tie of blood kindred (womb—rahm)
and affection for relatives and oblige beneficence and sympathy for them.

[4]   *A man came to the prophet and asked him, "Which deeds are most loved
by God?" He replied: "Belief in God." He asked, "What else?" He replied: "The tie of kinship* (blood kindred)." *He asked, "What deeds are
most hated by God?" He replied: "Taking partners to God; then cutting
kinship* (blood kindred, the womb)." The best of men and the most beloved of God is he who persists in the tie of kinship (blood kindred,
wombs) and treats his kinsmen (aqarib) with beneficience. And the worst
of men and the most hated by God is the cutter of kinship (blood kindred,
the womb). *The Messenger was asked: "Who is the best of men?" He
replied: "The most fearfully obedient to God* (the most pious) *and the
most persisting in their ties of kinship and the most commanding of them
in the good and the most avoiding of them in the reprehensible."* And
God said: **Such as break the covenant of God after its solemn binding,
and such as cut what God has commanded should be joined, and such as
do corruption in the land—they shall be the losers** (2: 27, A).

[5]   Kinship (blood kindred, the womb—rahm) is one of the indicators of
mercy (compassion, pity, human understanding, kindness—rahma) and
it is derived from the name—the Compassionate (al-raḥmān). So the one
who persists in (maintaining ties of) blood kinship (blood kindred, the
womb) has great favor [with respect to] the mercy of God, to him belongs
glory and power. And the cutter of blood kinship (blood kindred, the
womb, rahm) is cut off from the mercy (compassion, pity, rahma) of God.
Verily, the mercy of God is always close to the doers of good (muḥsinīn).
Abd al-Rahman ibn 'Awf said "*I heard the Messenger say, 'God said, to
him belongs glory and power: I am God; I am the Compassionate* (al-
rahman); *I created mercy* (compassion, kindness, rahma) *and I coined for
it a name* [from among] *my names. I split off* (joined) *to it one of my*
[ninety-nine] *names). Whoever keeps persistingly to it* (rahma), *I keep
persistingly to him and whoever cuts it off, I cut him off.' "*

[6]   As for the kinship (blood kindred, the womb, mercy—rahm) which God
and his messenger ordained. It is divided into two types—special kinship
(blood kindred, rahmun khāssa) and general kinship (blood kindred,

3. Abu Hurayra and Abd al-Rahman Ibn Awf were among the Prophet's intimates and
companions who are often cited as the last link in the chain of authorities for Hadith.

mercy, *raḥmun, ʿāmma*). General kinship (blood kindred, mercy) is the kinship (blood kindred, mercy) of religion founded upon genuine brotherhood among true believers, for the true believers are brothers. It is incumbent upon the Muslim to keep persistingly to his brothers in religion and to show affection toward them and to avoid all that leads to their injury and to the cutting of their kinship (*raḥmihim*, womb) and that he fulfill his obligations toward them. As for the special kinship (blood kindred, mercy), it is what involves relatives (aqarib) and kinsfolk (ahl). Islam has confirmed its ties and warned against its cutting. [They—special kindred] are the most deserving of men, of good kinship (*ḥusn al-ṣila*) and kindness (birr). Treating them with beneficience and charity is a religious obligation. After that, there enters into special kinship (blood kindred, mercy) brothers and sisters and paternal uncles and maternal uncles and paternal aunts and maternal aunts and their children and the grandparents and their branches from [among] their ancestors and descendants. With these one has the obligation of continuing the relationship, and that by visiting them and asking about their circumstances and spending on those of them who are needy and uncovering their anxieties and tragedies.

[7] God, may He be exalted, said: **and fear God by whom ye beseech one another; and** (respect) **women** (wombs, kinship—arham) (4: 1, S). Abu Hurayra said, the Prophet said: "*God, may he be exalted, created the creature so that when he had finished, the womb* (al-rahm) *said* [metonymically]: *'Is this the place of refuge* [in you—God] *from that which is severed* [the umbilical cord]?' *God replied: 'Yes, don't you approve of my* [re]*joining you to those who are connected with you* [i.e., your kinsmen] *and parting you from those from whom you are* [already] *cut off* [i.e., strangers of nonkin]?' *The womb said, 'Oh yes, Lord.' God said: 'Then that shall be for you* (your lot).' *Then the Prophet said: 'Obey, if you will. If you had the authority would you do the evil of severing ties with kinsmen* (wombs, arham)?' "

[8] What is worthy of the complete Muslim is that he keep persistingly to his blood kindred (relationships, kinship, womb, compassion—rahm) and relatives (*qarābatihi*) even if they cut him off and act with evil intent toward him. A man came to the Prophet and said, "*Oh Messenger of God, I have relatives who repay my social intercourse by social boycott, my good works with injury, my forbearance with foolishness* (ignorance)." The Prophet said: "*If you have been as you said, it was as if you fed them hot ashes. And God continues to be your auxiliary against them as long as you continue in this manner.*"

ANALYSIS

During the course of this sermon several forms of the Arabic root *r-h-m* are referred to. These forms have various meanings stretching from those whose denotations and connotations are physiological and organic to those that are socioethical to those that are sociopolitical to those that are theological. The most commonly referred to form is rahm, which is translated as "womb," "blood kindred," "kinship," and "relationship."4 The phrase, *dhu al-arham*, using the plural form of rahm, is translated as "relatives on the maternal side." The second most commonly referred to form is rahma, translated as "pity," "compassion," "human understanding," "sympathy," "kindness," and "mercy." The third most common form is al-rahman, translated as "the Compassionate," "the Merciful," and "the All Merciful" in all cases referring to God. Al-rahman is a term of considerable theological significance, being one of the recognized ninety-nine beautiful names of God. It is the first attribute of God mentioned in the Quran whose first verse begins, "In the name of God, the Compassionate, the Merciful" (*bismallah al-raḥmān al-raḥīm*). A number of other forms of the triliteral root, though not occurring in the sermon, should be mentioned to round out the range of denotations and potential connotations. Various verb forms have the meanings of "to spare or let off," "to ask God to have mercy (on someone)," "to plead for God's mercy (for what has happened)," "to love and respect one another," "to forgive," "to die of childbirth (woman)," "and to express pity for." A verbal noun, *tarḥīm*, refers to an intercessory prayer for the dead (for Christians) and a participle, *marḥūm*, is used whenever a deceased person is mentioned. Other noun forms refer to a disease of the womb and to Mecca (*umm al-raḥm*, literally, mother of mercy).

The sermon begins with an initial focus on the ethical:

> Give the kinsmen his rights . . . and do not slander him. Kinship and right conduct are linked and placed at the center of God's concern.
> . . . God has made the link of kinship among the best of relationships. He has sanctioned it with the greatest of acts of forgiveness and made it the key to good, the lock of evil.

But we are immediately confronted with the physiological denotations and connotations of the root in a framework of ethical negation and conditional salvation:

> *Blessing hurries as a reward after righteousness and the link of rahm* (kinship, the womb), *and wickedness hurries as punishment after the oppressor and the cutter of rahm* (the womb, kinship).

Already at the end of the first paragraph physiological, social relational, and soteriological meanings have been introduced and juxtaposed.

---

4. The dictionaries used are J. G. Hava, *Arabic-English Dictionary* and Hans Wehr, *A Dictionary of Modern Written Arabic*.

The first paragraph also introduces the image of cutting the womb (kinship) and the linked concept of disobedience, along with the positive act of keeping kinship and the linked concept of blessing. The act of keeping kinship (persistingly) and the image of cutting (off) kinship are carried along to the final paragraph of the sermon.

The second paragraph makes brutally specific, organic, and intense ["cut to pieces their wombs" (blood kindred, kinswomen)] the act of ethical negation and its worldly (deafness and blindness) and soteriological (painful torture) implications.

The third paragraph introduces another term, *rahma*, whose denotations and connotations are ethical and emotional. God specifies social relations as the proper arena of compassion: "God, may he be exalted, has placed among people different kinds of ties (silat) by which they may express pity (compassion, understanding, sympathy) amongst themselves and aid one another in repelling harm and bringing benefits in its place."

This paragraph also stipulates a number of other terms indicating particular modes of social relations: qaraba, kinship generally construed; nasab, agnation or partrilineality; and musahara, affinity or ties through marriage. Ahl, a term introduced later in the paragraph, denotes family, house, household, or people belonging to a community or locality, but it also denotes kinsfolk, relatives, and wife and in its verb form means to marry. But even given this proliferation of terms indicating modes of kinship and kinship-propinquity, it is still the mode of rahm (the womb, blood kindred, close kinship) that "concentrates" or "amasses" the others.

This image is immediately followed by a statement that has been foreshadowed in the previous paragraphs, an outright declaration of the link between the ethics of kinship and salvation: "Muhammad said, *"the cutter of rahm* (blood kindred) *will not enter paradise. . . ."*

This paragraph, then, while on the one hand diluting the meaning of the symbol, rahm, by associating it with relatives (aqarib), partrilineal pedigrees (ansab), affinity (musahra), and community and locality (ahl), on the other hand enriches it by extending it over a wider social structural range. However, the multivocality of the symbol is contained and returned to its image base by the almost physiological notion of "concentration" or "amassing."

It is clear, then, that rahm is a "root metaphor," as Ortner says, "sorting out complex and undifferentiated feelings and ideas and making them comprehensible to oneself."[5] In sorting out experience, such metaphors place it in cultural categories and help the individual think about how it

5. See Sherry Ortner's article, "On Key Symbols," *American Anthropologist*, Vol. 75, No. 5, October 1973 for a description of root metaphors.

hangs together. The sorting out process here is in the domain of kinship in which various rights and obligations attach to relations of patrilineal descent, marriage, family, household, and matrilaterality.

This paragraph is also the first of only two that specify in any way what the obligations to kinsmen in fact are:

> demonstrating affection for relatives and meeting their needs in wealth and high rank and sickness, and lightening their burdens in tragedy and joining in the celebration of their joys and their sorrows and laying bare their anxieties and executing their requirements.

The fourth paragraph associates ethical affirmation and ethical negation of kinship with the constitutive element in the belief system, monotheism, and its negation, polytheism:

> *A man came to the Prophet and asked him, "Which deeds are most loved by God?" He replied, "Belief in God." He asked "What else?" He replied, "The tie of kinship* (rahm)*." He asked, "What deeds are most hated by God?" He replied, "Taking partners to God; then cutting kinship."*

The end of this paragraph links worship, social relations, and for the first time, ethicopolitical responsibilities, for the "most fearfully obedient to God" is engaged in "commanding . . . the good and . . . avoiding . . . the reprehensible." For Muslims, man is his brother's keeper.

The fifth paragraph begins by pairing two of the key symbols of the organizing metaphor:

> Rahm (womb, blood kindred, kinship) is one of the traces (signs) of rahma (mercy, compassion, pity, kindness, understanding). . . .
>
> But immediately these two symbols are linked with a third: . . . and it [rahm] is derived from the name—the Compassionate (al-rahman).

The three key symbols derived from the trilateral root, rahm, rahma and al-rahman, denoting and connoting the physiological, social relational, ethical, and theological components of the organizing metaphor are now brought together for the first time. It is God that has made the linkage (not man):

> *I am God; I am the Compassionate (al-rahman); I created mercy (rahma) and I coined for it a name* [from among] *my names* [i.e., al rahim, the Merciful]. *Whoever keeps persistingly to it (rahma), I keep persistingly to him and whoever cuts it off, I cut him off.*

At this stage in the development of the sermon there has been a mutual transposition of meanings between the three key symbols, the organic-physiological but simultaneously social relational term, rahm, the ethical-emotional term, rahma, and the theological-soteriological term, al-rahman, a transposition, literally accomplished by God. Now he who is cut off from the womb, is cut off from his kindred, is cut off from right conduct, and is cut off from God. From this point on in the sermon the three separate terms denote and connote one another.

Although the symbol, rahm (or more precisely the triliteral root, r-h-m elaborates, categorizes, and sorts out ideas and feelings about kinship through its various forms, denotations, and connotations, it simultaneously clusters and condenses meanings and feelings and, in the process, crystallizes attitudes not only about the whole field of kinship but also about religion as well. In this respect r-h-m is, in a contradictory fashion, a "summarizing" as well as an "elaborating" symbol.[6]

The sixth paragraph returns to the specification of rahm, classifying with greater refinement its social relational implications. It is divided into the "general kinship" of religion and the "special kinship" of consanguinity which in turn is divided into aqarib (relatives) and ahl (kinfolk and neighbors) on the one hand, and close kinsmen (siblings, uncles, aunts, grandparents, and cousins) on the other. Affection, refraining from injury, and maintaining friendly contact is prescribed for the former and kindness for the latter with close kinsmen deserving of charity, beneficence, and constant solicitiousness regarding their economic welfare and psychological health.

In the mentonym (or more precisely synecdoche) introduced in the next paragraph [7] the womb (i.e., Man) speaks:

> The Prophet said, "God, may he be exalted, created the creature so that when he had finished, the womb (rahm) said: 'Is this the place of refuge (in you, God) from that which is severed (i.e., the umbilical cord)?' God replied, 'Yes, don't you approve of my rejoining you to those who are connected with you (i.e., your kinsmen) and parting you from those from whom you are (already) cut off (i.e., strangers or nonkin)?' The womb said, 'Oh yes, Lord.' God said, 'Then that shall be for you (your lot).' "

In this image, man, who has been severed from his organic link (i.e., born) and thereby at one and the same time severed from compassion and

6. See Ortner, "On Key Symbols" for a description of the two forms of "elaborating" symbols"—"root metaphor" and the "key scenario" as well as the contrasting "summarizing symbol." Ortner's description and analysis suggest that a symbol cannot at one and the same time be "elaborating" and "summarizing" in function. In the case of rahm, the simultaneous existence of a root, r-h-m, and its various forms (e.g., rahman, rahma, rahim, marhum), may explain the anomaly. See chapter 8 for further discussion of "summarizing symbols" in relation to the Prophet's night journey and ascent.

made independent and accountable seeks refuge in God which, from the transposition previously referred to, is also the womb. But that relinking now cannot be on the organic-physiological level but must be on the social relational-ethical level. That is, since birth has severed man from his source of physiological compassion, the womb, man must now seek God through ethical compassion (service to his fellowman, his kinsman, and co-religionist). The womb as the kinship group, is the refuge, the source of compassion and the object of compassion, and the means toward reunification with God.

The final paragraph [8] restates the relationship between the social relational, the ethical, and the theological components of meaning in a causal nexus whose primary implication is soteriological: Right conduct toward kinsmen brings God as an auxiliary; cutting kinship brings damnation.

The organizing metaphor of this sermon, then, comes at the critical point of mutual transposition of meanings between the three key symbols:

> I am God; I am the Compassionate (al-rahman); I created mercy (rahma) and I coined for it a name from among my names (i.e., al-rahim, The Merciful). Whoever keeps persistingly to it (rahma), I keep persistingly to him and whoever cuts it off, I cut him off.

Although rahm, the third key symbol, is not mentioned in this passage it is clearly present in the image since, as the beginning of paragraph 5 states, rahm is one of the traces of mercy and as the end of the paragraph concludes, God cuts him off who cuts it off. Following the image, injuring kinsmen, injures the body, cuts off life at the point of its inception (the womb), reverses the order of the social universe at its most intimate level, and leads to spiritual death. Taking this metaphor in conjunction with the metonym that succeeds it, the underlying meaning is as follows: Man's physiological trauma (his birth, his separation from the womb) which is also a spiritual trauma (since thereby man is made free and yet accountable) can only be overcome through ethical behavior. Man's individual salvation is linked with his group's destiny. Most simply put, separation from God can only be overcome through connection to man.

Arguing "logologically" and at some remove from the images analyzed above, that is, following the logical implication of concepts, a further implication of meaning can be derived. The first sentence and the last sentence of this sermon refer either directly or indirectly to acts of disobedience, and disobedience and its consequences—almost always with respect to rahm—are a prominent theme: as indeed are its opposites—obedience, good works, and reward. The positive principle of kinship involves its own negation (disobedience) and punishment (death, separation from God).

The Articulation of the Islamic Sermon with Its Social Structural and Cultural Context

Is the Islamic sermon just analyzed and others of its genre an example of formal speech and, if so, how is that formal speech articulated with other institutions in its social milieu? Bloch (1975) has distinguished as an ideal type "formalized" (as opposed to "everyday") speech acts according to seven attributes: fixed loudness patterns, extremely limited choice of intonation, some syntactic forms excluded, partial vocabulary, fixity of sequencing of speech acts, illustrations only from certain limited sources, and stylistic rules consciously applied at all levels. Informal or everyday speech, on the other hand, allows choice of loudness, intonations, syntactic forms, vocabulary, and sequencing. Bloch argues that the effect of formalized speech is to strengthen hierarchical social relationships, to reduce the possibility of challenging traditional authority, and to prevent the speaker from tackling specific issues or dealing with particular divisive actions (1975: 16). With respect to loudness and intonation the sermon is divided into the long substantive part and the short terminating part, divided by a pause in which the preacher sits down for a few moments and then rises to speak again. As indicated above, Islamic tradition officially recognizes the division by giving each part separate titles—"the sermon of admonition" followed by "the sermon of epithets." In this preacher's sermons, variation in loudness and intonation is greater in the first than in the second part. With respect to syntactic forms, the sermon in all its parts must be delivered in classical Arabic automatically excluding elements of colloquial syntax of all Arabic dialects. The same rule excludes all colloquial vocabulary items, although as observed above Luqman occasionally lapses into colloquial Arabic to make a point. The classical vocabulary used, moreover, is very selective, one skewed toward legal, ritual, and soteriological issues and content. Sequencing of speech acts is restricted by numerous prayer formulae which must be introduced after certain words or phrases. For instance, after the mention of God, "May he be exalted" or "May he be glorified" follows; after the mention of Muhammad, "May God have mercy on him and grant him peace" follows; and after the mention of one of the earlier prophets (Abraham, Moses, Jesus), "On him be peace" follows.[7] Illustrations are largely from

7. Frequently in the process of transliteration the preacher omitted these set formulas in his reading of the sermon because they were so frequent. This accounts for their occasional omission in the sermon translated above and in other sermons I recorded and translated. It

limited sources as the above-mentioned sermon indicates: the Quran, Traditions of the Prophet (some specified as to transmission, e.g., by the companion, Abd al-Rahman ibn Awf). The stylistic rules of classical Arabic are applied and within that linguistic tradition, the stylistic rules developed by Islamic scholars for over a thousand years. For instance, no new content should be introduced into the sermon of epithets and both the initial and the ending sermons should be concluded with either a reference to the Quran or to the Traditions of the Prophet.

In considering the degree of formality of the Islamic sermon it should also be remembered that it is ensconsed within a traditional Islamic ritual that takes place in the mosque where the Islamic ethos is most powerful. The Friday congregational service begins with the call to prayer heard by believers as they walk to the mosque, clicking the beads of their rosaries and reciting silent prayers; they have previously performed ritual ablutions and on entering the mosque perform several ritual prostrations. Immediately after the sermon, all worshipers stand in uniform rows behind the preacher—now doubling as imam or prayer leader—to perform the congregational prayer. Not to be forgotten either is the paradigmatic aspect of the Friday congregational prayers and sermon: Muhammad was the first prayer leader in Islam and its first preacher and the locus of his activity was the mosque. Although the speech acts described above may not be as formalized as many of the examples referred to by Bloch in Bali, Madagascar, and New Guinea, there is considerable formalization with respect to syntax, vocabulary, sequencing, illustrations, and style, and some with respect to loudness and intonation.

Do the consequences predicted by Bloch for such formalization follow? Does such formalization prevent the handling of specific issues, particularly divisive ones? Or in Parkin's (1975) terms, is formalized speech necessarily associated with an "ideological" appeal as opposed to a "quasi-plan" or "plan" approach, that is, is the lavish use of symbolism, an emotive mode, multivocally incompatible with the delivery of unambiguous messages presuming decision making and action by a defined audience? The sermon presented above suggests a negative answer to both questions. This sermon had as its efficient cause the visit of a village woman to the preacher; she came to him to complain that her kinsmen did not provide the help that was urgently needed. The question of the provision of help by kinsmen was a divisive issue in the village. The village was divided into three patrilineal clans clustered by and large in clan quarters, and these three clans were cross-cut by numerous ties of matrilaterality, affinity, friendship, and propinquity. The question of aid to

should be recognized that Muslims recognize Jesus as a prophet or, more strictly, a messenger (like Muhammad).

kinsmen was a sensitive one in a community in which incipient economic differences were emerging in terms of wealth and occupation. The preacher met the issue head-on and stipulated that obligations to kinsmen involved kindness, constant visiting, material aid, emotional support, and aid in life crises; estrangement and social boycott were unequivocally condemned. Within a distinctly formalized speech framework the preacher took on a divisive issue and recommended a clear line of action—perhaps not that specified by a "plan." Indeed, the sermon does have certain attributes of an "ideology," appealing to an audience in terms of common denominator idioms and values. But it is precisely the combination of extremely formal speech elements and clear-cut calls for action that are of interest and call into question the relationship posited by Bloch and Parkin, among many others, between speech forms and their social structural and cultural context.

What, then, is the mode of articulation of the Islamic sermon with its social structural context? Along with propinquity and age, kinship plays a critical role in organizing the life of the village. But the subject of most sermons is not kinship or its obligations. In fact the sermon analyzed above was the only one devoted exclusively to this subject. One other was given on the subject of good treatment of parents. That is not to say that the village preacher did not focus on ethics. On the contrary, sermons dealing with right conduct by far outnumbered those whose focus was on ritual, theology, or religious history. But the focus of these sermons was on "general kinship," that is, the obligations of "Muslim" brothers. The message of the preacher, generally speaking, is one that conflicts with the basis of village life: religion and not kinship or clanship is deemed by him as the overriding tie.

Rahm as enunciated in the sermon refers to both men and women. Indeed in a patrioriented society, rahm is a completely bilateral principle. When the preacher designated the kinship roles involved he mentioned sisters as well as brothers, maternal uncles as well as paternal uncles, maternal aunts as well as paternal aunts, and cousins and grandparents (of both sexes).[8] When I asked the preacher sometime after the sermon whether he could spell out who was designated by rahm, he replied with an organic bilateral metaphor: the father, mother, and grandfather (unspecified) he referred to as the origins or head, the son and daughter as the limbs, and the sister, the paternal uncle, the maternal uncle, the paternal aunt, and the maternal aunt as the hands and feet.

In the culture of the village, however, partrilineal descent is the dominant social structural symbol. This is indicated by a number of idioms

8. Father and mother are unmentioned; they are excepted as a special category and treated separately in a special sermon on filial piety.

used to stress the importance of patrilineal descent: "The son of the father's brother has priority" to indicate that the first claim to a girl's hand in marriage is held exclusively by her patrilineal cousins; "Blood begets among itself; the blood is one; after five grandfathers the blood is lost" to indicate the cohesion of the patrilineal descent group within five generations; and "It (the patrilineal descent line) is a staff—immersed but never wet" to indicate the solidarity of patrilineal kinsmen against other groups.

Moreover, in village life patrilineality has certain social structural and functional implications. The name of each individual is his patrilineal pedigree. Members of patrilineal descent groups usually live in adjacent houses and tend to have adjoining land plots. Disputes are mediated within the descent group, if at all possible. Both inheritance rules and guardianship rules—which are the Islamic rules—recognize agnates with the nearer excluding the farther. Patrilineal kinsmen are expected to be given priority in the sale of land, in the marriage of daughters, and in consultation on political matters, though such expectations are not always realized. One is obliged to visit one's patrilineal kinsmen on a regular basis. Finally, social control is the primary concern and the firm obligation of patrilineal kinsmen. That is, it is they who must pay compensation in cases of murder, rape, elopement, assault, and burglary, and the closest kinsmen to the culprit among them must evacuate their homes, suffering banishment pending a peaceful reconciliation.

It is not that other social structural models are not recognized in the village or that other social structural ties do not affect behavior. Indeed, the preacher referred to the importance of marriage ties in his sermon. And in other sermons in defining an individual's social obligation he referred to the right of the neighbor (*haqq al-jār*), the right of the Muslim (*haqq al-muslim*), and the right of kinship (*haqq al-rahm*).

But the striking fact about this sermon is that it makes central what is a minor, peripheral, or alternate symbol in the life of the village. Rahm is hardly mentioned at all by villagers while nasab, qaraba, and ahl are often mentioned. Why was rahm chosen as the dominant condensed symbol by the preacher? The answer is clear. Rahm is a maternal symbol par excellence, and in its social relational denotation it is bilateral. Rahm represents the principle of "complementary filiation," stressing the maternal line and at the same time the balanced lines of kinship—both female and male, mother and father.[9] William Robertson Smith pointed out many years ago in *Kinship and Marriage in Early Arabia* that in a complex patrioriented society, the most effective symbol of unity was a woman;

9. See Meyer Fortes, *The Web of Kinship Among the Tallensi* (1949), for an elaboration of the concept of complementary filiation.

whereas paternity could always be questioned, maternity was unimpeachable. Therefore, Bedouin tribes with corporate patrilineal descent groups not unusually claimed a female ancestress. In a village with three clans and numerous (twenty-eight) patrilineages the preacher chose the womb, the most intimate maternal symbol, to stress the kinship of all.

THE ARTICULATION OF SYMBOLIC ARENAS

The important question remains: What is the mode of articulation of the khutba with other speech codes found in the community or, more broadly put, what is the symbolic mode of articulation of the institutional focus represented by the mosque with the two other significant public institutions resorted to by villagers—that represented by the village guest house (madāfa) and that represented by the bureaucrat's office in town? Table 4.1 outlines the articulation of the three major symbolic loci for public ritual in Kufr al-Ma.

Although there is only one mosque in Kufr al-Ma there are many guest houses in the village and many bureaucratic offices in town to which villagers resort; however, the ethos, symbolic form, and mode of legitimization are more or less uniform within each institutional type regardless of the particular edifice selected.[10] The village guest house serves as a public meeting place where men meet in the evening to pass the time, exchange information, gossip, drink coffee and tea, and, most important, examine divisive issues and through the process of "encounter-through-mediation" resolve them.[11] That is, the vociferous give-and-take of the parties to a dispute is gradually converted through dyadic diplomacy (taking a person aside and convincing him he must compromise for the sake of his kinsmen, the village, and his family), the pressure of respected elders, and the emerging consensus as to the merits of each side's argument, into successful mediation. The guest house is also the locus of lavish hospitality to honored guests and strangers—the tray of rice and meat traditionally caps all major reconciliations (sulhas) and is served at all marriages, funerals, religious festivals, and important graduations; the meat is always lamb, mutton, or goat meat, an indication of the host's willingness to destroy capital in order to honor the guest, kin group, or village as the case may be.[12]

10. During the period when the sermons analyzed in this book were delivered there was only one mosque in the village. A second mosque was built in 1984.

11. For further information on the ethos, social structure, and function of the guest house among Jordanian peasants see Antoun 1972 and 1979; chapter 2.

12. This was the case at least from 1959–1967. Recent changes in the occupational structure of Jordan after OPEC'S raising of oil prices in 1973 has changed this pattern of hospitality or at least altered its scope. For a more detailed description of "encounter-through-mediation" and the "politics of hospitality" see Antoun, Low-Key Politics, 1979.

TABLE 4.1
Major Symbolic Loci for the Public Ritual System of Kufr al-Ma

	Mosque	Guest House	Bureaucrat's Office
SYMBOLIC FORM	God's Word: the Quran; the Khutba (Friday Congregational Sermon)	Shawl and Head-band; Tray of Rice and Meat: Patrilineal Pedigree	The Files
ETHOS	Religious: Piety; Entreaty; Compassion; Justice; Equality	Tribal: Honor; Encounter-Through-Mediation; Hospitality	Arbitrary Power; Progress; Superiority of Status; Civilitas (minor mode)
LEVEL OF REALITY	Eternal; Paradigmatic History; Soteriological Time	Social Relational	Contemporary Governmental
MODE OF POWER	Spiritual	Demographic and Military	Office; Military Force
MODE OF LEGITIMATION	God's Law: sharī'a (Islamic Law and Ethics)	Tribal Law; Village Custom	State Law; Military Force
SOCIAL OR-GANIZATIONAL FOCUS	Village; 'ulemā' (Muslim Scholars)	Patrilineal Descent Groups: Clan, Lineage, Close Consultation Group	Local Bureaucracy
RITUAL FOCUS	Friday Congregational Prayer	Coffee Ceremony and Attached Politeness Formulas	Rites of Status Affirmation (bifurcate: the elite vs. the generality)
CADENCE	Call to Prayer, Sequential Prayer Formulas; Clicking of the Rosary	Mortar and Pestle	Clerk-Ushers Call
GENDER	Exclusively Male, social relationally; Bilateral, symbolically	Exclusively Male, social relationally and symbolically	Dominantly but not Exclusively Male
MARITAL IMAGE	Married Men	Married Men	Household Heads
AGE	Middle-Aged Men and Elders (majority); Postpubertal Single Men (minority); Prepubertal Males (smattering)	Middle-Aged Men and Elders (great majority); Younger Married Men (minority)	Adults

TABLE 4.1 (cont.)
Major Symbolic Loci for the Public Ritual System of Kufr al-Ma

	Mosque	Guest House	Bureaucrat's Office
MODE OF INTERCULTURAL ACCOMMODATION	Compartmentalization and de facto Tolerance, behaviorally; Ignorance and/or Repudiation, ideologically	Compartmentalization and Cooperation, behaviorally; Incorporation, ideologically	Oscillating Condemnation and Cooperation; behaviorally but not ideologically
CENTRAL ACTOR	Khatib (Preacher)	Shaykh (Elder)	Subdistrict officer
CLOTHING	Red Fez, White Turban	Shawl, Headband, and Cloak	Western Suit, White Shirt, Tie, Polished Black Shoes, No Headress

Table 4.1 was inspired by Grimes (1976: 262). In several respects, however, table 4.1 organizes the data differently. First, some categories appearing in his chart have been omitted and vice versa. Second, the organization of the data in the table is in terms of symbolic loci rather than key symbols. Third, the multivocality of symbols is represented in table 4.1 whereas it is elided in Grimes's positional presentation. Finally, some terms used in Grimes's chart are used in table 4.1 but in a different sense.

In the guest house the shawl and headband must always be worn; that they are the symbol of the tribal ethos is indicated by the fact that when a man is desperate and wishes to appeal to the honor of another man (for instance, to accept the veracity of his statements or to support him in a critical matter), he pulls off his shawl and headband (ordinarily a violation of guest house etiquette) and thrusts it in front of the sitting place of the man being appealed to, bending down in front of him in a sacrificial stance. Guest houses are usually the gathering places of patrilineal kinsmen (though not exclusively so) and the agnatic relationships between men as spelled out by their patrilineal pedigrees (known by most at least through the fifth generation) has an important bearing on their economic, political, and strictly social relations. Tea is always served to a visitor in the guest house and on most important occasions, coffee. The coffee beans are pounded by pestle in a wooden mortar, mixed with cardamon seed, and then brewed in several brass pots over a charcoal fire housed in an open frame in the center of the room. The coffee is served in a small demi-tasse size cup without a handle one-third full. A maximum of three sips is allowed before the pourer passes the cup to the next man—all men are sitting on cushions on the floor, legs tucked under them, back straight, against the wall—to serve him. The pourer moves around the room until all are served, then begins the circuit again. In the guest house numerous politeness formulas are observed—after prayer, sneezing, departure, and arrival. For instance, after a man enters the guest house he must greet every man separately in turn and each person greets him; only then can normal conversation continue. The rhythmic pounding of the pestle in the mortar—there are special beats—can be heard throughout the neighborhood and constitutes a general announcement and invitation to the impending *soirée*.

By contrast, the bureaucrat's office is just that, "official." He represents the state and its universalistic norms, and his files represent the authority of that state. However, the subdistrict officer, the most powerful local bureaucrat, also represents the government which often exercises arbitrary power. Some villagers go to the subdistrict officer to demand their rights as citizens. But most approach him as a representative of government which is powerful and capricious and has to be approached with craftiness, suspicion, and flattery. The bureaucrat's clothing immediately stamps him as a stranger and as a superior to all peasants. Although they aspire for themselves or their sons to exactly what the bureaucrat has—position, wealth, education—peasants rarely have the same commitment to progress in an ideological sense.

The village mosque, on the other hand, is primarily the focus of God's Word in several senses. The Friday congregational sermon is the centerpiece of the ritual; it is punctuated by Quranic verses that provide pivots for the argument and the imagery; and the "Names" of God are reiterated in the call to prayer, the sermon, and both individual and congregational prayers. The emphasis on God's Word is particularly striking inasmuch as the village mosque itself is devoid of decoration or embellishment. Although the sermon analyzed above focuses on compassion in a complex manner, many other sermons emphasize justice and equality as well as piety. Whereas the activity of the guest house—whether hospitality, mediation, or politiking—is totally immersed in the web of village social relations, and the activity of the subdistrict office is centered on government plans and proposals, the mosque's messages are eternal—God's Word coexisted with God himself, before man's creation, in the Preserved Tablet (*al-lawḥ al-maḥfūTH*) and will exist after his passing. Insofar as they concern history these messages relate the events and model behavior of the first generation of Muslims ("our master, Muhammad, and his family and companions who were with their arham always in touch") or they concern the individual's quest for salvation ("the noble Quran has promised the cutter of kinship painful torture") Whereas the descent groups in the guest house establish their preponderance nowadays through numbers (and votes on the village council) and formerly established it through numbers of men with guns, the subdistrict officer exercises authority and, as a last resort, military force, and the preacher threatens God's retribution. And whereas the elders in the guest house appeal effectively to village custom and tribal law in cases of dispute and the subdistrict officer applies civil law and government fiat as well as military force in emergencies, the preacher invokes "The Way" (al-sharia), the thousand-year corpus of Islamic law and ethics.

Differences in gender, age, and marital image also exist among the three symbolic loci, but the differences range along a continuum, overlap, or contrast in a subtle and complex manner in contrast to the sharper differences outlined above. Married men in fact make up the great majority of those present in all three loci at any given moment in time; however, in the case of the bureaucrat's office it is crucial to have the head of the household present on most occasions; he may occasionally be a single man or exceptionally a woman. Although the guest house is the appropriate arena for the operation of wise men and thereby fitting for the middle-aged and elders (the repositories of wisdom), younger married men who aspire to be men of influence, and even single men if they cultivate the proper attitude of sobriety may be permitted to attend important meetings if they sit in inconspicuous positions and hold their tongues.[13] In the mosque during the Friday congregational prayer, the majority are middle-aged married men and elders, but there are a substantial minority of single men and some children. Regarding age of attendance at Friday prayers, a Tradition of the Prophet recommends to fathers of males: "*Urge them* (to attend) *at eight and beat them* (if they don't) *at fifteen.*" Although women do attend bureaucratic offices, particularly Islamic and civil courts where their testimony is required and critical particularly in matters of marriage, divorce, inheritance, and property—since Islamic courts deal mainly with matters of personal status most cases involve women—invariably they are accompanied by a male who speaks for, or more accurately, attempts to speak for them. Women are excluded from the village mosque by custom, but their presence may be dominant symbolically as the analysis of the above-mentioned sermon attests, and they may be an important and conscious reference group for the preacher who often exhorts his audience with respect to different subjects: "Go tell your women." Women are excluded from the guest house both personally and symbolically; no item of women's clothing or other personal possessions should remain in the guest house (which often is used by family members as an ordinary room in the house in the absence of guests) when the men are assembled there. Women past the age of menopause (and, therefore,

13. Of course, economic and political changes since World War II have given much greater importance to young men and changed the age composition of the guest house somewhat. In particular, in the 1960s single men who were soldiers in the Jordanian army—with position, a salary, and good marriage prospects—were welcome in the guest house.

symbolically men) are allowed to come into the guest house to plead their case on important matters.

Finally, the mode of intercultural accommodation differs. That is, the way in which each of these three institutions takes account of the other behaviorally and symbolically differs. The subdistrict officer, of course, accepts the Islamic ethos although he may not be convinced that its propagators have a firm commitment to progress. His attitude toward the tribal ethos and its symbolic forms is more complex and ambivalent. He oscillates between participating in the cultural performances indicative of that ethos-squatting, rolling up his sleeve, and eating with his hand from the tray of rice and meat alongside peasants in the guest house of the village or participating as a prominent public official in tribal peacemaking (sulha); and endorsing the tribal mode of legitimation (referring cases brought to him back to the village for mediation or ordering the involved kinsmen in a case of honor to produce a written patrilineal pedigree and enforcing the terms of banishment based on that pedigree) on the one hand—and on the other hand, repudiating that ethos and its associated groups and symbols, denouncing villagers for their clannishness, and accusing particular agnatic groups and their prominent men for impeding the way of progress by placing kinship ahead of community and nation.

The elders of the guest house totally incorporate the Islamic ethos and its symbols as their own; tribal peacemaking takes place in the presence of Islamic scholars and judges and reconciliation at the village level takes place in the presence of the village preacher who opens and closes the proceedings with an appropriate prayer. Both the tribal and Islamic ethos endorse justice, equality, generosity, and magnanimity, and there is some overlap with respect to specific legal norms. However, the Islamic and the tribal codes of law and ethics conflict at many points, and they in turn conflict with civil law. For instance, the tribal code calls for self-help in cases of murder and adultery, and revenge is always preferable to compensation; the State cannot tolerate such self-help and moves quickly to interdict revenge by banishing the close kinsmen of the culprit's family and jailing others pending a tribal peacemaking; in effect, the State accepts many components of tribal law (plea of protection, truce, banishment, compensation, peacemaking) and rejects others (revenge, destruction of property) in order to control events; the civil and tribal proceedings run concurrently and in an interdependent fashion until the final settlement. From the point of view of Islam—specifically, the judge of the Islamic court—both civil and tribal proceedings with respect, say, to adultery are not *shar'ī* (i.e., legal in terms of God's law which stipulates very strict rules of evidence—four witnesses of good character to the act—testified to under oath in the Islamic court before the Islamic punishment can be carried out). Moreover, even if the verdict of guilt is proved according to Islamic norms of procedure, the Islamic ethos recommends forgiveness rather than revenge for all violations with the exception of those five for which the Quran has stipulated penalties.[14] Behaviorally, then, "compartmentalization" reflects the mode of accommodation of the mosque and the guest house to one another and of both toward the bureaucrat's office.[15] That is, the representatives of each institution take superficial account of the other's traditions, but each set of representatives turns a blind eye toward the other's traditions, and all traditions continue to be resilient and relatively self-contained. This attitude explains how representatives of the Islamic tradition, such as the preacher, condemn the violation of Islamic norms in no uncertain terms (e.g., "cutting kinship") or refuse to recognize the existence of alternative norms (say, as to the usefulness of nicknaming and gossip in small communities) and at the same time recognize and tolerate considerable deviation from such norms (e.g., gossip or the fact that fathers do not give their daughters the prescribed marriage payment).

One more point needs to be made about the Islamic sermon and its articulation within the context of the mosque with other symbolic foci. It has been argued by too many social scientists to justify enumeration (Durkheim and Marx would be an early, Radcliffe-Brown a middling, and Bloch a latter-day example) that religious ritual and symbols exist either to reflect community or societal norms or to reinforce them and validate existing social structural claims. The sermon analyzed above does not simply reflect a patrioriented community and society. On the contrary, it focuses on an alternative and minor symbol in the life of the community, rahm, and, in doing so, reveals aspects of that life that would otherwise have remained obscure.

14. These five stipulated violations, categorized as *ḥudūd allah* "the limits of God" in the Quran, are theft, adultery, highway robbery, false accusation of adultery, and the drinking of wine and other intoxicating beverages.

15. This term is borrowed from Singer (1972) who developed it in analyzing the relations of Indian businessmen who had contrasting styles of life, seemingly inspired by contrasting values depending on whether they operated in their home or work (factory) milieus. See Antoun 1980 and chapter 1 for a further discussion of compartmentalization, particularly with respect to Islamic law and local custom in Jordan as witnessed in the Islamic court.

5

The Islamic Sermon (Khutba),
The Islamic Preacher (Khatib), and Modernity

Although the process of Islamization has proceeded in the Middle East for over 1300 years little is known about the process by which Islamic norms have been transmitted (or mistransmitted) to the vast bulk of the peasant population (fellahin).[1] Little is known about the content of these norms, the character of their transmitters—the Islamic preachers—or about the implications of these norms for social change and the transformation of the families, communities, and polities to whom they are addressed.

It may well be that the most significant change that has occurred in the Middle East since World War II is not demographic, economic, or political (though overpopulation, oil, and revolution are in the forefront of our consciousness) but cultural and social—the accelerated process of Islamization. To give two examples from my own research, when I arrived in the subdistrict of Al-Kura, Jordan in 1959 only four of its twenty-five villages had an Islamic preacher. When I returned in 1965 every village had a preacher. In 1959 a single family in the village of Kufr al-Ma, Jordan stipulated a deferred marriage payment (*mahr mu'ajjal*) for its daughters in the marriage contract, as required by Islamic law and ethics. By 1965 every family did so. In 1972, in the province of Gorgan, Iran, when I asked an opportunistic sample of villagers how often they had gone on the pilgrimage to Meshed, the greatest Shi'a shrine in Iran, I discovered that before 1960, if they had gone at all, they had gone once in their life.[2] Twelve years later it was not uncommon for small landowners to go every year and for sharecroppers to have gone once or twice.

What are the implications of the process of Islamization for the modernization and development of the Arab world and the Middle East?[3] The implications are not really clear since the in-depth investigation of the

1. The term *peasants*, fellahin, is defined here in terms of cultural rather than economic criteria, that is, in terms of style of life (diet, clothing, dialect, recreation, education, and outstanding personality traits). In these terms nearly all the residents of Kufr al-Ma were peasants in the 1960s, although only a minority tilled the land for a living.

2. Field work was conducted in Iran during the summer of 1971 and for six months in a village in the Gorgan area in 1972. An opportunistic sample is one which seizes on the informants who are available and willing to answer the researcher's questions.

3. See chapter 9 for an extended discussion of the concept of Islamization and its relation to Islamic resurgence.

process of Islamization, or as Srinivas would have termed it, parochialization, at the local level has just begun. But we can begin to examine the scanty evidence available and draw some tentative conclusions.

Borthwick, one of the few political scientists to have given any thought to the matter, on the basis of an analysis of Friday congregational sermons delivered in the urban mosques of Damascus, Amman, and Cairo, states that "the preachers are promoting 'nationalism' but they are not furthering political modernization" (1965: 108). He observes that "the rhetorical, exhortative and affective character of the sermon [with rhymed prose, melodious passages, and strings of adjectives] make it a suitable channel in which to communicate 'nationalism' but not political modernization. . . . Political modernization involves the development of skills rather than emotions" (1965: 189). He argues that although the Islamic sermon can contribute significantly toward the development of affective loyalties, it contributes little toward the development of the skills required for modernization:

> It is far easier to interweave the history of Arab "nationalism" with Islamic history and to show the unifying effect which Islam can have on Arabs than to demonstrate the relevance of the zakat in the modern world, the Islamic inspiration of the Aswan dam or the Islamic legitimacy of President Nasser. (1965: 193)

These skills, he argues, are learned through formal secular education, independent reading, and experience. This view is not an unfamiliar one in the literature of modernization and development. To evaluate it one must define a term such as "modernization" more precisely. For Borthwick, following Deutsch, modernization is a process with two aspects: (1) technological innovation—the introduction of modern science, technology, and industry, and (2) social mobilization—the mobilization of people out of a traditional society into a modern society (1965: 8).[4] The introduction of the term *modern* presents a problem since it does not sug-

4. See Karl Deutsch, "Social Mobilization and Political Development," *American Political Science Review*, Vol. 55, September 1961. For other views of modernization see Marion Levy, *Modernization and the Structure of Societies: A Setting for International Affairs* (Princeton University Press, Princeton, 1966); W. E. Moore, *Social Change* (Prentice-Hall, Englewood Cliffs, 1963); Manning Nash, "Industrialization: The Ecumenical and Parochial Aspects of the Process," in *Social Science and the New Societies*, Nancy Hammond, editor (Michigan State University Press, Lansing, 1973) and "Modernization: Cultural Meanings—the Widening Gap Between the Intellectuals and the Process," *Economic Development and Social Change*, Vol. 25, Supplement, 1977, and N. E. Smelser, "Essays in Sociological Explanation," in *Industrialzation and Society*, W. E. Moore and B. F. Hoselitz, editors (UNESCO, Paris, 1963). For another view of modernization that does not suggest a single center for its diffusion see Fred von der Mehden's recent book, *Religion and Modernization in Southeast Asia* (Syracuse University Press, Syracuse, 1986).

gest a principal concern for economic growth and the variant conditions under which different societies attain it, but rather a concern for values and their implications, that is, the attitudes necessary for such growth whether such attitudes pertain to knowledge, economic activity, the social structure, or the nature of reality. Manning Nash, an anthropologist who has focused on the study of economic development and social change in Central America, Burma, and Malaya has insisted on the necessity of distinguishing these two aspects of change, of distinguishing modernity from modernization:

> Modernity is the social, cultural and psychological framework which facilitates the application of tested knowledge to all phases and branches of production. Modernization is the process of transformation toward the establishment and institutionalization of the framework of modernity. (Nash 1977: 21)

For Nash, modernization focuses on the "historically chancey" process of economic growth and its "different routes, timetables and strategies" (21) together with the political and social changes that are its necessary concomitants. Modernity focuses on the values which are its prerequisites such as the relatively unhampered search for new knowledge, a positive stance toward innovation, a fostering of social mobility, and an achievement ethic which channels rewards to high performers (20). Nash's distinction immediately opens up the possibility (not pursued by him) that an institution—here, the Islamic sermon and its accompanying role, the Islamic preacher—may forward modernity without necessarily forwarding modernization and vice versa. Whereas the skills required to pursue science, technology, and industry may not be passed on by the Islamic preacher in his sermon, the attitudes necessary to such pursuits may be inculcated or reinforced.

My own collection of Friday congregational sermons in the village of Kufr al-Ma, Jordan, has led me to make some tentative inferences in this regard, as indicated in chapter 3. First, and rather surprisingly, the sermons delivered in the village mosque—in stark contrast to Borthwick's urban sermons—had minimal political content. Of the twenty-six sermons analyzed, over half (fifteen) dealt with ethical concerns: filial piety, the necessity of mutual aid among co-religionists and co-villagers, the doing of good deeds, the necessity of equal treatment to wives and siblings, the obligations of kinship, and women's immodesty and men's honor (see table 3.1, pp. 90–92). Seven dealt with theological concerns (e.g., death, the night of the divine decree [*laylat al-qadr*]); six dealt with ritual obligations (e.g., pilgrimage, fasting); six with religious history[5] (e.g.,

---

5. From an anthropological perspective this type of sermon would be classified as "myth,"

Muhammad's prophecy and struggle, the night journey and ascent [al-isra' wal mi'raj]); and only one with politics—a sermon on Palestine, delivered, interestingly enough, three days before the commemoration of the night journey and ascent.

One might infer, then, from the subjects of these sermons that although they may have implications for Arab nationalism and, thereby, for nation-building, they have few implications for modernization or modernity. However, along with the sermons referred to above were a number of others whose themes centered on subjects not unrelated to modernity: education, justice, work, magic, marriage and marriage payment, and the obligation of reconciling the estranged.

With respect to education the khatib argued that knowledge is revelation and Muhammad is the model teacher:

> And Muslims will not again have power (*'izz*) and glory unless they return to practicing their religion and hold fast to the book of their Lord. Verily, God sent Muhammad to an illiterate people who did not know anything about life's matters. And God, most high, said: **It is He who has raised up from among the common people a Messenger from among them, to recite His signs to them and to purify them, and to teach them the Book and the wisdom, though before they were in manifest error** (62: 2, *A*). So God sent Muhammad as a teacher (*mu'allim*) and a guide to these people who were ruled by ignorance and foolishness. . . .[6]

Furthermore, this knowledge is wisdom and the path to salvation:

> Oh people, knowledge (*'ilm*) is the basis of all virtues and the source of light and wisdom. In it there is immunity from error and safeguarding from faltering in the abysses of contention and damnation (*halāk*).

Knowledge is the key to national power and glory and to individual happiness as well as the guide to right conduct:

> For it is by knowledge that nations (*umam*) became mighty and attain their ends and investigate what will help and strengthen them and raise their status and honor and freedom and independence. Verily, the ignorant nation, retarded in knowledge and ideas, is the nation which attracted to itself contention and affliction . . . it having no dignity and no power . . . States colonize it and exploit its physical

---

a myth being an account of events regarded as having taken place by the narrator with no implication by the analyst one way or the other about their historicity.

6. This and the following excerpts are from a sermon on education, delivered in Kufr al-Ma, Jordan, in April 1960.

resources. . . . Knowledge (ilm) brings forth from a nation a rightly guided life and a people who know how to organize the affairs of a happy life. So the schools are the things which lead to honest service for the good of the people. In the schools students learn their lessons and their culture, and they learn what makes them happy and what they must avoid for its harmful consequences and what brings wretchedness. The schools are the foundation of learning and urbanity. Knowledge is the weapon of the nation and the symbol of its life and its glory and its happiness.

The religious tone, idiom, and meaning of this treatment of education is unmistakable. However, what is interesting from the viewpoint of modernity is the symbolic transposition of certain key terms and the symbolic transposition that occurs in the sermon itself. Throughout the sermon knowledge is seen as advancing the power and glory of the umma (pl., umam). The traditional referrant of umma is the religious community of Muslims founded by Muhammad and lasting to the present day to the extent that Muslims continue to inform their lives by Islamic law and ethics. It also has as its modern referent the sovereign nation-state as reflected, for instance, in the Arabic phrase for United Nations, *hay'at al-umam*. The term *knowledge* (ilm) also has a double meaning: a traditional referent, the heavenly knowledge contained in the Quran as well as the secular knowledge taught in the schools. Therefore, any reference to education using such terms carries with it a dual tone and meaning.

The symbolic transposition is reinforced at the end of the sermon. Just after referring to "heavenly knowledge" and to the light brought by its first teacher, Muhammad, the preacher closes with the statement:

Oh ye people, inhabitants of this village, there is an obligation placed on your shoulders: it is the creating of a school for the instruction of your children and their education (*tathqīfihim*). It is incumbent upon you to take up this command with striving and sincerity. Leave ignorance and selfishness and proceed as a collectivity to raise the money needed for constructing a new school in your village even if its cost is great.

The village needed to decide whether it would raise money for a new school. But the school contemplated was a secular school; its teachers were trained in secular teachers' colleges, and they were official members of the secular bureaucracy. Religious education was part of the school's curriculum but only a very small part. Thus, a basically religious message delivered by a religious leader in a religious idiom and in a singularly religious edifice was martialed for the support of a secular system of education.[7] This was an educational system in which not only the attitudes implied by modernity are propagated but also certain basic skills—reading, writing, and arithmetic—without which the more sophisticated skills required for modernization could not be taught.

The support given by local-level religious leaders for the secular educational system does not indicate, however, that all values and social structures associated with that system are applauded. Indeed, local-level religious leaders are quick to note the excesses of the system when it contravenes religious law and ethics. In a conversation the preacher specifically condemned the secular school system for the political party activity it encouraged:

> [During the party period] there were many political parties in Deir Abu Said [where the junior high school for the area was located]. Teachers were not on speaking terms with one another and each had their own coterie of students who were always quarreling on the playground; and education went by the boards. Teachers went around flunking students not of their party.

He also criticized the rending of the social fabric it entailed:

> Colonialism—it was what gave birth to the parties. There is a saying "Divide and rule." The English are the origin of the parties. This happened in the time of the English; the father was for a party, the son was for [another] party, and the daughter was for [another] party; and when they sat down at the table together to eat, they fought with one another.[8]

The fact is, however, that parents continue to send their children to secular schools; and they do so enthusiastically for the opportunities in the modern world they believe are opened up by such schooling. Preachers endorse the quest for secular knowledge in traditional terms and in

7. It is interesting to note as indicated in chapter 3, that the village preacher's secular education was terminated by his father over his own and the schoolmaster's objection at the end of the sixth grade. The preacher's father, a man with ample land in a land-short village, wished his son to till the land like his brothers, marry like his brothers, and accept a responsible position in village society. It may very well be that his own struggle to continue his studies (which he did secretly with the preacher in the next town after the official termination of his schooling) against his father and without much support from the community, gave the preacher a special commitment to education. For further life history information on this preacher see *Ethnology*, Vol. 6, July 1967. I have quoted at length from one of his sermons in an article appearing in the *American Anthropologist*, Vol. 70, August 1968. References to the preacher and a few short extracts from his sermons are also found in an article appearing in *The Muslim World*, Vol. 58, No. 1 and 2, January and April 1968.

8. As quoted in Richard Antoun, *Low-Key Politics: Local-Level Leadership and Change in the Middle East* (State University of New York Press, Albany, 1979), 128–29.

doing so they encourage the attitudes associated with modernity and, thereby, help lay the groundwork for modernization.

Another aspect of modernity is its giving meaning to cultural creativity in worldly pursuits, more specifically, its inculcation of attitudes conducive to economic activity. As Khuri (1968) has pointed out, Islamic tradition is bifurcate with respect to its attitude toward work. On the one hand some branches of the Islamic mystical (sufi) tradition have regarded work and worship as inversely related. On the other hand, many Sunni Muslim scholars have given priority to work over worship as reflected in such hadiths as, "*Earn your bread first, then devote yourself to worship.*"

The khatib dealt specifically with this subject in a sermon in which the obligation to work was based solidly on the Prophet's example and on that of his companions:

> This Prophet of Islam excited an interest in working for the sake of a livelihood. He said, *No one has eaten food at all, better than he who eats the food of his own hand.* The Prophet of God, Da'ud, who was obeyed by the angels, used to eat of the work of his own hand [only]. Those of most acute discernment, the Companions [of the Prophet], worked for this world as they worked for the next. The just caliph, Omar ibn al-Khattab, said: *Don't sit, any of you, and ask God for a livelihood, for you must know that heaven does not rain down gold—or silver.* The man who takes up a trade profits from it and finds freedom, thereby, from [other] men and from beggary. He who spends on his wife and children is better than the poor who begs from men and lives on the [work of] others.[9]

As he did with respect to the subject of education, the preacher linked work at one and the same time to the religious community and the destiny of the nation-state:

> The religion of Islam is a religion of work and striving and activity— not a religion of inactivity and indolence. It is incumbent on the religious community to create and strive and resuscitate the country with cultivation and the proliferation of factories and companies which will work for the augmentation of wealth and blessings.

In dealing with the subject of work, the preacher dealt with the more general philosophical and theological question of what kind of relationship should prevail between striving in this world and striving for salvation:

> Now, then, worshipers of God, some people are seduced by the world, craving after its pleasures, and they are preoccupied with it

9. The following are excerpts from a sermon on work delivered by the preacher in the village in January 1960.

[the world] away from their obligations. They are of those who will perish on the Day of Judgment. And there are some people who stand aloof from the world; they leave the world completely, devoting themselves to worship endlessly and giving up the striving for a livelihood. They are the vagabonds, the astray. There is no goodness in him who neglects the hereafter for the world. And none for him who neglects the world for the hereafter. As the Prophet of Islam said: *The world is the abode of work (ʿamal) and exertion (jadd) and endeavor (saʿy) and earning (iktisāb). The hereafter is the abode of requittal/penalty and reckoning, reward and punishment. The world is the planted field of the hereafter and its path.* [God], may he be exalted, said: **seek, amidst that which God has given thee, the Last Abode, and forget not thy portion of the present world** . . . (28: 77, A). In the words of the companions: *Work in the life of this world as if you will live forever and work for your hereafter as if you will die tomorrow.*

What is of interest here, again, with respect to religion and modernity is the kind of balanced view presented by the khatib—neither complete neglect of this world or the next; neither complete immersion in the affairs of this world or complete immersion in preparation for the next.[10] Robert Bellah, a scholar who has studied religious transformation in Far Eastern as well as Western and Middle Eastern cultures has argued that at the symbolic level the religious ideology that optimizes modernity involves a balance between this and other-worldly concerns:

Two conditions seem especially unfavorable for the religious encouragement of progress (here defined as an increasing ability to learn to

---

10. In 1983 I recall hearing a Unitarian Protestant minister in the United States discuss the problem of an unbalanced world view (unbalanced with respect to concern for this as opposed to the next world) for the ethos (emotional tone) of the culture and the psychological state of the individual. She was chiding her fellow "liberal" Unitarians for their too strong ever-on-the-go, ever-optimistic, socially conscious religious orientation which she characterized as "monkey-hold religion." And she was suggesting that they might profit by moderating their ethos in the direction (but not the extreme) of the ever-pessimistic, sin-ridden, yet relaxed traditional religion which she characterized as "cat-hold religion." She urged her co-denominationalists to get over the notion that they could set everything right, and that they must frantically go about setting it right. Rather, it would be better to adopt the view of the kitten held in his mother's teeth, above it all, who enjoys the view from the top, confident in the Creator's omniscience. The monkey, on the other hand, despite the constant solicitations of his mother, cannot overcome the apprehensions that his oversensitive reactions to his environment bring. In Judaism the problem of the unbalanced world view is often expressed in terms of the dilemma between spirit and matter. See Daniel Meijers, " 'Civil Religion' or 'Civil War'? Religion in Israel" in *Religion, Power and Protest in Local Communities*, Eric Wolf, editor (Mouton, Amsterdam, 1984) for this particular version of unbalance. The problem of the unbalanced world view, then, cross-cuts several religious traditions within the general monotheistic orientation.

learn): too close a fusion between religious symbolism and the actual world and too great a disjunction between them. Where religion simply sanctifies a given socio-cultural situation it provides little leverage to change it. . . . On the other hand, where religion stresses the utter disjunction between what is religiously valuable and the activities of this world, the ability to contribute to progress may be equally weak. (1965: 193).

Although other sermons of the preacher go to great lengths to stress the ritual obligations of Muslims—prayer, fasting, pilgrimage—this sermon goes to great lengths to stress the insufficiency of ritual behavior for the religious man:

Some Muslim brothers believe Islam is a religion of prayer and fasting. On the contrary, piety is not in prostration, not in kneeling, not in prayer. Build a mosque. Build schools. Build hospitals. Your land is richer than America. You have complained about the wheat distribution [from the United States]. If you would excel in the doing of good (birr) and piety (taqwa) you would be sending wheat and barley to America and they would not be sending it to you.

From a village perspective the work of the world, therefore, is as important as worship and the preparation for salvation. There is no question that in this sermon the khatib has phrased the religious symbol system in such a way as to give meaning to cultural creativity in worldly pursuits.

The brand of Islam propagated by the preacher in his sermons supports modernity in another if somewhat negative sense. Weber, Bellah, Geertz, and a number of other scholars who have paid attention to the relationship of religion and modernization have stressed the "rationalization of religious symbolism." The spread of the historic religions has involved the "disenchantment" of the world. To quote Geertz: "The locus of sacredness was removed from the rooftrees, graveyards and road-crossings of everyday life and put, in some sense, into another realm where dwelt Jahweh, Logos, Tao or Brahman [or Allah]" (Geertz as quoted in Bellah 1965: 177).

In his sermon on, or rather against, magic, the preacher condemns such practices of local religious particularism as sorcery, divination, geomancy, prediction through the reading of cups, and hypnosis. The strength of the condemnation is communicated by identifying wizardry and magic as among the seven great sins (kabā'ir), including the sin of polytheism for which there is no forgiveness:

The Messenger of God, God's prayers and salutations be upon him, said: "Avoid the seven things that bring disaster." They said, "Oh

Messenger of God, what are they?" He said, "Polytheism, magic, killing a soul which God has forbidden except by right, taking usury, taking the wealth of orphans, fleeing on the day of battle and slandering true-believing innocent married women."[11]

The preacher continued to present his bill of particulars against magic in its many forms:

Knowledge of sorcery and magic (*sihr*) used to exist in ancient times; there is no trace of it today. All that we see today in our own time—what we hear of divination (*kahāna*) and geomancy (*raml*) and prediction through the [reading] of cups (*fath*) and hypnosis (*tanwīm*) and informing about the future—it is all falsehood and imposture and deception and the plundering of the people's wealth with falsehood and without right. The intelligent person does not accept the deceptions and nonsense which dominates minds and causes men to be in perplexity about their religion and in doubt about their beliefs. The Messenger warned people and said, *He who comes to the diviner and questions him and believes what he says has become an unbeliever with respect to what was revealed to Muhammad.*

The opposition of the preacher to sorcery and magic is made somewhat problematic by the Quranic recognition of the class of preternatural beings, the jinn, to whom recourse is often made by village diviners and sorcerers. The preacher has dealt with this problem, as noted above, by suggesting that such knowledge is obsolescent and also by referring to the Quran itself in its account of the death of Solomon:

They [imposters and artful deceivers who pretend to know hidden things] do such and such by way of constraining the jinn and the jinn follow their orders and inform them of the future of the individual and what will strike him of good and evil. They cure the sick and create mischief between a woman and her husband. They bring about good [things] between friends [i.e., reconcile them] or they work miracles. They ornament their works before men so that they may reach their wealth and plunder it and eat it without right. If the jinn had known divine secrets (*al-ghayb*) they would have known about the death of Solomon—that time when he was standing resting on his cane while the jinn were operating between his hands. God, may he be glorified and exalted says, **When we decreed Solomon's death, they (the jinn) were not alerted to his death except [after] termites ate his cane away; when it fell, it [his death] became apparent**

11. The following are excerpts from a sermon on sorcery and magic delivered in the village in April 1965.

**to them. If they had known divine secrets they would not have con-
tinued in their tortured work (34: 14 *a*).**

Here, even the purported Quranic support for certain magical beliefs and
practices is dealt with effectively by the preacher.

The description and analysis of excerpts from these three sermons delivered in a rather obscure Jordanian village that in the 1960s could
hardly have been considered at the forefront of modernization certainly
does not support Borthwick's view that the Islamic sermon is effective
only for the communication of emotional messages. It is also effective for
the communication of rational messages conveying the ethic of modernity
and for circumscribing behavior inimical to such an ethic.

THE FILLING OF EMPTY FRAMES

This analysis has proceeded thus far as if the preacher is not operating
within the great religious tradition of Islam on the one hand and the great
political tradition of the nation-state on the other; that is, as if the
preacher is not constrained in his selection of topics for sermons and in
the way he develops them by the government bureaucracy and the formal
religious hierarchy. It is well known that collections of traditional
"canned" sermons are available for use by all preachers in all social milieus. Moreover, various publications produced by the departments of religious endowments of various Middle Eastern governments and privately
by religious scholars give guidance to local village preachers. Those that
are not handed out gratis by the departments of religious endowments or
various religious universities are available cheaply in the marketplace.
One of these small books, entitled *Instructions to Preachers*, listed certain
topics as appropriate (see table 5.1).[12]

Many of the subjects certainly have potential implications for the inculcation of the attitudes appropriate to modernity (e.g., learning, utilization of time, the role of cooperation, work, opposition to racial discrimination, the value of the young). More important, no weekly
schedule of sermon topics is stipulated; the khatib is free to choose appropriate sermon topics on the occasions he deems suitable, taking into account the day-to-day events of village life. Most important, these suggested sermon topics are empty frames into which a variable content can
be poured. Rather than being constraints, these topics are, on the contrary, relatively open to interpretation. Even a topic such as pilgrimage
with its strong ritual implication or the midnight journey and ascent with

12. I wish to thank my colleague, Akbar Muhammad of the State University of New York
at Binghamton for translating and discussing excerpts from this book in a graduate seminar
on the social organization of tradition jointly taught by us in the autumn of 1976.

TABLE 5.1
List of Appropriate Sermon Topics

I. *Beliefs and Works*

Faith in God
Faith in the Final Judgment
The Divine Decree
Prayer
Fasting and Spiritual Training
Repentance
Pilgrimage and Its Rationale in Islam
Holy War in Defense of Sacred Rights

II. *Ethics*

Truth
Trustworthiness
Loyalty
Sincerity
Ethics of the Prophetic Tradition
Protection of the Heart from Envy
Forbearance and Forgiveness
Generosity
Patience
Resolution and Virtue
Cleanliness
Beautification and Health
Life
Brotherhood
Muslim Brotherhood
Strength in Unity
Self-Respect
Compassion
Learning
The Utilization of Time
Bravery
The Bravery of the Predecessors

III. *The Family and Society*

Duties to Parents and Kinsmen
The Rights of Spouses
The Rights of Neighbors
Work and Professional Pursuits
The Role of Cooperation in Strengthening Islamic Society
The Ordering of the Good and the Forbidding of the Wrong
Justice and its Various Manifestations
Deliberation
Freedom Within the Limits of Religion
The Pillar of General Enlightenment

IV. *Religious Occasions and General Matters*

Hijra: A Turning Point and Victory
The Birth of the Prophet
The Midnight Journey and Ascent
The Great Battle of Badr
The Night of Power
Islam: Faith and Deeds
Arabism and Islam
Racial Discrimination
The Danger of International Zionism
The Unity of Mankind
The Value of the Young
The Islamic View of Wealth
How Can Muslims Regain Their Glory
Islam and the Rights of Mankind
Islam and Peace
The Feast of the Breaking of the Fast of Ramadan
The Feast of the Sacrifice

its strong theological implications can be turned in directions not strictly foreseen by the title or its connotations. The topic of pilgrimage could stress compassion, forgiveness, and equality on the one hand or salvation and the gaining of paradise on the other; the latter topic could become a political call for action against Zionism on the one hand or to an examination of the nature of miracles on the other. (See chapters 6 and 8 for evidence.)

Although the three sermons quoted above refer to education, work, and magic, other subjects relating to the social structure itself lend themselves directly to the reinforcement of modernity. For instance, the topic, the rights of spouses, can be easily interpreted in such a way as to strengthen the conjugal family (husband, wife, and children) against the claims of parents and wider kinship groups. The shift in emphasis from parent-child to husband-wife relationships has been regarded as a critical aspect of modernity.[13] Ample support for this interpretation is found in the Islamic corpus of law and ethics, in the Muslim court in Jordan, and in Luqman's sermons. The Quranic inheritance rules themselves single out conjugal family members as a social unit deserving special attention in their provision for "possessors of fixed shares," *dhu al-farā'id*.[14] Quranic norms also guarantee to the wife a marriage payment from the husband, and the Muslim court in Al-Kura, Jordan, has ruled in favor of daughters and wives and against fathers who attempt to claim this payment for themselves.[15] Moreover, in his own sermons on marriage and marriage payment Luqman has stressed that the mahr is the wife's and not her father's:

> (Formerly), the Arabs did not respect their wives' right of ownership of their marriage payments; her father used to seize the mahr (for himself) and left nothing for the woman. (In Islam) it is not permitted for the guardian of the bride to dispose of her mahr or to consume it.[16]

Neither patrilineal pedigree nor wealth are unalterable qualifiers for marriage:

> He (Muhammad) said: *You marry a woman for four* (reasons)—*for her wealth; for her noble descent; for her beauty; and for her religion; take the possessor* of *religion and you will be the possessor* (of all four).[17]

Luqman also condemned the saving of agricultural surplus and livestock for expenditure on honored guests, usually relatives and kinsmen from out of town, an accepted practice in a tribal area, if that meant depriving the conjugal family, which had to be recognized and given its due.

Considering social structural modernization in Islamic societies, it is interesting to note that even such traditional religious organizations as

13. See Marion Levy (1966) for a general statement of this view and James Peacock, *Rites of Modernization: Symbolic and Social Aspects of Indonesian Proletarian Drama* (University of Chicago Press, Chicago, 1968) for a discussion of this transition in Java.

14. See the article on *farā'id* in *The Shorter Encyclopaedia of Islam*; and N. J. Coulson, *Succession in the Muslim Family* (Cambridge University Press, Cambridge, 1971) for details.

15. See Richard T. Antoun, "The Impact of the Islamic Court on Peasant Families in Jordan," in *The Politics of Law in the Middle East*, Daisy Dwyer, editor (Bergin and Garvey, in press).

16. Sermon on Marriage and Marriage Payment, Kufr al-Ma, Jordan, July 22, 1966.

17. Ibid.

Islamic mystic (sufi) orders have demonstrated the capacity to modernize their associational structures and to act within the framework of modernity. Gilsenan has described in vivid detail the organization of the Hamidiya Shadhiliya Order in Egypt. This order developed a written "constitution," record-keeping at a central office, regular inspection of all branches, a system of promotion based on successful recruitment, regular reporting of the branches to the central office, a seven-tier hierarchy of privilege and responsibility with lines of authority stipulated both laterally and lineally, an elaborate machinery for conciliation and settlement, regulations for processing and penalties for absenteeism, and the policy of advertising in newspapers to widen recruitment.[18] Is religion always so irreconcilable with modernity?

THE MOLDING POWER OF SERMONS

The village preacher whose sermons have been the focus of discussion and analysis did not have the benefit of any formal religious training. As chapter 3 indicates, he was taught by a series of teachers who happened to pass through the village, staying for a year or more and passing on to him a knowledge of the particular books on law, ethics, or theology with which they were acquainted. When I first came to the village in 1959 he chose all the subjects of his sermons himself, and he prepared them himself. To my knowledge, he never gave a "canned" sermon. He delivered them from his own hand-written text although he occasionally extemporized from that text. At the time, he was hired and paid entirely on an annual basis in measures of grain by the residents of the village, each household paying a share according to the number of its male members. Insofar as any religious organization could be said to exist at the village level it was clearly congregational rather than episcopal. Although he had frequent contact with the judge of the subdistrict Islamic court and with the marriage officer (ma'dhun) of the subdistrict and occasionally with other preachers, no official body or designated individual instructed him as to what sermon topics to prepare, how to prepare them, or when to deliver them.

By 1964, the Jordanian Department of Religious Endowments had begun sending out a monthly newsletter in which suggested sermon topics were specified, and preachers were asked to preserve a written copy of their sermon (the khatib had always done so in any case). In 1965 in response to my query, the preacher told me that sometimes he chose one of the suggested topics for a sermon and sometimes he did not. I asked

18. See Michael Gilsenan, *Saint and Sufi in Modern Egypt: An Essay in the Sociology of Religion* (Oxford University Press, London, 1973) for details.

him whether he had introduced new sermon topics from the government list between 1959 and 1965. He said he thought not. My own comparison of the sermon topics he covered in 1959–1960 with those he covered in 1965–1966 supported his statement. I found no substantial change either in the subjects of the sermons or the content introduced. Therefore, although the village preacher must be affected by governmental policy and the pronouncements of religious dignitaries in the bureaucracy, he possesses a considerable degree of autonomy with respect to the subjects of his sermons and their content. Even in such centralized polities as Egypt where party organizations, cooperatives, and various government bureaucrats operate at the local level, there is no guarantee of control. The drive for family planning in Egypt has been underway for a number of years now, and directives for appropriate sermons have been delivered to village preachers. A correspondent for the *New York Times* reported that in one Egyptian village the preacher "dutifully read a sermon about the need for birth control. When he finished he said, 'This sermon was sent to me by my superiors in Cairo. May God forgive them' " (*New York Times*, April 26, 1977).

While it may be that the Friday congregational prayer sermon has an often realized potential for supporting many of the attitudes favorable to modernity, what evidence is there that in fact Muslims internalize the attitudes expressed in such sermons or, to go a step further, follow them up with action? Peacock (1968) has raised a similar question with respect to proletarian theater in Java which, he argues, constituted a "rite of modernization" for the audience which observed it. He points out that the relationship of symbolism to social life can be of four kinds: symbolism can reflect social life; it can reveal aspects of social life which cannot be seen by observing that life; it can influence social life and encourage change; or, even more strongly, it can mold values, ideas, and emotions of participants (Peacock 1968: 236ff.). It is certainly true that in sermons on pilgrimage, fasting, the giving of alms, the reconciliation of estranged kinsmen, and the doing of justice, Muslims learn by noting the model behavior of the Prophet, his companions, and the rightly guided caliphs and possibly, as well, by some degree of empathetic roleplaying. Moreover, the sermons are not ambiguous about the direction action should take. Unlike Javanese proletarian theater, the call to action is prominent in many sermons (e.g., "Build a school! Work, and God will make easy your endeavor! Go seek her in marriage, even with an iron ring [directed to a poor man who hesitates to marry because of the absence of a substantial marriage payment]," or, negatively, "He who comes to the diviner and questions him and believes what he says has become an unbeliever"). Such calls to action delivered on a regular basis in an optimally legitimate cultural and social context—in the mosque, face-to-face on the occasion of the Friday congregational prayer with the sermon punctuated by numerous religious prayer formulae—the *tahlīl* ("I bear witness that there is no god but God"), the *basmala* ("In the name of God, the compassionate and the merciful"), the *takbīr* ("God is greater"), the *tasbīḥ* ("I proclaim the glory of God"), the *taḥmīd* ("May God be praised"), the *taʿawwudh* ("I take refuge with God from Satan the accursed"), and the *taṣliya* ("May God call down blessing on our lord Muhammad and on the family of our lord Muhammad and greet them with peace")—such calls cannot but be persuasive for a substantial part of the congregation.

Conclusive evidence of the molding power of sermons remains, however, in the consequent actions of believers. Such observed efficient causal chains are hard to come by, but inferences on the basis of observed behavior are possible. In 1960, the village improvement officer (*murshid rīfī*) came to Kufr al-Ma to encourage the villagers to borrow money for a school. His mission was repudiated by a number of village elders because it involved usury (the paying of interest). When I returned to the village in 1965 I discovered that a native villager, the clerk-usher of the religious court, a respected and pious man, had borrowed money from the commercial bank and bought a tractor. He was now earning a living with his youngest son, driving the tractor and ploughing the land for a fee in the Jordan Valley—this to earn enough money to keep his eldest son, who was in Turkey, in medical school.[19]

One of the most prominent villagers in 1960 was the village magician (*ḥajjāb*). He was believed to have control of the jinn, and not infrequently clients from as far away as Amman came to seek his services. When I returned in 1965 I found that he had purchased a grocery shop as well as a tractor. He hired his tractor out on a piece-work basis. I discovered, incidentally, that in the interim he had purchased the saint's tree in the lower quarter of the village, chopped it up, and sold it for firewood in his shop. His occupational role as a magician, it seemed, had lapsed into the background compared with his other entrepreneurial activities.

On one of my last visits to the village in 1979 I counted thousands of olive trees as well as eighty-five automobiles and trucks, noted that the entire village had been electrified, and that all the houses had piped running water. Thirty students from this dusty village in what had been an economic backwater of Jordan were now studying in universities in seventeen different foreign countries including two in the Soviet Union, six in Greece, and three in Houston, Texas! Of course, most—but not all—

---

19. The clerk-usher's paying interest was not necessarily an irreligious act since various legal devices available in Islamic law can be invoked to legitimize it. What is of interest here is the fact that options are built into the corpus of Islamic law and ethics such that an individual over a short period of time can initiate a change which was previously considered reprehensible.

of this change was enabled by the 1973 OPEC price rises. But at no point in my discussions with villagers or religious specialists about the changes taking place was there an inkling that the pursuit of professional education or technological modernization was in any way inimical to Islamic law or ethics. On the contrary, Islamization and/or religious resurgence were proceeding apace with the building of a dome for the main mosque (1971), the establishment of a Quranic school (1977), the building of a new mosque (1983), and the hiring of a second preacher (1984).

If modernization is the adaptive process of transformation according to various routes, timetables, and strategies—transformation of the institutions that permit and encourage economic growth—and if modernity is the social, cultural, and psychological framework which supports and facilitates that transformation, it is by no means clear that Islamization and/or religious resurgence works against such a transformation or its cultural and psychological underpinnings. Indeed, since one of the main fora for Islamization is the Friday congregational sermon and its main purveyor is the Muslim preacher, the evidence both from the minbar and from the changing village over the last fifteen years clearly suggests a positive relationship. One might argue that the simutaneous progression of modernization and religious resurgence simply indicates the capacity for people to compartmentalize their lives.[20] However, as chapter 1 indicated, it is precisely the development of this capacity that is a hallmark of modernity and a catalyst of modernization.

20. I wish to thank Helen Rivlin for this suggestion.

View of nucleated village from surrounding fields
with domed mosque and western hills in the background

143

Traditional entrance (rough-hewn stone and adobe)
of courtyard with new-style house in background

Old nucleated village with zig-zag blind alleys

Stonecutter (1960)

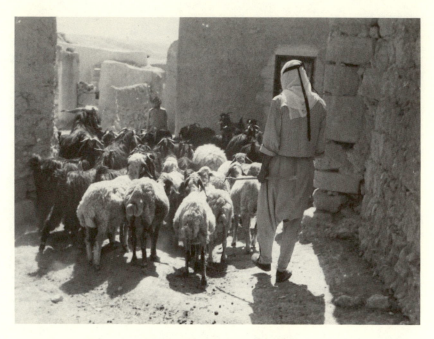

Shepherd returning with flock
through alley of nuclear village (1960)

The expanded village:
new housing on land formerly planted with grain (1987)

Old courtyard gate and new Mercedes II (1987)

Municipality driver. Note new-style house in background
with water tank and solar panels (1987)

Entrance to the village with new mosque in background

Preacher with driver in front of new bus

Paved main street with domed central mosque in background

Interior of new mosque with radio-tape recorder for announcing prayer, individual prayer carpets, stacked Qurans, reading stool with Quran (left) and photograph of Al-Aqsa Mosque. Inscription above prayer-niche reads: "God, the light of the heavens and the earth."

Preacher collecting his salary
on the threshing ground from one household (1960)

Village children with a
traditional bread-baking oven on the left

151

Villagers relaxing in front of village grocery shop (1986)

Anthropologist taking notes from the mayor of the village (1960)

Preacher reading in his study (1987)

Villagers meet for early morning festival prayer after Ramadan

6

Islamic Ritual and Modernity:
The Pilgrimage (Hajj) Interpreted

The Pilgrimage to Mecca (*ḥajj*) is one of the five pillars of Islam.[1] Muslims commemorate it every year in their home communities irregardless of those who are going on the Hajj themselves. The preacher is a key figure in focusing the ethical, motivational, and social structural implications of the Pilgrimage in his Friday congregational sermons during the Pilgrimage season. As a focus of piety and ritual devotion by millions of Muslims on an annual basis, directly by participation and vicariously by celebration, the Hajj is also a rich focus for symbolic interpretation. This chapter will first document and illustrate that commemoration by presenting two sermons delivered by the village preacher in the mosque during the Pilgrimage season. Second, it will briefly compare and contrast the themes of the two sermons. Third, it will discuss Pilgrimage in the lives of villagers in terms of its personal and social impact. Finally, it will examine the possibilities of interpreting the Hajj by referring to the analysis of one lay Muslim scholar in order to demonstrate the richness of the Pilgrimage as a multivocal symbol.

THE SERMONS

In more than one sense the preacher dramatically reenacts the Pilgrimage itself in his sermons during the pilgrim season. First, in preaching he plays Muhammad's paradigmatic role since Muhammad was the first Muslim preacher, and he gave his last recorded sermon while on Pilgrimage from the Mountain of Mercy at Arafat. In the mosque the Prophet spoke authoritatively, and not only on what Westerners would consider "religious matters" but also on social relations and important political issues. The contemporary village preacher continues to speak in a wide-ranging manner in his Friday sermons, linking ritual, soteriological, and ethical themes, even in treating a strict worship obligation such as Pilgrimage. Second, sermons such as those recounted below reenact the Pilgrimage by vicariously tracing the steps of pilgrims at the various ritual stations: the

1. When the Pilgrim/Pilgrimage to Mecca is referred to, Pilgrim/Pilgrimage will be capitalized. Non-Islamic and non-Meccan pilgrimages will not be capitalized. Hajj, the proper reference to the Meccan Pilgrimage in Arabic will, likewise, be capitalized. The reference to the returned pilgrim in Arabic, *ḥājj*, which is also the title he bears thereafter will not be capitalized.

Ka'bah, Safa and Marwa, Mina and Arafat.[2] These sermons also allude to the mystical experiences that accompany the Pilgrim's prayers, and to the entreaties for forgiveness and euphoria in retracing the steps of the Prophet in Mecca and its environs and, later, in Medina, the City of Light. The beatific religious experience, the intertwining of worship with ethics, the emphasis on paradigmatic history, and the symbolic multivocality of the Pilgrimage are all revealed in the sermons delivered by the village preacher during the pilgrim season of 1960.

The Soteriological, Ethical, and Mystical Significance of Pilgrimage

Praise be to God who ordained the pilgrimage to his sacred house for his worshipers. And they started out on the journey and he [God] called them to its vicinity. And on account of their love for him they did not consider it [the journey] long nor did they find it inconceivable [hardship]. I bear witness that there is no god but God, [to him] are prostrate in adoration those who are in the heavens and those on earth . . . and their shelter in the early morning and the evening.[3] And bear witness that our master, Muhammad, is his servant and his Messenger, a Prophet of compassion, a Messenger of guidance and peace. And [may you bestow] on his family and companions precious things.

Now then: God, may he be exalted, and he is the truest of the sayers, said: **Pilgrimage thereto is a duty men owe to God—those who can afford the journey; but if any deny faith, God stands not in need of any of his creatures** (3: 97, YA). Oh ye Muslims, God has ordained for his worshipers the pilgrimage to his sacred house [the Ka'bah] on condition that the person has the wherewithal and the means of transport; if so the pilgrimage is incumbent on him; he who does not make the pilgrimage is of the sinners. As for him who is unable [to make the pilgrimage], **On no soul doth God place a burden greater than it can bear** (2: 286, YA). After adversity God will bring ease [i.e., perhaps he will be granted the means to make the Hajj later]. God has ordained the pilgrimage once for every Muslim man and woman. He ordained it for those with sufficiency in order that they may return to the Muslim community with charity and blessings. On the Pilgrimage Muslims from the eastern and western limits of the earth meet in single bliss and they become acquainted with one another and harmonize and consult on matters that concern them and make them happy and cooperate on the improvement of their circumstances and the management of their affairs. Oh what felicity for he

---

2. If the reader wishes a more detailed description of the Pilgrimage rites at this point he may wish to skip ahead to the section on "The Hajj" (pp. 171–76) and then return to the description and analysis of the sermons on Pilgrimage.

3. It was not possible to decipher the meaning of the missing phrase in the original handwritten text of the sermon.

whose Lord has given success in making the Pilgrimage to the sacred house. He meets there with his brothers, the true believers, who have come from the ends of the earth saying, "There is no god but God," "God is great," humbling themselves to God, may he be exalted, saying with one voice that softens hearts and seeking the favor of the knower of the hidden: "Here I am, at your service; all your felicity and blessing are in your hands" (*Labbayka, labbayk, labbayka, wa saʿdayk wa khayru kuluhu fi yadayk*). On the Pilgrimage Muslim brotherhood appears in its most glorious manifestation when the rich and the poor and the princes and the kings stand in one spot shouting with one voice and calling one Lord with pure hearts. It [the Pilgrimage] is the manifestation of unity and brotherhood and equality. During the Pilgrimage he sees new countries and many nations and he becomes familiar with their circumstances and their customs, and he witnesses the sacred places and the [place of] death of the noble prophet and the tracks of the companions who raised the standard of Islam and carried the standard of guidance. In the Pilgrimage is an opportunity for trade and the succoring of the wretched from among the inhabitants of the holy lands. Oh ye people of felicity, he who spends on the Pilgrim a dirham, it is as if he has spent a thousand dirhams. And he who is able to make the Pilgrimage and does not is penalized for his omission in Hell.

He who makes the Pilgrimage with unlawful wealth—the wealth of usury, the wealth of plunder, of theft, of [usurped] marriage payment—and says, "Here I am good God at your service (*labbayka, allahuma labbayk*)" is called before God [who says]: "You are not here. You are not at my service. Yours is not felicity and your Pilgrimage is thrown back on yourself." The achievement of these peoples is due to God: their Lord called them to his side and they journeyed to his house tired and dirty. These are the ones in whom the angels take pride, the close companions (intimates); they spread his mercy, and his works are made general [by completing the Pilgrimage]. [God said]: *Oh my angels, you are seeing [none] except my worshippers. They left the comfort of their homes and they came to me whether riding or on foot. They filled the land with, 'There is no god but God' and 'God is great' (La illaha ill allah wa allahu akbar—i.e., with my praise). Bear witness I shall smooth the way for them with a hospitable reception [on the Day of Judgment]; I shall entrench their successors [on earth] and I shall place them in paradise.* Oh ye who have neglected (omitted) the pilgrimage and carry a heavy burden of sins, hurry to the Pilgrimage of the sacred house of God. God, may he be exalted, said: **Pilgrimage thereto is a duty men owe to God—Those who can afford the journey . . .** (3: 97, *YA*). He who makes the Pilgrimage receives repentance and attains profit, and good tidings are for he who drinks from the water of Zemzem and trots between Marwa and Safa and enters into the [enclosure of the black] stone a noble-minded Muslim. There is a people on whose hearts is written faith and on whose works [is written] mercy and [God's] favor. While they were paying their last respects by circumambulations [of the Ka'bah] and resolving on a return, they were impelled by yearning [to visit Medina] [as seen] by the rapidity of their walking to the [home of] the chosen Prophet. There [in Medina on Judgment Day] they will be encompassed by the light (grace) of Muhammad and they will be included in the prophetic blessing. The Messenger of God said: *He who makes the pilgrimage and does not speak obscene speech and does not commit obscene acts, his sins are taken away and he emerges as he did on the day his mother gave him birth.* And he, may God's prayers and salutations be upon him, said: *The Pilgrimage of good faith, there can be no reward for it but paradise.*

Pilgrimage: The Religious History of Muhammad's Struggle

Praise be to God who makes successful whom he wishes of his worshipers in carrying out the rites of Pilgrimage. And he guides them to the most rightly guided of paths. Praise him for his beneficence. Seek forgiveness from him, turn to him in repentance and solicit his help for the performance of good works [*ṣāliḥāt*]. And testify that there is no god but God. Alone, there being no partner for him. He confers plentitude and reckons [everything] great and small. **And who so doeth good an atom's weight shall see it then** [on Judgment Day] **and who so doeth ill an atom's weight, shall see it then** [on Judgment Day] (99: 7–8, P). And testify that our master, Muhammad, is his servant (*'abd*) and messenger (*rasūl*) and chosen one (*ṣafiyyu*) and his true friend (*khalīl*) whom God has ordained as the seal of his prophets. He sent him in compassion to the worlds. God bless our master, Muhammad, and all the prophets (*anbiyā'*) and messengers and their followers with goodness until the day of religion (reckoning).

Now, then, God may he be blessed (*tabāraka*) and exalted (*ta'āla*), he being the truest of speakers says: **And warn, for warning profiteth believers** (51: 55, P). Oh ye people, which person is most favored with happiness, greatest in prosperity, most highly rewarded and most perfect in faith (belief) of those for whom God, may he be exalted, has smoothed the way with the most illustrious benefits of Islam? It is the Pilgrim to his sacred temple in Mecca and his visitation of his beloved one, Muhammad, may he be blessed and preserved, and (his) enjoyment of the sights of the holy lands and the chaste spots on whose surface he has erected the most noble of the houses of God. Its regions have been made fragrant by the presence of the lodgings of the seal of the messengers of God. Its pathways have become glorified by the actions of his rightly guided successors and companions. Its power has become great by tenacious adherence to the religion of God. Oh how great is the impression which the mention of these beloved lands in the minds of men exerts—[these lands] in whose skies the sun of Islam has risen. There walked on its earth the learned heroes whom God selected to lead the confused ([and] pagan) peoples. And he chose from among them, Muhammad, to convey the final message. And he met with hardships and obstacles as the other prophets struggling [in the way of God]—the steadfast ones, the march warriors—until God crowned his cause with victory and he spread his message to the four horizons. **Surely we will help our Messengers and those who have believed, in the present life, and upon the day when the witnesses arise** [Judgment Day] (40: 51, A). How majestic respect [becomes] and how great recollection [grows] before the tomb of the Prophet when the onlookers remember what happened on the night of his noble birth in the land of Mecca, the venerable—of the cleaving of Kisra's palace and the splitting of Caesar's seat, and of what these sovereigns heard [in their dreams on that night] when an invisible man whose voice was heard cried out: Today an epoch ends and an epoch begins. After today there will be no kings or diviners or chiefs (*sayyid*s). Verily, worship is to God and sovereignty (*siyāda*) is to the religion of God and leadership (*qiyāda*) is to the seal of the Prophets of God and government (*ḥukūma*) is to the successors (*khulafā'*) of God and the world is to all God's worshipers—justice and freedom and brotherhood and equality. How majestic estimation becomes when the onlookers at the tomb of the Messenger proliferate [and they recollect] how he was sent at the time when people were scattered in disputing fragments (*ashtāt*) with no leader to unite them, all the while taken up with committing evil deeds and abominations such as the killing of boys and the burying alive of newborn girls; the persistence in the worshiping of idols and the oppression by the strong of the weak and burning enmity and hatred. He [Muhammad] contended with them with the message of his Lord, there being no army to support him and no authority to back him up. For, they turned away from him and grew conceited and confronted him with stubbornness. They injured him severely and boycotted him and his followers in the valley of Shi'ab, refusing to eat with them or drink with them. [The reference is to the seven-year boycott of the tribes of Mecca of Beni Hashim.] Finally, he fled to Ta'if with his relatives who sought to protect him from injury by the Quraysh. But he was greeted there with worse [treatment] than [he received from] the Quraysh. They cursed him and pelted him with stones until he bled. *An angel descended from the heavens saying to him: "Oh Muhammad, God has commanded me to obey you in what your people desire. If you wish me to crush them [the inhabitants of Mecca] between the two mountains [of Mecca], I shall do it." He, may the blessings of God and his salutations be upon him, replied: "I desire that God produce from their* *loins those who worship God. Oh God, guide my people rightly for they do not know better."* The angel said: *"He spoke the truth who named you the compassionate [ra'ūf] and the merciful [rahīm]."* He met their injuries with patience (*sabr*) and their curses with forbearance (*hilm*) and their coarseness with compassion (*rahma*), practicing what God had taught him: **Keep to forgiveness (O Muhummad) and enjoin kindness, and turn away from the ignorant** (7: 199, *P*). **For thou art of a noble disposition** (68: 4, *S*). Thus, Muhammad did not leave his people (*qawm*) in their state of infidelity (rebellion) against God. On the contrary, he met them with exhortation. With these qualities of character and with this manliness Muhammad alone triumphed over the Arabs. And this manliness [in turn] brought victory to the Arabs over the whole world and God the great sayeth the truth: **God will certainly aid those who aid His [cause]. For, verily, God is Full of Strength, Exalted in Might** [able to enforce His Will]. [They are] **those who, if we establish them in the land, establish regular prayers and give regular charity, enjoin the right and forbid wrong; with God rests the end** [and decision] of [all] **affairs** (22: 40–41, *YA*). How illustrious the regard, how great the memory when the onlookers before the tomb of the Messenger, the most great, recall the event of the prophetic flight to the city of light. The emigrants (*muhājirūn*) and the supporters (*ansār*) gathered round him [there]. With them he flung [himself] at the abodes of polytheism (*shirk*) and destroyed them and raised the standard of Islam and made fast the throne of the Quran. There [in Medina] monotheism (*wahdaniyya*) triumphed over paganism and humanitarianism (*insaniyya*) over fanaticism (*'asabiyya*) and Islam over the ignorant. The individual came to know the worth of his brother and souls perceived the superiority of justice (*'adāla*) and beneficence. And the caravan of life [thenceforth] wended its way to safety [along an] immortal path. How majestic the regard when he [the Pilgrim] recalls his [Muhammad's] victorious entrance into Mecca. How God made possible [his victory] over the Quraysh who injured him and plotted his destruction. Verily, he said to them when they (Meccans) gathered round him to see what their fate would be: *"Oh people of Quraysh, how do you think I shall treat you?"* They said, *"With goodness generous brother, generous nephew."* He said to them: *"Go, for you are free. I shall say to you only what Joseph, upon him be peace, said to his brothers—you are not under suspicion today; God forgive you and he is the most compassionate of forgivers."* Oh ye Muslims this is what our righteous ancestors used to say when God permitted them to speak. What is to be the answer by which we can defend ourselves? There is no excuse after today when the Book of God, may he be exalted, is between our hands opening before us the treasures of the earth and extending to us the tempers of heaven. In it our righteous predecessors found what helped them. They afforded the world the bounty of knowledge and the fruits of urban life and the happiness of civilization. It is an obligation upon all Muslims to shake themselves out of their sleeping places that they may repel tyranny and the people of injustice and error and expel the Jews and the Communists— striking them a hard strike—that the world perceive that Islam is a firm religion which God favored for the world and that they retrieve its ancient glory until the banner of Islam waves across the world and men feel secure and tranquil in their lives. Verily this [sermon] is a reminder for he who wishes to take it as a path to his Lord. Verily, for those who hold fast to the Book and perform the ritual prayer we need not broadcast the reward of the righteous. There has come from God light and a clear Book by which God guides he who seeks his favor—[to] paths of peace. He removes them from the darkness into the light, by his permission, and guides them down the straight path (al-sirat al-mustaqīm). A tradition (of the Prophet) runs: *The Messenger of God said: "I've left with you two things of high estimation; what—if you hold fast to them, you will not go astray, ever. The Book of God, may be exalted, and his [Muhammad's] Traditions."*

The first sermon (18 Shawwal) has a triple focus—social structural, ethical, and soteriological—with minor legal and mystical emphases. The worldly, social, and economic functions of the Hajj are stipulated: mutual consultation, trade, and egalitarianism ("the rich and the poor and the prince and the kings stand in one spot . . . shouting with one voice"). But these worldly functions are balanced by the significance of Pilgrimage for salvation: "There [in Medina, on Judgment Day] they will be encompassed by the light (grace) of Muhammad and they will be included in the Prophetic blessing." And again: *"The Pilgrimage of good faith, there can be no reward for it but paradise."*

The connections between the three foci are not, however, simply those of juxtaposed functions; rather, they are causal chains linking this world and the next. The religious and the ethicolegal significance of the Pilgrimage is intertwined since usury, plunder, theft, and usurped marriage payment render the Pilgrimage unacceptable to God on the one hand, and on the other, he who makes the Pilgrimage an ethical endeavor by refraining from obscene speech and acts, "his sins are taken away and he emerges as he did on the day his mother gave him birth."

The sermon of 3 Dhu al-Qa'da, on the other hand, focuses on paradigmatic history and its mystical implications and, secondarily, on its ethical implications. In addition, it introduces a short but powerful revolutionary political theme. Unlike the previous sermon which dwells on the ritual and legal aspects of the Hajj (e.g., drinking from the water of Zemzem, trotting between Safa and Marwa, circumambulation, ritual prayer (*tal-*

biyah), and acts that cancel the Pilgrimage's efficacy), this sermon is a sketch of the trials and tribulations of Muhammad's prophetic career. In the course of that sketch the listener is taken vicariously on a journey where he enjoys the "sights of holy lands"—"its regions hav(ing) been made fragrant by the presence of the lodgings of the seal of the messengers of God; its pathways . . . glorified by the actions of his rightly guided successors and companions." This sermon alerts the senses of the listener to the religiomystical experiences to which he can look forward—or which he can enjoy in pale reflection if he is already a hajj. Here, the beatific vision of the Pilgrim is regarded as a key to his appreciation of the Pilgrimage. But into this essentially mystical discourse are woven ethical implications. Muhammad's paradigmatic ethical acts are recounted—patience, forbearance, magnanimity to defeated enemies—and contrasted to the abominations of his opponents (e.g., persecution, factionalism, idolatry, and female infanticide).

In this sermon, however, in the process of recounting paradigmatic religious history, a political message completely lacking in the Shawwal sermon is introduced. The birth of the Prophet results in "the cleaving of Kisra's palace" and "the splitting of Caesar's seat," symbols of political revolution:[4] "After today there will be no kings or diviners or chiefs . . . leadership is to the Seal of the Prophets of God and government is to his successors. . . ." Here, Muhammad was challenging the rulership of the two dominant empires of his day, the Sassanian and the Byzantine.

These two sermons, then, both focus on Pilgrimage and its significance; they both demonstrate the intertwined ethical, mystical, soteriological, and social structural strands found in the ethos and world view of popular Islam; ethics and salvation are inextricably tied in the action the Muslim must take before undertaking the Pilgrimage, the action he must take during its performance, and the action he must take after its completion. And both sermons underline the basic view that as believer, man's chief obligation is to testify to the unity of God in the darkness of this world: "They fill the land with, 'There is no god but God,' and 'God is great.'" Here, devotion to God and the unity of God, (tawhid) implying rejection of all rivals, are the keys to the faith.

But the sermons are quite different in their organizing framework and the content of their messages. The first sermon seeks to influence behavior through its stress on the egalitarian ethos of Pilgrimage and it aims at molding the behavior of pilgrims through a number of negative provisos regarding family obligations and slander. The first balances a this-worldly (but nonpolitical) social structural emphasis with distinct soteriological

4. Kisra represents the ruler of the Sassanian Empire and Caesar the ruler of the Byzantine Empire, the two dominant imperial domains of Muhammad's day.

concerns in a ritual and legal framework of argument. The second sermon pursues mystical and to a lesser degree ethical significance through paradigmatic history, or, otherwise stated, myth, and plucks a contemporary political message out of religious history.[5] The two sermons do not illustrate variations on a theme. Rather, they illustrate the different directions a resourceful preacher can go with a seemingly rigid ritual subject—the Pilgrimage to Mecca.

The second sermon seeks to mold behavior through the description of the model acts that marked the Prophet's career: compassion, manliness, generosity, magnanimity. But the second sermon goes beyond an attempt to mold. It is an unmistakable call for political, more, military action against named opponents:

> It is an obligation upon all Muslims to shake themselves out of their sleeping places that they may repel tyranny and the people of injustice and error and expel the Jews and the Communists—striking them a hard strike—that the world perceive that Islam is a firm religion which God favored for the world. . . .

The Islamic sermon, then, ranges across a number of perspectives—mystical, mythological, ethical, political, military—and seeks certainly to influence, to mold, and sometimes to call for action of a particular kind. These two sermons on a seemingly straightforward "religious" subject, Pilgrimage, remind us again, this time with respect to ritual rather than education or work as was demonstrated in the last chapter, that Islam in its local environment at the popular level is neither passive and inflexible, nor ethically unelevated or irrelevant in its message for the modern world.

THE PILGRIMAGE IN THE LIVES OF VILLAGERS

How do villagers incorporate the fact and significance of the Pilgrimage including the richly textured themes of the preacher's sermons into their own lives? To answer this question requires placing the Pilgrimage in its diachronic, spatial, and social structural context. Hajj in its full sense does not begin with the entrance of the pilgrim into the environs of Mecca or end with his departure from "The Noble City." The two months preceding the Pilgrimage itself have a significant preparatory character and are known as "the pilgrimage season" (*mawāsim al-ḥajj*).[6] During this

---

5. "Myth" here refers to beliefs held to be true about man, his relation to his fellow men, to nature, and to the invisible world—without any judgment implied about the veracity of such beliefs.

6. William Roff has stressed the importance of the preparatory aspects of Pilgrimage in understanding its religious and social significance. See Roff, "Pilgrimage in the History of Religions: Theoretical Approaches to Hajj," 78–86, in *Approaches to Islam in Religious Studies*, Richard C. Martin, editor (University of Arizona Press, Tucson, 1985).

period villagers provide for their households, pay their debts or attempt to do so, arrange for transportation, sometimes organizing caravans with buses and drivers, and attend to necessary formalities such as obtaining passports and visas. Quite often they invite or are invited by relatives and friends for a communal meal. The prospective Pilgrim seeks information from previous pilgrims on practical matters pertaining to domicile and the journey and from the preacher on ritual obligations. By the 1970s the latter had for distribution a large number of printed tracts detailing the ritual requirements of the Pilgrimage that he had brought back with him from previous trips to Mecca and Medina. These leave-taking social events indicate that the prospective Pilgrim is about to enter a liminal period—marking a sharp break with his everyday routine and its attendant interests.[7]

The pilgrim journey itself is an important part of the Pilgrimage and the subject of some discussion before going and after returning.[8] The journey from Amman to Mecca is 1669 kilometers and pilgrims discuss the stops and the distances between them. Many of the stops on the Pilgrim road are the loci of significant events in Muslim history filled with rich denotations and connotations (e.g., Tabuk and Badr where critical battles were fought and Medina, the locus of the Prophet's flight, tomb, and mosque).

Many observers have commented that Islam is linked symbolically and historically with movement including the Prophet's flight from Mecca to Medina which is commemorated at the beginning of the Muslim calendar/year. The Pilgrimage is an annual reaffirmation of movement, but it is important to note that movement is always circular with traditional visits to Medina (and formerly Jerusalem) on the return trip, almost always ending with the arrival of the Pilgrim with his new title, hajj, and his new social status back in his home community.[9]

On his return the Pilgrim is visited and congratulated by his relatives, friends, and neighbors. Customarily, the visitor addresses him, on entering, with the words, "May your Pilgrimage (Hajj) be blessed." In the

---

7. Roff suggests that these leave-taking events sometimes have a testamentary or funerary character.

8. Bharati has suggested for Hindu pilgrimages in India that the journey is as important as the rituals at the pilgrimage site itself. See Bharati, "Pilgrimage Sites and Indian Civilization" in *Indian Civilization*, J. W. Elder, editor (Kendall-Hunt Publishers, Dubuque, 1967); and Bharati's autobiography, *The Ochre Robe* (1970).

9. There are a few exceptions to this circular route of migration. Hurgronje noted in the last century (1884) that many Javanese pilgrims had settled permanently in Mecca, and my own contact with Pilgrims from Chad who had reached Beirut in 1966 verified that many had been living in Beirut for sixteen years. Economic circumstances sometimes delay the return of the migrant for a very long period, but this pattern is unusual, particularly today in the age of vehicular traffic and air travel. The overwhelming majority of Pilgrims from Kufr al-Ma make the round-trip within a two-week period.

event that he has made the "Little Pilgrimage" ('*Umra*), a supererogatory religious observance that can be made individually at any time of the year, and which includes the circumambulation of the Kaaba and the running between Safa and Marwa but not the standing at Arafat or the subsequent ritual slaughtering, the visitors greet the returnee with the words, "May your Little Pilgrimage ('Umra) be blessed."[10]

The returnees come back with vivid descriptions of the Pilgrimage, usually filled with happiness and a plethora of comments on the journey and on Arabian society generally.[11] For instance, one returned Pilgrim recounted the large number of rest houses and restaurants along the road, estimated that he had seen a thousand buses from Jordan along the way, praised a group of Saudi Arabian hosts who had received them in Medina—they had slaughtered three sheep for them and cooked them whole—and stated that they had visited Arafat and the stations of stoning (even though it was not part of their Little Pilgrimage) as well. This Pilgrim, the schoolmaster of the boys' junior high school, had received twelve books from the religious university in Medina for the library in the village school and had purchased a kerosene heater, at a saving, as well as a telephone operated by buttons and with a key. He said that it had been a splendid trip and that next year he would take his wife with him. It is interesting to note that all three comments were on "the Little Pilgrimage," that is, the economic, social, and recreational aspects of the trip were incorporated with the ritual as part of a single profound experience.

The preacher himself had returned from the 'Umra a few weeks before and had brought with him a newspaper entitled, *Muslim World News* and a load of books including a Quranic commentary by the great religious scholar, Ibn Hanbal, and another by al-Rabbani in fourteen volumes and twenty-four parts given to him by friends at the religious university in Medina where his son had graduated three years before. On my inquiring as to how these volumes would be used he replied that they would be consulted only by university graduates in the village, for they were too sophisticated for the use of others.

Among those returning from the Pilgrimage or those intending to go discussions occur, particularly in the home of the preacher, concerning ritual and legal matters pertaining to particular acts of Pilgrimage. For instance, on one occasion Shaykh Luqman gave me a small handbook

10. See the next section for a more detailed discussion of the difference between Hajj and 'Umra. See also the article on 'umra in the *Shorter Encyclopaedia of Islam*.

11. On the other hand, in a (1986) paper on "The Hac: Sacred and Secular," Delaney recorded that the Turkish Pilgrims from a central Anatolian village who returned from Mecca found the experience of the Pilgrimage disorienting; it was the "secular Hac"—the return to Turkey after long absences working in Europe—that was "transformative" and emotionally charged.

evaluating all acts on the Hajj according to five degrees of necessity/approval: basic element (*rukn*), prerequisite (*shart*), required (*wājib*), Tradition of the Prophet (*sunna*), and recommended (*mandūb*). We began to discuss different acts of Pilgrimage in terms of those categories of approval. The preacher said that the Shafi'is (a school of law) regarded the following as basic elements: the statement of intention (*niyya*) before each ritual, the standing at Arafat on the eighth day of the Pilgrimage, the "exuberant circumambulation" (*tawāf al-ifāda*) of the Ka'bah, the running (*saʿy*) between Safa and Marwa, the shaving of all the hair or most of it (as part of consecration), and following the proper succession of rituals. Luqman said that a "basic element" was absolutely required and that a shart act cancelled all subsequent acts if not performed; an act that was wajib was required and, if not performed, had to be atoned for, and the act or its absence is still counted (for or against the person); he said the nonperformance of a rukn act voids all subsequent acts. I pointed out that the standing at Arafat was classified as sunna, a Prophetic Tradition but not an absolute requirement. This comment triggered a debate with all present expressing surprise at such a statement and attempting to explain it. The preacher then consulted various works on Islamic law in his library and finally said that the categorization of the standing at Arafat as sunna referred only to the hour of the day when it began (about which there were various legal opinions) and not to the act itself which is absolutely required.

Then the villagers began to discuss the question of when the Hajj and/or ʿUmra properly began, that is, with what ritual formula and at what station. Shaykh Luqman said that three alternative ritual strategies for initiating the Pilgrimage were possible, depending on the statement of intention selected. First, one might say, "Here I am awaiting your command, oh God. Oh God, I intend to perform the Little Pilgrimage." Then the Pilgrim can begin to perform his ʿUmra at Abar Ali on the outskirts of Medina. After the Pilgrim finishes the rites of the Little Pilgrimage, he can doff his consecrated clothing and put on regular clothing until the eighth day of Dhu'l-Hijja, the Pilgrimage month, when he must reconsecrate himself, put on his consecrated clothing, and recite the ritual prayer of the Hajj. He then maintains his state of consecration until he arrives at Mina on the tenth day of the month. After the stoning of the Pillars at Mina he may put his regular clothing back on and perform the circumambulation of the Ka'bah in them. A second ritual option is for the Pilgrim on arrival at Abar Ali to make a linked statement of intent, "Oh God, I intend to perform the Hajj and the ʿUmra," in which case he maintains his state of consecration including pilgrim clothing until the Festival of Sacrifice on the tenth day of the month. A third option is for the Pilgrim, on reaching Abar Ali, to say, "Oh God, I intend to perform the Hajj."

And only after the rites of Pilgrimage proper are over at the mosque of Aisha (the Prophet's wife) does he make the statement of intent to perform in addition the Little Pilgrimage.

Someone raised the question of what a poor Muslim who could not afford to buy a sacrificial animal for slaughter at Arafat (as required by the Hajj) on the tenth day of the Pilgrimage month could do to render his Pilgrimage acceptable to God. The preacher said that it was possible for him, instead, to fast thirty days in Mecca and seven days when he returned home.

The preparatory acts of Pilgrimage, the Pilgrimage journey, the rites of Pilgrimage themselves, and the post-Pilgrimage commemorations and discussions, then, make a profound impression on both the individual and his society. This impact is great not only in terms of beatific religious experience and social communion but also in terms of widening horizons of knowledge: of Islamic law and ritual, the geography and ethnography of Islam, and the marketplaces of other countries.

The brief account recorded above of one Pilgrim's reflections on the Pilgrimage experience leads to another question, not about the functions of the Pilgrimage, but rather about the way the Hajj and by extension pilgrimages in other cultures are viewed by pilgrims in the course of pilgrimage and afterwards in their home communities. Several intertwined perspectives are involved. Although Muslim culture defines the Hajj and the ʿUmra as religious events par excellence, and the individual Muslim Pilgrim accepts that view without question, in the course of the Pilgrim journey, the rites of Pilgrimage, and the return journey several perspectives—religious, aesthetic, commonsense, and ludic—alternate in dominance.[12] One might argue as Bharati (1982) does that a commonsense economic perspective characterizes much activity at the religious fairs (*melas*) accompanying most Hindu pilgrimages. He has also stressed that seeking an auspicious vision (*darshan*) from an icon or holy man, commerce, and "fun and games" are all parts of a single pilgrimage experience in India, and that cameras, radios, and tape recorders are commonly brought along on pilgrimages.

Although such activity seems not to take place for consecrated Muslim Pilgrims on the Hajj, after their emergence from consecration (*iḥrām*) and often during their visits to other Muslim pilgrimage sites, they purchase the same kind of equipment in the various bazaars abutting on the shrines themselves. Historically, we know that Mecca itself was an entrepot at a

12. See Geertz, "Religion as a Cultural System," in *Anthropological Approaches to the Study of Religion*, Michael Banton, editor (Tavistock, London, 1966) for a brief but illuminating discussion of the different perspectives that characterize human behavior. See also Bharati 1967, 1980 and in press for a discussion of how such perspectives shift in the process of pilgrimage in India.

caravan crossroads and that much of the opposition of Muhammad's own clan, Beni Hashim, to his religious mission was out of concern for its impact on the trade by which they earned their living.

Traditionally, many Muslims on the Hajj worked their way across a continent, particularly in Africa, over a period of years and worked their way back.[13] I have met Pilgrims from Bahr al-Ghazal and Chad who had worked their way across Africa to Port Sudan, thence to Mecca and on to Medina, Jerusalem, and Beirut, where I met them in the course of their jobs as peanut peddlers in the central square. Commonly, they married along the way and their children were born enroute. They all intended to return home, but their income from peddling did not permit it. When I met them in 1966 some had been living and working in Beirut for fourteen years. In these instances a commonsense economic perspective was necessarily part and parcel of the Pilgrimage.

Turner, an anthropologist who has studied pilgrimage cross-culturally, has described the pilgrim route, on the one hand, in terms of its ever-increasing sacredness (Turner 1973: 214), but on the other, in terms of simultaneously increasing secular concerns:

> He (the pilgrim) meets with more shrines and sacred objects as he advances, but he also encounters more real dangers such as bandits and robbers; he has to pay attention to the need to survive and often to earn money for transportation; and he comes across markets and fairs, especially at the end of the quest, where the shrine is flanked by the bazaar and by the fun fair. (Turner 1973: 204–5)

What becomes clear from these comparative comments and from statements of returned pilgrims is that several perspectives juxtapose (or mesh) with one another in the course of the Pilgrimage.

Sax's description of the various occupations and castes witnessing the religious drama of Ram Lila in India suggests something more, namely, a tendency for certain social categories to favor certain perspectives—for example, those engaged in business (Vaisyas in general caste identity) to take a religious perspective and to pursue it more intensely; local agricultural workers (Shudras in caste identity) to take a ludic-aesthetic perspective; and, interestingly enough, the sadhus or holy men to take a commonsense economic perspective (they were extremely concerned and apprehensive about the size of the Maharajah's impending distribution of food to their number at the shrine) (Sax 1981: 13–17). One could argue that the holy men were simultaneously and preeminently moved by a religious perspective since they had renounced home and family and devoted their lives to the search for release from the chain of transmigration

13. Ahmed B. Yusuf, n.d.

(*moksha*). Probably, however, the relationship between perspectives is not synchronic and social structural with certain occupations, classes, castes, or family types pursuing certain kinds of perspectives and not others; nor do individuals pursue certain perspectives to the exclusion of others over long periods of time. Rather, what one might expect from pilgrims is transient commitment to particular perspectives in a sequential fashion with reversal of perspectives not only possible but commonplace.

This brief discussion of different perspectives applicable to pilgrimage experience on a cross-cultural basis would be misleading, however, without one important caveat. When the pilgrim reflects on his Pilgrimage he does not divide it into component parts. For him it is all of a piece. The schoolmaster referred to above was moved by the entire experience. The witnessing of a thousand buses proceeding to the Holy Ka'bah, the hospitality received from friends in Medina, and the books received for the village school merged with the beatific rites of the 'Umra as parts of the splendor of the Pilgrimage whose ultimate meaning was religious.

In considering how villagers incorporate the fact and significance of the Pilgrimage into their own lives the diachronic dimension must not be overlooked. Both the village community and the world around it have been changing and that change has been reflected in the frequency of Pilgrimage and the breadth of its social structural scope. In 1959 when I first undertook fieldwork in Kufr al-Ma I recorded nineteen adult men who had made the Hajj and bore the title and five women who had done likewise. The average age of the men was sixty-five, although two were in their forties. To my knowledge, none had made the 'Umra as a separate Pilgrimage. Today (1986) hardly a week goes by during the three-month pilgrim season when someone from the village is not going or returning from the Little Pilgrimage, and many men and women have made the Hajj and the 'Umra a number of times. Today many young men have made the Pilgrimage, and perhaps because so many men have made it, they are not always addressed as "hajj" in public by those who know them.

In part this intensification of Pilgrimage in both numbers and social scope is a result of the ongoing process of Islamization by which the religious institution stabilizes and expands.[14] However, Islamization has been given impetus by two other factors. First, the rise in annual income, with many villagers working in Arabia after the 1973 oil-price boom, has allowed many villagers to realize their religious goals for the first time. Second, the central government has encouraged the Hajj by co-opting local preachers as "pilgrim guides" who help to organize the Pilgrimage in their home communities and then accompany pilgrims during the rites in Mecca. As indicated in chapter 3, Shaykh Luqman was one of those co-

14. See chapter 9 for a more detailed discussion of the process of Islamization.

opted, and he has led groups of pilgrims to Mecca for twelve consecutive years with the exception of one year (1974). Furthermore, as part of what one might call "administrative religion" the army itself leads pilgrims to Mecca. Several of the younger villagers who had enlisted in the army performed the Pilgrimage under these auspices.

Related to the change in frequency and scope of Pilgrimage is a change in its ethos. In 1960, young men were not encouraged to make the Pilgrimage. There was an implicit assumption that the status of hajj required traditional headdress, sober demeanor, a sense of community responsibility—entering into the guest house as an elder who took it upon himself to mediate among kinsmen and estranged co-villagers—and increased piety. Any man, identity unknown, with graying temples, traditional headdress and sober demeanor is, still today, addressed as hajj in the marketplace in town. In 1960 it was thought that the normative constraints demanded by the status of hajj would be too much for young men to observe. Today, however, young men, particularly educated young men, those attending junior colleges and universities as well as teenagers attending Quran school in the village, are encouraged to make the Hajj or the 'Umra, and many do so. Indeed, one might argue that today it is the young men, those below the age of forty, who are most active in asserting their religious identity.

The traditional reluctance to encourage the young to perform the rites of Pilgrimage is related to the view that the Pilgrimage is inextricably tied to ethical action before its undertaking, during its performance, and after its completion. The sermons cited in this chapter point out that performing the Pilgrimage is conditional upon several ethical considerations: not bringing hardship on one's family, making it with lawful wealth (and not usury, theft, or usurped marriage payment), and not making it at the expense of depriving one's neighbor, the poor, or one's fellow Muslims. A Tradition of the Prophet recounted by the preacher in 1960 dramatized the conditional ethical nature of Pilgrimage.

There was once a Muslim who gave alms every day to his poor neighbor. When the Pilgrimage season approached he stopped giving alms and began saving for the Pilgrimage. The poor man spent three days with his wife and family without food. On the morning of the fourth day he left the house early and after walking a short distance came upon a dead lamb abandoned along the roadside. He slung it on his shoulder and returned with it to his house where he told his wife to prepare it for the children. The wife of the rich neighbor smelled the odor of cooking and savored of the meat. She went next door with a cooking pan in her hand and asked to sample the dish. The poor man's wife turned towards her and said "Oh my neighbor, this food is permitted for us but prohibited for you." [Carrion is forbidden food for Muslims except in case of dire necessity]. The rich man's wife returned in anger to her house and informed her husband of what had happened. Her husband went to the house of his neighbor and reproved him for his wife's behavior. The poor man replied, "Oh my neighbor, this food is not permitted for you. We have spent the last three days in hunger, and on the fourth I came upon a dead lamb and brought it home for consumption." When he heard this the rich man took his neighbor to his house, fed him, and after the meal, gave him the purse full of money which he had saved for the Pilgrimage. That year those Pilgrims absorbed in their devotions witnessed two angels descend on 'Arafāt and overheard the one ask the other, "How many have made the Pilgrimage this year?" The other replied, "Six thousand." "And of those who made it, for how many has it been accepted [by God?]". The other replied, "All of them by virtue of the man who could not make it."

Behavior on the Pilgrimage must also be ethical. The sermons condemn Muslims who stint on the expenditure of alms during Pilgrimage or who perform obscene acts or use obscene speech. Furthermore, the sermons stress the Quran's extirpation of the abomination of infanticide and factionalism and Muhammad's ethical behavior in practicing forgiveness and magnanimity toward defeated enemies as well as patience and compassion toward fellow Muslims.

After Pilgrimage the hajj is obliged to lead a moral life as befitting his new purified state. He now has a title he must live up to in his home community. He must take his place as a respected elder in the guest houses of the village, set the moral tone for reconciliation, pay all his debts promptly, and apologize to those he has angered without due cause.

The fact that many Pilgrims do not live up to ethical norms established for them by their religion is not surprising, and is, in fact, commented on both by the residents of their home communities and by satirical literature. Mary Hegland reported (1986) that an oppressive landlord never known for his piety in a village in southwestern Iran, a landlord who had allied with the shah's regime (and was, among other things, a large opium dealer), fell out of favor after the 1979 revolution. In order to reinstate himself in the good graces of both the city's new administrative hierarchy and the residents of his own village, he abruptly decided to make the Pilgrimage. The village custom was that all the residents of the village went out to welcome the returned hajj on the road outside the village and accompanied him in a festive manner into the village. The villagers not only did not greet the landlord in the accustomed manner, they did not allow him into the village, and he was forced to sneak back in after midnight as befitting his status as village hypocrite.

Sadeq Hedayat in *Haji Agha* (1979) satirizes the hypocrisy of an Iranian wheeler-dealer whose behavior made a mockery of his title. His own father had made the Hajj on ill-begotten income and he himself had never made the Hajj, though bearing the title. He drank, gambled, pledged alms payment without fulfilling the pledge, pretended to fast, and illegally retained the marriage payments due to his wives. These tales, fictional or ethnographic, of religious hypocrites who are also hajjis only reinforce the Islamic paradigm of Hajj as highly ethical and inextricable from its ritual and soteriological components.

Shaykh Luqman, who focused on the importance of Pilgrimage in his sermons and who had led Pilgrims to Mecca was not unfamiliar with religious hypocrisy and dealt with it in a telling manner. In a 1960 sermon the shaykh had condemned a villager (unnamed) who had persisted in repeating the Hajj when his economic status was weak and his family suffered deprivation as a result. In 1986, on my most recent visit as we were discussing the Hajj and ʿUmra, I mentioned that, in Iran, a Shiʾa Muslim received a separate title after a visit to each of the shrines at Meshed and Kerbala, as well as a title after making the Hajj. Luqman replied, "The worth of a person is found in two things: good deeds and fearing God (piety). Having made the Pilgrimage or not having made the Pilgrimage—that is all beside the point. If a man makes the Pilgrimage and does bad things, what is the benefit?" I asked, "But doesn't the Pilgrimage lead to the forgiveness of sins?" He smiled wryly and replied, "The Hajj lessens the sins of a person, but some pilgrims go on the Hajj and come back the same or worse!"

THE HAJJ

We have already explored the richness and multivocality of the organizing metaphor of rahm in chapter 4 where the alternate separation and fusing of physiologial, social, ethical, and theological meanings was demonstrated in a rhetorical form. The key rituals of a religion, the pillars of the faith, are also open to symbolic interpretation and to multivocality despite their doctrinal definition. This fact may be due to their very centrality, their complexity, and the intensity with which they are focused on by a multitude of worshipers who are called on to perform them. We shall now explore the multivocality of the Hajj in the work of one lay Muslim scholar, Ali Shariati. In order to understand the symbolic significance of his interpretation, it will first be necessary to recount in a capsule fashion the rites of Pilgrimage as they take place in Mecca and its environs during the first thirteen days of the holy month of Pilgrimage, Dhu'l-Hijja.

The Hajj comprises the rituals of consecration (ihram), vigil (*wuqūf*), lapidation, circumambulation (tawaf), running (saʿy), and sacrifice (adha). These rituals take place during the first thirteen days of the month of Dhu'l-Hijja. The Little Pilgrimage, or ʿUmra, comprising the rituals of consecration, circumambulation, and running, may be performed at any time of the year, but if it is to be performed in conjunction with the Hajj it must be performed during the Hajj season, the Muslim months of Shawwal, Dhu'l-Qaʿda, or Dhu'l-Hijja. Certain other acts such as the ritual haircut (*tahallul*), are not regarded as obligatory by all Muslim law schools as are the above-mentioned rituals, but they are nevertheless regarded as customary and observed by most pilgrims.[15] In the brief description that follows, it will be assumed that both the ʿUmrah and the Hajj are performed in a linked fashion with the former preceding the latter. Arrival circumambulation (*tawāf al-qudūm*) and running (saʿy) take place, respectively, inside and just outside the sacred enclosure (*haram*) in Mecca sometime before the ninth of the month of Dhu'l-Hijja; the standing (wuquf) takes place in the plain of Arafat about twelve miles east of Mecca on the ninth of the month. The "rushing" (*nafrah*) takes place from Arafat to Muzdalifah, a small town about four miles away (from Arafat) in the direction of Mecca after sunset on the ninth. The stoning of pillars takes place in Mina, about four miles west (from Muzdalifah) toward Mecca on the morning of the tenth, and it is there that the ritual takes place initiating the four-day festival of sacrifice (*ʿīd al-adha*). The ritual haircut also takes place there. The pilgrim then returns to Mecca to perform the "exuberant circumambulation" (tawaf al-ifada). On the eleventh and twelfth he returns once again to Mina to continue the stoning and finally on the thirteenth (or, if not then, just before he leaves Mecca) he returns to Mecca to perform the farewell Pilgrimage (*tawāf al-wadāʾ*). (See figure 6.1 for the relative location of the rituals.)

A number of other religious events, ceremonies, and rituals occur during the Pilgrimage. On the eighth of the month, the covering of the Ka'bah is removed and a ceremonial washing of the Sacred House occurs, officiated by the king of Saudi Arabia. Immediately after the arrival circumambulation, pilgrims usually perform devotions at the Abrahamic complex: saying a prayer of two rak'ahs at the standing place of Ibrahim (*maqām ibrahim*), drinking from the water of the Zemzem well, and praying at the *hijr*, an enclosed area next to the Ka'bah where the tombs of Hajar and Ismail are said to be located. During the course of the Pilgrimage, the Pilgrim is likely to drink from the water of Zemzem three times, following each of the three tawafs. He is also likely to hear four sermons, one on the seventh in the Sacred Mosque, two at Arafat, and one in the roofless mosque of Muzdalifah on the evening of the ninth.

15. See David E. Long, *The Hajj Today: A Survey of the Contemporary Pilgrimage to Mekkah* (State University of New York Press, Albany, 1979), 11.

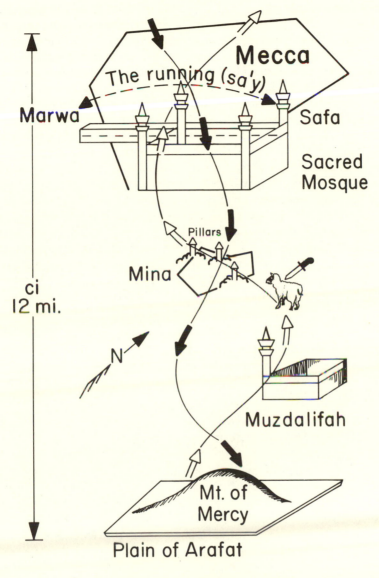

Mecca

The running (sa'y)

Marwa

Safa

Sacred
Mosque

ci
12 mi.

Pillars

Mina

N

Muzdalifah

Mt. of
Mercy

Plain of Arafat

Figure 6.1 Major Rituals of the Hajj

Although not part of the Hajj, the great majority of pilgrims go on to Medina after the thirteenth for a "visit" (ziyārah) to the Prophet's mosque. It is also customary to pray in the "Garden of Paradise" and to visit the Prophet's tomb, the tomb of the caliphs, Abu Bakr and 'Umar, and the tomb of Muhammad's daughter, Fatimah. Visits are also usually made to the Baqiyah cemetery where a number of Muhammad's early companions are buried, the mosque of the two qiblahs, and the battlefield of Uhud. The recommended stay in Medina is eight days in order to be present for forty prayers. Although the Islamic law schools do not agree on the obligatory nature of all the rituals, ceremonies, and events referred to above, most pilgrims attempt to perform all of them.[16]

Eligibility for the Hajj includes ethical prerequisites regarding debt, family support, and source of travel funds as well as physical (arrival at puberty) and mental (sound mind) qualifications.

The first ritual on arrival at one of the proper special stations on the outskirts of Mecca is that of consecration or ritual purification, ihram, whose six acts were described above. The special ritual prayer pronounced at the time of ihram, the talbiyiah, and repeated the most frequently during the course of the Hajj, is as follows:

> Here am I awaiting your command, O God, here am I!
> Thou has no peer (literally, associate), here am I!
> Yea, praise and grace are Thine, and Dominion!
> Thou has no peer, here am I![17]

The pronouncement of this ritual prayer over and over by over a million pilgrims on the ninth day of Dhu'l-Hijja is regarded by some as the climax of the Hajj,[18] and involves simultaneously devotion, beatific vision, and "crossing" as well as testifying to faith and the peculiar Islamic emphasis on the belief in the unity of God (tawhid).

A substantial part of Pilgrimage devotion focuses on the rite of sevenfold circumambulation (tawaf) of the Ka'bah. This ritual is performed three times during the Pilgrimage including its beginning and end. The first three circuits are made at a jog and the last four at a walking pace. The circumambulation is of the Ka'bah located in the center of the Sacred Mosque. It is toward the Ka'bah that Muslims, wherever they are, face when praying, and the prayer niche (mihrab) in each mosque, wherever it is, points toward Mecca. The Ka'bah itself is built of stone and is about fifty feet high, forty feet long, and thirty-three feet wide. Imbedded in its eastern corner is a black stone encased in a silver band. Following the

16. Ibid.
17. Ibid., 159.
18. See ibid., 8; and Ali Shariati, Hajj, R. Campbell, translator (Mizan Press, Berkeley, 1980), 72–108.

statement of intention made at the black stone to perform the tawaf, the pilgrim begins the circuit, always in a counterclockwise direction. Each successive circuit is begun by kissing or at least touching the black stone. During each circumambulation special prayers are said praising God, seeking his refuge, and asking his forgiveness and acceptance of the Hajj. In assessing the significance of these rituals it is important to remember the immense crowds that perform the tawaf and the following sa'y, the great press of people, and the fabulous diversity of languages and races that are literally brought together, cheek to jowl.[19]

The "running" (sa'y) consists of seven one-way trips between two small hills, al-Safa and al-Marwah, four hundred yards apart near the Sacred Enclosure. It repeats symbolically Hajar's (the biblical Hagar) frantic search for water for her child, Ismail, after having been abandoned in the desert by Ibrahim (the biblical Abraham) at God's command. Again, the Pilgrim must make a statement of intention (niyyah) to perform the ritual before initiating it. Ritual deconsecration (tahallul) is possible after sa'y for those who arrived early in the Pilgrimage season and wish to resume a consecrated state and perform the Hajj after the lapse of several days or weeks.

The Hajj proper begins with the wuquf, the standing (day) at Arafat, which lasts from noon through sunset. During this period two sermons, khutbahs, are delivered from the pulpit atop the Mountain of Mercy. It is important to note that during Muhammad's "Farewell Hajj" in the Muslim year 10 (A.D. 652), three months before his death, he delivered a sermon from atop this mountain and that the customary rituals of the Hajj are based upon the Traditions of the Prophet, hadith, relating in detail his last Pilgrimage observances. Pilgrims at Arafat and elsewhere, then, are following in the tracks of the Prophet, and their devotion and witness to their faith is matched by their reception of blessing through following the very steps of the founder on the pilgrim trail.

Following the "pouring forth" (ifadah) to Muzdalifah and the night of prayer and meditation, again, in the massed company of thousands of devotees, the Pilgrims arrive in Mina on the tenth to perform the stoning of the first three pillars (jamrahs). This stoning is the subject of rich symbolic interpretation focusing on the various temptations of Satan to Ismail and to man generally.[20] The stoning of the pillars represents man's struggle against temptation.

The tenth, eleventh, twelfth and thirteenth of Dhu al-Hijjah constitute the Feast of Sacrifice ('id al-adha) and are keyed to the slaughtering of an

19. See *The Autobiography of Malcolm X* (1964) for an instance of the religious impact of the Hajj and the vast gathering of diverse Muslims at Mecca, on a prominent Muslim from the United States.

20. For an instance, see Shariati, *Hajj*, 99ff.

unblemished sacrificial animal, again, a symbolic reference to the original Abrahamic sacrifice. But here, again, the ritual is a rich and varying source of religious symbolism. Pilgrims generally wish to slaughter an animal on the first day of the festival, though it is permissible on any of the four days. Unlike the other rituals of the 'Umrah and Hajj, the Feast of the Sacrifice is celebrated throughout the Muslim world by visiting, gift-giving, and special prayers.

The closing ceremonies of the Hajj are marked by three degrees of deconsecration: the cessation of the special ritual prayer of the Hajj, talbiyah, after the stoning of the first pillar at Mina; the freedom from all ihram restrictions except sexual intercourse after the ritual haircut; and complete deconsecration after the cirumambulation of Exuberance in Mecca on the tenth day of Dhu al-Hijjah. This deconsecration process again highlights the significance of pilgrimage as "crossing" into and out of sacred space and time.

ISLAM AS AN INTERPRETED RELIGION: ALI SHARIATI AND THE HAJJ

The Hajj is by far the most elaborate ritual prescribed for all Muslims in terms of number of separate and differing acts required, movement over space, and expenditure of time, energy, and material resources. Western descriptions of the Hajj have tended to focus either on its ritualistic and legalistic aspects, its social structural implications, or, more recently, the administrative problems it raises for Saudi Arabia.[21] That it is a rich source of symbolism and ethics is largely overlooked.

The following section explores the symbolic and ethical implications of the Pilgrimage in the work of one educated lay Muslim, Ali Shariati. Shariati's interpretation of the Hajj is by no means representative of interpretations of Muslim religious scholars at large.[22] Shariati is an Ithna 'Ashari Shi'a Muslim. Though exposed to traditional Islamic learning, he is not a product of a law college (*madrasa*), as, for instance, Muhammad 'Abduh or Ayyatollah Khomeini. Furthermore, he continued his higher education in Paris at the Sorbonne where he read Gide, Kafka, Marx, and Wilde, among others. There is no question of his being a "mainline" represen-

21. See, for instance, the article on the *Hajj* in *The Encyclopedia of Islam*, for the ritualistic-legalistic emphasis, Hurgronje's *Mekka in the Latter Part of the 19th Century* for the social structural emphasis, and Long's *The Hajj Today* for the administrative emphasis.

22. The work explored here is Shariati's *Hajj*, translated by Ali Behzadnia and Najla Denny, 1980. Other translated works of Shariati include *On the Sociology of Islam* (1979) and *Marxism and Other Western Fallacies* (1980). For another, perhaps more mainline interpretation of Hajj by a well-known twentieth-century Muslim fundamentalist see chapters 24–27 of Sayyid Abu A'la Mawdudi's *Let Us Be Muslims*.

tative of Islam. But, on the other hand, his status as a thinking and true Muslim and a scholar is evident for those who read his works. The significance of his interpretation of the Hajj is its appreciation of the "multivocality" of Hajj rituals, its implications for the conduct of Muslims, its relation to fundamental Muslim beliefs, and its relevance for the modern world.[23]

Shariati's sensitivity to the many meanings imbedded in key words and rituals is reflected in his treatment of ihram. Ihram is the pilgrim's seamless dress. It is also the state of consecration which the pilgrim assumes from the time he dons that dress. It also stands for reversal—physiological, social structural, psychological, and symbolic. Shariati describes the consecrated state symbolized by the seamless garb:

> Do not give orders to anyone. Therefore, exercise a sense of brotherhood! Do not harm animals or insects. Therefore, for a few days live as Jesus! . . . Do not indulge in lovemaking and intercourse, therefore, be inspired by real love! . . . Do not use makeup. Therefore, see yourself as you are! . . . Do not sew your Ihram. Therefore, evade self-distinction! . . . Do not stay in the shade. Therefore, be exposed to the sun. Do not cover your head (males). Do not cover your face (females). (Shariati 1980 17–18)

Moreover, the seamless pilgrim dress is also, Shariati notes, the *kafan* or shroud for the dead, accentuating the liminal implications of pilgrimage.

The Abrahamic complex in the sacred enclosure in Mecca is a rich source of symbolism of the Hajj. Pilgrims stop at the standing place of Ibraham after circumambulation and pray there. Ibrahim's footprint is believed to be imbedded in a large stone where he stood with his son, Ismail, raising the foundation of the Ka'bah at God's command. At Ibrahim's position the pilgrim "shakes hands with" God, that is, touches the black stone (Shariati, 37). The "running" of Hajar, Ibrahim's concubine, back and forth from Safa to Marwah is part of this complex. The semicircular short wall which faces the Ka'bah on its western side is called Ismail's *hujr*. "Hujr" denotes enclosure, lap, or skirt—the semicircular wall resembles a skirt. The hajj must touch this wall when circumambulating the Ka'bah. Hajar's grave is said to be near the third column of the Ka'bah. In the Quran and the Traditions of the Prophet Ibrahim is the great rebel who established monotheism in its purest form. Ibrahim's absolute devotion to God and his belief in tawhid, the unity of God, is attested to by his absolute submission to God in his demand for the sacrifice

---

23. "Multivocality" is a term coined by Victor Turner to emphasize the fact that particular symbols, especially when they are key symbols in a ritual or a culture, have not one but many meanings. See Turner, *Chihamba the White Spirit: A Ritual Drama of the Ndembu* (1962) and *The Forest of Symbols* (1967).

of Ismail, Ibrahim's son. For Shariati, tawhid symbolizes collective unity and the perfect society, one in which each individual "has turned away from himself to face Allah [God]" (Shariati 1980, 11). The three pillars to be stoned at Mina represent the temptations Satan cast in front of Ibrahim and Ismail to divert them from God's injunctions. Since it was at Mina that they were tempted, it is there that the symbolic struggle against temptation must take place. In the first instance, these pillars are three faces of oppression: the oppression of wealth, symbolized by Croesus; the oppression of hypocrisy, symbolized by Balam; and the oppression of power symbolized by Pharaoh. All three are summed up under the master symbol of oppression, their progenitor Cain (Shariati 1980, 101ff.). For Shariati the stoning of the pillars at Mina symbolizes man's struggle in this world (*jihād*) against oppression.[24] But the stoning at Mina also has a wider meaning for Shariati, a meaning for the modern age. The idolatry of today, the "new polytheism" as he calls it, the devotion to other than God takes on many new forms:

> At times it is exhibitionism, nationalism and racism while at other times it is nazi-facism, bourgeoisism and militarism. It may be . . . love for ideas (idealism), love for matter (materialism), love for art and beauty (romanticism), love for nothing (existentialism), love for land and blood (racism), love for heroes and central government (fascism), love for individuals (individualism), love for all (socialism) . . . love for wisdom (philosophy) . . . love for heaven (spiritualism), . . . love for history (fatalism), love for God's will (determinism), love for sex (Freudianism). . . . (Shariati, 142)

For Shariati, tawhid and sacrifice is giving up whatever is most beloved: "Who is your Ismail or what is it?—Your position? Your honor? Profession? Money? House? Farm? Car? Love? Family? Knowledge? . . ." (Shariati, 84).

As important as Ibrahim, Ismail, the sacrifice, and the stoning of pillars are for Shariati, the symbolism of Hajar and the "running" (sa'y) are equally if not more important. Shariati declares that Hajj is "a decision for eternal movement in a certain direction" (Shariati, 39); he notes that the trilateral root of Hajar's name, *h-j-r* signifies "migration"—from unbelief (*kufr*) to submission to God (*islām*). In "running" between Safa and Marwah, all pilgrims must play the role of Hajar. Shariati observes that Hajar was a woman not honored enough to be a wife—she was Ibrahim's concubine—though she was a mother of prophets. She was a slave; she was black and yet she is the only person buried inside the Sacred En-

---

24. It is not accidental that the Iranian revolutionary organization which calls itself the *mujāhidūn*, or "strugglers in the way of God," comprises many followers of Shariati.

closure at Mecca. In circumambulating God's House, the Ka'bah, one must circumambulate her grave. "Why," he asks? She was a mother and a model of submission, but she did not sit idly, crying helplessly, bewailing her abandonment. She was a responsible woman, "constantly searching, moving, and struggling, she decided to rely on her self, her feet, her will and her mind" in search for water (Shariati, 40). Sa'y is "not metaphysical, not love, not submission, not obedience, not soul, not a philosophical view of life, not in heaven. . . . No, no, no. . . . In this world and it is drinking water! . . . It is the way of finding heaven in this world and enjoying its fruit in this earth. Sa'y is physical work . . . running after water and bread in order to satisfy your thirst and feed your children" (Shariati, 41).

For Shariati, the meaning of sa'y is activism. The Muslim must live to the full in the world, and struggle in that world for his material life, his bread and his water, and against oppression in all its forms—economic, political, and ideological.

But sa'y, "endeavor," is linked to tawaf, circumambulation. This link is first of all positional and spatial since, Shariati notes, sa'y is only a few steps and a few moments removed from tawaf in the ritual cycle. They are linked but contrasting. Tawaf is:

> Love, worship, spirit, morality, beauty, goodness, holiness, values, truth, faith, righteousness, suffering, sacrifice, devotion, humility, slavery, perception, enlightenment, submission, Allah's might and will, metaphysics, the unseen, for others, for the hereafter, and for Allah [God]! And whatever the easterner's spirit is motivated by and in love with. (Shariati, 42)

Sa'y is:

> Wisdom, logic, needs, living, facts, objectives, earth, material, nature, privileges, thinking, science, industry, policy, benefit, joy, economy, civilization, body, freedom, will-power, mastery, in this world—for the self. And whatever the westerners struggle for. (Shariati, 42)

Sa'y is "searching for water"; tawaf is "searching for thirst [meaning]" (Shariati, 42). Shariati notes that all Hajar's efforts were useless. After her frantic and fruitless search for water, she returned to find, to her astonishment, the Zemzem well—that God had provided. The lesson drawn from "running" and its succeeding event, the appearance of Zemzem, is that although man must strive, God alone grants.

On the other hand, Shariati points out that Husayn, Muhammad's grandson and the Third Imam of Ithna 'Ashari Shi'a Muslims, broke off his Pilgrimage in Mecca (i.e., his tawaf to go to Qerbala). That is, in the presence of oppression, performance of worship does not receive priority. Tawaf and sa'y are of equal importance, but the former must be subordinated momentarily when human beings suffer from tyranny in any of its forms. Therefore, for Shariati, "Hajj is the COMBINATION of tawaf and sa'y." It symbolizes living "not for the sake of living but for the sake of Allah [God]" and "trying your best not just for yourself but for people" (Shariati, 44). This message of spiritually informed activism is certainly pertinent to Muslims concerned with economic development, social welfare, and cultural identity in the modern world.

The other linked symbol of Pilgrimage, tawaf, has two foci of meaning. The first, quoted above, is its spiritual significance. The circumambulation is around the Ka'bah, God's house. God is the center of existence, and man is a "moving particle around that center" (Shariati, 27). The Ka'bah, literally, the "Cube," is nondirectional, encompassing all directions. Shariati quotes the Quran here: "**Unto Allah belongs the east and west, and whether-so-ever you be will be facing Allah**" (2: 115, Shariati, 23).

The Ka'bah "symbolizes the constancy and eternity of God" (Shariati, 27). Man's touching the black stone in the course of each circumambulation symbolizes his taking the right hand of God—making a commitment to tawhid, the cancelling of previous allegiances that conflict with loyalty to God.

But tawaf has another meaning which Shariati underlines early in his book: "Although you are here to see God, you find yourself busy with people" (Shariati, 31). Not only busy with people—pressed on all sides by people during every circumambulation. To approach God "you must first approach people!" (Shariati, 27). The Ka'bah is known not only as God's house but also as the "house of people" (*bayt al-nāss*). In the course of circumambulation it is impossible for the individual worshiper to stop, enter the Ka'bah singly, or engage in individual worship. One must continue circumambulating, "shoulder to shoulder with the people" (Shariati, 31). This was the first house of the people in history. How does one "approach people?" One approaches people by "becom(ing) involved in the problems of people, not as a monk who isolates himself in a monastery but by becoming actively involved . . . practicing generosity, devotion and self-denial, suffering in captivity and exile, enduring torture. . . ." (Shariati, 28).

Both circumambulation and the Ka'bah are symbols of an ethos that one might label "democratic theism." God's will and God's work can only be done by and with the people. It is at Mina, Shariati reminds us, on the eleventh and twelfth of the month after the dramatic ritual events of the Hajj are over and the pilgrim has earned the title *hajj*, and entered the deconsecrated state, that Muslims must camp in one place for two whole days. What do they do during these two days—the ritual stonings take only a brief time. This is the time when the people get together as people, fellow-Muslims, and talk about their mutual affairs and their mutual problems. These are "people's seminars"—not university seminars or government fact-finding commissions.

A number of Shariati's interpretations of Hajj symbolism have distinct political implications that should now be brought out more fully. As mentioned above, Shariati declares that Husayn, the Prophet's grandson, cut off his Pilgrimage in order to fight the oppressive ruler, Mu'awiyah. He declared that those Muslims who remained circumambulating the Ka'bah while Husayn went to his martyrdom at Qerbala "were in fact circumambulating around the green palace of Muawiyah" (Shariati, 152). They were, in fact, idolators supporting political oppression. In discussing Ibrahim's sacrifice of Ismail, Shariati says:

> Put the knife to his throat with your hands. Save the throat of the people from being cut—the people are always sacrificed at the doors of palaces of power and temples of torture. Put the blade at your son's throat so that you may take the blade from the executioner's hand! (Shariati, 150)

This is a clear call to Muslims for martyrdom against political oppressors, a call for political action in its most extreme form—violence and the surrender of one's own life. Shariati is also forthright in condemning religious rationalizations for the passivity of Muslims in the face of political oppression. Those who say, "the hell with the world, let's work for the paradise of the hereafter" in fact "turn their backs to the Ka'ba. . . . Feeling happy with the joy of the life after death they are sound asleep on the warm ashes of the master's kitchen floor and enjoy the leftover of the plunderer's table!" (Shariati, 154).

The revolutionary implications of Shariati's interpretation of the Hajj is not least of all for the established religious leaders of Islam, the 'ulema. He includes the 'ulema among the oppressors of the people under the symbol of Balam, hypocrisy, and enjoins Muslims to read the Quran themselves and not to allow others to interpret it for them: "Since some of Cain's descendants are commentators for the Quran, you should read the text yourself and comprehend what it says because it is the only document which has been saved from their embezzlement" (Shariati, 134).

Finally, what is perhaps most interesting about Shariati's view of the Hajj is his notion that it is unfinished business. He notes that the Hajj is full of pauses (e.g., beginning with the miqats, stations, and consecration and ending with the stops at Arafat, Muzdalifah, and Mina) to pursue comprehension followed by hurried leave-takings. The Hajj is not a journey completed with the end of the ceremonies. The Muslim has the duty of going on into the world and "making the earth a sacred mosque" (Shariati, 150). After visiting God's mosque in the Sacred Enclosure at Mecca this duty is magnified since the forces of evil represented by the sneaky whisperer (*waswās khannās*) continually threaten the conscience of the responsible individual (Shariati, 143).

The Hajj is unfinished business in another sense. Its meaning is open. The symbols of the Hajj—the three pillars at Mina—are not completely obvious:

> Everytime I went to the Hajj, I tried to correct some of my previous undertakings, that is, to complete my interpretations, but I discovered new codes and considerations. During my last Hajj, I asked myself, "Why should I specify something which not even the stage-manager has specified. Had it been necessary to identify each idol, the stage manager would have done it. (Shariati, 105)

For Shariati, God has left the full meaning of the Hajj open for Muslims to discover.

Religion and Politics:
"Parties" (*Aḥzāb*), Processes,
and the Complicated Relationship between
"People's Religion" and "Government Religion"

Unless one appreciates the inextricable religious quality of polity, history, and society for believing Muslims, one not only misses but also misconstrues the significance of events in the Muslim world at the end of the twentieth century. From a Muslim perspective the good life is the next life, and life in this world, though not devalued since it is part of God's creation, is preparatory for the next. The community exists to bear witness to God in the darkness of this world, darkness compared to the light of the next.[1] Every mundane act of the community, therefore, as W. Cantwell Smith has expressed it, has meanings-consequences for this world (right conduct) and the next (salvation).[2] This dual set of meanings and consequences permeated many of the institutions of the medieval Muslim world including guilds, lodges, sanctuaries, and fairs. It still permeates the Jordanian peasant's and postpeasant's view of government and king.[3] In order to appreciate the religious quality of polity and social structure for many Muslims it is useful, by way of contrast, to outline briefly the opposite assumptions made by many Americans about the relationship between religion and government in the United States.

The first amendment of the U.S. Constitution states that "Congress shall make no law respecting an establishment of religion, or prohibiting the free exercise thereof. . . ." This doctrine of the separation of church and state, as it has come to be known, received one of its most recent affirmations and interpretations by the Supreme Court of the United States in 1971. The court declared that a law is unconstitutional if (1) its primary purpose is to promote religions, (2) its effects are to advance

1. The symbols of contrasting darkness and light are a central focus in the Quran's Surat al-Nur (chapter on light).

2. See Wilfred Cantwell Smith, *Islam in Modern History* (Princeton University Press, Princeton, 1957).

3. This perspective permeates Islamic militancy among Shi'a Muslims in the 1980s, as Robin Wright in her important book, *Sacred Rage* (1986), has documented. In her study Wright explores the political and international implications of this religious perspective for Islamic militancy among Shi'a Muslims in the states of Lebanon, Bahrain, Kuwait, Saudi Arabia, Israel, and Iran. Specifically, she notes the omnipresent theme of martyrdom among militants of all groups.

religion, or (3) it entangles government excessively in religious affairs.[4] Furthermore, the court ruled that taxes cannot be used to support religious institutions. Government aid to parochial schools and sectarian colleges has also been struck down. Such rulings do not surprise social scientists who have long argued that secularization is an ongoing and continuing process characteristic of the modern world.[5]

As recently as September 1984, Governor Mario Cuomo of New York in a major address at the University of Notre Dame argued that in a pluralistic society all religious-based values do not have an a priori place in public morality. He added, referring to American Roman Catholics, "While we always owe our bishop's words respectful attention and careful consideration, the question whether to engage the political system in a struggle to have it adopt certain articles of our belief as a part of public morality is not a matter of doctrine; it is a matter of prudential judgement."[6] The year before, after President Reagan had addressed the National Convention of Evangelicals, asking them to support the policy of nuclear arms superiority over the Soviet Union, Baptist preachers in one upstate New York city voiced reservations about the president's soliciting support from clergy, by direct implication from their pulpits, for his policies. One preacher said, "My pulpit is a sacred place for God's word. I will not use it for politics." Another stated, "I am not a political expert. I can and do preach from the Scriptures. That is what I am trained to do." A third stated, "politics does not belong in the pulpit," and he proceeded to say that he did not like to discuss political issues publically. These statements and those of the governor seem quite in line with the long-standing separation doctrine.

A substantial part of the American clergy, identified broadly with the "Moral Majority,"[7] has rejected these views. They have preached in the pulpit, particularly in the election year of 1984, for and against particular

---

4. As reported by *New York Times* reporter Lindsey Gruson, spring 1984.

5. See, for instance, Donald Eugene Smith, *Religion and Political Development* (Little, Brown, Boston, 1970).

6. *New York Times*, September 13, 1984.

7. The term *Moral Majority* has a narrow and a broad reference. The narrow reference is to the group identified as followers of the Reverend Jerry Falwell. The broad reference is to all those adherents of American religious denominations, including Jews as well as Christians, who support conservative positions on public issues and who tend to be fundamentalists in their interpretation of Scriptures (i.e., who tend toward a literal interpretation of Scripture). Fundamentalists also tend to view the world, nations, men, and issues in terms of moral dichotomies, good and evil. The broad reference also includes conservative laypersons who are mobilizing support for or against particular items of legislation in Congress with no necessary affiliation to particular denominations. The use of the term in this chapter refers to the broad conservative religiously inspired politically activist movement rather than the specific organization led by Falwell.

legislation and for and against particular candidates for political office. They have opposed the ERA (equal rights amendment) and vociferously supported a constitutional amendment to ban abortion, legislation for tuition, tax credits for religious and private schools (despite the above-mentioned Supreme Court decision), and the transfer of jurisdiction over school prayer from federal to state courts. One of their leaders, the television evangelist, M. G. Pat Robertson, addressing the Republican National Committee on August 17, 1984, stated, "It's time for God's people to come out of the closet, out of the churches and change America."[8] Another conservative religious leader and theologian, John Newhaus, stated, "When religion is banned from public life the public square is left naked to a takeover by the State."[9] It is clear that the clergy of the Moral Majority aims to sacralize society—to unsecularize it—and their followers have demonstrated every intention of implementing that goal, using a variety of techniques: setting up political action committees, monitoring voting records of congressmen, producing millions of "report cards" for distribution, registering voters, urging followers to boycott TV programs featuring sex and violence, working for state legislation that requires employers to give workers their Sabbath Day off if they request it,[10] and lobbying for legislation to recognize student groups meeting in public schools after hours for religious purposes.

Fundamentalist conservatives deny that their positions and tactics violate the doctrine of separation of church and state and deny that their aim is to expand the arena of religion to encompass education, law, the economy, and the polity. Rather, they argue that it is government that has intruded itself into the legitimate (traditional) religious arena and that the solution is to get them out of it.[11] Nevertheless, historically the effect of their preaching and public activity is to increase the scope of religious activity and, seemingly, to reverse the process of secularization that both U.S. social scientists and U.S. politicians have assumed to be one of the hallmarks of modernity.

The debate about the role of religion in society in the United States at the end of the twentieth century and its focus on the separation of church and state and on the issue of the danger of overlapping arenas, dramatizes and clarifies, by way of contrast, the entirely different set of suppositions Muslims hold about the relation of religion and politics in Islam. This set

8. *New York Times*, August 18, 1984.

9. *New York Times*, September 8, 1984.

10. See *The Evening Press*, Binghamton, New York, November 8, 1984.

11. This view was enunciated by Edward McAteer, former director of the Conservative Caucus and founder of Religious Roundtable, as reported by Don Campbell in *The Evening Press*, Binghamton, New York, March 25, 1981. McAteer said: "The problem is that government got into religion, and we've got to get it out."

of suppositions arises out of the circumstances of Islam's history and the content of its Scriptures. As chapter 3 indicated, Muhammad was both prophet and statesman, and as the first Muslim preacher he enunciated public policy as well as the call for salvation in the Friday congregational sermon delivered in the mosque. Moreover, beginning with his emigration to Medina in A.D. 622, attendance at the Friday sermon was a political as well as a religious act since it marked adherence to the newly formed umma or Muslim community. Evidence for this interpretation is the fact that attendance in one place, one particular mosque, was regarded as obligatory for all free adult believing men (but not women or children), that is, for all free men bearing arms, the protectors of the community par excellence.[12] Moreover, Muhammad's political successors, the caliphs, and their deputies, the governors of provinces, made political pronouncements in the mosque on the occasion of the Friday congregational worship, and while doing so they often leaned on a bow, sword, or staff, the symbol of their political authority.[13]

Frequently, the name of the ruler was mentioned in the Friday sermon during the invocation of the blessings, conferring legitimacy on his reign. In later historical periods as mosques began to proliferate they became differentiated: the official mosques in which the Friday congregational prayer was expected to be performed, often called *jawāmiʿ*, became separate in political function and significance from the smaller private and popular mosques often called *masājid*. Indeed, some Muslim jurists regarded performance of the Friday congregational prayer as appropriate only in provincial capitals or only in one main mosque in each town.[14] Moreover, Muslim jurists, preachers, and teachers were co-opted into the state bureaucracy as judges, law college professors, jurisconsults, and government ministers during many Muslim dynasties. The instance of Ibn al-Jawzi discussed in chapter 3 is one example.

12. See S. D. Gotein, "The Origin and Nature of the Muslim Friday Worship," in *Studies in Islamic History and Institutions* (E. J. Brill, Leiden, 1968) for a development of this argument.

13. Grabar argues that the mutual implication of religious and political authority was clearly demonstrated immediately after Muhammad's death. Since Muhammad, during his lifetime, had appointed Abu Bakr as imam of the mosque in his own absence, Muslims inferred in the *shūra* (consultation of notables) following Muhammad's death that Abu Bakr should become their political leader since he had already been chosen as their prayer leader. Since prayer (i.e., salvation) ranked ahead of political leadership (i.e., of worldly affairs), the selection of the political leader should be modeled on the selection of the prayer leader. See Grabar, "Architecture of the Middle Eastern City," in *Middle Eastern Cities*, Ira M. Lapidus, editor (University of California Press, Berkeley, 1969).

14. See Grabar 1969; Gotein 1968; and Abner Cohen, *Custom and Politics in Urban Africa* (University of California Press, Berkeley, 1969), particularly chapters 4 and 6 for variations on this argument.

The significance of the facts outlined above is that the separation of religion and politics or religion and government has no traditional place in Muslim society and still has no place as recent events at the end of the twentieth century are making all too clear.[15] Muslim societies in all of their social structural and cultural variety are, as D. Eugene Smith has pointed out, "organic" societies.[16] Organic societies are characterized by organic religious systems. That is, in these societies the primary collective expression of religion is found in "societal" as opposed to "religious" structures. Organic religious systems have, according to Smith, three defining attributes: an "integralist" religious ideology, internal societal mechanisms of religious control, and a dominant political authority.[17] An integralist religious ideology fuses religion and government at many points: the king is guardian of the cosmic order (as well as the kingdom); religious functionaries legitimate the king's authority; law is the expression of the divine command; and education is the transmission of divine teaching. Internal societal mechanisms of religious control are the product of small-group sanctions and custom.

In the Muslim Ottoman imperial case, for instance, monitoring of violations of socioreligious obligations such as fasting the month of Ramadan or giving the required alms-tax or *zakāt* was the job of every small-size local unit—urban quarter, village, or nomadic camp—and not the job of the government or private formal associations. The dominance of political authority over religious affairs in the Ottoman Empire was reflected in the sultan's responsibility for the preservation of the sacral order in such a way that the various estates (men of knowledge, warriors,

15. A historian of the modern Middle East, Helen Rivlin, has reminded me (June 1986) that the institution of the religious endowments (*awqāf*) were, in fact, quite separate and independent from the State in many Muslim polities, for example, in Egypt where Muhammad Ali only brought them under the control of the State in the first third of the nineteenth century and in Iran where the shah only brought them under state control in the 1960s (perhaps at the cost of a revolution). Moreover, Hamilton Gibb has stressed that large areas of human behavior in Muslim polities were gradually removed from the jurisdiction of Muslim courts (e.g., criminal law, commerce) and dealt with by civil courts, rulers' courts, or the police (Hamilton Gibb, Lectures on Islamic Institutions, Harvard University, autumn 1957). Nevertheless, normatively, this separation and autonomy was never—and still is not—recognized as legitimate by many devout Muslims as attested to by the demands for the restoration of the Shari'a by many militant Muslim movements at the end of the twentieth century. Moreover, historically, as Gibb and Bowen's *Islamic Society and the West* points out, by the nineteenth century the Ottoman Empire in its core areas had become a classic case of the bureaucratization of the religious institution in nearly all its aspects.

16. See D. E. Smith's *Religion and Political Development* (1970) for a comparative analysis of the development of "organic" and "church" societies. Smith briefly compares the historical cases of Latin American Christianity, Middle Eastern Islam, Theravada Bhuddism, and Hinduism.

17. Ibid. 60.

businessmen, and peasants) were held together in a complementary fashion.[18] The sultan's religious role as defender of the faith was reflected in the title he claimed, *khalīfat rasūl allah* ("Successor of the Messenger of God"—in his political role) or as it has been rendered in the West, caliph; in his organization of religious minorities into religious communities or millets to insure that they kept their place in Muslim society but also to insure that they had proper religious autonomy; in his capacity as defender of the Shari'ah or religious law; and in his appointment of religious judges (qadis) and a supreme jurisconsult or Grand Mufti. The fused or organic nature of Ottoman Muslim society was reflected by the fact that the Grand Mufti made final pronouncements on matters of interpretation involving taxes, war, marriage, divorce, and the introduction of tobacco, coffee houses, and printing presses—as well as the obligations of prayer, fasting, ritual ablutions, and pilgrimage.[19]

According to Smith, as secularization proceeds constitutional recognition is given to the fact that the political system does not derive its legitimacy from religion, and religious symbols are abandoned (e.g., the use of Arabic, the language of the Quran, the title of caliph, the traditional dress of the religious estate, and the form of religious law though perhaps not its substance, as in contemporary Egypt, where Muslim law is still applied but in civil courts and according to nonsharʿi procedures). As secularization proceeds, major areas of social life (education, law, and the economy) pass from religious regulation to the jurisdiction of the State. The final stage of secularization consists in the "transvaluation of political culture." Secular ideologies such as nationalism and socialism become dominant and, overall, nontranscendent temporal goals such as modernization replace the goal of salvation. Social structurally, secularization implies the separation of the political from ecclesiastical structures and religious ideologies and the expansion of the polity to perform regulative functions in the socioeconomic sphere.[20]

In the nineteenth and twentieth centuries in many Muslim countries, there is no doubt that the State, first under the control of colonial powers and subsequently under the control of nationalists of various persuasions and diverse social backgrounds (military, tribal, fundamentalist religious, modernizing, professional, or some combination thereof) expanded its regulative functions in many directions. In Jordan, for instance, when I initiated my research in the subdistrict of Al-Kura in what was an economic backwater of the country in 1959 the central government had al-

18. See H.A.R. Gibb and Harold Bowen, *Islamic Society and the West*, vol. 1, parts 1 and 2 (Oxford University Press, London, 1950 and 1957) for details. See also Norman Itzkowitz, *Ottoman Empire and Islamic Tradition* (Alfred A. Knopf, New York, 1972).

19. See Smith, *Religion and Political Development*, chapter 3 for further details.

20. Ibid. 11ff.

ready placed numerous representatives in the subdistrict center as chapter 2 indicated. They included judges of the civil and religious courts, a subdistrict officer, a forest ranger, an agricultural inspector, a land registry officer, a health officer, a tax agent, and the local police. This expansion of government functions at the subdistrict level was unprecedented in the modern era.

But such expansion of state power and influence has had unpredictable consequences for secularization. In Afghanistan at the end of the nineteenth century, for instance, the expansion of state power and centralized administration under Amir Abdur Rahman actually increased the power of the religious institution since part of that expansion was the spread of a regular Islamic court system throughout the country and the provision of a sound financial base for it through taxation.[21] Likewise, in Jordan today the expansion of state power from Amman includes the education, training, and confirmation of local preachers and their partial bureaucratization through emoluments from the Ministry of Religious Endowments. This process has been traced for its impact on Shaykh Luqman's career in chapter 3. The point of importance here is that no conception of a proper separation between religion and government exists, even in a modernizing Muslim state such as Jordan. Responsibility for the care of the main mosques and their staffing rests with the government as it did in the time of the rule of the early caliphs. Policies of afforestation, irrigation, and secular education move forward without any concomitant implication of the reduction of the scope of religion in society. The separation of church and state is irrelevant as an issue in Jordan not only because there is no "church," that is, a formal ecclesiastical organization, from which to separate but also because government and religion are perceived as mutually implied. What may be perceived as paradoxical from a Western perspective—Jordan's simultaneous development in the 1970s and 1980s of an economic boom and rapid modernization (occupational mobility, international migration, the spread of secular education at all levels, the quadrupling of incomes, the rapid expansion of consumer purchases [including TV's, automobiles, and trucks], a construction boom in village housing and urban real estate, agricultural modernization [use of tractors, fertilizers, and new modes of cropping and irrigation])—together with Islamic resurgence (proliferation of religious specialists, religious books, new mosques, and Quranic schools and religious fundamentalists seeking and gaining political office) is not at all surprising once the "organic" character of Jordan's religious system is appreciated. King Husayn, after all, is a descendant of the Prophet or *sharīf* as well as a king,

21. See Ashraf Ghani, "Islam and State-Building in a Tribal Society in Afghanistan: 1800–1901," *Modern Asian Studies*, 1978.

and all of his appointments including those of religious officials through the Ministry of Religious Endowments bear the seal of religious legitimacy as well as the legitimacy gained from effective prosecution of material modernization.

If the expansion of the State in the last two centuries has to be viewed within the context of Muslim society and culture to appreciate its significance, so much the more must the transvaluation of political culture, the last claimed stage in secularization, be viewed in that context. By "political culture" D. E. Smith refers to the beliefs, expressive symbols, and values which define the situation in which political action takes place. Smith himself realizes that the process of secularizing political culture is much more complex than that of polity separation (from religion) or polity expansion. The latter two processes can be initiated and implemented by modernizing elites and do not have to be referred to the people for approval (e.g., land reform, civil service reform, educational reform, abolition of polygyny, and the ban on intercaste marriage [in India]). But the transvaluation of cultures—the instilling of new attitudes reflecting new values and new identities such as cross-religious egalitarianism, humanism, materialism, skepticism, a positive stance toward innovation, an achievement ethic which channels rewards to high performers, and the sense of citizenship of a nation—can only work its way through the population gradually.[22] Smith, like other students and almost inevitably proponents of modernization and secularization, assumes that the process is one of gradually sloughing off the beliefs and symbols of an "organic society" on the one hand or "church" on the other and replacing them with a new set.[23] He and they have no doubt about the successful unfolding of the process, only about its length.

For organic religious systems, however, the problem of the transvaluation of political cultures is precisely that of the fusion of meanings-consequences such that the transcendental and the worldly are mutually implied in many roles, institutions, and symbols. To illustrate this problem I shall pursue the meaning-consequence of one symbol utilized by peasants, postpeasants, urbanites, tribesmen, religious scholars, and shopkeepers in Jordan, the symbol of *ḥizb* or "party."

Hizb is one of the "deeply flawed symbols" referred to by Hudson in his 1977 study:

The poignancy of the imperialist legacy for modern Arab politics is that the implanted values and instruments of social modernity were contaminated through the modalities of implantation. The new modes of thought, politics, production, and commerce were of

22. See Smith, *Religion and Political Development*, 113ff.
23. For an elaboration of the argument see ibid., chapter 4.

course disruptive in themselves, but because they were thrust upon a weaker, backward society in a manner that was inevitably brutal and manipulative, they became for generations of educated Arabs symbols of legitimacy yet, at the same time, deeply flawed symbols.[24]

Among the flawed institutions and symbols that emerged out of European colonialism in the Middle East one might include not only political parties but also parliaments, banks, and the liberal democratic tradition of minority rights; the latter is deeply flawed since the colonial powers discriminated in favor of religious and ethnic minorities by giving them special economic opportunities and preferred positions in the bureaucracy (e.g., the Copts in Egypt, the Maronites in Lebanon, the Assyrians in Iraq, the Jews in Morocco, and, today, the Druze in Israel).

The case of the symbol, *hizb*, is more complex, however, than the analysis of Hudson suggests since hizb was an important symbol in the Quran, long before its reintroduction during the era of European colonialism, and it was a deeply flawed symbol even then as the following analysis demonstrates.

HIZB (PARTY) IN THE QURAN

The Quran refers to the term *hizb* variously translated as "party," "partisan," or "sect" in many different verses in both the Meccan and Medinan periods of Muhammad's prophecy.[25] One verse (5: 48, A) indicates that such divisions are part of God's divine plan and a test for man:

If God had willed, He would have made you one nation; but that He may try you in what has come to you. So be you forward in good works; unto God shall you return, all together; and He will tell you of that whereon you were at variance.

The term has very positive denotations and connotations in some verses, particularly when associated with God's supporters: "Whoso makes God his friend and His Messenger, and the believers—the party (hizb) of God, they are the victors" (5: 56, A). And again:

Thou shalt not find any people who believe in God and the Last Day who are loving to anyone who opposes God and His Messenger, not though they were their fathers or their sons or their brothers, or their

24. Michael Hudson, *Arab Politics: The Search for Legitimacy* (Yale University Press, New Haven, 1977), 107.

25. References to the term *hizb*, are found in the following suras of the Quran: 56: 5, 53: 23, 32: 30, 19: 58, 22: 58, 6: 35; reference to the term, *hizbayn* in 12: 18; to the term *ahzab* (plural form of *hizb*) in 17: 11, 36: 13, 37: 19, 20: 33, 22: 33, 11: 38, 13: 38, 5: 40, 30: 40, 65: 43.

clan. Those—He has written faith on their hearts, and He has con-firmed them with a Spirit from Himself; and He will admit them into gardens underneath which rivers flow, therein to dwell forever, God being well-pleased with them, and they well-pleased with Him. Those are God's party (hizb); why surely God's party—they are the prosperors. (58: 22, A)

In a verse preceding that quoted above, God's party is juxtaposed to Satan's: "Satan has gained mastery over them, and caused them to forget God's Remembrance. Those are Satan's party (hizb); why, Satan's party, surely they are the losers!" (58: 19, A)

The transcendental consequences of belonging to Satan's party are made unequivocal in another surah: "Surely Satan is an enemy to you: so take him for an enemy. He calls his party (hizb) only that they may be among the inhabitants of the Blaze" (35: 6, A). In these verses God's party is singled out, its obligations are specified, its motivating spirit underlined, and its transcendental rewards—eternal abundance and par-adise—glorified and juxtaposed to those of the followers of Satan.

In other verses of the Quran, hizb has a different but still positive de-notation:

> They think the Confederates (ahzab) have not departed; and if the Confederates come, they will wish that they were desert-dwellers among the Bedouins asking for news of you. If they were among you, they would fight but little. (33: 20, A)

Here, ahzab refers to the allies of Muhammad who aided him in a critical battle. In still another verse, ahzab has a neutral referent simply indicat-ing two groups: "Afterwards we raised them up again, that we might know which of the two parties (ḥizbayni) would better calculate the while they had tarried" (18: 12, A).

However, by far the largest number of references to hizb have negative connotations and denotations. Some of these references are very general; referring only to those whose "hearts are in perplexity" (23: 60, A) or to "the parties after them" (40: 5) or to "the day of the parties" (40: 30, A). In one verse those who vacillate in support of the confederates, the allies of Muhammad, and wish to flee the scene of battle are identified as "the hypocrites" (munāfiqun) (33: 12, A).

In another verse those who oppose God's party are identified more spe-cifically as "those of them, who were given the Book before you" [i.e., Christians and Jews, (5: 57, A)]. A subsequent verse reaffirms the identi-fication: "Say: 'People of the Book (ahl al-kitāb), do you blame us for any other cause than that we believe in God, and what has been sent down to us, and what was sent down before, and that most of you are ungodly?' " (5: 59, A).

Another verse groups peoples of the Book (Christians and Jews) with unbelievers who mock the true religion: "O believers, take not as your friends those of them, who were given the Book before you, and the unbelievers, who take your religion in mockery and as a sport—and fear God, if you are believers . . ." (5: 57, A). Although the term *peoples of the book* generally refers to Christians and/or Jews depending on the context, Al-Baydwi's commentary of the Quran in one instance makes the reference more specific in interpreting the phrase, "**But the parties [ahzab] have fallen into variance among themselves**" (19: 37, A).[26] The commentary mentions the Jews and the Christians but more specifically the sectarianism associated with theological disputes among Christian sects: the Nestorians said that Jesus was the Son of God; the Jacobites said he was God descended to earth then ascended to heaven; and the Malkaniya said he was one of the three (Father, Son, or Holy Ghost)—this is in contrast to the Muwahhidun (Muslims) who said he was the servant of God and his prophet.[27] In interpreting another Quranic verse,

> **And those to whom we have given the Book rejoice in what is sent down unto thee; and of the parties (ahzab) some reject some of it. Say: "I have only been commanded to serve God, and not to associate aught with Him. To Him I call and to Him I turn."** (13: 36, A)

Al-Baydwi's commentary states that some Jews and Christians rejoiced and converted to Islam when they heard its message. Others, the unbelievers (*kuffār*), united against (*taḥazzabū*) the message.[28] In this context, the ahzab are those who deny part of the Quran.

By far the largest number of Quranic verses mentioning hizb, however, are even more specific. Members of "parties" are not simply members of "God's party" or "confederates" on the positive side or "those whose hearts are in perplexity," "peoples of the book," "hypocrites," or members of "Satan's Party" on the negative side; they are the people who declared false successive divine revelations of which Muhammad was only the final and culminating one:

> **And what of him who stands upon a clear sign from his Lord, and a witness from Him recites it, and before him is the Book of Moses for an example and a mercy? Those believe in it; but whosoever disbelieves in it, being one of the partisans (ahzab) his promised land is**

26. Nasr al-Din al-Baydawi, *tafsir al-baydāwi*, *Al-Baydawi's Commentary* (of the Quran, commentary in Arabic), Cairo, n.d., 406.

27. Ibid., 153.

28. Ibid., 333. In this sense they are "countergroups." This term has been used by Fazlur Rahman in his article, "Pre-Foundations of the Muslim Community in Mecca," *Studia Islamica*, June 1976: 5–24.

the Fire. So be thou not in doubt of it; it is the Truth from thy Lord, but most men do not believe. (11: 17, A)

And again,

Cried lies before them the people of Noah, and Ad, and Pharaoh, he of the tent-pegs, and Thamood, and the people of Lot, and the men of the Thicket—those were the parties (ahzab); not one, that cried not lies to the Messengers, so My retribution was just. These are only awaiting for a single Cry, to which there is no delay. (38: 11–15, A)

Parties (ahzab), then, are associated with every messenger; the message they deliver is always unheeded and distorted; the members of parties are unbelievers who declare prophets false and hatefully seek to spread error in the presence of known truth; these members are finally seized and suffer divine retribution. In these verses there is an intimate connection between belief and unbelief and their transcendental consequences on the one hand and their social consequences on the other: social dissension and schism. Those who spread error in the presence of the known truth, the sectarians, cut up the community, destroy its unity, and threaten its existence:

O Messengers, eat of the good things and do righteousness; surely I know the things you do. Surely this community of yours is one community, and I am your Lord; so fear Me. But they split in their affair between them into sects, each party (hizb) rejoicing in what is with them. So leave them in their perplexity for a time. (23: 51–54, A)

The most radical manifestation of this social dissension is the military activity mounted by opponents of prophets. In the case of Muhammad, these opponents included in one instance—the attack on Yathrib in the year 5 A.H.—the clans of Quraysh and Ghafatan as well as the Jewish clan of Beni Qureyzah. The thirty-third sura of the Quran refers to this event. All the negative connotations of factionalism, social dissension, blasphemy, and their logical conclusions conspiracy, military confrontation, and damnation—are captured in the title of this sura, al-ahzab.[29]

Although the term *hizb*, has a variety of denotations and connotations,[30] some of which are positive or neutral, the main thrust of the sym-

29. This is so even though the specific denotation of the term in this surah is to the "confederates" who aided Muhammad.

30. For instance, it refers to a special part of the Quran (which is divided into sixty "parts" or ahzab); Sufi brotherhoods have selected certain "parts" as regular prayer formulae; the term has been extended to particular non-Quranic prayer formulae, originating from Sufi saints recited on special occasions; the term has also been used to refer to Sufi brotherhoods themselves. Another form of the root, *hazzāb*, referred in Algeria to a reciter of the Quran (literally of its parts) attached to a particular mosque. In the early part of the

bol, "party," in the various forms of its Quranic usage (e.g., hizb, ahzab, and hizbayn) is negative. It refers to those who spread error, who ignore the call of God's prophets, and who factionalize into sects even within particular religious traditions. Fazlur Rahman has termed such groups "countergroups."[31]

In the last historical case recorded in the Quran such groups denied the Messenger of God, Muhammad, denied the authority of the Quran, and denied God. The theodicy of such opposition to prophets over the ages is indicated in the first Quranic verse quoted above: "**if God had so willed, He would have made you but one community but** [He has not done so in order] **that He try** [all of] **you. . . .**"[32] Testing man is part of God's divine plan. The struggle is essentially a moral struggle between God's party and Satan's party, a struggle cutting across intimate kinship ties and having soteriological consequences as Surah 58: 22 quoted above indicates. Followers of God's party will be admitted "**into gardens underneath which rivers flow . . . forever**" while followers of countergroups will become the tortured inhabitants of hell. According to one Quranic commentary merely reading the Quranic chapter, *al-mujādila*, "The Disputation," in which the insidious acts of countergroups are described, will allow one to be written on as of "**the party of God**" on Judgment Day.[33]

The struggle between good and evil suggested by these Quranic verses and their interpretation by contemporary traditional Muslims has been termed by Munson in another (North African) context, "innate fundamentalism."[34] The intensity of Muhammad's opposition to such groups, particularly to those hizbs of Jews (of whom there were many in Medina) and Christians was due to his firm belief in the identity of the messages of all the prophets. All the Scriptures, including those of the Jews, Christians, and Muslims were from one source—the preexisting "Heavenly Archetype," "Mother of Books," or "Hidden Book" as it was variously called in the Quran.[35] The Quran, he believed, was from the same source as the Torah and the New Testament; the opposition of Jews and Chris-

---

nineteenth century, W. E. Lane used the term *hizb* to refer to a company of men assembling themselves on account of an event that had befallen them. See the article on hizb in the *Encyclopedia of Islam*, 513ff.

31. See Fazlur Rahman, "Pre-Foundations of the Muslim Community in Mecca," *Studia Islamica*, June 1976: 1–24.

32. The translation of this Quranic verse is Rahman's translation. See Rahman, "Pre-Foundation," 19.

33. Al-Baydawi, "tafsīr," 723–24.

34. See Henry Munson's perceptive account of Muslim fundamentalism viewed through the eyes of a Moroccan peddlar and European guest worker in *The House of Si Abd Allah: The Oral History of a Moroccan Family* (1984).

35. See Fazlur Rahman, *Major Themes of the Quran* (Bibliotheca Islamica, Chicago, 1980) for an elaboration of these concepts.

tians could only be due, then, to distortion and error perpetrated by their leaders. This fundamentalist view of religion, as expressed by Munson, regarded the world as an arena for the struggle of good and evil; regarded the Scriptures, here the Quran, as "the divine and inerrant word of God"; insisted that all believers conform to the literal text in their everyday lives, and argued that the world of men must be forced to conform to the word of God, implying rejection of social and cultural innovations. In addition, in both the Quran and in recent Muslim history the dominance of infidels (European colonialists and in the latest historical instance, the State of Israel) is regarded as God's punishment for immoral behavior, heedlessness, and the repudiation of Scripture.[36]

For political culture, the implications of the Quranic meanings of hizb are clear. Divisions within the community can only be factions dividing and weakening it.[37] There is no basis in these Quranic verses for a pluralistic political community in which adherents of different religions or, indeed, different sects of the same religion, are accorded equal worth and equal political participation.

HIZB IN THE MODERN WORLD:
THE NONPARTY ORIENTATION OF JORDANIAN PEASANTS

We must now consider the meaning of the symbol, hizb, in the context of some Muslims living in the twentieth century at the end of a period of Western colonialism and Western cultural penetration. To do so I shall examine the beliefs and attitudes of twenty village residents and two local-level bureaucrats as reflected in an opportunistic sample[38] taken by the author in the village of Kufr al-Ma in 1960. The sample included an agricultural inspector, the two village mayors, the village schoolmaster, the village carpenter, a village shopkeeper, the village preacher, a village watchman, a soldier, a student, a court clerk, and eleven cultivators of various economic status. What is striking about the beliefs and attitudes of these residents is their similarity to those just quoted in the Quran.

36. See Munson, *House of Si Abd Allah*, 17ff.

37. See Bruce Borthwick's interesting development of this theme in a modern context, "Religion and Political Development in Israel and the Arab States," paper delivered at the annual meeting of the Middle East Studies Association, 1974. See also Borthwick's "Religion and Politics in Israel and Egypt," *The Middle East Journal*, Vol. 33, No. 2, Spring 1979: 145–63.

38. An opportunistic sample is a convenience sample. It is composed of informants who were available and willing to answer the questions posed. Since the questions were of a controversial and politically sensitive nature, as some of the responses indicate, in a nonparty state systematic sampling proved to be impossible. The responses are not out of line with the author's perceptions of village attitudes and beliefs after sixteen months of research in the village at several points in time.

Respondents were asked the following question:

Of the following persons, which is closest to being the exemplar: the able, successful merchant; the God-fearing and pious Muslim; the devoted revolutionary who struggles for his country's interests; the obedient, contented citizen; the military hero; the man working quietly and with deliberation for his people?

Nine out of twenty-two selected the man working quietly for his people although in answer to another question nine out of twenty-two picked military force as the most important factor in history; five selected the pious Muslim; and two the revolutionary; one each selected the merchant and military hero.

In answer to the question, "Of the following which factor has had the largest effect in history: military strength; thought; economic factors and classes; political leadership?" nine selected military strength, four economic factors, four thought, and only three political leadership. One peasant in amplifying his selection of military strength said, "What is politics? Politics has been overturned." Of the four respondents who selected thought, only one, the agricultural inspector, attached political implications to it. He said, "Great Britain used political ideas to dominate; when people wake up and use their minds they will free themselves from imperialism."

The rejection of political leadership as a significant factor in history is striking in view of the importance attributed to foreign powers, foreign threats, internal insecurity, politics (al-siyāsa), and internal disunity with respect to other issues of the day. Respondents were asked, "What is the greatest problem facing Jordan today?" Of the twenty-one replies, five cited Israel, two communism, one Algeria, one the United Arab Republic, one the enmity between the Arab countries, three internal security, and one "the choosing of ministers—we need to pick only a few." In contrast to the fourteen who selected politically related problems only four—and these the more highly educated—cited economic problems: the agricultural inspector cited lack of water, the schoolmaster, the economic problems of poverty, ignorance, and disease, a bureaucrat the problem of want and the settlement of debts, and the preacher the economic dilemma of the lack of money. One respondent, the student, cited a geographic factor—the small size of the country.

Respondents were asked, "What is the cause of the loss of Palestine?" Nine respondents blamed the English; three England and America; four an Anglo-Jewish conspiracy; and one Zionism. A significant minority, however, blamed the Arabs themselves: two blamed the Arab character; two the treachery of the Arabs to one another; and three the lack of Arab unity. One respondent cited the lack of arms. Two respondents specifically cited politics in their explanations: (1) "politics lost us Palestine—the politics of Britain"; (2) "politics—the politics of the English only." Prominent in the above answers was some version of a conspiracy theory (e.g., "The Jews used to work for the English without pay on the condition that they would take the lands of Palestine," or "When the English were here they worked at corruption," or "The English sold the land of Palestine"). A significant number, however, rejected the conspiracy theory for the naïveté theory: (1) "The simplicity of the Arabs [is at fault]; Abdullah was misled by the British; he thought they were going to allow the Arabs' independence and unity"; (2) "The Jews came like refugees and we trusted them; they asked to buy land, or rent land and we gave them; then they dug their roots in."

When respondents were asked, "What is the best practical solution to the Palestine problem," three cited war, four the return of the refugees, two Arab unity, one the tightening of the Arab boycott, and one the perserverance of Arab countries. However, the largest number (five) related the solution to God: (1) "If God wills, it will be solved in peace"; (2) "God will proclaim it. When our Lord, may He be exalted, wishes, it will be solved"; (3) "I don't know if there is a solution; if God wills the refugees should return to their homes"; (4) "God is more knowing."

On the other hand, when respondents were asked, "What is the solution to the greatest problem facing Jordan today?" half of the respondents (five) mentioned ethical solutions, such as "work" or "peacemaking" or "the purifying of the people" or "cooperation among themselves" or "for leaders to reject the coveting of offices"; only one cited force and only one God.

At this point, a number of important observations can be made. First, although almost half of the respondents selected military force as the most important factor in history, only one selected the military hero as exemplar and only three cited war as the solution to the Palestine problem.

Second, ethical factors assume great prominence in positing solutions even when the behavior is manifestly political. For instance, national unity and pan-Arab solidarity were frequently cited as solutions but the solution was phrased in ethical terms suggesting the underlying change of heart that was the prerequisite of successful political behavior (e.g., "for leaders to reject the coveting of offices," "for Arabs to be as one hand," "only with the perseverance of the Arab countries," "the purifying of the people," "winning support of a people which has cleansed itself from imperialism," "faith of Arabs in their homeland," "when the Arab countries become a single hand, it will be solved," "cooperation among ourselves"). The importance of ethical considerations is also revealed in the fact that by far the largest number selected "the man working quietly and with deliberation for his people" as the exemplar. This focus on ethics is the obverse of the belief in the domination of current political life by external conspiracy and internal treachery. Moreover, it is all of a piece with the village preacher's own emphasis as the analysis of sermons in the last four chapters has demonstrated.

Third, the nonpolitical character of informant responses cannot be overstressed. Despite the salience of national and international politics for the problems facing Jordanians, only two picked the revolutionary as the exemplar and only one the obedient citizen. The man working quietly for his country was by implication neither a politician, nor a political leader, nor a bureaucrat. Thus, all the overt political roles were selected against, even the passive role of obedient citizen. Furthermore, as the answers to the questions relating to Palestine demonstrate, politics is synonomous with external (Western) conspiracy and internal (Arab) treachery and the loss of Palestine. Politics, then, is associated with destructiveness and very little if at all with constructive political action, national glory, or ethical behavior. Finally, respondents' answers indicate the importance if not the domination of religious beliefs and attitudes. Five of eighteen respondents selected the God-fearing pious Muslim as the exemplar and five of sixteen respondents cited God's will as a solution to the Palestine problem.

The importance of religious beliefs and attitudes, the focus on ethics, and the nonpolitical orientation of village informants becomes more apparent in the answers of respondents to the questions, "What are the basic principles of Islam? democracy? capitalism? socialism? communism?" In defining the basic principles of Islam eleven respondents referred to ritual: (first informant) "profession of faith, fasting, prayer, and almsgiving"; (second) "profession of faith, prayer, almsgiving, and pilgrimage"; (third) "prayer, fasting, almsgiving, and reading the Quran"; (fourth) "Islam is compounded of the five: profession of faith, fasting, prayer, almsgiving, and pilgrimage"; (fifth) "the religion with God is Islam [submission to God], fasting, prayer, and the refraining from the disapproved." Three respondents referred primarily to belief: (first) "That one profess that there is no God but God and Muhammad is his Messenger and the seal of the prophets; the preceding prophets must be recognized and believed in; belief in his angels and books and messengers and the resurrection and one's share (lot) and hell and the Fire"; (second) "The Prophet, Moses, and Jesus"; (third) "God is one; He has no partner; religion and honor and nation; and Muhammad and Jesus are his Messengers and Moses is his Messenger." Four respondents referred primarily to ethics in defining Islam: (first) "strength of bonds; honesty of intentions; avoidance of the 'limits' [flagrant violations of Islamic norms, e.g., adultery, theft, highway robbery, apostasy]"; (second) "fulfillment of

agreements"; (third) "tolerance, loving others than oneself, not interfering in others' affairs, equality"; (fourth) "equality, generosity to the
guest, preservation of rights, rebellion against tyranny." Two of the four
respondents who responded in an ethical vein were lower-echelon bureaucrats, and one was the village preacher. On the other hand, many of
the peasants who responded in terms of ritual, the eleven cited above, and
social solidarity, cited below, added an ethical component (e.g., almsgiving, refraining from the disapproved, cooperation, doing right). Two informants responded in terms of social solidarity: (first) "All Muslims are
brothers; doing right among ourselves; agreement among ourselves";
(second) "Walking according to the Book of God and the traditions of
the Prophet; cooperation; social intercourse among Muslims." Only one
respondent, the school teacher, related Islam to political action, citing rebellion against tyranny.

The most frequent response to the question on capitalism was either a
nonreply (seven of twenty) or a statement, "I don't know," or "I haven't
read about it" (four of twenty informants). Of those who did make a
substantive reply, most connected it with commerce and/or the United
States: (first) "the big merchants"; (second) "commerce"; (third) "This is
what you have in America; the capitalists are over there; there are no
capitalists in Jordan"; (fourth) "This is the rich merchant; America";
(fifth) "America; they always want work to be going on; wealth and commerce and not liking war and it [America] doesn't oppress the people."
The two bureaucrats responded in a significantly different way, one citing
"oppression of the people" and the other "exploitation and the imperial-
izing of weak peoples."

The most frequent response to the question on democracy was either
some form of the "don't know" answer (seven of twenty) or a nonreply
(four of twenty). Varieties of the "don't know" answer included "I don't
know, I've never heard of it"; "I don't know anything about it"; "I
haven't studied it, I can't answer, every person interprets it according to
his fancy"; "I haven't studied about them nor have I ever seen one dem-
ocrat" (this last being the reply of a lower-echelon bureaucrat who is also
a native villager). Substantive replies by village residents included: (first)
"No imposition by force; in Jordan there is democracy today; Jamal (Abd
al-Nasser) has a dictatorship; the right to complain to the district attor-
ney" (village mayor); (second) "Alms to the poor"; (third) "That one
walk according to the right path and equality"; (fourth) "They lean to
the people; they favor peace; America is our friend; it gives us everything
we need; our students go and learn there; we work there"; (fifth) "The
state of Britain; from the side of religion it [democracy] does not contra-
vene it; politics deceives the people, but they do not lay themselves open
to violation of honor; America is a nation, always neutral; it loves peace

more than war—why, because it is a commercial nation." Again, the two
nonresident bureaucrats' responses differed significantly, one citing "social justice, equality, and noninterference in the affairs of others," and the
second "freedom of the individual to speak his own ideas, general freedom, and freedom to represent the people." At another point in the inter-
view all twenty-two informants were asked a related question: "If you
were in a public meeting and a citizen rose to defend a point of view that
you and the majority of the assembled considered contrary to the interest
of the country and the people, do you believe that he has the right to be
heard?" Only one informant, interestingly, the village preacher, responded in the affirmative.

The most frequent response to the question on socialism was either a
nonreply (nine of twenty) or a form of "don't know" answer (six of
twenty). Substantive answers stressed its similarity with communism:
(first) "Like communism; in Islam's view communism and socialism are
the same"; (second) "The socialist is a cursed one; he is a communist."
The two other substantive answers among village residents included:
(third) "People who get together and amass money and use it"; and
(fourth) "It's close to communism; the Shadhiliyya, a sect of northern
Syria, are socialist; they bring a woman in naked and she dances in the
circle and then they all enjoy her." Again, the two nonresident local-level
bureaucrats' answers were distinctive. One said, "There is Arab socialism
and communist socialism; communist socialism is not fit for us; Arab socialism stands for equality—all working and the raising of the standard
of living." The other said, "I don't know; I'm afraid to tell."

The informants' responses on communism reflect most clearly the non-
and even antipolitical orientation of the village population, its focus on
ethics, and its religious commitment. Interestingly, only one informant
did not reply and only one gave an uncomplicated "don't know" answer.
Even those who gave no substantive answer made an evaluatory reply: "I
don't like it" or "I don't know; it's bad but I don't know why; we only
hear of parties, communist and socialist" or "They threaten the world; I
haven't studied them at all," or "Anything that opposed the will of his
majesty, the king, we don't know anything about it nor do we want to
know" (soldier). By far the most common theme in the responses was
communism's antireligious orientation: (first informant) "They are
marching against Islam—more I don't know"; (second) "They make war
on the revealed religions"; (third) "They desire oppression of people; they
transgress the principles of religion; we don't know their works";
(fourth) "They have no religion or foundation"; (fifth) "It contravenes
Islamic and religious principles as destroyer; it cannot stand the heavenly
religions; there is no religion which they do not deny." A second common
theme stresses communism's undermining the family structure: (first)

"They divide the people, separating father and son"; (second) "We will not stand mixing; the father doesn't know his daughter." Three village informants gave more complicated responses combining a number of themes: (first) "They make war on the revealed religions; that all in the land of wealth and land and real estate and companies is the property of the state"; (second) "A destroyer; it insults honor; honor is prized; it contravenes religion; it contravenes honor; it contravenes country; one does not know his children or his sister; they take them; a destroyer; everything becomes the government's; one has no honor; you become a son of the country"; (third) "Religion is to the state; the prohibition of people from religion except in special circumstances; the forced separation of families from their sons; no property to the individual—all to the State; complete freedom to the woman—neither her husband nor her brothers nor her father can control her" (village mayor). Again, the two nonresident bureaucrats differed somewhat in their responses. One said, "The forming of classes and the oppression of the weak by the strong; the clamping down on freedom and the clamping down on thought." The second said, "I am afraid to tell my thoughts."

The statements of the last two village informants quoted above dramatically demonstrate the close connection in the minds of the village residents between political activity, religion, ethics, and social solidarity. Certain political beliefs are regarded as destroying religion, undermining society's foundations, and depriving the individual of his basic identity, leading to the loss of family lines, the undermining of familial discipline, the loss of property, the institutionalization of immorality, and the destruction of the sexual identity of the individual, for a man or a woman without honor has forfeited his or her claim to act as a human being. Although the linkage of politics, ethics, social solidarity, and religion may be accentuated in the case of communism, it is a linkage that village opinion extends to all political party belief and action as the next section will demonstrate.

THE GREAT TRADITION INTERPRETED: THE PREACHER AS CULTURE BROKER

The second section of this chapter described the Quranic view of "party men" as distorters and repudiators of prophets, spreaders of error, and agents of social dissension and schism, and the last section demonstrated the remarkable compatibility and, to a large extent, agreement between the beliefs and attitudes reflected in verses of the Quran and those of Jordanian villagers. Political roles are selected against, politics is associated with destructiveness, and much activity associated with it is regarded as antireligious, immoral, and injurious to the social fabric. How has such agreement been achieved among peasants who have had, until recently, a high rate of functional illiteracy and little or no connection with Islam's formal institutions—its courts and brotherhoods? One answer is the Islamic preacher.

The most significant fact about his sermons for the theme pursued in this chapter is that out of the approximately sixty-five that I myself heard, only one dealt with an overtly political theme (the loss of Palestine) and, to the best of my knowledge, only one other that had been given by the preacher related to a political theme (the struggle in Algeria). In contrast, two-thirds of the sermons dealt with subjects that were ethical in content.

Preachers in this subdistrict in Jordan rarely address political matters. When they do, however, and particularly when the subject is political parties, the idiom adopted is the negative one with which we are now familiar, uniting the traditional religious view of parties with the condemnation of their modern counterparts. The preacher of the subdistrict center in a guest sermon delivered in Kufr al-Ma stated the following:

> At the end of time (Judgment Day) there will be a proliferation of followers of contending parties (ḥizbiyun). The heretical parties (al-aḥzāb al-mulḥida) which have come to our country—and if they had [not] believed and if the king, our redeemer, Husayn, who is our protector at the head of the community (umma), had not warned against them, then God's word and his [the Prophet's] traditions could not have remained firm.

He continued:

> Nationalism, this newborn, this modern nationalism! What is it, nationalism (al-qawmiyya)? God has called you. The faller before truth is the devil. What unites people is religion. Language does not unify people. Walid ibn Mughira, 'Ubay ibn Khalaf, Abu Lahab and Abu Jahl were all patrilineal kinsmen of the Prophet and speakers of Arabic; they did not accept his message while Bilal, the Ethiopian did so. The most honorable among you with God is the most God-fearing (pious). Help your (Muslim) brother, oppressor be he or oppressed. If we remain quiet [in the face of unbelief] there is no happiness for us and no comfort [on the Day of Judgment]. The Muslim is the brother of the Muslim; he does not oppress him or forsake him or humiliate him. Every Muslim is to his fellow Muslim a doer of good.

Although he did not mention political matters—whether at the local, national, or international levels—frequently in his sermons, the village preacher made his attitude toward modern political parties and their activities quite clear to the villagers and to me on several occasions in the course of casual conversation: "The National Syrian Party, the Resurrection Party, the National Socialist Party, the Communist Party—they're all the same, communist." When I asked the preacher why these parties were so popular, he replied:

> Colonialism—it was what gave birth to the parties. There is a saying, "Divide and rule." The English are the origin of the parties. This happened in the time of the English; the father was for a party, the son was for (another) party, and the daughter was for (another) party; and when they sat down at the table together to eat, they fought with one another.

As indicated above, foreign parties and foreign knowledge (*'ilm ajnabi*) were associated and considered, alike, corrupting. This association was strengthened by the widely held belief, with considerable evidence to support it, that it was the school teachers who were mainly responsible for propogating political party opinions in rural areas. The preacher made the connection explicit:

> [During the party period] there were many political parties in Deir Abu Said [where the Junior High School for the area was located]. Teachers were not on speaking terms with one another and each had their own coterie of students who were always quarreling on the playground; and education went by the boards. Teachers went around flunking students not of their party.

The events recounted by the preacher relate to local political history. During the mid-1950s, a period known in Jordan as "the party period," there was a proliferation of political parties and one of the few free openly contested national elections took place. Branches of Jordanian, inter-Arab, socialist, communist, and Muslim parties were formed in the cities and large towns. However, by the late 1950s the activities of these parties were curtailed and in most cases suppressed by the central government by the early 1960s. Even candidates for local offices such as the village mayorship were disqualified if evidence of previous political party activity was revealed. However, their sympathizers, mainly educated and often operating clandestinely, remained. Villagers came into contact with their views mainly through their children whose teachers often were partial to one party or another, if not actual members. In the 1950s and early 1960s teachers often made active attempts to win over their students to their point of view. The reaction of the adult villagers in Kufr al-Ma to this kind of political party activity was, as indicated above, overwhelmingly negative. An indicator of the degree of opposition to such activity is that the Liberation Party, a Fundamentalist Muslim party, was condemned along with other parties, and many villagers viewed with considerable satisfaction the arrest of the village's primary school teacher—he had been caught in town distributing propaganda for this party.

During "the party period" becoming a "party man" (*ḥizbi*) could open up many new resources outside the village if the individual's party proved successful at the election box. On the other hand, being a party man in a State that became, increasingly, a nonparty State, could bring great misfortune. One villager is a living example of such misfortune. He had been a lieutenant in the Arab Legion and an adherent of a political party. He continued to be vociferous in announcing his political opinions in spite of the increasing hostility of the State to such public statements. Finally, he was jailed, first for a short period and after a second attack on the government for a prolonged period. He returned to the village, practically penniless, borrowed some money, and was raising chickens when I left the village. Moreover, he was a social isolate in the village. He did not visit others and they did not visit him; this avoidance relationship extended to his own brothers, one of whom was the mayor of the village. Conversations with him revealed him to be as psychologically alienated from village values and the village way of life as he was, by his own choice, socially isolated.

Thus, when the village preacher told me quite dogmatically, "There are no parties in the villages," he was quite correct and his preaching was in some measure responsible for that situation. However, he went on to say, "We do not know their principles" which was only a half-truth; a garbled version of the principles of some were known, if only through the children of the adult generation and, negatively, through the preachers. He went on to explain this absence—both of party affiliation and knowledge of party principles—by the absence of newspapers. This statement was certainly true and the inference he made from it had some credence since newspapers were often associated with and sometimes subsidized by particular political parties. In the 1960s I knew of only one villager, the clerk of the local civil court, who bought the newspaper on a regular basis. Hardly anyone else ever bought it at all.

The judges of the religious court in the subdistrict center also addressed themselves to the subject of parties in a somewhat different manner. One judge said that Islam did not need parties (ahzab) because in a Muslim state the ruler is just; therefore, there was no need for opposition to check injustice. He went on to say that there was no necessity for parties since Islam was "the party." On the other hand, he said that Islam was "political" (*siyāsi*): it must take on all the problems of society.

There is no doubt that the opposition of villagers to political parties and their activities is rooted in the nature of their social structure and their mode of decision making. Ties between villagers are multiplex, serving many interests—economic, religious, kinship, political, recreational.

Bonds between villagers, therefore, tend to be ethical rather than instrumental and follow the line of a single interest. Political party activity forces people knit together in so many different ways to take sides and to accentuate differences. This is particularly so on the occasion of elections. Villagers traditionally settle their differences through dyadic diplomacy and the extended, often raucous give-and-take of debate in the guest houses of the village. A consensus is eventually reached; although none leave these meetings entirely satisfied, none leave the losers—or winners for that matter—either. Party activity and elections contested by political parties jeopardize the multiplex relations of village-mates and make the art of compromise more difficult. One of the most serious consequences of political party activity in the villager's mind is exactly this weakening of the social fabric and the basic value which underlies it—the necessity for social harmony within the community. Thus, when villagers used the word, "party man" (hizbi), it was not to be taken as a simple pejorative term; it indicated strong condemnation of the individual because in their view it connoted lack of solidarity among kinsmen, co-villagers at odds, and even the split of the nuclear family. Moreover, it was used to describe not only individuals known to be affiliated with political parties but also individuals with views that were at all similar to those enunciated by party members or party sympathizers.

There can be no doubt that one profound source of hostility to political party activity is the Islamic belief system as interpreted for peasants by judges in religious courts in rural areas and especially by village preachers. The ideology of consensus and reconciliation is fundamental to the brand of Islam propagated at the local level as, indeed, it is at the formal institutional level.[39] One might well argue that there is no philosophical

---

39. Shaykh Luqman delivered a sermon on reconciliation in August 1966 (see table 3.1) in which the positive themes of religious brotherhood and consensus were arrayed against the negative themes of schism and disputation. On the positive side he said, quoting the Quran, **The believers are naught else than brothers. Therefore make peace between your brethren and observe your duty to Allah that haply ye may obtain mercy** (49: 10, P). And the preacher continued, saying, "Verily, the union of ranks and the unity of expression (*tawḥīd al-kalima*) and the direction of unified effort has in it joy for the individual and the collectivity and good for the worshipers and the country." And getting down to cases, as he usually did in his sermons, he said, "God commanded man to reconcile in many places—in the family, between the two spouses. He laid down for man the way of peace with his words, **If you fear a breach between them twain** (the spouses), **appoint** (two) **arbiters, one from his family and the other from hers. If they wish for peace God will cause their reconciliation: For God hath full knowledge and is acquainted with all things.**" (4: 35, YA). On the negative side the preacher said, quoting a Tradition of the Prophet, *The corruption of concord is the shaver. I don't mean the shaving off of the hair, rather, the shaving off of religion.* And later in the same sermon he said, "A proverb goes, 'The passer over truth in silence is a deaf Satan.' That is the state of those who pass up (the opportunity of) peacemaking between enemies. What (then) is the state of those who feed the face of enmity and loathing among

basis to the rule of plurality at the local level and that there can be no justification of a bare majority's rule. The Quranic message is social solidarity, the preachers have delivered that message, and the villagers have enunciated it.

The preachers stated clearly, and the villagers echoed in their proclamations the grounds of opposition to political party activity: it accentuates traditional rivalries; it disturbs the educational process; it breaks up kinship ties including the ties of the nuclear family; it confounds religion; and it undermines the difficult process of consensus by which social harmony is achieved in the community.

Most important, it is the preachers who unite the Quranic view of party men as hypocrites, agents of the devil, repudiators of prophets, spreaders of error, and agents of schism with the modern evaluation of political parties as destroyers of family lines, underminers of family discipline, sowers of community dissension, demeaners of individual honor, and losers of sexual identity—uniting them in such a way that the many meanings of the term *hizbi* fuse to form a powerful multivocal symbol whose halo is destructiveness and immorality.

Borthwick has recently considered the relationship between political development and religion by examining the policies and pronouncements of modernizing Arab elites and the constitutions of their national states.[40] He has concluded that from a Muslim perspective individual liberty is only conceived of in relation to the Muslim community, umma. The source of power is God, not the people. Therefore, "consultation," shura, an accepted Sunni Muslim principle of government dating from the days of the immediate successors of Muhammad (the four "rightly guided caliphs" who were selected after consultations with the notables of the community), is for the purpose of discovering God's will and not the people's will.[41] Since God's will is single and unitary, only one party and one leadership is possible. Although Borthwick's evidence is drawn from mainly secular Arab states, they are also Muslim states and that fact is indicated in their constitutions. Indeed, what is significant is the fact that the constitution of a substantively secular state such as Algeria should have a provision that insists on precisely the kind of unity for the nation that is insisted on by the modern hizbollahis of Iran, the followers of the "party

men and add clamor to the fire of separation? They are gathering the firewood of discord (*fitna*) to fuel it when it is sleeping, and spreading its flames when it is already running. God says about the just desert (*al-haqq*) of these spreaders: **Civil discord is worse than carnage** (killing) . . ." (2: 191, R).

40. See chapter 5 for Borthwick's views on the effectiveness of the Islamic sermon as a legitimizer as opposed to its weakness as a modernizer.

41. See Borthwick, "Religion and Political Development," for an elaboration of this argument.

of God" who are the arch-supporters of Ayatollah Khomeini. The Algerian constitution states: "No person shall make use of the rights and freedoms enunciated above to impair the independence of the nation . . . the institutions of the Republic . . . the principles of the singleness of the Front of National Liberation."[42]

The hizbollahis of Iran, on their side, throughout 1980 and 1981 conducted a series of demonstrations and counterdemonstrations, invariably disrupting the meetings of other Muslim parties such as the Mujahidin al-Khalq. They conducted pitch battles in the street against various liberal and leftist parties and against students on university campuses, using fists, knives, sticks, and guns. They also led the attack on President Bani Sadr, once he began to criticize religious scholars with prominent roles in the government and to use his presidential office to challenge their appointments to various government ministries. They attacked and closed down newspapers of various parties after they had been banned by the government, and after supporters of President Bani Sadr took to the streets to protest the revolutionary prosecutor's banning Bani Sadr's newspaper, they attacked them in various parts of Teheran.[43] Earlier they had called for Bani Sadr's trial and execution. This occurred after Ayatollah Ruhollah Khomeini had warned that he would remove any politician from power who continued to challenge Iran's Islamic authorities. Significantly, Khomeini charged Bani Sadr with being a would-be "dictator" for opposing "the Prosecutor-General's office, the Parliament and other institutions." The Ayatollah said, "If a group shows itself in contradiction with the law, this is dictatorship."[44]

The counterpoint to Khomeini's pronouncements was the constant rhymed chant of the hizbollahis during their public demonstrations, a chant that became the hallmark of the movement and from which its name was taken: "The only leader is Ruhollah, the only party is the Party of God." As events unfolded in Iran over the two years when the incidents reported above occurred, it became clear that political parties, universities, and the press were to be subordinated to the single leadership of the "Party of God" as represented in the dominance of "the religious guide," al-faqīh, Khomeini himself, and the Islamic Republican Party as represented in the duly elected parliament and in key government positions such as the prosecutor-general.

What is clear whether one examines the symbol, hizb, in its Quranic context, its modern context among peasants in Jordan, or its contemporary revolutionary context in Iran is that it is a powerful multivocal sym-

42. The Algerian Constitution as quoted in Borthwick, "Religion and Political Development," 20.

43. See *New York Times* reports on the activities of the hizbollahis for December 30, 1979, March 22, 1980, April 28, 1981, June 8, 9, 16, 22, 1981.

44. *New York Times*, June 9, 1981.

bol with various connotations and denotations. What may not be so clear is that this symbol is only one of a patterned cluster of symbols that carry the message of "innate fundamentalism," the struggle between good and evil. This becomes apparent when one analyzes a sermon by Shaykh Luqman on the theme of reconciliation (*islāḥ*).[45] It was quite easy to divide the symbols in this sermon between those that related to the party of God and those that related to the party of Satan. On the one side, islah (making peace, reconciliation—related to happiness, security, and social bonds), salah (goodness), birr (good works), taqwa (piety), *khayr* (the good), rahma (compassion), tawhid al-kalima (union of speech or expression), *ikhwān* (brothers), umma (the Muslim community), and *jamā'a* (society). Other phrases that related to this side of the moral dichotomy included "arbitration between estranged spouses," "union of hearts," "single cohering bloc," "single hand," and "concord."

On the other side, related to the party of Satan, were *ahzab* (parties, divisions), *fitna* (discord—related to fire and killing), *fasād* (perversion, corruption), *shiqāq* (schism), *tanāfir* (contention), *dhat al-bayn* (enmity), *talāq* (divorce), *ithm* (crime), *dhanab* (sin), and *shī'a* (factions). Other phrases related to this pole of meaning included "disputation," "suicide of the family," and "passer over truth in silence," that is, a man who has the opportunity to make peace and does not do so.

The organic metonym dominating this sermon was the umma as a diseased and fevered body:

Are not all the true believers like the one body and every individual of them like one of the limbs of this body? The whole feels the pain of the part and the part feels the pain of the whole. Our noble Messenger, our protector from separation . . . said, *The example of the true believers in their mutual affection and compassion is like the body—if one of its members becomes diseased the whole body becomes afflicted with sleeplessness and fever.*

The remedy for factionalism is twofold. The first is revealed in a Quranic verse: "**And if two parties of believers fall to fighting then make peace between them. And if one party of them doeth wrong to the other, fight ye that which doeth wrong till it return unto the ordinance of Allah**" (49: 9, P), that is, until the party that obfuscates the settlement cooperates and makes peace.

The second remedy is revealed in a Prophetic Tradition that capped the sermon:

Help your brother, oppressor be he or oppressed. If he is the oppressor restrain him from his oppression; in that there is for him victory [in Paradise].

45. Sermon on reconciliation, Kufr al-Ma, Jordan, August 19, 1966.

The methods used to end oppression were spelled out by the preacher for "Mr. Everyman" on more than one occasion in the following Prophetic Tradition:

He among you who sees a denier [of truth] *must correct him by his hand* [by force]. *If not possible by his tongue* [by argument and persuasion]. *If not possible by his heart* [by steadfast fortitude]. *The latter is the weakest remedy.*

The judge of the local religious court in interpreting this tradition emphasized that opposition by the heart was not to be construed as passivity but as boycott and public scorn.

These two Traditions of the Prophet highlight again a theme pursued in the last four chapters: the ethical focus in the brand of Islam being preached by Shaykh Luqman. Moreover, it is important to note that the obligation of peacemaking is the obligation of every man—the Muslim is his brother's keeper—and it involves peacemaking at all levels: the family, the community, and the nation.

The focus on oppression and by implication, its opposite, justice, in these two Traditions and in the Quranic verse quoted above reintroduce in another way the theme pursued in this chapter, the relationship between religion and politics. Politics is the vocation of all men in the sense that all Muslims are obliged to resist injustice. Moreover, the conflict between God and Satan is described in a specifically political manner—the struggle between the oppressor and the oppressed. In the Muslim Middle East in the twentieth century resistance to oppression has been to a large degree resistance to Western colonialism in its cultural as well as its military and political forms. The statements of Jordanian peasants quoted above make this clear. However, political activity does not require political parties or, to state the case more precisely from a Muslim point of view, it requires only one party, the party of God. So stated all legitimate political party activity is religious activity against the factions that disrupt and pervert God's single message. "Union of speech," therefore, is taken seriously and applied to all fora: universities, schools, the press, parliament, village communities, the family and, indeed, to the party of God itself. The hizbollahis of Iran may be the most publicized examples of such attitudes and the actions implied by them, but other fundamentalist Muslim movements such as the Muslim Brotherhood in Syria, Takfir and Hijra in Egypt, and Hizb al-Tahrir in Jordan reflect similar attitudes. Divergent views threaten social solidarity, and the remedy is for the party of God to seize control of the State and restructure civil society.[46] The last

46. Eric Davis has made the same point about religious movements in the Middle East in his essay, "Religion Against the State: A Political Economy of Religious Radicalism in Egypt

two sections of this chapter have documented similar attitudes for Jordanian peasants. This fact is significant because it demonstrates that the values and attitudes described are not simply those of modernizing sectors of urban populations caught in an economic squeeze or socially disoriented through rural-urban migration as many social scientists and contemporary historians have suggested.

I do not wish to argue that Jordanian peasants refrain from political party activity solely because of an Islamic ethic that condemns factionalism and strongly supports mutual discourse, compromise, and consensus politics at the community level—an ethic that is effectively institutionalized through the role of the preacher and the religious judge. The social structural context of life in a multiplex village community characterized by cross-cutting ties (see chapter 2 for details) in and of itself promotes a mode of conflict resolution that aims to achieve community harmony and suppress factionalism: developing partible allegiances (so that one can be on both sides of the fence at once), dyadic diplomacy (private one-on-one parleys), and the free give-and-take of debate in the guest house with consensus formation as an outcome ruling out winners and losers.[47]

Mary E. Hegland has pointed to an alternative interpretation.[48] She argues that peasants in Jordan do not participate in politics because in a nonparty state participation in political parties does not bring rewards—jobs, roads, schools, bureaucratic positions—but punishments, ostracism, and arrest. Moreover, she argues, even in a party state villagers judge their own resources as being too scarce, including a paucity of necessary connections into urban hierarchies, to engage in the gamble. Why should they divert their time, effort, and resources away from their investment in kinsmen and neighbors who are their substantive social and economic insurance? I might even strengthen Hegland's argument by adding that peasants have known for some time that the Jordanian government has been engaged in a policy of material modernization that willy-nilly will bring, indeed, has brought, roads, schools, water, and electricity to the village. Again, why then take the risk of joining or supporting parties? Multiple causation is clearly at work here.

The main interpretive thrust of this chapter, nevertheless, remains valid. Overwhelmingly, these peasants evaluate political party activity negatively, and in this evaluation they do not distinguish between hizb as God's party or Satan's party and hizb as modern political party. Hizb, as defined by the preacher and interpreted by the peasants, is a multivocal

and Israel," in *Religious Resurgence: Contemporary Cases in Islam, Christianity and Judaism*, Richard T. Antoun and Mary E. Hegland, editors (Syracuse University Press, Syracuse, 1987).

47. See chapter 2 and Antoun, *Low-Key Politics*, for details.
48. Mary Hegland, personal communication.

symbol in which the Quranic transcendental and social structural implications of the term are interwoven with its modern nationalist and colo-
nialist implications. This interpretation of the symbol, insofar as it is a
transvaluation of political culture, is one oriented not toward secularization of society but rather toward its sacralization, an outcome not anticipated by Eugene Smith and other students of religion and modern politics.

THE COMPLEX RELATIONSHIP
BETWEEN GOVERNMENT ISLAM AND PEOPLE'S ISLAM

This chapter has proceeded thus far as if Islam, whether it is "separating,"
"expanding," or undergoing "transvaluation," is a single set of beliefs,
rituals, and institutions. The argument of the first chapter and the evidence of succeeding chapters do not support such a conclusion. To take
an instance cited above, Amir Abdur Rahman's centralization of authority in Afghanistan at the end of the last century also expanded Islam
through the appointment of religious judges in various districts. But the
Islam that was being spread was "government Islam," an Islam that bore
the brand of Abdur Rahman's centralizing policies, stressing the legitimacy of monarchy on the one hand and state taxation against a recalci-
trant countryside on the other. Daniel Crecelius has argued that the modernization of Al-Azhar, Egypt's ancient religious university, particularly
after the Egyptian revolution of 1952, sought to foster particular national
goals and policies such as education of a certain kind, science and technology, and later, socialism and population control. The administrators
of Al-Azhar were selected by the central government with regard to their
willingness to support such policies.[49] "Government Islam" is associated
with many religious scholars and judges who accept permanent government positions. It is associated with particular mosques, usually the largest congregational mosques in the capital cities, closely administered by
the Ministry of Religious Endowments or equivalent ministries in various
states. In Iran during the reign of the recently deposed shah certain
mosques were clearly identified as representing *dīn al-dawla* (the religion
of the state) as opposed to others representing *dīn al-millat* (the religion
of the people).[50]

   As one examines the content and form of religion in various local areas,

49. See Daniel Crecelius, "Nonideological Responses of the Egyptian Ulama to Modernization," in *Scholars, Saints and Sufis*, Nikki Keddie, editor (University of California Press,
Berkeley, 1972) for details.
50. See George Wilbur Braswell, "A Mosaic of Mullahs and Mosques: Religion and Politics in Iranian Shi'ah Islam" (Ph.D. diss., University of North Carolina, 1975) for an elaboration of these concepts.

however, the dichotomy remains pertinent but twists in its emphases and becomes a much more complex phenomenon. Patrick Gaffney, for instance, has described two preachers in southern Egypt in the city of Minya with sermons of quite different styles and contents.[51] One preacher presided over a shrine mosque that was a center of Sufi (Islamic mystic) activity; but the preacher himself was not a Sufi, and he usually discussed current national issues such as socialism and Camp David, openly criticizing in sharp terms the president, Anwar Sadat. Clearly, his stage was Egypt. His sermons were evangelical and didactic, delivered in a traditional grandiloquent style. The second preacher preached in a much newer mosque built with government assistance. The mosque had no connection with Sufi saints; on the contrary, it was used to serve a variety of practical and economic functions: dormitory, clinic, workshop, and food cooperative. This preacher had been imprisoned in his earlier days for his activities in the Muslim Brotherhood, but at that time he was an employee of the Ministry of Education. His sermons dealt mainly with matters of specific community interest: for example the obligation of the alms tax (zakat), family planning, and the status of women. Moreover, his style was low-key and informal, a considerable departure from normal preaching norms. He did not sit on or stand near the minbar. Rather, he sat cross-legged on the mats on the floor of the mosque without head dress and discussed in conversational tones Islamic ethics and their implications for the contemporary life of the community.

One might argue that the first preacher represented "people's Islam" in that he denounced government policies and delivered his sermon in a mosque associated with Sufism, a "popular" religious movement. But he dealt with "national" issues and had been known to shift his opinion as local opinion shifted. Was his Islam, "local influential's Islam" rather than people's Islam or government Islam? The second preacher, on the other hand, was a local-level government employee and had been in that sense co-opted into "government Islam." But his sermons did not deal with national issues either by way of direct praise or criticism of government policies. He was concerned with the application of these policies at the local level and their impact on the needs of the community. Moreover, unlike the first preacher, his preaching style did not separate him from his congregation, from the "sons of the mat," as he called them. Was not his Islam the true "people's Islam?"[52]

51. See Patrick Gaffney, "The Local Preacher and the Islamic Resurgence in Upper Egypt: An Anthropological Perspective," in *Religious Resurgence: Contemporary Cases in Islam, Christianity and Judaism*, Richard T. Antoun and Mary E. Hegland, editors (Syracuse University Press, Syracuse, 1987) for details.

52. See Fouad Ajami, "In the Pharaoh's Shadow: Religion and Authority in Egypt," in *Islam in the Political Process*, James Piscatori, editor (Syracuse University Press, Syracuse,

Or, take Shaykh Luqman. He legitimized King Husayn's rule by mentioning his name in the khutba, and he himself had been somewhat co-
opted into the state by degrees as he took on the positions of ma'thun and
pilgrim guide along with their concomitant stipends. Moreover, increasingly he received literature from the Ministry of Religious Endowments,
including a monthly journal suggesting the propagation of a certain
brand of Islam. In his sermons he stressed the religious legitimacy of the
ruler in the strongest terms and the necessity of obedience on the part of
the subject:

> The Sultan is the shadow of God on earth; there seeks refuge with
> him every oppressed worshiper. If he renders justice he receives the
> reward [in the after life] and the thanks of his subjects. If he goes
> astray and oppresses, then on him is sin and incumbent on his sub-
> jects is patience. If the governors go astray the heavens dry up and
> . . . the flocks perish.[53]

The ruler is not only a dispenser of justice but also a keystone of society
and a critical actor in the cosmos as is appropriate to his role in an organic
society. The consequence of the sultan's injustice ("the heavens dry up
and . . . the flocks perish") testifies to this fact. He is also a model for
household management and control: "The head of the family is the ruler
of the household. He is obliged to render equally between its members.
He must not prefer a boy to a girl or an elder over a younger or one wife
to another."[54]

But there was another side to Luqman's preaching. Luqman had collected the tapes of the well-known anti-establishment Egyptian preacher,
Shaykh Kishk. In his sermons he had also made it perfectly clear that it
was not kingship that conveyed authority but rather divinity and that, by
implication, kings, when they departed from divine ordinances and rendered injustice were subject to divine retribution. There was a historical
example of such retribution in the birth of Muhammad and his prophecy:

> How majestic respect [becomes] and how great recollection [grows]
> before the tomb of the Prophet when the onlookers remember what
> happened on the night of his noble birth in the land of Mecca, the
> venerable—of the cleaving of Kisra's palace and the splitting of Cae-
> sar's seat, and of what these sovereigns heard [in their dreams on that
> night] when an invisible man whose voice was heard cried out: "To-

---

1983) for a brief but perceptive analysis of the relations between the Egyptian State and
government Islam on the one hand and people's Islam on the other. See also Gilles Kepel,
Muslim Extremism in Egypt: The Prophet and the Pharaoh (University of California Press,
Berkeley, 1985), for an analysis of greater length and depth on the same issues.
   53. Sermon on justice, Kufr al-Ma, Jordan, July 1966.
   54. Ibid.

day an epoch ends and an epoch begins. After today there will be no kings or diviners or chiefs (sayyids). Verily, worship is to God and sovereignty (siyyada) is to the religion of God and leadership (qiyada) is to the Seal of the Prophets of God and government (hukuma) is to the successors (khulafa') of the Messenger of God and the world is to all God's worshipers—justice and freedom and brotherhood and equality."[55]

Muhammad's religious prophecy undermined two great empires, the Sassanid and the Byzantine, symbolized by the reference above to Kisra and Caesar, whose leaders were paying for their sins with a collapse of their political fortunes, as innate fundamentalism predicts.

This sermon excerpt certainly cannot be regarded as support for "government Islam." On the contrary, it has revolutionary implications for the relationship between religion and government. Luqman, moreover, as indicated in chapter 3, composed his own sermons and did not recite "canned" ones prepared in classical sermon texts or sent out in contemporary journals from the Ministry of Endowments.[56] Only two of his sermons that I heard, read, or had reported to me over several research trips, those on Palestine and Algeria, concerned the fate of the "Arab nation" in any direct way. Most were focused on ethical issues of concern to community, family, clan, husband, wife, parents, children, neighbors, orphans, and co-believers. Furthermore, as chapter 3 demonstrates, his interpretation of his own role was an egalitarian one. Although he did not go as far as the second preacher described by Gaffney—he wore the traditional dress of the preacher and spoke from the minbar in the formal style—he stressed an egalitarian interpretation of religious obligation. All free adult Muslims not only had the capability and the obligation of performing the required pillars of the faith—prayer, fasting, alms-giving, and pilgrimage—but they also had the obligation of performing special religious duties such as the ablutions and rituals connected with death and burial. And, most important, they had the obligation of being their brother's keeper in hand, tongue, and heart. His was a priesthood of all believers.

Luqman's career and sermons weave together various strands of government Islam and people's Islam with various meanings: legitimacy of the ruler, co-opted functionary of the state, obedience of the subject, dispenser of justice, divine retribution for injustice, model for the family, perversion of the establishment, brother's keeper, priesthood of all believers, corruption of parties, passer over truth in silence. The communica-

55. Sermon on Pilgrimage, April 29, 1960.
56. This is not to say Luqman was not influenced by some of the ideas in these sermons as he was by other religious books in his library.

tion is complex, but its emergent pattern contains a clear message: political obedience is conditioned on orthopraxy, justice, personal piety, and regard for Muhammad's community (umma).

In certain historical cases and in the life and writings of certain individuals, "people's religion" emerges much more clearly and sharply counterposed to "government religion" or "establishment religion" than indicated in our Jordanian and Egyptian examples. The black preacher referred to in chapter 3 is one such case. Eugene Genovese has vividly described how plantation owners and white preachers in the antebellum South attempted to restrict the operation of the black preacher particularly after 1831.[57] Fears of a black rebellion against slavery inspired state laws forbidding black preaching and requiring registration and control of black preachers, monitored through the required presence of white "patrollers" at black worship services. Genovese describes how the slaves resorted to dissimulation to preserve their own religion and, in doing so, their own hope, dignity, and capacity for spiritual resistance. After white preachers led them in prayers for the Confederacy black preachers held secret prayer sessions for the Union. Indeed, the slaves themselves and, particularly, their preachers, insisted on separate religious services in which they could develop their own style of worship, "the frenzy," and their own theology to counter that of the establishment. They rejected sin for luck as an explanation of misfortune, insisted that Christianity proclaimed all men brothers, and declared that there was a Master above their masters. One slave preacher described this constant tension between establishment religion and people's religion in his description of what white plantation owners told black preachers and exhorters and what black preachers and exhorters in fact did: "And he say, 'Tell them niggers iffen they obeys the massa they goes to heaven,' but I knowed there's something better for them, but daren't tell them 'cept on sly. That I done lots. I tells them iffen they keeps prayin, the Lord will set em free."[58]

Ali Shariati's interpretation of the Pilgrimage described in the last chapter also reveals clearly and sharply a view of "people's Islam" as opposed to "government Islam." Ibrahim (Abraham) for Muslims, the first monotheist, was for Shariati also a great rebel (against polytheism) and Hagar was a symbol of the struggle of two oppressed minorities, women and blacks. The stoning of the three pillars at Mina symbolized man's struggle against the three faces of oppression: wealth, tyranny, and hypocrisy. The latter symbolized the body of established religious scholars and religious specialists in Iran whom Shariati had declared in other works to have

57. See Eugene D. Genovese, *Roll, Jordan, Roll: The World the Slaves Made* (Vintage Books, New York, 1976), particularly book 2, part 1, "The Rock and the Church."
58. Ibid., 263.

corrupted Islam and betrayed its spirit.[59] Polytheism, for Shariati, referred to taking as an end rather than a means any of the human desires, physical or sublimated (e.g., love of land, sex, knowledge, power, and honor). Shariati's Islam was people's Islam: "Although you are here to see God, you find yourself with people." It was a religion of acts rather than ritual or meditation: "becom(ing) involved in the problems of people, not as a monk who isolates himself in a monastery but by becoming actively involved . . . practicing generosity, devotion and self-denial. . . ." It was a religion of martyrdom, resistance, and revolution as a response to injustice.

> Put the knife to his throat with your hands [following the model act of sacrifice by Abraham of his son, Isaac]. Save the throat of the people from being cut—the people are always sacrificed at the doors of palaces of power and temples of torture. Put the blade at your son's throat so that you may take the blade from the executioner's hand. (Shariati 1980)

Shariati's view of people's Islam was rejected by the government establishment who harassed and arrested him on a number of occasions and by the religious establishment who refused to credit his interpretations and teaching with legitimacy since he was not a product of the standard Islamic law college or madrasah. Indeed, his message of condemnation and defiance toward both political and religious establishments made cooperation with them impossible.

Indicative of the existence of these two Islams is the fact that during the year-long events that preceded the Iranian Revolution in January 1979, the tapes of Shariati's lectures rivaled those of Khomeini in their dissemination in urban and rural milieus. In many areas the younger generation preferred those of Shariati.[60] After the revolution and the accession of the new religiopolitical establishment as represented by the domination of the Islamic Republican Party in the parliament and the bureaucracy and of the "religious guide," Khomeini, in the constitution and the life of the nation, it is significant that the severest ideological, political, and military clash between the new establishment and its opponents was that between the Islamic Republican Party and its popular supporters, the hizbollahis and the Mujahidin al-Khalq, one of whose principal sources of inspiration are the writings of Ali Shariati. In this instance people's Islam was defeated by government Islam or, to put it another way, people's Islam

59. See Ali Shariati, *On the Sociology of Islam*, Hamid Algar, translator (Mizan Press, Berkeley, 1979).
60. Mary Hegland, personal communication.

did not prove to be as popular as government Islam or as powerful.[61] But then, the terms *people's Islam* and *government Islam* are themselves time-bound, and one can become the other. The roots of the present Saudi Arabian dynasty began in the last century as a revolt of "people's Islam" in the form of the Wahhabi Movement. But in the course of events and certainly after the accession of the Saudi dynasty to power in the first part of the twentieth century, the Wahhabi Movement became "government Islam" which may have been challenged by a new "people's Islam" as the seizure of the Grand Mosque in Mecca in November 1979 may already have indicated.

61. William Shepherd has, with some justice, cautioned against the usage of "people's Islam" in this context. In a personal communication (September 1985) he said: You speak of Shari'ati's Islam as "people's Islam." Insofar as this is meant as a contrast to "Government Islam" you are, of course, right, but perhaps a phrase like "opposition Islam" would be better. "People's Islam" suggests to me something like popular Islam (say in the sense of "little tradition": as opposed to "great tradition"), and this would not describe Shari'ati. Also . . . I suspect that the present Iranian government has at least as good a claim to represent the religion of the people as does the Mujahidin. Both Ali Shari'ati and the Mujahidin represent middle class intellectuals' efforts to identify with people more than something actually coming from the people. . . . Shepherd's corrective is well taken. However, it is necessary to distinguish between the actual class composition of religious movements and their appeals. Although Shariati's following seems to have been of the middle class and particularly of the young, its appeal was "populist," that is, to the generality of Muslims. One must also distinguish between the pre-(1979) revolutionary situation and the post-(1979) revolutionary situation. In the prerevolutionary situation the unity of all opponents to the shah's regime—as Muslims—was stressed by all religiously inspired groups. Only in the postrevolutionary situation was the question of who represented "people's Islam" raised and, afterwards, fought out in the streets.

The Interpretation of Islam
by Muslim Preachers in the Modern World:
Five Views of the Prophet's Night Journey and Ascent

Oh worshipers of God, oh ye who follow the path of the Messenger of God, on the morning after the night journey, the Messenger of God, may God bless and grant him salvation, said to Umm Hani, the daughter of his uncle, Abu Talib, while he was in her house after the night journey: *"Oh Umm Hani, I prayed the last supper prayer with you in this valley, then I was taken [by God] to Jerusalem and I prayed there. Then I returned and prayed in your house the noon prayer." Umm Hani said, "Don't tell people what you've told me or they'll call you a liar." The Messenger of God said: "I shall tell them and God will safeguard me from the people." She grabbed his gown so that he could not leave, but the Messenger loosened his gown from her [grip]; then he left for the Ka'bah and stood with courage between it and Nadwa Valley and called the clans of the Quraysh. They hastened toward him and surrounded him and said: "What's the matter, Muhammad?" He said, "God took me with him on a Night Journey." They said, "Where?" He said, "To Jerusalem." They said, "And you returned in one night?" Muhammad said, "Yes." They were taken aback and astonished and said to him, "Are you telling us that you made this trip in one night when it takes our caravans two months?" He said to them: "My Lord is all-powerful." They said, "Your story is astonishing. Your deeds before this were trivial. But today what you have said is bad and what you have perpetrated is prattle." Some of his relatives felt sorry for him and some of the Muslims recanted and some men were fascinated by his account. Abu Bakr did not recant and repeated his words: "I believe, I believe, oh Messenger of God."* (Friday sermon excerpt, radio broadcast, Jerusalem, July 8, 1977)

The night journey and ascent is one of the miracles of our Prophet, Muhammad, May God bless and grant him salvation, [a miracle] which has and still does stimulate great discussion and lends itself to many meanings. What is the debate about? It centers around two matters: the first of them relates to the wondrous occurrence of the miracle. The second of them relates to whether one of them (the night journey and ascent) or both of them were spiritual [odysseys] alone or both spiritual and corporeal together. With respect to the nature of the miracle's occurrence, the Muhammadan miracle addressed the mind, unlike the miracles of previous prophets which addressed the senses. Moses' miracles, on him be peace—**Then he flung down his staff and Lo! it was a serpent manifest; and he drew forth his hand** [from his bosom], **and Lo! it was white for the beholders** (7: 107–8)—these are visual miracles witnessed by spectators and astonishing them. And they led either to belief or stubbornness (denial). The miracles of Jesus, on him be peace, in bringing to life the dead and curing the blind and the lepers, these too were visual miracles that led either to conviction or denial. But the miracle of Muhammad, the blessings of God and his salutations be upon him, God, may he be glorified, did not wish the miracle of Muhammad to be on this material plane. He made it to converse with the mind and to stir thought. (Friday sermon excerpt, radio broadcast, Acre, Israel, July 15, 1977)

Oh ye Muslims, let us ask one another why the night journey and ascent from Mecca, the honorable, to heaven wasn't direct? Why this aside on the road to heaven which Muhammad followed, praying as imam and leader with the prophets and messengers, then ascending to the high heavens? Why didn't he descend directly to Mecca? On the contrary, he returned to Jerusalem and from there to Mecca, the honorable. (Divine) messages and prophecies occurred before, most of them being in Palestine and to the Beni Israel, that is, to the descendants of Isaac. But the Jews disbelieved the signs of God, declared false the prophets, and killed them unjustly. God, most high, wished to transfer prophecies from one people to another and from one country to another and from the descendants of Israel to the descendants of Ishmael. And that is what happened. God, may he be glorified, confirmed that all prophecies are from a single source and that all prophets pray to a single Lord and a single religion. God gathered them all together and brought the seal of the prophets, may God bless and grant him salvation, to direct them and lead them in their prayer till it became clear to all mankind that all the prophets called for surrender to God (Islam). (Friday sermon excerpt, radio broadcast, Amman I, Jordan, July 8, 1977)

Oh worshipers of God, Palestine is a part of the lands of Islam. In it there is the Farthest Mosque, the blessed, which he ennobled with sanctification. He gathered in it the prophets on the night of the ascent out of regard for our Prophet, Muhammad, may God bless and grant him salvation. He made it (the sacred area) the third of the noble sanctuaries just as he made it the beginning of the Muhammadan mission, the direction of prayer for the people of Islam. There is blessing in it and what is around it. The Quran has informed us of that by his words, may he be exalted: "**In the name of God, Most Gracious, Most Merciful. Glory to (God). Who did take His Servant for a Journey by night from the Sacred Mosque to the Farthest Mosque, whose precincts we did bless—in order that we might show him some of our signs: for He is the One who heareth and seeth** (all things)" (17: 1, *YA*). Is it fitting for us, then, as Muslims—this being the great matter of Palestine—that we leave in it the base band of Zionists? (Friday sermon excerpt, Kufr al-Ma, Jordan, January 22, 1960)

With his insight he (Salah al-Din) was convinced that he had to unite the Muslims in order to defeat the Crusaders. He began his war against Muslims. Do not find it surprising. If you want to build a house, you eliminate the ruins first, then you level the land and build a house on a solid foundation. He (Salah al-Din) did not take long. He united all the standards under his own and the principalities under his own authority. Then he proceeded with power made firm by God and the power of the sword calling on whomever was able to fight the Crusaders. He and his army accomplished astonishing feats. Oh ye Muslims the period of his rulership over Syria was less than nineteen years. He and his army embarked boldly during this period on seventy-four battles, all victorious. Do you know what that means? That they fought a battle every three months. They used every kind of arms in their battles: the sword, the spear, the arrow. They used the tank—yes, the tank! They used the battering ram, a huge vehicle which had a head in its center that demolished walls. They used the mangonel, resembling an artillery piece today. They used Greek fire. They used trickery. They used cunning. They used courage. They used manliness. They used generosity. They used amnesty. They did not leave a weapon God permitted and that they had access to, unused. (Friday sermon excerpt, Amman II, July 15, 1977)

The five sermon excerpts quoted above were all delivered as part of the Friday congregational prayer service during the Muslim month of Rajab in commemoration of the Prophet's night journey and ascent, one of the most important religious occasions in the Muslim calendar. The sermons were delivered by preachers in two cities, a town, and a village in the Israel-Palestine-Jordan area, all within a radius of about sixty miles, one in 1960 and four in 1977.¹ Each of the sermons assumes a knowledge of basic events constituting the night journey and ascent: Muhammad was awakened one night as he lay sleeping in the vicinity of the Ka'bah in Mecca by the angel, Gabriel, who took him to a winged steed, Buraq, which he mounted, and they proceeded together to Jerusalem. On the way they witnessed various scenes presaging the fate of the damned (e.g., misers swallowing red-hot stones, adulterers devouring foul meat, usurers swimming in rivers of blood, and spreaders of dissension lacerating their faces and breasts). They stopped to perform ritual prayers at Medina, Mount Sinai, and Bethlehem. At Jerusalem they met the previous prophets and Muhammad led them in ritual prayer, affirming his precedence. Then, with Gabriel he ascended a ladder through seven consecutive heavens. In each heaven they met one of the previous messengers of God: Adam in the first, Jesus and John in the second, Yusuf in the third, Idris (Enoch) in the fourth, Harun (Aaron) in the fifth, Moses in the sixth, and Abraham in the seventh. Finally, Muhammad appeared before God's throne in the seventh heaven and, on Moses' advice, asked repeatedly for a lessening of the ritual prayer obligation on Muslims, an obligation which was finally reduced from fifty prayers a day to five. Then they returned to Jerusalem and thence to Mecca—on the same night.² All five sermons agree on the basic theological, soteriological, and religious significance of the night journey and ascent: its confirmation of the seal of the prophets, its charter for the obligatory ritual prayer, its reminder that the first direction for Muslim prayer is Jerusalem, its linking of the three sacred mosques—the Sanctuary at Mecca, the Prophet's Mosque at Medina, and the Farthest Mosque (including the Dome of the Rock as well as al-Aqsa) in Jerusalem—and its message of salvation and damnation. What is remarkable about the sermons is the different weighting placed on the religious, theological, ethical, psychological, and political implications of the event and the quite different approaches used to advance the argument.

The Jerusalem preacher, for instance, in his first substantive sermon (each Islamic sermon is formally broken into two parts, the first and main part which constitutes most of its length and the second short, usually benedictory sermon) focused on the soteriological implications of the night journey and ascent:

1. I wish to thank Muneera Salem-Murdock and Sami Salem for recording the four sermons broadcast on the radio from Acre, Jerusalem and Amman during the summer of 1977. I also wish to thank Sohair Muhammad for painstakingly typing the tapes thus recorded and my colleague, Akbar Muhammad, for aiding in the translation of difficult passages.

2. Of course, numerous variant accounts of the night journey and ascent occur in Muslim sources. The capsule account referred to here is that of Imam Najm ad-Din al-Ghaiti, translated from his *al-mi'rāj al-kabīr*, Cairo, 1906, by Arthur Jeffrey and appearing in his *Reader in Islam* (Mouton, New York, 1962), 621–39.

It is related from Ibn Mas'ud, may God show him favor, that the Messenger of God, may God bless and grant him salvation, said, "*I saw Abraham on my Night Journey and he said, 'Oh Muhammad, greet your community a greeting from me and inform them that paradise is sweet and its earth fertile, sweet of water, and [its topography is] a plain and its vegetation is: Glory be to God, and Praise be to God, and There is no God but God, and God is greater, and There is no power and no force except by God's [will].'* "

This preacher completely excluded any mention of the political implications of the night journey and ascent. Such implications can even appear when soteriological themes are prominent. Thus, the village preacher from Kufr al-Ma linked salvation and paradise with holy war (jihad):

Muhammad . . . urged the true believers to fight against those who fought them and occupied their homes by force; he made that (holy war) to be among the highest purposes of Islam, and he guaranteed for the strugglers the highest place in paradise.

And again: "we are the sons of Islam, created for the holy war, born for struggle. Death on the road to glory and honor is the most illustrious part of our faith. . . . The happy life is not of this world."

The preacher from Acre, on the other hand, dwelt mainly on the theological implications of the night journey and ascent:

If we look at the night journey and ascent in relation to the Prophet, we say it was a miracle because it was Muhammad who traveled by night and was raised to the high heavens and it was he who saw the majesty of God and the exaltedness of creation and the true nature of existence. People did not see anything; they only hear about events which he only witnessed. They were obliged to believe, if true believers, or remain unconvinced if unbelievers. These were not miracles to lead to the affirmation of the Prophet or to belief or the stamping out of unbelief.

And by extrapolation on its religiopsychological significance:

One of the significances of this immortal event is its strange timing. It occurred after the Messenger went to Thaqif to preach Islam and after he had suffered injury from the Quraysh for nearly ten years. After his circumstances straitened following the death of his uncle [and protector] Abu Talib and his wife, Khadija, may God show them favor, he thought that he might find supporters in Taif. But they greeted him with evil and they deceived him and they sent the insolent among them and their slaves to rain stones on him till his legs

bled and he cried. . . . The night journey and ascent were an assurance and a consolation for him—that divine power stood by his side.
. . . It was as if the power of God conversed with him on his journey,
saying, "Oh Muhammad you shall overcome difficulties with our
protection and our compassion just as (certainly as) the earth and
heavens (will) advance with our power and solicitude."

And on its religiohistorical significance:

The second meaning of the night journey is that the Quran spoke as
a testing for the true believers and as a winnower for those weak in
faith and as a purifier of ranks. . . . This divine purification of the
elements of weakness in the ranks of the true believers (was) a necessity as a preparation for what the power of God had begun of a new
stage in the struggle of the Prophet and his companions—a struggle
that began with the flight to Medina [hijra].

The Acre preacher's detailed functional analysis of the night journey
and ascent contrasts with the rather brief soteriologically oriented sermon
of the Jerusalem preacher, but it is similar to it in excluding contemporary
political themes. The exclusion is even more pronounced since it extends
not only to the first substantive sermon (as in the Jerusalem case) but also
to the second extended benedictory sermon which includes not only blessings for the Prophet and his family collectively, and the companions of
the Prophet and for Abraham and his family, as is usual, but also for the
four rightly guided caliphs (political successors to Muhammad), and by
name for the Prophet's grandsons, his wives, and his daughter, and for
the followers of the companions.

By contrast, the political implications of the night journey and ascent
are drawn out in two consecutive Friday sermons by the Amman
preacher. What is particularly interesting about these sermons is that the
second benedictory part of both is used to carry a primary political message. Indeed the first part of the initial Amman sermon (July 8) does not
differ significantly from the Jerusalem and Acre sermons in its predomi-
nant religious and theological themes (as the third introductory quotation
indicates) though it does emphasize the political significance of the linking of the three mosques: "Perhaps in this linkage between the three
mosques Muslims feel that to some extent they are responsible for the
protection of all three (equally), and their rescue from the hands of the
enemies of God and the enemies of the prophets and the enemies of mankind."

But the political implications of the night journey and ascent are spelled
out clearly in the benedictory sermon immediately after the invoking of
blessings on the Prophet and his family:

Good God, make victorious he who makes victorious your religion. Good God, forsake he who forsakes the Muslims. Good God, bring us victory over the unbelieving folk. Good God, martial to your farthest mosque the servants of the true believers who will return it to the protection of Islam, oh Lord of two worlds. Good God, make us powerful with Islam. Good God, make us victorious with religious faith. Good God, deal with the enemies of this religion. Good God, deal with the Jews and those who aid them, oh Lord of two worlds. Good God, free the farthest mosque and the holy land from the (many) kinds of criminals, by your strength and power oh Lord of two worlds.

This sermon is "political" in the fullest sense since it deals openly with the theme of power and beseeches God, the source of power, to strengthen individual Muslims and through them the polity to overcome its enemies.

The Amman preacher's following Friday sermon (July 15) takes a very different tack to explore the same theme. He devotes the entire sermon, mentioning the night journey and ascent only in the introduction, to outline a capsule life history of Salah al-Din (Saladin), wishing to present a historical paradigm for the solution of Muslims' contemporary political problems. However, in doing so he makes clear that the political and the religious problems are intertwined, for Salah al-Din begins his political career with a religious turning:

Salah al-Din came after Nur al-Din, the martyr. He used to follow his own desires and amuse himself in play. When he succeeded to authority and commanded the Muslim community (umma) he returned to God and abandoned what he had been involved in and endeavored to obey his Lord, firstly, and then to unify the Islamic principalities, secondly, and then to fight the crusading kings, thirdly. He returned to his Lord and used to pray in the mosque, congregationally, or with the army, congregationally. He did not skip prayer in his (whole) life except in the last three days of it when he was unconscious and dying.

The formula for the solution of political problems is, then, first, religious awakening, second, the political and if necessary forcible unification of Muslims, and, third, military action against the enemy. The political fragmentation of the Muslim world then (and now) constituted a critical weakness:

After he took command of Syria after the death of Nur al-Din, what did he find? Don't be surprised? In every country there was a (separate) principality: in Damascus, Hama, Baalbek, Aleppo, Jericho,

Hilla, Mosul, Sinjar, a settlement close to Mosul. In the mountain
there were principalities in Shawbak, in Kerak, in Aqaba. Wherever
a country was found, that country was a (separate) principality.

Again, and unusually, the second benedictory sermon is used to pro-
pound a specific political message with respect to a particular issue. But
the political message is inextricably linked with a religious message:

Now then, oh ye Muslims, there were the heroic deeds of Salah al-
Din and his faith and the faith of those before him and those with
him. God gave victory to them—all of them. Do you know why?
They found a book. They found a wondrous book in which there
was a plain road for life, there not following it anyone but that he
will emerge victorious in war and peace. . . . Verily, if there were
among literate Muslims those who would be able to find a copy of
this book in order to lead us to read it and understand it and act on
its basis and follow its wisdom, then we will cleanse our country
from the defilement of colonialism and the filth of Zionism and take
back the farthest mosque and the glory of our ancestors and occupy
once again the place of eminence in the world. There is nothing between us and this result except that we act on the basis of this book.
Do any of the literate Muslims and their leaders have a copy of this
book? Do they know the name of this book? It is the noble Quran.
Good God, turn us back to your book, oh Lord of two worlds. Good
God, illuminate our hearts with the generous Quran and block our
errors with the wisdom of the noble Quran. Enclose us with your
book. Make our rulers rule by the noble Quran. . . . Good God, inspire your servant and the son of your servant, Husayn ibn Talal that
he may proceed according to the noble-hearted Quran.

In this sermon political leaders are singled out as having dual religious
and political responsibility for following the historical paradigm and
leading a simultaneous political and religious reawakening. The village
preacher from Kufr al-Ma also singled out "the grandchild of the glorious
Prophet," the Hashemite, King Husayn of Jordan, for responsibility and
incipient heroism:

Verily, in the near future Husayn and his courageous army will hold
the first historic session in the life of the Islamic nation in the second
capital of the Kingdom, Jerusalem,[3] from where the first star and
light ascended into the high heavens to the Lote-tree of the Boundary
to the Paradise of the Mansion, and fire the first salvo for the rescue

3. In 1960 Jerusalem had been officially designated as a second capital of the Hashemite
Kingdom of Jordan along with Amman.

of Palestine—to make the world understand that the voice of the holy land has not ceased to speak and says, "Begone oh ye impure ones from my land. For this is Husayn—who will purify me from the filth of unbelief and restore Palestine as an Arab Muslim land in which the call to prayer shall ring out from the mosques of Jaffa and Haifa: God is most great! God is most great!"

Even the Jerusalem sermon which was the most thoroughly apolitical in its substantive part, as befitting a Muslim community in the capital city of a Jewish state, communicated a resonant political message, albeit general, in its benedictory part:

God, make Islam and the Muslims victorious. God, make Islam and the Muslims victorious. God, make Islam and the Muslims victorious. Good God, support the power of Islam. Good God, support the power of Islam. Good God, support the power of Islam. And destroy the cunning unbelievers. Good God, make victorious all who walk in his path in order to raise the banner of Muhammad, may God bless and grant him salvation.

Now it may appear strange that a religious "sermon" should assume in whole or in part a political complexion, pursuing themes of power, fragmentation/unity, military valor, and effective leadership. But this may be only because the medieval European Christian doctrine of "the two swords"—the conception of society under dual control, presided over by twin hierarchies, having distinguishable jurisdictions—of which the U.S. doctrine of separation of church and state is only an extreme variant (see previous chapter), has befuddled our thinking about Islam. For Muslims, the community (umma) is simultaneously a religious and a political community under a single jurisdiction headed by God. From the beginning, the sermon (khutba) was delivered by the head of the community, Muhammad, and after him by the rightly guided caliphs and by the governors of provinces in their names. The oral presentation in the mosque delivered by the preacher during the Friday congregational prayer service covers— and always has covered—a much wider range of topics than would be indicated by the English gloss, "sermon." In the early Islamic period the content of the "sermon" would as likely have been a diatribe against the enemy, a pronouncement of views on political questions, or an announcement of legal decisions as an edifying moral discourse, a laying down of ritual obligations, or a theological lecture. This wide-ranging content can be understood better when it is realized that the mosque was a multifunctional institution: house of worship and meditation, assylum for the accused, gathering place for the community, place of daily prayers, and focus of collective action. Moreover, the preacher's mounting the pulpit connoted the beginning of some kind of authoritative statement even when the preacher himself had no political office or, indeed, much influence in the community from sources other than religious learning. Even though religious roles have undergone differentiation and the Muslim preacher has become more specialized, the scope of his discourse continues to be wide-ranging and cast on the paradigm of the Prophet: the first leader of the Muslim community, the first preacher, and the first exhorter to the good. The fact, then, that a sermon on an ostensibly theological event becomes a capsule life history of a Muslim commander and political leader or that the night journey and ascent becomes confounded with the issues of colonialism and the modern history of Palestine is not surprising particularly since, as observed in the previous chapter, from a Muslim point of view religious and political achievements and events are inextricably linked.

Political themes are not the only ones that reflect the wide-ranging societal concerns of the Islamic preacher. The Amman preacher's focus on the life history of Salah al-Din, particularly his military career, had as its aim not just the glorification of leadership, piety, and heroism. It also carried the hardly veiled message that innovation, borrowing, and technological modernization were among the essential ingredients of societal health and self-preservation.

Ethical concerns are pursued as minor themes in four of the five sermons. The Acre preacher's largely theological sermon still points out one of the ethical functions of the night journey and ascent: to dramatize the consequences of unethical behavior—the taking of interest, fornication and adultery, consuming the wealth of orphans. Most of the sermons highlight Muhammad's courage, piety, and forbearance in persecution, and the Amman preacher stresses Salah al-Din's perseverance and self-control in the course of struggle and his magnanimity in victory. Only the village preacher's sermon completely neglects reference to specific ethical traits considered praiseworthy for the true believer. His sermon is perhaps the most political of the five, stressing victory and power at the beginning and the end: "Praise be to God who gives victory to the followers of his religion and renders mighty the true believers. . . . He extends to them his insuperable power and aids them with his unchallengeable authority." He commends holy war and martyrdom, and calls for the forcible expulsion of the enemies of Islam under the command of a contemporary leader, King Husayn of Jordan, on the model of Saladin. This call is surprising in view of Luqman's focus on social orthopraxy as indicated in preceding chapters. But it is also instructive in two senses. First, it cautions us against drawing conclusions about the typicality or atypicality of the themes pursued by particular preachers without having a substantial corpus of that preacher's sermons available for analysis. I witnessed sixty-five of the sermons of this village preacher in 1959, 1960, 1965, 1966, and 1967 and recorded twenty-six of them over fifteen months of field research. Of the twenty-six sermons, over half (fifteen) dealt with ethical concerns as the major organizing theme of the sermon—filial piety, the necessity of mutual aid among co-religionists and co-villagers, the doing of good deeds, the necessity of equal treatment to wives and siblings, the obligations of kinship, the proper mode of marriage payment, and women's immodesty and men's honor—and most of the remaining sermons dealt with ethical concerns as a minor focus. Only five of the twenty-six sermons dealt with theological concerns such as death or the night of the divine decree (*laylat al-qadr*); only three dealt with ritual obligations (e.g., pilgrimage, fasting); three dealt with religious history (e.g., Muhammad's prophecy and struggle); and only one, the sermon excerpted here, dealt with political questions. Thus, the sermon quoted here is completely atypical of the dominant orthopraxic focus of Luqman's sermons viewed in terms of the annual religious calendar.

In another sense, however, the village preacher's sermon had a thoroughly ethical focus, and this focus was expressed in the general obligation of Muslim brotherhood, here expressed in relation to the particular plight of the refugees created by the successive Israeli-Arab wars:

> They come seeking your sustenance in order to save them and protect them. . . . We are your brothers in religion and the responsibility of the brother is to aid his brother and defend him from injury. He who is not concerned with the [pressing contemporary] affairs of Muslims is not one of them.

Here, ethics is defined in terms of the comprehensive societal obligation of protecting the life and limb of one's co-religionists and restoring their economic sustenance through the return of their homeland rather than the specific ethical imperatives directed to family and home, kinsmen and neighbors.

THE SERMON AS A PERSUASIVE FORM

Thus far this analysis has dealt almost entirely with the content of Islamic sermons and very little with their form. As indicated in chapters 3 and 4, the sermons do have an established form set generally by the tradition of the Prophet's own practice and specified much more narrowly by the practices of the rightly guided caliphs, their successors, and the scholars of Islam. For instance, the first sermon is long and the second short. Both end with a reference to a Tradition of the Prophet (hadith) or a verse from the Quran. The first sermon begins with praise to God and praise to the Prophet followed by a set phrase which indicates the beginning of the substantive part of the extended sermon. The second sermon enjoins the blessing of God on the prophet, his family, and the believers. The second sermon is even more formal than the first in the sense that there is no room in it for modification or addition—no new subject is introduced in it.[4] The body of both sermons usually contains references to the Quran and the Traditions of the Prophet. Moreover, both sermons are punctuated with numerous religious prayer formulae that occur at certain points in the sermon or, automatically, after certain phrases, as many of the excerpts quoted above indicate. For instance, after the mention of God, "May he be exalted" or "May he be glorified" follows; after the mention of Muhammad, "May God bless and grant him salvation" follows. After the mention of the names of other prophets such as Moses and Abraham, "On him be peace" follows; and after the mention of the name of a companion of the Prophet, "May God show him favor" follows. "God is greater" (the takbir), "May God be praised" (the tahmid), "I take refuge with God from accursed Satan" (the ta'awwudh) and "I bear witness that there is no god but God" (the tahlil) are prayer formulae occurring again and again throughout the sermon.

As indicated in chapter 4, Maurice Bloch (1975) has called attention to the attributes of formalized language with particular reference to its implications for social control in traditional societies. For him the attributes of formalized language or formalized speech acts include the following: fixed loudness patterns, extremely limited choice of intonation, some syntactic forms excluded, partial vocabulary, fixity of sequencing of speech acts, illustrations only from certain limited sources (e.g., scriptures, proverbs), and stylistic rules consciously applied at all levels.[5] Informal speech, on the other hand, allows choice of loudness, intonation, syntactic forms, vocabulary, and sequencing.

We must consider further here the implications of Bloch's analysis for Islamic sermons. Whereas formal speech only allows the initial choice—to accept or not accept (by withdrawing from the presence of or avoiding the speaker) the subsequent "arthritic" speech forms—informal speech involves linguistic choice and renegotiation of every speech act. Bloch argues that the effect of formalized speech is to strengthen hierarchical social relationships, to reduce the possibility of challenging traditional authority, and to prevent the speaker from tackling specific issues or dealing with particular divisive (and hence possibly innovative) actions. He ar-

4. Not all Muslim law schools are agreed on this point. The Hanafi School, for instance, allows interpolation of new material in the second sermon. Other schools allow elaboration of material in the second sermon between prescribed ritual formulae under certain circumstances (e.g., forgetfulness of the preacher). Akbar Muhammad, personal communication.

5. See Maurice Bloch, *Political Language and Oratory in Traditional Society* (Academic Press, New York, 1975).

gues further that "the effect of always comparing particular events to the same general illustrations reduces the specificity of utterances so that all events are made to appear as though they were alike."[6] The merging of events in this manner "transforms the dangerous and uncertain present into the fixed eternal and orderly past."[7]

Although the Islamic sermons quoted above are not as completely formalized speech acts as many of the examples referred to by Bloch (in Bali, Madagascar, Polynesia, and New Guinea) there is no doubt that restriction occurs in terms of loudness, intonation, selection of vocabulary, fixity of sequencing, and choice of illustrations. With respect to the latter, for instance, the village preacher's juxtaposition of the indigenous Jews, driven out of Medina by Muhammad in the seventh century after they refused to accept his message, the Crusaders driven out of the near East by Saladin in the twelfth century, and the Jews inspired by Zionism in the modern state of Israel makes it appear that all are alike and, therefore, subject to a similar fate. Or, for instance, the juxtaposition of Muhammad, Saladin, and the latter-day Hashemite, Husayn ibn Talal, by the Amman preacher makes it appear that the problems faced by these societies were essentially the same and that therefore the solutions are the same, namely, heroic leadership. In terms of persuasion, the paradoxical result of this assault on the historicity of events is to make them alike, in some sense scripturally anticipated, and to enhance the feelings of unity and solidarity of the audience not only with their historic past but also with one another in the living present.

Another characteristic of these Islamic sermons does not, however, support Bloch's conclusion that formal oratory precludes the tackling of specific issues. That characteristic is the brief introduction of a specific event, issue, or person into the flow of formal speech; for instance, in the excerpt quoted above, the introduction of King Husayn as the future liberator of Palestine right after the contours of heaven including the Sacred Lote-Tree and the Paradise of the Mansion have been mentioned and right before two successive takbirs ("God is great") are uttered. Or take the excerpt quoted above in the second brief (and most formal) sermon delivered by the Amman preacher:

> Good God, illuminate our hearts with the noble Quran and block our errors with the wisdom of the noble Quran. Enclose us with your book. Make our rulers rule by the noble Quran and our community (umma) proceed by the munificent Quran. Good God, give us victory over our enemies while we battle under the standard of the noble-minded Quran, with your compassion oh Lord of two worlds. Good

6. Ibid., 15.
7. Ibid.

God, inspire your servant and the son of your servant, Husayn ibn
Talal that he may proceed according to the noble-hearted Quran.
Inspire him to act in accordance with what pleases you, oh Lord of
two worlds. Good God, forgive Muslim men and women and true-
believing men and women, living and dead. Good God, prayer for
our master, Muhammad, and all the prophets and messengers the
most excellent of prayers and peace be upon you and the mercy of
God and his blessings.

The formality of this sermon excerpt, in Bloch's terms, is apparent:
there is excessive repetition of particular words and phrases, that is, a
"partial vocabulary" and a fixity of sequencing of speech acts with certain
stylistic rules consciously applied. What is not obvious from the text is
the relative fixation of the loudness pattern in the second sermon (as compared with the first extended sermon), the restricted intonation pattern
(given in a beseeching tone of voice), and the alliterative and onomato-
poeic effects in part as a result of the restriction on vocabulary and sequencing. Ensconced in the middle of this benedictory sermon with all its
religious and soteriological denotations and connotations are several specific messages relevant to the contemporary scene and the modern world:
an injunction to rulers to rule justly; a further injunction, hardly veiled,
that to rule justly they must lead successful military action against the
enemies of the community; and a singling out of King Husayn for particular responsibility, fixing on him the mantle of legitimacy.

One more example of this common tendency to introduce one cultural
or social specific into the midst of the flow of formal speech and next to
the inculcation of general values will suffice: "Worshipers of God, God
commands justice and benificence and giving to kinsmen. He prohibits
abominations and the reprehensible. He admonishes you in order that
you may remember. Remember God, the great, that he may remember
you." Doing justice and avoiding the reprehensible are unspecified categorical imperatives; giving to kinsmen is a specific ethical norm. Such a
juxtaposition gives the latter the same weight as the former.

The conclusion to be drawn here is not simply that formalized speech
acts or formal oratory does allow the tackling of specific issues but that
such oratory and even particular ritual formulae included in such oratory
convey important political messages about the modern world, and that
such messages are all the more effective for being ensconced in formal
speech acts. Muhammad's night journey and his witnessing the scenes of
hell, ostensibly a warning to the believers about the jeopardy of their salvation, his leading the prophets in prayer in Jerusalem, ostensibly a theological charter for Islamic precedence, and his ascent through the heavens and his conversation with God, ostensibly a ritual charter for the five

obligatory prayers, all encode an underlying message concerning the re-siliency of the contemporary Muslim community in the modern world.

The five views of the Prophet's night journey and ascent analyzed above demonstrate beyond doubt the richness of the khutba, even in its most formal parts, its "thickness"[8] and its "multivocality"[9] for Muslim wor-shipers. The night journey and ascent is no doubt a "summarizing sacred symbol,"[10] a clustered, "condensed,"[11] and crystallizing commitment. Yet at the same time it is, itself, a "key scenario,"[12] a significant action by a prophet formuating a model, not only an actable form within a strictly religious context (pilgrimage) but also an actable form in the modern world generally (movement through space for action with intent to unify a divided world).

What is remarkable about these sermons is the different weighting placed on the religious, theological, ethical, psychological, and political implications of the same event and the very different approaches used to advance the argument. These sermons provide convincing documentation of the diversity of the Muslim preaching corpus in terms of both content and interpretation within a quite narrow geographical range.

More generally, they suggest that the meaning of symbols, even and

8. "Thick description" is a term coined by Clifford Geertz to refer to the analysis of symbols in such a way as to uncover the layer-upon-layer of meanings encoded. See Geertz, *The Interpretation of Cultures* (Basic Books, New York, 1973), chapter 1 for details.

9. "Multivocality" is a term coined by Victor Turner to indicate that many ritual symbols stand for many things at once—the "fan of meanings" being contributed by explanations of informants, social structural implications from treatment and usage of ritual objects by performers, and spatial and hierarchial positioning of ritual objects independent of exegesis or usage. See Turner, *Chihamba the White Spirit: A Ritual Drama of the Ndembu* (Man-chester University Press, Manchester, 1962); "Three Sermons of Passage in Ndembu Cir-cumcision Ritual," in *Essays on the Ritual of Social Relations*, Max Gluckman, editor (Manchester University Press, Manchester, 1962); and *The Forest of Symbols* (Cornell Uni-versity Press, Ithaca, 1967) for details.

10. Sherry Ortner has formulated the provocative distinction between "summarizing" and "elaborating" symbols. See Ortner, "On Key Symbols," *American Anthropologist*, Vol. 75, No. 5, October 1973, for details.

11. Ortner's use of the term *condensed* is probably drawn from Victor Turner's concept of "condensation." See Turner, *The Ritual Process: Structure and Anti-Structure* (Cornell University Press, Ithaca, 1969), and *Forest of Symbols* for details.

12. Ortner has coined the terms *key scenario* and *root metaphor* to describe the two types of "elaborating" as opposed to "summarizing" symbols. The two are contrasted mainly in terms of their functions for cultural and social systems. Summarizing symbols shape atti-tudes and crystallize commitment; elaborating symbols formulate relationships either by placing experience in cultural categories (root metaphors) that clarify that experience or by providing actable forms (key scenarios) for achieving the valued states of the culture. The night journey and ascent is in these terms quite clearly and powerfully both a "summariz-ing" and an "elaborating" symbol and makes Ortner's distinction somewhat problematic, although Ortner recognizes that the contrast between the two types of "keyness" and their two modes breaks down in practice.

perhaps particularly "key" or "core" symbols is always versional and partial. To that extent the search for such core symbols, a search which has preoccupied many anthropologists for a number of years, apart from their spatial, social, and diachronic contexts confers a false stable semantic content on symbols and leads away from the most interesting questions of interpretation.[13]

13. One of the most brilliant attempts to delineate the meanings of core symbols is Clifford Geertz's analysis of the three symbols, *haqq* (real, right), *dharma* (duty, order), and *adat* (outlook, local consensus making) in the Islamic, Indic, and Malaysian cultures, respectively. It is a rich and textured analysis. Yet it suffers in the same way as Ortner's analysis from an absence of and perhaps an unwillingness to come to terms with versional meanings. (See Geertz's *Local Knowledge: Further Essays in Interpretive Anthropology* [Basic Books, New York, 1983], chapter 8.) Victor Turner has, perhaps, come closest to accommodating the drive to identify core meanings and core symbols with the recognition that all meaning is versional in his concept of the "dominant symbol" whose dominance is relative and situational. That is, the meaning of symbols for Turner is "episodic" though a symbol may carry a halo of meaning from one situation to the next. See Turner's *Chihamba the White Spirit* and *Forest of Symbols*.

Islamization,
Islamic Fundamentalism, Islamic Resurgence,
and the Reinterpretation of Tradition in the Modern World

Discussions of Islam in the modern world often use a number of phrases which presume to describe a phenomenon, a process, and a set of beliefs without defining the terms in a clear-cut fashion or noting their relationship with one another. The two most commonly used phrases are "fundamentalist Islam" (sometimes referred to as "militant Islam," "neofundamentalism," or "faith-driven politics") and "Islamic revival" (otherwise referred to as "Islamic resurgence," "renewal," "awakening," or "reassertion").[1] One term that has rarely been used in these discussions

1. Some of the most significant and/or recent references for the usage of these terms are the following: Fazlur Rahman, *Islam* (1960); "Islamic Modernism: Its Scope, Method and Alternatives," *International Journal of Middle East Studies*, October 1970; "Islam: Legacy and Contemporary Challenge," in *Islam in the Contemporary World*, and "Roots of Islamic Fundamentalism," in *Change in the Muslim World* (1981); Bruce Lawrence, "The Fundamentalist's Response to Islam's Decline: A View from the Asian Periphery," in *Islam in the Modern World* (1980); "Muslim Fundamentalist Movements: Reflections Toward a New Approach," in *The Islamic Impulse* (1987); John Voll, "Hadith Scholars and Tariqas: An Ulema Group in the 18th Century Haramayn and Their Impact in the Islamic World," *Journal of Asian and African Studies*, Vol. 15, Nos. 3–4, July–October 1980; and "Islamic Renewal and the 'Failure of the West'," in *Religious Resurgence: Contemporary Cases in Islam, Christianity, and Judaism* (1987); Henry Munson, Jr., *The House of Si Abd Allah* (1984); Steven Humphreys, "Islam and Political Values in Saudi Arabia, Egypt and Syria," *The Middle East Journal*, Winter 1979, and "The Contemporary Resurgence in the Context of Modern Islam," in *Islamic Resurgence in the Arab World* (1982); Ira Lapidus, *Contemporary Islamic Movements in Historical Perspective* (1983); G. H. Jansen, *Militant Islam* (1979); Richard Dekmejian, "The Anatomy of Islamic Revival: Legitimacy Crisis, Ethnic Conflict and the Search for Islamic Alternatives," *Middle East Journal*, Winter 1980; Mumtaz Ahmed, "Islamic Revival in South Asia" (in press); William Ochsenwald, "Saudi Arabia and the Islamic Revival," *International Journal of Middle East Studies*, August 1981; Nazih Ayubi, "The Political Revival of Islam: The Case of Egypt," *International Journal of Middle East Studies*, December 1980; Nikki Keddie, "Iran: Change in Islam; Islam and Change," *International Journal of Middle East Studies*, July 1980; Detlev Khalid, "Islam and the Future of Civilization," in *Islam and Civilization* (1982); Mohammed Ayoob, *The Politics of Islamic Reassertion* (1981). See also Michael Fischer's "Islam and the Revolt of the Petit Bourgeoise," *Daedalus* Vol. 3, No. 1, 1982, for a stimulating discussion of the relationships between the problems of political legitimacy, symbolic interpretation, class formation, and Islamic resurgence. See also William Shepard's thoughtful 1987 essay, "Islam and Ideology: Towards a Typology," which attempts to compare, contrast and relate ideologies labeled as "secularism," "Islamic modernism," "radical Islamism," "traditionalism," and "neo-traditionalism."

but is nevertheless familiar to students of Islam is "Islamization." In the discussion that follows I shall seek to clarify the concepts of Islamization, Islamic fundamentalism, and Islamic resurgence and go on to explore the relationship of these concepts to the problems of the moral state of Muslim society, the flexibility and breadth of the Islamic corpus of law and ethics, the persistence of religion as a force in the modern world, and the reinterpretation of tradition.

Let us begin with the term most familiar to us, fundamentalism, which is derived from the American Protestant tradition rather than Islam. As Bruce Lawrence has pointed out, etymologically there is no Arabic term for fundamentalism, although Arabic terms do exist for "reform" (*iṣlāḥ*), and "revival" (*nahḍa*) (and one might add for "renewal" [*tajdīd*] and "modernity" [*tahdīth*] as well). Moreover, no Muslim group refers to itself as "fundamentalist."[2] Generally speaking, in the Quran those who commit themselves to the full implementation of Islamic norms are labeled *mu'minin*, "true believers"; those who claim to be Muslims according to formal criteria without the accompanying moral intensity and acuity are labeled *muslimin*, "Muslims"; and those who assert Muslim identity while contradicting such assertion with morally repugnant acts are termed *munāfiqin*, "hypocrites."[3]

Nevertheless, historically, as Rahman (1966), Voll (1980), Lapidus (1983), and Lawrence (1984) have pointed out, Muslim individuals and groups, particularly since the eighteenth century, have called for sociomoral reconstruction on the basis of a return to Holy Scripture, the Quran, and the Traditions of the Prophet. Fundamentalists aim "to rediscover the original meaning of the Islamic message without historic deviations and distortions and without being encumbered by the intervening tradition. . . ."[4] In this regard, Voll in particular has stressed that Islamic fundamentalism emerges out of "traditional" Islamic institutions such as the study of the hadith and the practice of Islamic mysticism interpreted in an activist sense.

And yet, as the above-mentioned quotation indicates, fundamentalism is incompatible with the conservative, traditional stance of many Muslim scholars since it regards the intervening 1300-year cumulative tradition of Islamic scholarship as an encumbrance. It is not accidental, therefore,

2. Lawrence, 1987.

3. Hundreds of verses in the Quran use the terms, *mu'minin*, *muslimin*, and *munafiqin* or other words related to the respective triliteral roots: *a-m-n*, *s-l-m*, and *n-f-q*, as any index of the Quran will reveal. However, for some of the more significant verses in this context see the following: 49: 14–17; 74: 31; 57: 13–14; 63: 1–5; 2: 7–9; 3: 102; 2: 132; 3: 52; 29: 133; 26: 81.

4. Rahman, "Roots of Islamic Neo-Fundamentalism," in *Change in the Muslim World*, P. H. Stoddard, editor (Syracuse University Press, Syracuse, 1981), 33.

that in the twentieth century Islamic fundamentalism has been spread by teachers and preachers such as Hasan al-Banna, Shaykh Kishk, and Shaykh Luqman, and by emotionally and morally intense lay Muslims such as Ali Shariati rather than by professionally committed Muslim scholars such as Ayatollah Khomeini (the exception). Fundamentalism, then, represents a sharp break with established religious tradition at the same time that it calls for a return to the past. But it is to be a past reaffirmed in a different light, a past dispensing with significant traditions of law, theology, and mystical practice.

Henry J. Munson (1984) has concisely stated the fundamentalist world view: "the belief that a specific set of sacred scriptures are the divine and inerrant word of God and that all believers must conform to the literal text of these scriptures in their everyday lives. . . ."[5]

For the fundamentalist, Munson holds, moral choice is central—the choice between God and Satan. In the Islamic case fundamentalism is driven by outrage at Western cultural and economic penetration perhaps even more than by political subjugation since the former is pervasive and insidious. Fundamentalist Moroccans who are the subjects of Munson's study are as outraged by Muslims speaking French, sending children to French schools, marrying French women, and wearing short skirts and low-cut blouses in the streets as they are by the fact that the factories are still controlled by Christians long after the official end of French colonialism.[6] Furthermore, fundamentalists place a particular construction on colonialism (overt political and military domination by foreign powers) and neocolonialism (economic domination and covert political domination): they regard foreign domination as a sign of the wrath of God and liberation as only possible by a strict return to the precepts of scripture (the Quran).[7]

As Rahman indicates and Lapidus and Jansen stress, Muslim fundamentalists regard Islam as central to every aspect of life, as being comprehensive, including politics; any reforms or legislation contemplated by them are with a view to the consequences for both this world and the next. Their goals are in Lawrence's words, "utopian," nothing less than "to be fully authentic Muslims in a world which cares little about religion."[8]

The historical context in which Islamic fundamentalism has arisen is intertwined with its content and style. It grew in strength in the nineteenth century in relation to the breakdown of Muslim empires and it grew in

5. Munson, *The House of Si Abd Allah: The Oral History of a Moroccan Family* (Yale University Press, New Haven, 1984), 19.

6. Ibid., 21–22.

7. Ibid., 23–24.

8. Lawrence, 1984, 21.

the twentieth century in relation to the rise of modern national secular states. Detlev Khalid (1982) has stressed that its growth is related to a crisis of identity brought about by the challenge of an alien Western civilization, and the social and economic disruption left in its wake. This crisis of identity has led to a "nativistic" response in which Islam has the attraction of the genuine and the familiar. Stephen Humphreys (1979) has stipulated the alien context more specifically as that of secularism: the novel and overwhelming impact of mass communication, health care, education and, most important, nationalism, has aroused a "militant" (Jansen's term) response first of all—and still—to foreign armies and colonial and neocolonial economies, but second and equally, if not more important, to an alien world view encompassing relations between the sexes, the family, education, law, and economic life.[9] Most exasperating for fundamentalists is that this alien world view seems to have captured not only the political establishments of Muslim states but also the religious establishment identified in chapter 7 as "government Islam."

Rahman (1966, 1970, 1980, 1981) has charged fundamentalists and "neofundamentalists" with intellectual sterility, with failing to argue about issues, mechanically declaiming on subjects and, along with "Islamic modernists," with failing to engage in the systematic interpretation (through *ijtihād*, independent judgment) of scripture, religious law, and religious traditions—the systematic interpretation necessary to relate Islam to the modern world.

Lawrence has observed, however, that Islamic fundamentalists are committed to ideology rather than theology. That is, they are looking for ways to authenticate the powerless rather than for ways to rethink the implications of scripture.[10] Islamic fundamentalism, then, is nothing if not activist. It wishes to move religion out of the mosque, which is still a proper locus for worship, into markets and banks, into the forum and the streets, and into athletic clubs, scout groups, women's auxiliaries, school hallways, and factories—even on to the city walls (for religious graffiti) and the battlefields (as in Iran today). Phrased another way, Islamic fundamentalism is an attempt by local-level religious specialists and religious laymen as Jansen has phrased it, "to remodel their public and private life—politics, economics, law, social mores—according to the precepts of

9. On the other hand, both Voll (1987) and Ochsenwald (1981) have stressed the failure of the secularizers and secularism in explaining the rise of "neofundamentalism," rather than its overwhelming impact. Ataturk, Nasser, and the ruling Baath party of Syria and Iraq, Ochsenwald holds, failed to realize their own basically secular goals: political legitimacy, economic development, social justice, and military parity. Voll, on the other hand, relates Islamic resurgence in the last quarter of this century, partially, to the realization by Muslims of "the failure of the West" to solve the social and economic problems in its own baliwick.

10. Lawrence, 1984.

their faith"[11] at the same time that they come to terms with an alien way of life that has implanted itself by force in their land, undermined their dignity, and called into question their identity.

This call for movement of Islam out of the strict formal worship setting so eloquently exemplified in the work of Shariati discussed in chapter 6, and the willingness of Islamic fundamentalists, more, their eagerness to embrace science and technology—without its attendant secularism and materialism—is what sets them off sharply from traditional Muslims and marks their movement in the latter part of the twentieth century as something new.

"Islamic resurgence" or "revival," what Jansen calls "militant Islam," describes a broader phenomenon, process, and set of beliefs than "fundamentalist Islam." Resurgence can be defined in terms of the increase in the power, prosperity, and international respect paid to Muslim states (Pipes 1980; Wenner, 1980), the intensification of the role of Islam in public life, a change in the hearts of men (Danner 1980), the return to the fundamentals of religion and their sources (Dekmejian 1980; Keddie 1980), or cross-culturally and primarily, in terms of the growth of a social movement actively involved in the recruitment of others, responsive to personal and societal crisis, and implementing some form of personal or social change (Gerlach and Hine 1970).[12] In whatever way that resurgence is described, it is distinct from a second process, the process by which Islamic institutions such as courts, mosques, preachers, and mystic orders, have been and continue to be diffused throughout the Muslim world. Although Islamic identity may have been initiated more than a thousand years ago with the conversion of the population, its institutionalization is a continuing process with many ebbs and flows.

Since World War II, the process of Islamization in the parts of the Middle East with which I am most familiar, Jordan and Iran, has been continuous. It has proceeded in terms of Islam's orthoprax focus, that is, in terms of judges, marriage officers, and preachers as well as in terms of worship. When I arrived in the subdistrict of Al-Kura, Jordan in 1959, only four of its twenty-five villages had an Islamic preacher. When I returned in 1965 every village in the subdistrict had a preacher. The Islamic court had been established in the adjoining village of Deir Abu Said only

11. Jansen, *Militant Islam* (Harper & Row, New York, 1979), 15.

12. Islamic resurgence is a huge and complex phenomenon which cannot be investigated in any detail within the scope of this work. The author hopes to do so in a future work devoted to socioeconomic change in rural Jordan and its impact on religious institutions. For a description and analysis of the phenomenon see the readings mentioned in footnote 1. See also *Religious Resurgence: Contemporary Cases in Islam, Christianity and Judaism*, Richard T. Antoun and Mary E. Hegland, editors (Syracuse University Press, Syracuse, 1987).

six years before (1953). In 1960, almost one-quarter of all marriages recorded in the village were sister-exchange marriages (*tabādal*), marriages
proscribed by Islamic law and ethics since they did not stipulate a marriage payment (mahr).[13] In 1967 when I asked Luqman who in the meantime had been appointed marriage officer (ma'thun) how many sister-exchange marriages he had registered in the previous year he said only two
out of one hundred marriage contracts. When I initiated my research in
1959, hardly a single family in the village of Kufr al-Ma, Jordan, stipulated a deferred marriage payment (*mahr muajjal*), an ethical norm encouraged by Muslim judges; by 1965 every family did so. I have already
discussed Luqman's cumulative religious occupational specialization, the
cumulative growth of his library (e.g., from three traditional commentaries of the Quran to the commentary of al-Tabari in thirty-eight parts and
twelve volumes, and from traditional works on religion to a library including the fundamentalist and modernist writings of Sayed Qutb and
Khalid Muhammad al-Khalid), the Islamization of the village in terms of
the addition of a new mosque and a second preacher, and the establishment of a Quran school.

In Iran, Islamization has also proceeded, but, based on my research in
the province of Gorgan in 1972, it has accentuated worship rather than
Islamic law and ethics. When I asked a convenience sample of villagers in
"Haftabad" how often they had made the pilgrimage to Meshed, the
greatest Shi'a shrine in Iran, I discovered that before 1960, if they had
gone at all, they had gone once in their life.[14] By 1972 pilgrimage had
accelerated to the degree that it was not uncommon for small landowners
to go to Meshed every year and for sharecroppers to have gone once or
twice. I had intended as part of my study of Shi'a Islam to record the
elegies (*rawḍeh-khaneh*) chanted in the Husayniyya during Muharram on
my tape recorder. However, I decided that it would be inappropriate for
me, a non-Muslim, to intrude myself into the religious life of the village
at the apex of the religious cycle and with a tape recorder in a community

13. Technically, this is incorrect since in the 1960s such exchange marriages did involve
a marriage contract (*aqd al-nikāḥ*) and the stipulation of mahr. They were, then, legal
(*shar'ī*) in that sense. However, since the linked marriages were usually simultaneously celebrated, there was no actual payment of mahr on either side.

14. Field work was conducted in Iran during the summer of 1971 and for six months in
"Haftabad" (the name of the village is a pseudonym) in 1972. Haftabad is a completely
Persian-speaking Shi'a Muslim village with a permanent nucleated population of three thousand that swells to five thousand at the peak of the agricultural season with the influx of
migrant labor. For further information about its social structure and system of social control, see Richard T. Antoun, "The Gentry of a Traditional Peasant Community Undergoing
Rapid Technological Change: An Iranian Case Study," *Iranian Studies*, Vol. 9, No. 1, Winter 1976; and "The Complexity of the Lower Stratum: Sharecroppers and Wage Laborers
in an Iranian Village," *Iranian Studies*, Vol. 14, Nos. 3–4, Summer–Autumn 1981.

where I was a recently arrived stranger. Therefore, I left my tape recorder in Teheran. On the occasion of my first visit to the Husayniyya on the third day of Muharram, I noticed a bearded patriarch of the village sidle up to the wall, just before the narrative chanter (*rawḍeh-khan*) began his elegy on the martyrdom of Husayn at Kerbala, and push something into it. I suddenly realized that he had plugged in his tape recorder and was about to record the chanting. I soon discovered that many villagers had tape recorders, and that their almost exclusive use was for taping elegies in the Husayniyya and sermons and/or lectures of leading preachers in the mosques of Meshed, Qum, and Tehran. This was seven years before the Iranian revolution and was not, I would argue, a precursor of the revolution or an index of Islamic "revival" but rather an example of ongoing "Islamization."

To argue that Islamization has proceeded continuously since World War II might seem to be contradicted by the well-recognized processes of secularization and centralization of state power that have taken place during the twentieth century, indeed, beginning in the nineteenth century in the Middle East and North Africa. One might argue, for instance, as Crecelius (1972) has argued for Egypt and Donald Smith (1970) generally for Asia and Latin America, that the process of polity-expansion secularization, that is, the process by which the State extends its jurisdiction into areas of social life formerly regulated by religious institutions, has reduced or eliminated religion from one sphere after another. In the case of Islam, the regulation of education and law might be regarded as crippling since it is in the Shari'a, the corpus of ethics and law, that Islam has undergone its greatest elaboration and organizational expression. However, the process of state centralization has had variable and often unpredictable effects on Islamization.

At the end of the nineteenth century, Amir Abdur Rahman, the founder of a dynasty in Afghanistan, proceeded with a relentless policy of centralization directed against all local and regional power centers, tribes, and ethnic groups. The religious institution was as relentlessly bureaucratized as other aspiring elites. Sayyids were given stipends and qadis (religious judges) were forbidden to teach or trade and were provided with manuals drawn up by the king stipulating which sources of the law were to be applied (Ghani 1978, and n.d.).[15] Paradoxically, Abdur Rahman's centralization policy at one and the same time weakened the religious institution by depriving it of autonomy, but also strengthened it by giving it organization and a regular financial base.

15. See Ashraf Ghani, "Islam and State-Building in a Tribal Society in Afghanistan: 1880–1901," *Modern Asian Studies*, 1978 and his "Order and Conflict: Consolidation of Power Through Law 1880–1901" (mimeographed) for details.

In Jordan in the last quarter of the twentieth century one might argue that village preachers like Luqman have become increasingly bureaucratized and financially dependent on the State (in this case through the Department of Religious Endowments), particularly as they take up ancillary duties (e.g., as marriage officials or pilgrim guides). However, in some respects the financial security provided by such bureaucratization has made them more independent to oppose local customs conflicting with Islamic norms and to oppose local power centers at odds with the religious institution. Moreover, as Crecelius points out for Egypt, although the 'ulama have not been able to resist the steady expansion of state power or to successfully defend their own prerogatives, through self-imposed isolation, compartmentalization, retroactive change (i.e., changing a little in unimportant spheres in order to maintain intact major spheres), and obstruction, they have successfully resisted the secularization of values that results in the secularization of society. Bureaucratized preachers at the local level are as capable as 'ulama at the national level of conveying their own message and at the same time confounding the message of the State, as indicated by the Egyptian village preacher referred to in chapter 5, who dutifully read the sermon prescribed by the government on birth control. Despite the expansion of state power, the secularization of education, and even the bureaucratization of religious specialists, the Islamic religious institution continues to transmit its own values to the great majority of the population through its judges, its preachers, its marriage officers, its pilgrim guides, its religious scholars, its narrative chanters, and mystic adepts in an ever-increasingly wider arc and, increasingly through the modern media (tape recorder, TV, and radio) as well as the traditional loci of religion (mosque, zawiyya, shrine, and husayniyya). Islamization was, is, and will be a basic and ongoing process in the Muslim world, apart from the rise and fall of fundamentalist movements or Islamic revival. It may be quickened by their energy or slowed by their lassitude, but as the engine of institutionalized religious activity and the mechanism for its survival, Islamization has a continuous and persisting quality that warrants separate analysis.

The relationship between Islamization, resurgence, and fundamentalism, then, can be expressed in the following way. Conversion to Islam initiates a process that has at once but to varying degrees cognitive (relating to the mind), orectic (relating to the senses and emotions), and conative (relating to the goal-oriented drive to action) components. The breadth and depth of each component differs from individual to individual. Islamization is the process of institutionalization, social organization, differentiation of roles, proselytization, and systematization of doctrine. Muslims who worship in mosques, appear as litigants in Islamic courts, and serve as initiates in Sufi orders or fighters in paramilitary organizations undergo constant and cumulative exposure to a Muslim society and culture such that their understanding of the Islamic world view broadens and their sensitivity to the Islamic ethos deepens. Islamic resurgence, a variegated response to the challenges facing Muslims in the modern world in all fields, perhaps quickens the process of religious institutionalization; it certainly deepens religious commitment on the part of some Muslims. Islamic fundamentalism is one form of Islamic resurgence with its own deep historical roots and its own peculiar sensitivity to the modern situation.[16] In social organizational terms, as one moves from conversion through Islamization to resurgence, there is a tendency for the Muslim to move from a peripheral or supporting role in various religious networks or groups to a central or core role.

It is interesting to note, as observed above, that the Quran itself uses terms that can be construed as relating to degrees of religious commitment, indicating the movement from peripheral to central, from nominal to profound, and from instrumental and manipulative to orectic and cognitive: the terms munafiq, muslim, and mu'min. It is interesting to note too that in Egypt's current Islamic resurgence as recorded by El Guindi (1981), the women recruited to local cells of the movement recognize three stages of increasingly "religious commitment," or *iqtinā'*, each marked in terms of increasing modesty and leadership: "the religious one" and wearer of scarf and headdress (*mutadayyina*); "the covered or sheltered one," completely covered with the exception of the face (*mutaḥajjiba*); and "the veiled one," completely covered including an opaque veil over the face (*mutanaqqaba*). El Guindi notes that a woman cannot wear any mode of dress without expression of the behavioral correlates of commitment.[17] Here, then, is an example, perhaps rare in its compre-

16. Another form of Islamic resurgence is "Islamic modernism." For the modernists the main problem is the adjustment of social institutions to the demands of modern life. A secondary but related problem is the relationship of reason and tradition. The Islamic modernist's approach to the first problem is or should be the rethinking of the ethic of social justice and its application to laws of marriage, divorce, the position of women, and economic life. The modernist's approach to the second problem is rethinking God's relationship to man, nature, and the afterlife. For a discussion and a critique of Islamic modernism see the works of Rahman cited above. "Islamic traditionalism" is, of course, a third response to the challenge facing Muslims in the modern world: a staunch defense not only of the Quran and the Traditions of the Prophet but also of the long tradition of Islamic law and mainline theology. Traditionalists reject, far more, cultural content considered to be alien in inspiration, than modernists or fundamentalists. All these categories, as described above, are oversimplified both in terms of behavioral and intellectual attributes.

17. These observations on religious resurgence in Egypt were made as discussant's comments by Fadwa El Guindi at the Conference on Religious Resurgence of Contemporary Islam, State University of New York at Binghamton, March 1981. See also El Guindi's article, "Veiling Infitah with Muslim Ethic: Egypt's Contemporary Islamic Movement," *Social Problems*, February 1981. Of course, the issue of backsliding would have to be addressed to develop a fuller understanding of the process of religious commitment.

hensiveness, of the broadening and deepening process of religious commitment accompanied and marked at once in terminology, style of life, personal conduct, and sociopolitical leadership.

ISLAMIC RESURGENCE

That Islamization has proceeded apace in the twentieth century may startle the students and advocates of modernization and secularization. That it should do so only indicates their too firm faith in the power of states and the influence of political elites. From a Muslim point of view, life lived on an non-Islamic basis is based on an absence of principle. As Gibb and Cantwell Smith have pointed out, in societies that have not undergone historical movements supportive of humanism such as the Renaissance and the Enlightenment, secularism proposed as such must fail and secularization, in so far as it is accepted, is accepted in terms of a religious idiom. Borthwick (1979) makes this point explicit for the recent history of Egypt where "Islamic" socialism was introduced in the 1960s. Operation "Badr," the surprise attack across the Suez Canal, took place in the 1970s and the Arab nation is referred to as the umma. Among the great majority of Middle Eastern people it is doubtful if the shift from a religious to a distinct nonreligious (national) identity and from religious legitimization for the State to nonreligious (ideological, popular, or pragmatic) legitimization has taken place. One index of this state of affairs is the continuing respect Muslims have for the personnel and the procedures of Muslim courts as opposed to indifference and/or suspicion they have for the personnel and procedures of civil courts in the self-same polities.

If Islamization is an undeniable and ongoing reality in the modern world, what, then, of "resurgence" or "revival'? Perhaps the easiest way to approach this question is to indicate what it is not. Manfred Wenner (1980: 143–44) speaks of revival in terms of the "increase in the power, prosperity and international respect paid to the Muslim states. . . ." He also regards the revival as involving a change of attitudes among the elites of Muslim countries such that their modes of expression reflect an increasing usage of "Muslim terms, expressions and referents in daily speech." Daniel Pipes (1980) has elaborated this theme by defining "revival" as the increase of political action in the name of Islam. He links the revival to the startling effects of the oil boom which have afforded vast resources, for instance, to Saudi Arabia and Libya who have supported the diffusion of Islamic beliefs through the export of religious literature and the sponsorship of international conferences and organizations. This oil boom has also led to social and economic disruption and, therefore, so the argument runs, to a turning toward Islam. Both Pipes and Wenner argue that the Islamic "revival" has nothing to do with an increase in the personal piety of the common man.

Unfortunately, Pipes and Wenner have taken the grain of truth that inheres in most arguments and made it into a mountain, thereby distorting the phenomenon under study and obscuring its significance. Worldly success for Muslims is "Muslim" success. As Cantwell Smith (1957) has pointed out, the course of history and its social shape are profoundly relevant for the quality of a Muslim's personal life. This is so because from the beginning the Muslim community (umma) had a dual religiopolitical nature: the religious functions of government—protecting the worship of the community of believers and the applications of Muslim law and ethics—were combined with its politicomilitary functions—protection of its citizens against internal and external violence. Every mundane act of the community has had two implications: meaning/consequence in terms of this world (for right conduct) and meaning/consequence in terms of the next (for salvation). As chapter 7 has demonstrated, religious acts have political implications (for instance, apostasy is often considered tantamount to treason) and political acts have religious implications (for instance, political weakness, the inability to defend the community of believers from colonial control, is often taken as an index of spiritual weakness). The clearest contemporary example of the simultaneous religio-socio-political nature of the Islamic community is the recently promulgated (1979) constitution of Iran, in which God is designated exclusively as the sovereign and the legislator (Chapter 1, Article 2), and one of the primary duties of government is declared to be the *ḥisba*, that is, "summoning men to good by enjoining good and forbidding evil" (Chapter 1, Article 8). The religious resurgence we are discussing, then, has not taken place because the Libyan or the Saudi Arabian or any other government has exported religious literature, has sponsored conferences, or has established chairs for the study of Islamic civilization. If that resurgence exists, it is because Muslims perceive that since the umma is gaining in economic vitality and political clout, its spiritual life is enhanced. From a Muslim point of view every mundane act of the community has a necessarily religious connotation if not denotation. Pipes's and Wenner's categorical claims as well as those of Victor Danner (1980)—that the "revival" we are witnessing has not to do with a change in the hearts of men—ought to be regarded as conjectures rejected on a priori grounds unless evidence is produced to indicate otherwise.

Whatever the inner and motivating content of Islamic resurgence, its social and political consequences as Lapidus (1983) has noted and Ayoob's (1981) volume has demonstrated, are varied and contradictory.[18] In Indonesia a social reform movement has taken root, in the Sudan a religious worship movement, and in Egypt Islamic resurgence has

---

18. Ira M. Lapidus, *Contemporary Islamic Movements in Historical Perspective* (University of California Press, Berkeley, 1983), 18.

been related to the adjustment of rural people to unsettling urban life.[19] During the 1970s in Iran and Syria Islamic resurgence was central to opposition to the established regime while in Pakistan, Egypt, and Malaysia it was related to efforts to legitimize the regime. But in the 1980s Islamic resurgence has become the bulwark of the "revolutionary establishment" in Iran while in Egypt it has increasingly played a major role in movements of opposition. The distinction between "government Islam" and "people's Islam" discussed in chapter 7 clarifies this muddle to a limited extent. The fact is that "Islamic revival" is a complex and variegated phenomenon involving various classes, ethnic groups, and political interests, all of which respond to change, both particular and local, and general and worldwide in the modern world.

ON THE MORAL STATE OF MUSLIM SOCIETY

This discussion leads directly into an important question which many scholars, both social scientists and humanists, wish to skirt. What is the moral state of Muslim society in the last quarter of the twentieth century? It would be presumptuous of me to suggest that I can answer such a question or that it can be answered. But, on the other hand, I am not satisfied with holding the position that no evidence is available. As a social anthropologist who has confined his research to two small peasant communities in Jordan and Iran, I can only report on the evidence that I have—and there is some evidence.

Before considering such evidence it would be well to remember the historical image of Islam developed in the Christian West over the course of a thousand years documented so well by Daniel (1960): the view that Muhammad was a licentious hypocrite; that polygamy and concubinage indicated the affirmation of self-indulgence; that Islam was a religion with a special propensity toward violence and power; the insistence on misunderstanding the content and meanings of Islamic ritual. Friday congregational prayers were seen as analogous to the Jewish Sabbath and the Christian Lord's Day, and the Muslim Fast as a travesty of Lent. Of course this historical image and moral evaluation has changed somewhat as power relations between European and Middle Eastern states changed and as our interest in and knowledge of other cultures has increased. But the negative moral evaluation of Islam so long in the making has had and continues to have an impact not only, to get down to cases, on U.S. public

19. See Henry Munson's (1987) analysis of the role of the petite bourgeoise in Islamic militancy in Egypt and Iran in chapter 10 of his *Islam and Revolution in the Middle East*. Munson challenges the view that Islamic militancy, particularly its leadership, is drawn from maladjusted low-middle-class urban migrants.

opinion but also on U.S. academic opinion. As late as 1947, Hamilton Gibb in reviewing Northrop's *The Meeting of the East and West* said:

> The most striking example of this deficiency is offered by his treatment of Islam and the Mohammedan world. Indeed, the omission of any study of Islam as a whole and its relegation to a few superficial and inaccurate paragraphs in the context of India, brings the student of Islamic culture up with a jolt. How has it come about that a philosopher who is so obviously in earnest in his study of world cultures has found nothing significant to say about the spiritual and philosophical foundations of Islam? To some extent Islamic orientalists have themselves to blame, by their failure to furnish non-orientalists with adequate materials for a study of this kind. Yet it is difficult to believe that if Professor Northrop had searched the available sources, he would not have found enough to correct his excessively political interpretation of Islam with its fantastic picture of 80 million Mohammedan Indians "instilled over the centuries with the dictatorial, frenzied, aggressive militant theism of a Mohammed." This refusal to extend to Islam the benefit of that charity and largeness of mind which is accorded to every other system of thought and belief is not only regrettable in itself, however. Within Islam there were made some of the earliest attempts to solve the very problem which he has set before himself, the integration of the positivist religious intuition with a theoretical analysis of the structure of things. (*The Middle East Journal*, Vol. 1, No. 3, July 1947)

Yet, Gibb himself, a giant in the field of Arab and Islamic studies in the West, in *Modern Trends in Islam* (1947), clearly indicated that parts of the Islamic world were in a state of moral breakdown.[20] What is of more interest, perhaps, is that some Muslim scholars have made the same moral evaluations. Fazlur Rahman, for instance, has declared that there is a tendency for contemporary Muslims "to emphasize the formal and nominal aspects of Islam at the manifest expense of its moral and spiritual content." He has argued that this kind of attitude "when combined with a

---

20. See H.A.R. Gibb, *Modern Trends in Islam* (University of Chicago Press, Chicago, 1947), 52, 103, 113, 119, 123, 125, and 136. In various places Gibb refers to the petrifaction of Islam's orthodox formulations and systematic theology and to its reform as being held up by emotional impulses. Many of its modernist reformers are, he says, "finding the strain of double-mindedness too severe to be borne or the social cost of modernism too high, [so that they] end up as ultra-orthodox bigots" (Gibb, 1947: 119). But he continues to hold that "Islam [apart from its orthodox formulations and social apologetic] is a living and vital religion, appealing to the hearts, minds, and consciences of tens and hundreds of millions, setting them a standard by which to live honest, sober, and god-fearing lives" (Gibb, 1947: 123).

predominantly deterministic doctrine, amounts to a sure fatality of the moral sense" (1966: 301).

A somewhat different but related line of thought espoused by Western scholars who have conducted research in Muslim countries, most notably Clifford Geertz, has argued that the world in general and Islam as part of it, has moved from a state of "religiousness" to a state of "religious-mindedness" (Geertz 1968: 18). That is, "the grasping power of the classical symbols has weakened" for many Muslims. This is not to say that they doubt their beliefs; rather they are disturbed by the inability of these beliefs to move them. "Religiousness," Geertz holds, "is not merely knowing the truth . . . but embodying it, living it . . ." (Geertz 1968: 16–17). Whereas, the religious-minded offer reasons for their beliefs—and they are still believers—the religious live their beliefs.[21]

Admittedly, the problem we are grappling with is a most difficult one, methodologically. How are we to determine, for instance, whether the building of new mosques, the establishment of government-sponsored religious publishing houses, the setting aside of special places in parliament for prayer, the establishment of religious political parties, or the establishment of bureaus to safeguard the Holy Quran are indications of religiousness, indications of religious-mindedness, indications of a shift in the attitudes of elites only, or simply an increase in political action in the name of Islam? Is an increasing use of Arabic, an increase in veiling, an increase in attendance at the Friday congregational prayer, or an increase in pilgrimage to be taken as an increase in piety, religious-mindedness, or hypocrisy? The fact that judgments must be qualitative does not relieve us from the obligation of making them.

My own study of the sermons of the Jordanian village preacher over the years 1959, 1960, 1966, and 1967 does not bear out the evaluations of Gibb and Rahman or even some of the inferences of Geertz. Although there may be some truth to Rahman's characterization of traditional Islam as deterministic, stressing political obedience (therefore leading to passivity and cynicism) and emphasizing justification by faith, it does not follow that Islam does not emphasize humanistic values, is not action-oriented, cannot or does not check despotism, and stresses nominal and formal aspects of religion rather than moral action and moral intent.

After hearing one of Luqman's Friday congregational sermons I was struck by the seeming moral obtuseness of his statement: "Help your [Muslim] brother, oppressor be he or oppressed (anṣar akhūka, thāliman kāna aw maTHlūman)." I said to him later, "How can Islam justify

21. Actually, Geertz's description and analysis is more complicated since he views men as constantly oscillating between a "religious" and a "religious-minded" perspective; one does not displace the other in a linear evolutionary fashion; rather, the frequency of the religious-minded perspective increases.

oppression?" He replied, "You do not understand. One aids the oppressed by struggling with him against oppression and one aids the oppressor by urging him to put aside his oppressive acts." As indicated in
chapter 7, at the end of my first period of research I put the following
question to twenty village informants: "If you were in a public meeting
and a citizen arose to defend a point of view that you and the majority of
the assembled considered contrary to the interest of the country and the
people, do you believe that he has the right to be heard?" The only villager to answer in the affirmative was the preacher. A number of sermons
before and during the month of Ramadan, focused on a pillar of the faith,
fasting. The preacher stressed that the fast was observed on three levels,
each higher than the preceding. There was the general fast: the abstention
from food, drink, and sexual intercourse. There was the special fast: the
abstention from slander, killing, and malevolence. And there was the elevated fast: the fast of the heart from all its vices. "The believer who fasts
all day," he said, "and thieves with his eyes and slanders with his tongue
gains nothing from the fast, nothing but hunger and thirst."

Of the twenty-six sermons transliterated and translated by me in four
separate periods of field work, one dealt with politics (Palestine), six dealt
with ritual obligations (e.g., pilgrimage, and fasting), six dealt with religious history (e.g., Muhammad's prophecy and struggle), seven dealt
with theological concerns, and fifteen—over half—dealt with ethical concerns: filial piety, the necessity of mutual aid among co-religionists and
co-villagers, the doing of good deeds, the necessity of equal treatment to
wives and siblings, the obligations of kinship, and women's modesty and
men's honor.

The preacher did not neglect subjects that related to the modern world
and to the modernizing aspirations of Muslim states. He gave a sermon
on education, as recorded in chapter 5. The sermon was not just a statement of high ideals, for the issue was a local and pressing one:

> Oh ye people, inhabitants of this village, there is an obligation placed
> on your shoulders: it is the creating of a school for the instruction of
> your children and their education (tathqifihim). It is incumbent upon
> you to take up this command with striving and sincerity. Leave ig-
> norance and selfishness and proceed as a collectivity to raise the
> money needed for constructing a new school in your village even if
> its cost is great.

The preacher gave a sermon on work:

> The Prophet of Islam excited an interest in working for the sake of a
> livelihood. He said, "*No one has eaten food at all better than he who
> eats the food of his own hand.*" The Prophet of God, Da'ud, who

was obeyed by the angels, used to eat of the work of his own hand
[only]. Those of most acute discernment, the companions of the
Prophet, worked for this world as they worked for the next. The just
caliph, Omar ibn al-Khattab, said: "Don't sit, any of you, and ask
for a livelihood, for you must know that heaven does not rain down
gold—or silver." The man who takes up a trade profits from it and
finds freedom, thereby, from [other] men and from beggary. He who
spends on his wife and children is better than the poor man who begs
from men and lives on [the work] of others.

As he did with respect to the subject of education, the preacher linked
work at one and the same time to the religious community and the destiny
of the nation-state:

The religion of Islam is a religion of work and striving and activity—
not a religion of inactivity and indolence. It is incumbent on the religious community to create and strive and resuscitate the country
with cultivation and the proliferation of factories and companies
which will work for the augmentation of wealth and blessings.

My research in Jordan, then, does not support Rahman's view of a
passive, formalistic, emotional Islam with a reduced moral standard leading to passivity rather than activism. On the contrary, it suggests an ethically oriented Islam emphasizing moral action and rejecting a formal definition of religious obligation in favor of an inquiry into moral intent.
My research in Iran, on the other hand, did record an Islam more oriented toward the formal aspects of religion—prayers, pilgrimages, visi-
tations to the tombs of the imams—and toward its emotional and soteriological aspects—elegies, flagellation, the martyrdom of Husayn, and
salvation. Two of the three religious edifices in the village studied, the
Husayniyya and the imamzadeh (the other being the mosque), were not
focused at all toward the solution of contemporary social, economic, or
political problems but rather toward that "other world to live in" that
marks "religious" experience. Yet the traditional soteriological and one
might argue hagiologic emphasis of Ithna 'Ashari (Twelver) Islam, as
Hegland has convincingly argued, has been capable—one might go further—is inherently capable of supporting moral action of the most extreme kind, calling for risking one's own life to oppose what is defined as
tyrannical rule.[22] A traditional, inward-looking, emotion-fraught Islam

22. See Mary Hegland's provocative argument based on local-level field research in Iran
in the following articles: "Two Images of Hosain: Accommodation and Revolution in an
Iranian Village," in *Religion and Politics in Iran*, Nikki Keddie, editor (Yale University
Press, New Haven, 1982); "Ritual and Revolution in Iran," in *Political Anthropology*, Vol.
2, *Culture and Political Change*, Myron Aronoff, editor (Transaction Books, 1983); and

not only provided the moral drive for a revolution but also was a leading factor in engineering the downfall of the regime. Such action surely cannot be the product of sheer "religious-mindedness." It is a product of the continuing pertinence of the moral-ethical revolution expressed in the Quran, a revolution that introduced individual responsibility and produced a new moral division of labor within the family and a new vision of the societal structure.

Mumtaz Ahmed's conclusion regarding a common reaction of the Muslims of West Pakistan in 1971 to the war with India, the loss of Bengal, and the separation of East Pakistan to form the independent state of Bangladesh is significant for the matter at hand. Many Muslims pointed out that East Pakistan was lost "because people had not been good Muslims in their personal . . . [or] collective behavior." Everywhere on the walls of big cities were posted the slogan, "What broke up the country? Liquor!" in reference to President General Yahya Khan's personal life and his reputation as a drunkard.[23] Of course, this view reflects the Islamic fundamentalist's assumption that all political and economic problems are essentially moral ones. But the direct implication is more specific. Responsibility for human action is placed squarely on individuals who are held accountable by God for their own conduct and their treatment of their fellow human beings. It would be difficult to construe the reaction of West Pakistani Muslims to the schism of their country as a "fatality of the moral sense."

Lest the above-mentioned remarks be taken as a "new apologetic" for Islam, it should be stated that the author is not unaware that the Islamic corpus of law and ethics and certain key Islamic symbols to be discussed in the next section, are not always elevating in their implications for human beings and for particular categories of the population. The discussion of the symbol, hizbi, or "party man" in chapter 7 should have made this fact painfully clear. Elsewhere I have devoted a rather long essay to the constraining implications of certain parts of the Islamic corpus for women, particularly peasant women in the Arab Muslim world.[24] Moreover, chapter 9 of the Quran (*Surat al-Tawba*) in its condemnation of ritually impure idolators including Christian monks and Jewish rabbis

"Islamic Revival or Cultural Revolution? An Iranian Case Study," in *Religious Resurgence: Contemporary Cases in Islam, Christianity and Judaism*, Richard T. Antoun and Mary E. Hegland, editors (Syracuse University Press, Syracuse, 1987). See also her Ph.D. dissertation, "Imam Khomaini's Village: Recruitment to Revolution," State University of New York at Binghamton, 1986.

23. See Mumtaz Ahmad's "Islamic Revival in South Asia," in *Fundamentalism, Revivalism and Violence and South Asia*, James B. Jörkman, editor (Riverdale Press, Riverdale, Md., 1987), 24 and footnote 33.

24. For details "On the Modesty of Women in Arab Muslim Villages: A Study in the Accommodation of Traditions," *American Anthrpologist*, Vol. 70, No. 4, August 1968.

provides the basis for religious and legal discrimination and persecu-tion.[25] These constraining implications are there and cannot and must not be hidden.

Two caveats are in order here. Elevating and constraining aspects can be found in all the great religious traditions including Bhuddist, Chris-tian, Hindu, Jewish, and Zoroastrian; particular investigations of con-straining or elevating aspects should not be taken as representative of the whole tradition. Second, judgments about particular aspects of religious traditions are always value-laden. As Geertz (1984) has reminded us, meaningful universals of culture and society are hard to come by. Defini-tions of the big words to which many religious traditions attach impor-tance such as "order," "salvation," "freedom," and "believer," are quite different and so it should not be unexpected that the view of the role of different social institutions such as government, family, party, and citizen should differ too. Moreover, as Shweder and Bourne (1982) have stressed, from whatever point of view the social scientist or humanist views the diversity of humankind—universalist, relativist, evolutionist, or even "confusionist"—that point of view inevitably, has both strengths and weaknesses for understanding ourselves, our societies, and, one might add, our religions.[26]

THE BREADTH OF THE ISLAMIC CORPUS

Part of the difficulty of Westerners' understanding the moral resiliency and continued social effectiveness of Islam in the twentieth century is an ignorance on the part of non-Muslims of the nature of Islam's enormous corpus of law and ethics, the derived capacity for diverse interpretations, and the possibilities of adaptation to various social structures and geo-graphic and historical circumstances. Perhaps no aspect of Islam's social legislation is so well known in the West as that pertaining to polygyny. The Quranic proof-text for polygyny is Surah 4, Verse 3:

And if ye fear that ye will not deal fairly by the orphans, marry of the women who seem good to you, two or three or four; and if ye

25. All these Quranic verses are open to interpretation, and what may seem like a con-straining verse can be construed as liberating and vice-versa. For instance, some villagers in Kufr al-Ma questioned the propriety and legality of my attending the Friday congregational sermon in the mosque since I had not performed the ritual ablutions required of Muslims for purification. When this question was brought up later to the visiting preacher who had delivered the Friday sermon, he quoted a tradition of the prophet, recounting that Muham-mad had put up visiting Christians from Najran in the mosque of Medina overnight. Shaykh Luqman had justified my presence earlier in response to similar questions by saying that there was always the possibility that I might convert to Islam.

26. For further details see Geertz, "Distinguished Lecture: Anti-Relativism," *American Anthropologist*, Vol. 86, No. 2, June 1984.

fear that ye cannot do justice (to so many) then one (only) or (the captives) that your right hands possess. Thus it is more likely that ye will not do injustice.

The statement is a conditional one with two clauses. Commentators of the Quran who stress the first clause emphasize the permissive implications of the verse and the right of polygyny; commentators who stress the second clause, on the other hand, emphasize the restrictive aspects of the verse and interpret it as requiring monogamy since they argue, no human being can treat several others equally in all respects. In fact there is a specific Quranic basis for this interpretation for elsewhere (Surah 4, Verse 129) the Quran says, **Ye will not be able to deal equally between** (your) **wives.** . . . Therefore, an institution that has been regarded as a hallmark of Islam, polygyny, is in fact open to question and even denial.

Much has been made of Islam's toleration of political autocracy and its stress on political obedience. Yet some form of representative government can be argued for on the basis of the Quranic endorsement of the shura, a consultative body, and on the basis of a principal source of Islamic law and ethics, *ijmā'* or consensus. Of course, as Rahman (1966: 296) has pointed out, that consensus would have to be oriented toward the future rather than the past. Indeed, we are not speaking here about potentialities. We have just witnessed the establishment of an Islamic "republic" in Iran with an elected parliament, a Council of Guardians, and stipulations for a Leadership Council and an Assembly of Experts to make key appointments and to handle the problem of succession (see Chapter 8 of the 1979b Iranian constitution). The Iranian case is an instructive one with respect to the flexibility of the Islamic corpus, inasmuch as Shi'a Ithna 'Ashari Islam has been regarded as one of the more conservative Islamic traditions. Keddie (1980: 533) has recently pointed out just how much ideological change has occurred within it:

> Khomaini's political position is not just a restatement of any past important line of thought in Shi'ism. Shariatmadari is, in his "moderation," more traditional than Khomaini, although in its specifics even Shariatmadari's tradition goes back less than a century; before 1905 no ulama argued for constitutions and before Khomaini, whatever the claims of some ulema to greater legitimacy than the kings, none argued that kings should not exist and ulema should rule Iran directly.

If we are to accept Keddie's analysis, then we must conclude that there has been considerable change in Ithna Ashari religious ideology from a belief in the non-necessity of following the consensus of *mujtahids* (religious scholars) to the belief that one must follow them in law to the belief that has evolved in our own time that they should be followed in government. In an earlier (1965) analysis, Binder has pointed out the distinctive features of Shi'a Islam in Iran—the greater authority accorded to its men of learning, the absence of a challenge to their authority, the greater centralization of the scholarly establishment, and their greater autonomy from government control. These characteristics are a reflection of the resilience of Ithna 'Ashari Islam today and its capacity to adapt to geographical, social structural, historical, and specifically Iranian circumstances. This adaptation was so successful that in 1978 and 1979 it was able to mobilize substantial elements of the population in a grass-roots revolution. To dramatize the historical possibilities of interpretation of the vast corpus of law and ethics, one need only recall Ghani's (1978) characterization of Amir Abdur Rahman's version of Islam a hundred years earlier in neighboring Afghanistan: jihad was the key military obligation, zakat became the key social obligation, obedience to kings became the key political obligation, and values supporting the ruler's policies of economic modernization and political centralization such as trustworthiness, keeping contracts, and paying taxes became the hallmarks of Islam.

The capacity of the Islamic corpus of law and ethics to reflect diverse meanings extends even to such key passages of the Quran as that which has been taken as a proof-text for political obedience: "**Oh believers, obey God, and obey the Messenger and those in authority among you** . . ." (4: 59, *P*). This verse has commonly been interpreted as demanding obedience by Muslims to political authority however arbitrary. But, on the other hand, the command to "obey those in authority among you" can be construed as implicitly conditional on their (those in authority) "obey[ing] God." Therefore, a ruler who in his actions and beliefs clearly violated God's word (the Quran) is not due obedience. Clearly, in the history of Islam the Kharijites, who were often in rebellion against established authority, did not interpret the above-mentioned verse as stipulating obedience to rulers irrespective of the morality of their behavior.

The proof-text for obedience of Christians to political authority is likewise open to interpretation: "Render to Caesar the things that are Caesar's and to God the things that are God's" (Mark 12:17). This verse can be construed as meaning that "since the major problem of the Jews [from Jesus' point of view] was not political [rather religious, one of religious decision], no political solution would be adequate for it."[27] Or, alternatively, the message can be construed as two-edged. If it calls for political submission to the powers that be, it also calls for the militant defense of the freedom of the spirit and the autonomy of the personality.[28]

27. H. C. Kee and F. Young, *Understanding the New Testament* (Prentice-Hall, Englewood Cliffs, 1957), 162.
28. See Genovese, *Roll, Jordon, Roll*, book 2, part 1.

Or, to take an instance of more specific application to "socialist" re-
gimes in the Middle East such as Nasser's Egypt, Asad's Syria, or Hussein's Iraq, Islamic law and ethics can be martialed against differences of
social stratification by relying on the Tradition of the Prophet:

People are equal as the teeth of a comb.

or in favor of such differences by relying on the Quranic verse:

**We have apportioned among them their livelihood in the life of the
world, and raised some of them above others in rank that some of
them may take labour from others. . . . (43: 32, P).**

Or, finally, consider the options and potential variable interpretations
of the Tradition of the Prophet quoted in the previous chapter:

*He among you who sees a denier [of truth] must correct him by his
hand. If not possible by his tongue. If not possible by his heart.*

Diversity of interpretation, then, does not occur only at the national
level and in urban centers among gifted scholars, or in the courts of kings
and in state capitals as some of the above-mentioned examples might suggest. It occurs at the local level too. The previous chapter demonstrated
the variety of interpretations of five Friday congregational sermons in the
Palestine-Transjordan area in four separate locations—all on the subject
of the Prophet's night journey and ascent. One preacher devoted almost
the entire sermon to the soteriological implications of the event (holy war
and salvation); a second devoted most of the sermon to discussing its
contemporary political implications (the restoration of Palestine to Muslim rule); a third focused on its theological significance (was it a miracle,
and, if so, what kind); and the fourth highlighted its religiopsychological
significance (the event occurred at a low point in Muhammad's career
after the death of his uncle and protector, Abu Talib, and his wife Khadija
and after the rejection of his mission at Taif). Moreover, two of the five
sermons were given by the same preacher on consecutive Fridays. The
first covered mainly religious and theological themes, but the second
made no allusions to such themes and was entirely devoted to a description of the career of Salah al-Din al-Ayyubi (Saladin). Its major theme
was political (the reconquest of occupied Muslim lands) and its minor
theme was modernization—Saladin triumphed in part because he was
quick to adopt whatever technological and social organizational improvements were available. Thus, diversity of interpretation is not only
between different scholars and different preachers but by the same
scholar and the same preacher on different occasions.

As the substance of this book suggests, the flexibility of the Islamic
corpus and its openness to meaning is never demonstrated more clearly

than in the interpretation of key symbols. This capacity for "condensation" can be illustrated by one more important example, that of jihad. Of course, jihad means "holy war," the collective obligation of the Muslim community to defend itself against aggression. But jihad also means the internal personal struggle of Muslims to achieve virtue. Lapidus has stated the significance of the matter succinctly: "both personal, religious and collective political goals [are expressed] in the same condensed symbols."[29] Built into the symbol of jihad are both an active and a passive mode, both an external and an internal orientation. Hegland's (1982) analysis of the symbol of "Husayn" (grandson of the Prophet and third imam of the Shi'a Muslims) in revolutionary Iran demonstrates this possibility of Muslims to shift gears, as it were, even more graphically. Husayn as patron and intercessor and, hence, symbol of political accommodation became in the new situation, Husayn, the martyr and symbol of political revolution. Both revolt and political accommodation to the unjust exertion of power are inherent in the single symbol.[30]

In the contemporary political situation in Israel, the concept of *geula*, redemption, like the concept of hizbi, "party man" in the contemporary political situation in Jordan has a similar labile character. Redemption, which in the biblical context referred to redemption of the ancient Hebrews from slavery in Egypt and from captivity in Babylon, has been reinterpreted by some Zionists to mean in the twentieth century settlement of the West Bank, land reclamation, and redeeming Jews from the Soviet Union (the external active mode); rather than the personal revolution of every Jew in way of life, vocation, and language (the internal active mode); or obeying the Law in all its details in preparation for the Messiah (the internal passive mode).[31]

Just as Judaism has built into its symbolic structure Maccabean Judaism as well as pharisaical Judaism, so Shi'a Islam has built into its structure the contrast of Imam Hasan (the elder accommodationist brother) and Imam Husayn (the younger revolutionary brother) or in another version, Husayn, the intercessor-accommodator, and Husayn, the martyr-revolutionary. The rich potential for interpretation of the key symbols of Islamic movements, their condensed quality, their capacity to unite mean-

29. Lapidus, *Contemporary Islamic Movements*, 46.

30. See Hegland 1982a, 1982b, and 1987.

31. See Borthwick 1979 and Paine 1984 for details. Deshen has extended the discussion of religious symbols in Israel into the analysis of multivocality in the political party campaigning occurring in and around the synagogue in relation to a Torah Scroll presentation. In this instance, an Israeli political party, Pai, used as its election symbol the capital letter, D—which also symbolized the central credo of the Jewish faith, "Hear, O Israel, the Lord is our God, the Lord is One (ehad)," repeated at least three times in daily prayers. See Shlomo Deshen and Shokeid Moshe, *The Predicament of Homecoming* (Cornell University Press, Ithaca, 1974), chapter 5.

ings from the past and present, for an active or a passive mode, and in relation to an inner personal experience or an external threatening civilization surely help to account for their persistence and the persistence of the movements they symbolize in the modern world.

THE REINTERPRETATION OF TRADITION

It is time now to return to the theme pursued at the beginning of this book, the interpretation of tradition. Chapter 1 broached the universal problem/process of the management of the two-way flow of ideas over the culture gap between the great and little traditions in a comparative cross-cultural framework. The chapter focused on the necessity of the linker, the culture broker, to exercise choice (interpretation) in presenting the tradition to his audience. The chapter called attention to various perspectives for studying the process including the perspective of the religious specialist as well as that of the folk (his audience). Although a cultural gap was assumed to exist between specialist and audience, quite often that gap was closed to a considerable extent, and an interpenetration of traditions took place, because of or in spite of such brokers. The study of the social organization of tradition was regarded as problematic as long as the process was conceptualized in unitary and global terms, personified in particular individuals, and pursued without contextualization in time, space, and relevant interest areas, for example, politics, economics, and religion.

With the benefit of our case study of the culture broker and his product (the sermon) behind us, let us pursue the problem of the interpretation of tradition further—particularly with respect to its contextualization in time and to changes in "intellectual technology,"[32] "mode of cultural reproduction,"[33] "articulation of cultural media,"[34] and the role of the in-

32. The concept of "intellectual technology," a phrase coined by Jack Goody, refers to the mode of storing information and involves the introduction and spread of literacy, more specifically, the degree to which there exists a technical (by the specialist) as opposed to nontechnical mastery of reading skills and a restricted as opposed to generalized command of writing skills. Goody's assumption is that changes in modes of thought are preceded by changes in techniques of storing information. See Goody, *Literacy in a Traditional Society* (1968) and *The Domestication of the Savage Mind* (1977).

33. Mode of cultural reproduction refers to the institutions that reproduce the norms and beliefs of a society which in turn place constraints on its practice. See Pierre Bourdieu, "Cultural Reproduction and Social Reproduction," in R. Brown, editor, 1973 and Bourdieu, *Outline of a Theory of Practice*, Richard Nice, translator (Cambridge University Press, Cambridge, 1982).

34. Articulation of culture media refers to the degree to which symbols, particularly ritual acts, convey precise as opposed to vague meanings. See Robert Hefner, *Hindu Javanese* for its usage in analysis of ritual form and meaning.

dividual believer in cultural transmission. To help in this task I shall draw on the work of Mottahedeh (1985), Nelson (1985), and particularly on the work of Eickelman (1985) and Hefner (1985).

Early in his book, *The Mantle of the Prophet, Religion and Politics in Iran*, Mottahedeh contrasts the old style of Islamic learning exemplified by the early eleventh-century scholar, Avicenna, with the new (later to become "traditional") style of learning exemplified by the Islamic law college (madrasa) established at the end of that century. Avicenna learned arithmetic, grammar, literature, and the Quran in his early years as well as Islamic law. He soon broadened his knowledge by the study of Aristotelian logic, Euclidian geometry, Ptolemaic astronomy, medicine, and philosophy. His practice of medicine was so accomplished that he became the king's royal physician in Rayy near modern Tehran. In this older style of learning, exemplified by Avicenna, the broad-gauge scholar wandered from teacher to teacher; taught in informal discussion circles in many different places; debated by principles of contrariety and contradiction other learned men who were "thrust into each other's presence by a bored or curious monarch"; and passed on the knowledge of particular subjects, such as medicine and philosophy, individually and informally.[35]

The new mode of teaching that replaced private dyadic learning and the informal discussion circle, at first in Mesopotamia and later in the Muslim world at large, was the madrasa. The madrasa was a charitable, corporate trust, founded by rulers and ministers, existing in perpetuity, taking on large numbers of students and providing a standard curriculum focusing on religious law (shari'a) and the subjects that would illuminate it: the relationship of the law to its sources (*uṣūl al-fiqh*), grammar and rhetoric (now taught as courses), the principles for deriving the law from its sources or jurisprudence (*fiqh*), logic (*mantaq*), and scholastic theology (using logic to reason about the creator's intention for his creation) or *kalām*.[36]

In his study of the education of a twentieth-century notable, *Knowledge and Power in Morocco*, Eickelman has spelled out what a traditional primary, secondary, and "mosque college" (madrasa) education entailed in Morocco before it was engulfed by French colonial policies in the 1930s. In the initial stages of education students were often taught at home by relatives—with rigorous discipline and little explanation of memorized material. Eickelman stresses that only the oral transmission

35. See Mottahedeh, *The Mantle of the Prophet* (Simon & Schuster, New York, 1985), 82ff.

36. See George Makdise, *The Rise of Colleges: Institutions of Learning in Islam and the West*, 1981 for a detailed treatment of the rise of the law college in Islam. See also his article, "The Guilds of Law in Medieval Legal History: An Inquiry into the Origins of the Inns of Court," *Cleveland State Law Review*, Vol. 34, No. 1, 1985–1986.

of knowledge was culturally legitimate; learning was reciting a selected text and being corrected by the teacher. Mnemonic knowledge was considered purer than writing since knowledge acquired exclusively from the study of books was considered unreliable. The Muslim primary school or kuttab did not teach reading and writing, and the primary school teacher usually had no printed or manuscript copy of the Quran; rather he wrote the verses to be memorized on the blackboard each day, and only many years later, if the student persisted in attaining a religious education—and most did not—would he gain some idea of the literal meaning of the verses. In order not to misconstrue the significance of Quranic memorization and recitation, however, one must remember that what was being inculcated by such recitation was "meaning" rather than "information."

Shaykh Abd al-Rahman, the rural notable studied by Eickelman, recalled that as a child he had been beaten by his father each night if he did not recite five parts (hizbs) of the Quran—other children were required to recite only one part—without error. He also told Eickelman that he felt no resentment toward his father for such beatings since they indicated the father's concern for his children, that is, for their salvation. Children were told that the parts of the body hit did not burn in hell.[37] Subsequently, after leaving the primary school taught by his elder brother, Shaykh Abd al-Rahman was placed in the care of a renowned teacher. Before finishing memorization of the Quran under the tutelage of this shaykh he was required to memorize two grammar books (one composed of one thousand rhymed verses) and subsequently several handbooks of Islamic jurisprudence—all between the ages of thirteen and fifteen.

Eickelman points out that there existed an underlying attitude toward the attainment of religious knowledge: Man was endowed with reason (ʿaql) which gave him the ability to discipline his own nature in accord with the code of conduct laid down by God. This discipline was, therefore, inculcated along with the memorization and recitation of the Quran and subsequent works, and also manifested in such religious obligations as the feast of Ramadan.[38] No explanation of Quranic verses was ever sought by the student since to seek explanation at this level was considered blasphemy. Explanation of the Quran was a science and required years of study, particularly of the exegetical literature (tafsīr).

Understanding of the Quran (or other texts) would later be evaluated by the ability to make practical reference to it in appropriate contexts. This underlying attitude toward religious knowledge was demonstrated on many occasions during the course of my field work in Kufr al-Ma. For

37. See Dale F. Eickelman, *Knowledge and Power in Morocco: The Education of a Twentieth-Century Notable* (Princeton University Press, Princeton, 1985), 50ff.
38. Ibid., 62ff.

instance, during the winter season I would often look up at the partly cloudy sky in the morning and ask a villager if he thought it was going to rain. He usually replied by reciting a verse from the Quran such as, **Hast thou not seen that God knows whatsoever is in the heavens, and whatsoever is in the earth** (58: 7, A). Once when a villager and I were discussing our respective back problems, I commented that man had a pronounced tendency to have such problems because unlike the rest of animal creation who walked on four legs, man was a strange two-legged creature who stood upright behind the plow or, as hunter, ran on two feet after his prey. The villager, by way of refutation of my invidious comparison, immediately quoted the Quranic verse: **Surely we created man of the best stature** (95: 4, P).

Education at the mosque-university in Marrakesh, the Yusufiya, involved sitting in various lesson circles in the mosque, led by particular scholars who doubled as father figures. Student life was intensely communal and simulated the family; younger students washed and did chores for older students in return for lessons. Eickelman points out that the mosque-university was not discretely set off from the life of the community. On the contrary, its activities "were intricately meshed with the wider social and cultural life of the community."[39] Townspeople were free to walk into the mosque-college and join any lesson circles taking place there. Students, on their part, recited the Quran for recompense in smaller neighborhood mosques and on the occasion of weddings, circumcisions, and funerals. The wealthier students at the university also developed special ties with well-known teachers through pan-regional family networks and, thereby, developed special patron-client relations in society at large. The madrasa itself was supported by gifts of produce and clothes from the people of the city, and by religious endowments established by lay Muslims, which provided water in fountains, stipends for Quranic recitations, and daily bread rations for students. Many lesser circles met in the city's religious lodges, shrines, and smaller mosques besides those meeting in the main mosque-college.

As in previous stages of education, the form of knowledge was the oral transmission of a series of texts students were expected to memorize after reception by dictation. No questions were asked in class;[40] this would

39. Ibid., 77ff. On this point see also Eickelman, "The Art of Memory: Islamic Education and Its Social Reproduction," *Comparative Studies in Society and History*, Vol. 20, No. 4, 1978.

40. The lack of questioning and development of a critical faculty is certainly not characteristic of the style of learning at the madrasa of Qum in Iran. Michael Fischer describes the mosque college education there as stressing argument and counterargument (*mujādala*). Therefore Eickelman's characterization of Muslim higher education in Morocco may not be typical of the Muslim word. See Fischer's *Iran: From Religious Dispute to Revolution* (Harvard University Press, Cambridge, 1980).

have been an insult to the teacher, and aside from the texts, note-taking was not expected. Eickelman observes that the effect of this form of cultural transmission was the deflection of "attention from awareness of historical and contextual transformations."[41] He stressed that no sharply defined body of students, faculty, administration, course examinations, entrance exams, curriculum, united source of funds (from a state budget or alumni), or "graduation" existed in the law college at Marrakesh. The definition of a "student" (*tālib*) entitled to reside in university housing was vague, and, to all intents and purposes, a talib (literally, "seeker of knowledge") was "anyone who had memorized the Quran (or claimed to have done so) and who was oriented toward life-long religious learning."[42]

As alluded to above, students acquired knowledge in two other milieus besides the lesson circle: through peer learning (on a one-on-one basis with a somewhat older student) or in literary circles; and through sponsorship by a man or men of learning who orally transmitted the texts they knew over a number of years and provided a certificate (ijaza) indicating the texts studied and the specified qualifications of the teacher. Eickelman comments that in many instances the religious knowledge gained through this traditional mode of education was used iconically and instrumentally rather than substantively. That is, it was used as a prestige marker and to establish a wide-ranging social network useful for business ties across Morocco, rather than to prepare and qualify students for posts as judges, teachers, and scribes.

The introduction of French colonialism into Morocco including French control (and thereby disgrace) of the mosque-university and the French-language educational system which provided privileged access to the bureaucracy and a reliable income in a poor country led in the 1930s to the collapse of the traditional form of premadrasa and madrasa education. By the time Islamic resurgence occurred in Morocco in the 1980s, the intellectual technology of cultural transmission had changed along with the code of cultural reproduction. The concept of knowledge as a fixed and memorizable truth was undermined as thousands of Moroccans moved after the 1930s through French or French-influenced secular schools or alternatively, since the 1960s, through government-controlled religious institutes. Eickelman observes that replacements for the older generation of shaykhs who progressed through the traditional educational system are now bureaucratically appointed specialists who, in the view of many Moroccans, "carry neither the authority nor the sense of legitimacy" possessed by the older generation of scholars.[43] Religious specialists no longer consider mnemonic learning received orally from a

41. See Eickelman, *Knowledge and Power*, 94ff.
42. Ibid., 85.
43. Ibid., 168.

chain of traditional transmitters as superior, and they have emancipated themselves from long-term apprenticeship to a shaykh.

With the dissemination of books, mimeographed tracts, waqf journals, and, most recently, cassette lessons and lectures, the printed word has become the foundation of religious knowledge for religious specialists, and the mass media the means for the dissemination of religious knowledge for the populace at large. This shift in intellectual technology has widened the scope of eligible carriers of religious knowledge, as Eickelman observes, to "anyone who can claim a strong Islamic commitment. . . ."[44] The shift has the further implication that "religious knowledge can be delineated and interpreted in a more abstract and flexible fashion."[45] Furthermore, this shift has been accompanied by a spatial and institutional shift of religious activity away from the mosque and into the school, the home and, in the 1980s the street.

The question of the implications of high as opposed to low popular participation in religious ritual and activity alluded to by Eickelman has been discussed by Robert Hefner at greater length in *Hindu Javanese: Tengger Tradition and Islam* (1985). Hefner describes, for certain villages of eastern Java, the unusual situation of a priesthood that performs many village and household rituals out of sight and/or earshot of the great majority of believers. Even when such rituals are performed within earshot they are usually not given close attention or, if attended and heard, not understood; or if understood, understood imperfectly in a variety of ways (e.g., the identity of guardian and family spirits are construed differently by different believers).[46] Hefner raises the question of how belief is sustained when the audience of believers is not present to hear "the magical power of [the priest's] words" in key rituals.[47] He argues by way of reply that "the efficacy of ritual speech" "does not depend on villagers' understanding what the priest says in prayer" nor does the villagers' spiritual welfare depend on their presence during the performance of priestly rites. The performance of such rites is addressed to the gods of Mount Bromo and to the ancestors and not to living mortals; villagers receive no additional blessing by attending priestly rituals and listening to their prayers.[48] The efficacy of ritual speech depends, rather, "on the prayers being performed by the right person in the right fashion under the right circumstances,"[49] that is, by the normative prescription and institutionalization of the priest's role in the community. Nonattenders and nonhearers

44. Ibid.
45. Ibid.
46. See Hefner, *Hindu Javenese: Tengger Tradition and Islam* (Princeton University Press, Princeton, 1985), 184.
47. Ibid., 212ff.
48. Ibid., 213.
49. Ibid.

nevertheless do believe that the priest's prayers invoke the ancestors and guardian deities who protect the village and its individual households; the priest's work with the gods does not require the participation or even the attendance of the believers.

In Islam, on the other hand, popular participation in religious ritual, normatively, must be high. Attendance at the Friday congregational prayer (ṣalāt al-jumʿa) is strongly recommended by the four Sunni Muslim law schools, the Shafi'i school holding that forty Muslims must be present in the mosque in order for the worship service to be valid.[50] In Muhammad's own time and still today in small rural communities in Jordan the absence of adult males from the Friday congregational prayers is regarded as disruptive of social as well as religious harmony.[51] Furthermore, the congregation must participate in the Friday prayer corporately and individually in the five daily ritual prayers (salat) for religious reasons. The ritual prayers have soteriological and, according to some scholars, sacramental significance. They are regarded as intimate conversations with God.[52] As Nelson's (1985) study, *The Art of Reciting the Qur'an*, suggests, from a Muslim point of view recitation of the Quran on the one hand and listening to its recitation on the other is religious experience in an ultimate sense: it engages the heart and clarifies the mind as only a brief audition/glimpse/sense of "another world to live in" can bring about.[53] For Muslims the Quran is divine, transcendent, and fluid, and its meaning cannot be captured by any single rhythm or recitation.[54] Thus, there is a drive for continued recitation on the one hand and audition on the other by Muslim worshipers.[55]

The Tengger Javanese example and the Jordanian Muslim example illustrate the problem of the congruence of belief/interpretation as between ritual specialist and lay audience by posing the two limiting cases: the private learning of the liturgy by the Tengger priest from his own father in his own home, and the absence or nonattention of worshipers in sub-

50. See the article on *Djum'a* in *The Shorter Encyclopaedia of Islam*, 93.

51. See S. D. Goitein, editor, *Studies in Islamic History and Institutions* (E. J. Brill, Leiden, 1968), chapter 5 on the sociopolitical significance of the Friday congregational worship service in Muhammad's time.

52. See the article on *salat* in *The Shorter Encyclopaedia of Islam*, 498. See also Padwick, *Muslim Devotions: A Study of Prayer Manuals in Common Use*, part 3, 1961.

53. The term *glimpse* is not inappropriate here since Nelson has pointed out that one of the aims of the professional Quran reciter, even though his medium is sound, is getting the hearer "to picture the meaning." See pp. 58–59, 63, 65. The phrase *another world to live in* is taken from Clifford Geertz, "Religion as a Cultural System," in *Anthropological Approaches to the Study of Religion*, Michael Banton, editor (Tavistock, London, 1966).

54. See Nelson, *Art of Reciting the Qur'an*, 181 and 178ff.

55. For an analysis of the religious significance of the Quran, including its theological significance, see Fazlur Rahman, *Major Themes of the Qur'an* (Bibliotheca Islamica, Chicago, 1980).

sequent public priestly rituals; and the public acquisition of religious knowledge in the madrasa or (today) junior colleges or state-run preachers' colleges with the necessary attendance of worshipers at weekly congregational prayers and prayer meetings. In the Jordanian Muslim case the degree of public participation in religion goes even further. In Kufr al-Ma in the 1980s many mature adult men and, increasingly, younger men train in private two-year junior colleges where they pursue religious studies, and have begun to play the role of culture brokers, a role that was formerly played by the preacher, the religious judge in the subdistrict, and a few other knowledgeable elders.

This dispersion of cultural brokerage in the field of religion is related to another important distinction Hefner has drawn between "less articulate" and "more articulate" cultural media.[56] By "less articulate" Hefner means "less capable of precise semantic communication" as compared with spoken media such as prayer.[57] Hefner has pointed out that "it is the less articulate cultural media [gesture, offerings, ritual implements (of the priests)] that are most directly accessible to non-priests during ritual performance."[58] Even when Tengger ritual is more articulate, for example, when the priest prays, and the believers are in attendance, the prayer is often "virtually inaudible to all those assembled."[59] Tengger priestly religion, then, is clearly characterized by less articulate cultural media with a low degree of participation in ritual while rural Jordanian Islam is characterized by more articulate cultural media with a high degree of participation in ritual. Prayer is not only open to all Muslims and normatively required, but it is also practiced widely in Kufr al-Ma.

The implications of high participation and high articulation in our Jordanian case go beyond ritual, however; they relate to interpretation as well. Both daily and congregational prayer, along with fasting, pilgrimage, and giving alms are the subjects of constant interpretation in the Quran, the Traditions of the Prophet, commentaries of the Quran, the weekly sermons of the preacher, and, more recently and frequently, in books written by lay Muslims. Hefner has hypothesized that the less articulate cultural media such as liturgical offerings or gestures, although they may evoke "powerful feelings or general attitudes," are imprecise semantically and, therefore, allow flexible interpretation of the liturgy by villagers in different historical periods in a way that would be precluded were the more articulate cultural media, that is, prayer, dominant.[60]

The Jordanian Muslim case is certainly one in which the more articu-

56. See Hefner, *Hindu Javanese*, 186.
57. Ibid.
58. Ibid.
59. Ibid., p. 156.
60. Ibid., p. 186.

late cultural media dominate, and yet the result is a greater degree of diversity of interpretation rather than a lesser degree as inferred by Hefner. Quranic commentaries provide quite diverse interpretations for the same passages, and Prophetic Traditions can be used to support minority points of view (as Khomeini's book, *Islamic Government* [*ḥukūmat-i islāmi*] indicates). In chapter 8 we clearly demonstrated in the analysis of sermons of four different preachers on the same subject on the same occasion the degree to which the Islamic sermon, as a more articulate cultural medium, allows for and facilitates considerable reinterpretation of tradition. Moreover, books by lay Muslims on women's rights, social justice, birth control, and tribal law espouse different points of view. As Kufr al-Ma becomes, with the growth of literacy and the advance of higher education in the 1980s, a more articulate, highly participant population, access to diverse interpretations becomes greater and not less. And as occupational differentiation and mobility proceed in tandem with the spread of higher education and increasing travel, more and more lay Muslims obtain copies of the Quran, collections of Prophetic Traditions, and manuals of Islamic law. Others have obtained formal religious training, either in Jordan or Saudi Arabia, though they return to pursue a variety of nonreligious occupations. Therefore, it would not be unusual to expect that the interpretations of now postfolk and postpeasants will not only vary from those of the religious specialist, the preacher, but also from one another. Given increasing opportunity for economic enterprise and higher education, high participant societies with highly articulated cultural media demonstrate the possibility of increasing flexibility of interpretation of ritual and belief, along with those at the other end of the continuum described by Hefner, a somewhat counterintuitive conclusion.

Even in the Tengger case in which insulation of the religious specialist from the generality of believers is maximized, Hefner recognizes the existence of two-way "seepage" or what I have referred to in chapter 1 as the two-way flow of ideas and interpenetration of traditions. That is, priestly liturgy does have some effect on public commentary in folklore and in myth. People do have glimmers of the meaning of priestly talk in terms of the existence of a pan-Javanese pantheon and, on the other hand, popular lay culture does have some impact on priestly liturgy as it attested to by the replacement of regional deities with the names of Adam and Allah in priestly prayers (in some villages). That is, the gradual Islamization of society has been, willy-nilly, recognized by some priests. If such seepage occurs at the end of the continuum represented by insulation of specialist from folk, how much more must such seepage occur at the other end of the continuum where such insulation does not exist. Indeed, at that end it is no longer seepage but a two-way flow and, sometimes, a confrontation, as indicated in chapter 1 by the example of the interpretation

of the funeral prayer in Kufr al-Ma by peasants, the village religious specialist, and the district judge.

Changes in intellectual technology have marked both Tengger Javanese
and rural Jordanian religious traditions. In the Tengger case since transmission of religious tradition was within the family from priest-father to
apprentice-son, the critical change involved the maintenance or loss of
literary skills between the generations.[61] Hefner discovered that in some
villages priests could both read and write the archaic script in which the
prayers were written. In others, priests could only read the script and had
to go to a rare writing specialist to replace the sacred text; in still other
villages priests could no longer read the archaic palm-leaf texts (since they
knew only the modern Javanese script and were taught religion by non-
priests in that script) and kept them only as sacred heirlooms to be dis-
played on the occasion of certain liturgies. Hefner found that the appren-
tice-priest, traditionally, learned the prayers only gradually, the full
corpus being mastered only in adulthood after marriage. Therefore, the
clash with popular understandings became apparent only very late in the
apprenticeship, and only after a mature sense of the complexity of priestly
religion and an appreciation of the fact "that the liturgy contains truths
too powerful for ordinary understanding."[62]

Hefner argues that it is the mode of cultural and social reproduction
(insulated, from father to son, in the intimate home atmosphere over a
long period of time) and the underlying attitudes inculcated in the process
of learning that are most responsible for the transmission and preservation of a religious tradition at odds with popular understandings rather
than any particular literate technology per se.[63]

In Kufr al-Ma the mode of cultural and social transmission has evolved
from a series of private or small-group teacher-student tutorial relationships within the village, usually in the home of the student or teacher in
the 1940s and 1950s; to classes in religion for students attending the secular primary school in the 1960s; supplemented in the 1970s and 1980s
by classes sponsored by voluntary private religious associations within
the village such as the Quranic school (dar-al-qur'an) which are held in
the mosque or in a room rented for the purpose and, in any case, fur-
nished with a modest library of religious books. At a higher level of learning, cultural transmission occurred on the basis of intimate dyadic oral
transmission between teacher and student, often by peripatetic teachers
in the student's home, as described for Shaykh Luqman in the 1940s and
1950s, to sporadic seminars for practicing village preachers staffed by

61. The critical nineteenth-century shift in intellectual technology in the Tengger case was
twofold: the shift in recording prayers from an archaic language to modern Javanese; and
the shift in the form of record from sacred palm-leaf sheafs to paper notebooks.

62. Hefner, *Hindu Javanese*, 209.

63. Ibid., 207, 256ff.

urban professors in the nearby market town in the 1970s, to formal classes, curriculum, and teaching staff at two-year preachers' colleges, controlled and financed by the central government and held in the capital of Amman in the 1980s; or, alternatively, formal classes, curriculum, teaching staff, and degrees at private two-year junior colleges in the market town (which is also the district capital); or, alternatively, formal classes, curriculum, teaching staff, and degrees from four-year religious universities in Saudi Arabia. What we have witnessed in Kufr al-Ma and in Jordan, generally, then, in the latter part of the twentieth century at both higher and lower levels of religious education is the extension of book knowledge into formal settings (institutes, universities, seminars, primary school classes, Quran schools) and the replacement of the old-time intimate, multiplex, dyadic, and privileged learning.

The underlying attitude to religious knowledge inculcated in the rural Jordanian Islamic case is twofold. On the one hand, the knowledge of the Quran is perfect and clear to all who seek understanding—which is possible because man is endowed with reason. On the other hand, the truths of the Quran are so deep as to be unfathomable by man. The first attitude allows Muslims of many ages, occupations, and degrees of learning to present themselves as missionaries and interpreters of Islamic beliefs, including shopkeepers, petty bureaucrats, truck drivers, high school students, cultivators, teachers in the secular school, as well as its custodian. The second attitude renders all interpretations tentative and open to reinterpretation just as one recitation of the Quran, even by a professional reciter and however beautiful and moving, is open to other and subsequent recitations that seek to capture its truth, emotionally and intellectually, in another fashion.

Perhaps the most significant contribution of Hefner's study of tradition in Java is its emphasis on the fact that, whatever the intellectual technology or the concatenation of symbols may be, interpretation of religious beliefs and rituals is always mediated by individual biography, personality, and social interests. On both the transmitter's side and the receiver's (audience's) side there are idiosyncratic factors bearing on the transmission of the liturgy and its interpretation. Hefner gives the example of the pan-literate (in old and new texts) father who transmitted a large (and not small) corpus of prayers, providing his son a unique (in the region) comparative analytic framework so that he could relate and synthesize the ideology and symbolism of the Balinese Hindu reform movement (a major religious movement in the outside world) to the insulated worship tradition of his own village. On the receiver's side Hefner discusses the priest (son) who didn't even read the texts his father had laboriously copied due to his dullness, lack of curiosity, and lethargy.[64]

64. Ibid., 207.

The analysis of the symbol of rahm (kinship/womb/compassion) in chapter 4 demonstrates the usefulness of analyzing a text (the sermon) independently as a concatenation of symbols, as rhetoric. But the contextualization of that particular symbolic arena within the local culture and social structure provided even more insight. There can be no question, furthermore, that the consideration of certain biographical facts relating to Luqman's position in the sibling order, family situation, kinship and class position, religious training, personality, and successive religious occupations, provided in chapter 3 the prerequisite knowledge and understanding by which to appreciate more fully certain themes in his sermons and to understand his idiosyncratic life history. In a patrioriented society it was not accidental that he took on his father and the village in a struggle to assert, simultaneously, his occupational and religious identity; or that he refused to become a preacher in another village; or that he often championed free expression; or that he sent his son to the religious university at Medina to receive higher education in religious studies before the current religious resurgence made it fashionable; or that near the end of his career he is demonstrating signs of becoming an entepreneur. To put it another way, all of the above was an accident of biography, social position, and individual inclination.

Bibliography

Abu-Lughod, Lila. *Veiled Sentiments: Honor and Poetry in a Bedouin Society*, University of California Press, Berkeley, 1986.

Ahmad, Mumtaz. "Islamic Revival in South Asia." In *Fundamentalism, Revivalism and Violence and South Asia*, James B. Jörkman, editor, Riverdale Press, Riverdale, Md., 1987.

Ajami, Fouad. "In the Pharaoh's Shadow: Religion and Authority in Egypt." In *Islam in the Political Process*, James Piscatori, editor, Syracuse University Press, Syracuse, 1983.

Akhavi, Shahrough. *Religion and Politics in Contemporary Iran: Clergy-State Relations in the Pahlavi Period*, State University of New York Press, Albany, 1980.

Algar, Hamid. *Religion and State in Iran, 1789–1906*, Mizan Press, Berkeley, 1969.

———, translator. *Constitution of the Islamic Republic of Iran*, Mizan Press, Berkeley, 1980.

Antoun, Richard T. "Social Organization and the Life Cycle in an Arab Village," *Ethnology*, Vol. 6, No. 3, July 1967: 294–308.

———. "The Social Significance of Ramadan in an Arab Village," *The Muslim World*, Vol. 58, January and April 1968a: 36–42, 95–104.

———. "On the Significance of Names in an Arab Village," *Ethnology*, Vol. 7, No. 2, April 1968b: 158–70.

———. "On the Modesty of Women in Arab Muslim Villages: A Study in the Accommodation of Traditions," *American Anthropologist*, Vol. 70, No. 4, August 1968c: 671–97.

———. *Arab Village: A Social Structural Study of a Transjordanian Peasant Community*, Indiana University Press, Bloomington, 1972.

———. "The Gentry of a Traditional Peasant Community Undergoing Rapid Technological Change: An Iranian Case Study," *Iranian Studies*, Vol. 9, No. 1, Winter 1976: 2–21.

———. *Low-Key Politics: Local-Level Leadership and Change in the Middle East*, State University of New York Press, Albany, 1979.

———. "The Islamic Court, the Islamic Judge and the Accommodation of Traditions: A Jordanian Case Study," *International Journal of Middle East Studies*, Vol. 12, No. 4, December 1980: 455–67.

———. "Key Variables Affecting Muslim Local-Level Religious Leadership in Iran and Jordan." In *Leadership and Development in the*

Arab World, Fuad Khuri, editor, American University of Beirut, Beirut, 1981: 92–101.

———. "The Complexity of the Lower Stratum: Sharecroppers and Wage Laborers in an Iranian Village," *Iranian Studies*, Vol. 14, Nos. 3–4, Summer–Autumn 1981: 215–46.

———. "The Impact of the Islamic Court on Peasant Families in Jordan." In *Law and Islam in the Middle East*, Daisy Dwyer, editor, Bergin & Garvey, Boston, in press.

Antoun, Richard T., and Mary E. Hegland, editors. *Religious Resurgence: Contemporary Cases in Islam, Christianity and Judaism*, Syracuse University Press, Syracuse, 1987.

Arberry, A. J. *The Koran Interpreted*, Macmillan, New York, 1974.

Ayoob, Mohammad, editor. *The Politics of Islamic Reassertion*, St. Martin's Press, New York, 1981.

Ayubi, Nazih. "The Political Revival of Islam: The Case of Egypt," *The International Journal of Middle East Studies*, Vol. 12, No. 4, December 1980: 481–99.

Baydawi, Nasr al-Din, al-. *tafsīr al-baydāwi (Al-Baydawi's Commentary)*, Cairo, n.d.

Bellah, Robert N. *Religion and Progress in Modern Asia*, Free Press, Glencoe, New York, 1965.

Bennett, John W. "Further Remarks on Foster's Image of the Limited Good," *American Anthropologist*, Vol. 68, No. 1, February 1966: 206–10.

———. "Microcosm-Macrocosm Relationships in North American Agrarian Society," *American Anthropologist*, Vol. 69, No. 5, October 1967: 441–54.

———. *Northern Plainsmen, Adaptive Strategy and Agrarian Life*, Aldine, Chicago, 1969.

Bharati, Agehananda. "Pilgrimage Sites and Indian Civilization." In *Indian Civilization*, J. W. Elder, editor, Vol. 1, Kendall-Hunt Publishers, Dubuque, 1967: 83–126.

———. *The Ochre Robe, An Autobiography*, Ross-Erikson, Santa Barbara, 1980.

———. "Theoretical Approaches to the Anthropology of Pilgrimage." In "Sacred Journeys: The Anthropology of Pilgrimage," E. Alan Morinis, editor, unpublished manuscript.

Binder, Leonard. "The Proofs of Islam: Religion and Politics in Iran." In *Arabic and Islamic Studies in Honor of Hamilton A. R. Gibb*, George Makdisi, editor, E. J. Brill, Leiden, 1965: 118–40.

Binghamton Evening Press, September 12, 1973, January 22, 1974.

Bloch, Maurice. "Introduction." In *Political Language and Oratory in*

Traditional Society, Maurice Bloch, editor, Academic Press, New York, 1975: 1–28.

Borthwick, Bruce M. "The Islamic Sermon as a Channel of Political Communication in Syria, Jordan and Egypt," Ph.D. diss., University of Michigan, 1965.

———. "Religion and Political Development in Israel and the Arab States." Paper delivered at the annual meeting of the Middle East Studies Association, Boston, 1974.

———. "Religion and Politics in Israel and Egypt," *The Middle East Journal*, Vol. 33, No. 2, Spring 1979: 145–63.

Bourdieu, Pierre. "Cultural Reproduction and Social Reproduction." In *Knowledge, Education and Cultural Change*, Richard Brown, editor, Tavistock Publications, London, 1973.

———. *Outline of a Theory of Practice*, Richard Nice, translator, Cambridge University Press, Cambridge, 1982.

Braswell, George Wilbur. "A Mosaic of Mullahs and Mosques: Religion and Politics in Iranian Shi 'ah Islam," Ph.D. diss., University of North Carolina, 1975.

Bujra, Abdullah. *The Politics of Stratification: A Study of Political Change in a South Arabian Town*, Oxford University Press, London, 1971.

Bulliet, Richard W. *The Patricians of Nishapur: A Study of Medieval Islamic Social History*, Harvard University Press, Cambridge, 1972.

Burke, Kenneth. *The Rhetoric of Religion: Studies in Logology*, Beacon Press, Boston, 1961.

Chicago Tribune, February 14, 1977.

Clark, David. *Between Pulpit and Pew: Folk Religion in a North Yorkshire Fishing Village*, Cambridge University Press, Cambridge, 1982.

Cohen, Abner. *Custom and Politics in Urban Africa*, University of California Press, Berkeley, 1969.

Coulson, N. J. *Succession in the Muslim Family*, Cambridge University Press, Cambridge, 1971.

Crapanzano, Vincent. *The Hamadsha: A Study in Moroccan Ethnopsychiatry*, University of California, Berkeley, 1973.

Crecelius, Daniel. "Nonideological Responses of the Egyptian Ulama to Modernization." In *Scholars, Saints and Sufis*, Nikki Keddie, editor, University of California Press, Berkeley, 1972: 167–210.

Daniel, Norman. *Islam and the West*, University of Edinburgh, Edinburgh, 1960.

Danner, Victor. "Religious Revivalism in Islam: Past and Present." In *Islam in the Contemporary World*, Cyriac K. Pullapilly, editor, Crossroads Books, South Bend, 1980: 21–43.

Davis, Eric. "Religion Against the State: A Political Economy of Religious Radicalism in Egypt and Israel." In *Religious Resurgence: Contemporary Cases in Islam, Christianity and Judaism*, Richard T. Antoun and Mary E. Hegland, editors, Syracuse University Press, Syracuse, 1987: 145–68.

Dekmejian, Richard H. "The Anatomy of Islamic Revival: Legitimacy Crisis, Ethnic Conflict and the Search for Islamic Alternatives," *The Middle East Journal*, Vol. 34, No. 1, Winter 1980: 1–12.

Delaney, Carol. "The Hac: Sacred and Secular." Paper delivered at the annual meeting of the Middle East Studies Association, Boston, Massachusetts, November 1986.

Deshen, Shlomo, and Shokeid Moshe. *The Predicament of Homecoming*, Cornell University Press, Ithaca, 1974.

Deutsch, Karl. "Social Mobilization and Political Development," *American Political Science Review*, Vol. 55, September 1961: 493–514.

Dozier, Edward P. "Rio Grande Pueblos." In *Perspectives in American Indian Culture Change*, Edward H. Spicer, editor, University of Chicago Press, Chicago, 1961: 94–186.

Durkheim, Emile. *The Elementary Forms of the Religious Life*, J. W. Swain, translator, Free Press, Glencoe; Allen & Unwin, London, 1926.

Eickelman, Dale F. *Moroccan Islam: Tradition and Society in a Pilgrimage Center*, University of Texas Press, Austin, 1976.

———."The Art of Memory: Islamic Education and Its Social Reproduction," *Comparative Studies in Society and History*, Vol. 20, No. 4, 1978: 485–516.

———. *The Middle East: An Anthropological Approach*, Prentice-Hall, Englewood Cliffs, 1981.

———. *Knowledge and Power in Morocco: The Education of a Twentieth-Century Notable*, Princeton University Press, Princeton, 1985.

El Guindi, Fadwa. "Veiling Infitah with Muslim Ethic: Egypt's Contemporary Islamic Movement," *Social Problems*, Vol. 28, February 1981: 465–85.

El-Zein, Abdul Hamid. "Beyond Ideology and Theology: The Search for the Anthropology of Islam," *Annual Review of Anthroplogy*, Vol. 6, 1977: 227–54.

Fernandez, James. "The Mission of Metaphor in Expressive Culture," *Current Anthropology* Vol. 15, No. 2, June 1974: 119–45.

Firth, Raymond. "Problem and Assumption in an Anthropological Study of Religion." In *Essays on Social Organization and Values*, Athlone Press, London, 1964: 225–56.

Fischer, Michael. *Iran: From Religious Dispute to Revolution*, Harvard University Press, Cambridge, 1980

———. "Islam and the Revolt of the Petit Bourgeoise," *Daedalus*, Vol. 3, No. 1, Winter 1982: 101–25.

Fortes, Meyer. *The Web of Kinship Among the Tallensi*, Oxford University Press, London, 1949.

Freund, Andreas. *The New York Times*, May 27, 1979.

Friedl, Ernestine. "Lagging Emulation in a Post-Peasant Society," *American Anthropologist*, Vol. 66, No. 3, June 1964: 569–86.

Gaffney, Patrick D. "The Local Preacher and the Islamic Resurgence in Upper Egypt: An Anthropological Perspective." In *Religious Resurgence: Contemporary Cases in Islam, Christianity and Judaism*, Richard T. Antoun and Mary E. Hegland, editors, Syracuse University Press, Syracuse, 1987: 35–63.

Geertz, Clifford. "Ethos, World-View and the Analysis of Sacred Symbols," *Antioch Review*, Vol. 17, No. 4, December 1957.

———. " 'Internal Conversion' in Contemporary Bali," mimeographed, 1961.

———. "Religion as a Cultural System." In *Anthropological Approaches to the Study of Religion*, Michael Banton, editor, Tavistock, London, 1966: 1–46.

———. *Islam Observed*, Yale University Press, New Haven, 1968.

———. *The Interpretation of Cultures*, Basic Books, New York, 1973.

———. *Local Knowledge: Further Essays in Interpretive Anthropology*, Basic Books, New York, 1983.

———. "Distinguished Lecture: Anti-Relativism," *American Anthropologist*, Vol. 86, No. 2, June 1984: 263–78.

Gellner, Earnest. *Saints of the Atlas*, University of Chicago Press, Chicago, 1969.

Genovese, Eugene D. *Roll, Jordan, Roll: The World the Slaves Made*, Vintage Books, New York, 1976.

Gerlach, Luther P., and Virginia H. Hine. *People, Power and Change: Movements of Social Transformation*, Bobbs-Merrill, Indianapolis, 1970.

Ghaiti, Imam Najd al-din, al-. *al-miʿrāj-al-kabīr*, excerpt translated by Arthur Jeffrey and appearing in his *Reader in Islam*, 621–39, Mouton, New York, 1962.

Ghani, Ashraf. "Islam and State-Building in a Tribal Society in Afghanistan: 1800–1901," *Modern Asian Studies*, 1978: 269–84.

———. "Order and Conflict: Consolidation of Power Through Law, Afghanistan, 1880–1901," mimeographed, n.d.

Gibb, Hamilton A. R. *Modern Trends in Islam*, University of Chicago Press, Chicago, 1947.

Gibb, Hamilton A. R. Review of "The Meeting of East and West: An Inquiry Concerning World Understanding" by F. S. Northrop, *The Middle East Journal*, Vol. 1, No. 3, July 1947.

———. Lectures in Islamic Institutions, Harvard University, autumn, 1957.

Gibb, H.A.R., and Harold Bowen. *Islamic Society and the West*, vol. 1, parts 1 and 2, Oxford University Press, London, 1950, 1957.

Gibb, H.A.R., and J. H. Kramers. *Shorter Encyclopedia of Islam*, Cornell University Press, Ithaca, 1953.

Gilsenan, Michael. *Saint and Sufi in Modern Egypt: An Essay in the Sociology of Religion*, Oxford University Press, London, 1973.

———. *Recognizing Islam*, Pantheon Books, New York, 1982.

Gluckman, Max. *The Judicial Process Among the Barotse of Northern Rhodesia*, Manchester University Press, Manchester, 1955.

Goldziher, Ignace. Article, *fikh*. In *Shorter Encyclopaedia of Islam*, Vintage Books, New York, 1976: 102–7.

Goody, Jack, editor. *Literacy in Traditional Societies*, Cambridge University Press, Cambridge, 1968.

———. *The Domestication of the Savage Mind*, Cambridge University Press, Cambridge, 1977.

Goitein, S. D. "The Origin and Nature of the Muslim Friday Worship." In *Studies in Islamic History and Institutions*, S. D. Goitein, editor, E. J. Brill, Leiden, 1968: 111–25.

Grabar, Oleg. "The Architecture of the Middle Eastern City." In *Middle Eastern Cities*, Ira M. Lapidus, editor, University of California Press, Berkeley, 1969: 26–46.

Graham, William A. "*Qur'an* as Spoken Word: An Islamic Contribution to the Understanding of Scripture." In *Approaches to Islam in Religious Studies*, Richard C. Martin, editor, University of Arizona Press, Tucson, 1985: 23–40.

Grannot, A. *The Land System in Palestine: History and Structure*, Eyre & Spottiswoode, London, 1952.

Grimes, Ronald L. *Symbol and Conquest: Public Ritual and Drama in Santa Fe, New Mexico*, Cornell University Press, Ithaca, 1976.

Gulick, John. *Social Structure and Culture in a Lebanese Village*, Wenner-Gren Foundation, New York, 1955.

Hardy, M.J.L. *Blood Feuds and the Payment of Blood Money in the Middle East*, Beirut, 1963.

Hava, J. G. *Arabic-English Dictionary*, Catholic Press, Beirut, 1951.

Hedayat, Sadeq. *Haji Agha*, G. M. Wickens, translator, University of Texas Press, Austin, 1979.

Hefner, Robert. *Hindu Javanese: Tengger Tradition and Islam*, Princeton University Press, Princeton, 1985

Hegland, Mary E. "Two Images of Husain: Accommodation and Revolution in an Iranian Village." In *Religion and Politics in Iran*, Nikki Keddie, editor, Yale University Press, New Haven, 1982.

——. "Ritual and Revolution in Iran." In *Political Anthropology*, Vol. 2, *Culture and Political Change*, Myron Aronoff, editor, Transaction Books, New York, 1983.

——. "Imam Khomaini's Village: Recruitment to Revolution," Ph.D. diss., State University of New York at Binghamton, 1986.

——. "Islamic Revival or Political and Cultural Revolution? An Iranian Case Study." In *Religious Resurgence: Contemporary Cases in Islam, Christianity and Judaism*, Richard T. Antoun and Mary E. Hegland, editors, Syracuse University Press, Syracuse, 1987: 194–222.

Hodgson, Marshall, G. S. *The Venture of Islam: Conscience and History in a World Civilization*, Vol. 1, University of Chicago Press, Chicago, 1974.

Homans, George C. *The Human Group*, New York, Harcourt, Brace & Co., 1950.

Honigman, John J. *Culture and Personality*, Harper & Brothers, New York, 1954.

Hudson, Michael D. *Arab Politics: The Search for Legitimacy*, Yale University Press, New Haven, 1977.

Humphreys, Stephen. "Islam and Political Values in Saudi Arabia, Egypt, and Syria," *The Middle East Journal*, Vol. 33, No. 1, Winter 1979: 1–29.

Hurgronje, C. Snouck. *Mekka in the Latter Part of the 19th Century*, E. J. Brill, Leiden, 1970.

Hussein, Taha. *The Stream of Days*, Hilary Wayment, translator, Longmans, Green, London, 1948.

Ibn Ishaq. *Sirat Rasul Allah (The Life of Muhammad)*, Alfred Gillaume, translator, Oxford University Press, Lahore, 1967.

Itzkowitz, Norman. *Ottoman Empire and Islamic Tradition*, Alfred A. Knopf, New York, 1972.

Izutsu, Toshihiko. *Ethico-Religious Concepts in the Quran*, McGill University Press, Montreal, 1966.

Jansen, G. H. *Militant Islam*, Harper & Row, New York, 1979.

Keddie, Nikki. "Iran: Change in Islam: Islam and Change," *International Journal of Middle East Studies*, Vol. 11, No. 4, July 4, 1980: 527–42.

Kedouri, E. Article, *hizb*. In *The Encyclopaedia of Islam*, rev. ed., Vol. 3, Leiden, E. J. Brill, 1967: 513–26.

Kee, Howard C., and W. Franklin Young, *Understanding the New Testament*, Prentice-Hall, Englewood Cliffs, 1959.

Kepel, Gilles. *Muslim Extremism in Egypt The Prophet and the Pharaoh*, University of California Press, Berkeley, 1986.

Khalid, Detlev. "Islam and the Future of Civilization." In *Islam and Civilization*, Mourad Wahba, editor, Ain al-Shams University Press, Cairo, 1982: 127–60.

Khuri, Fuad I. "Work in Islamic Thought," *Al-Abhath*, Vol. 21, December 1968: 3–13.

———. *Imāmat al-shahīd wa imāmat al-baṭl TanTHīm al-dīnī lada al ṭawā'if wa al-aqiliyāt fi al-ʿālim al-ʿarabī* (The Leadership of the Martyr and the Leadership of the Hero: The Religious Organization of Sects and Minorities in the Arab World), University Publishing House, Jounieh, Lebanon, 1988.

Khuṭab al-jum' a wal 'īdayn (Friday Sermons and Sermons for the Two Festivals), Cairo, 1974.

Lapidus, Ira M. *Contemporary Islamic Movements in Historical Perspective*. University of California Press, Berkeley, 1983.

Lawrence, Bruce B. "Muslim Fundamentalist Movements: Reflections Toward a New Approach." In *The Islamic Impulse*, Barbara Stowasser, editor, Croom Helm, London, 1987.

Levy, Marion J. *Modernization and the Structure of Societies: A Setting for International Affairs*, Princeton University Press, Princeton, 1966.

Linton, Ralph. *The Study of Man*, Appleton-Century, New York, 1936.

Loeffler, Reinhold. *Islam in Practice: Religious Beliefs in a Persian Village*, State University of New York Press, Albany, 1987.

Long, David E. *The Hajj Today: A Survey of the Contemporary Pilgrimage to Mekkah*, State University of New York Press, Albany, 1979.

Louisville Courier Journal, September 28, 1969, December 3, 1969, December 6, 1969, December 9, 1969.

Madi, Munib, and Sulayman Musa. *tārīkh al-irdun fi al-qarn al-'ashrīn* (*The History of Jordan in the Twentieth Century*) Ammam, 1959.

Makdise, George. *The Rise of Colleges: Institutions of Learning in Islam and the West*, Edinburgh University Press, Edinburgh, 1981.

———. "The Guilds of Law in Medieval Legal History: An Inquiry into the Origins of the Inns of Court," *Cleveland State Law Review*, Vol. 34, No. 1, 1985–86: 3–18.

Malcolm X. *The Autobiography of Malcolm X*, Grove Press, New York, 1964.

Marriott, McKim. "Little Communities in an Indigenous Civilization." In *Village India Studies in the Little Community*, McKim Marriott, editor, University of Chicago Press, Chicago, 1955: 171–222.

Mawdudi, Sayyid Abul A'la. *Let Us Be Muslims*, Khurram Murad, editor, Islamic Foundation, Leicester, 1985.

May, Henry F. *Ideas, Faiths and Feelings: Essays in American Intellectual and Religious History*, Oxford University Press, Oxford, 1983.

Meijers, Daniel. " 'Civil Religion' or 'Civil War'? Religion in Israel." In *Religion, Power and Protest in Local Communities*, Eric Wolf, editor, Mouton, Amsterdam, 1979: 137–62.

Mitchell, Henry M. *Black Preaching*, J. B. Lippincott, New York, 1970.

Moore, Wilbert E. *Social Change*, Prentice-Hall, Englewood Cliffs, 1963.

Mottahedeh, Roy. *The Mantle of the Prophet*, Simon & Schuster, New York, 1985.

Munson, Henry, Jr. *The House of Si Abd Allah: The Oral History of a Moroccan Family*, Yale University Press, New Haven, 1984.

———. *Islam and Revolution in the Middle East*, Yale University Press, New Haven, 1987.

Murra, John V., editor. *American Anthropology: The Early Years*, West Publishing Company, St. Paul, 1976.

Nash, Manning. "Industrialization: The Ecumenical and Parochial Aspects of the Process." In *Social Science and the New Societies*, Nancy Hammond, editor, Michigan State University Press, Lansing, 1973: 131–45.

———. "Modernization: Cultural Meanings—The Widening Gap Between the Intellectuals and the Process," *Economic Development and Cultural Change*, Vol. 25, Supplement 1977.

Nelson, Kristina. *The Art of Reciting the Qur'an*, University of Texas Press, Austin, 1985.

Ochsenwald, William. "Saudi Arabia and the Islamic Revival," *International Journal of Middle East Studies*, Vol. 13, No. 3, August 1981: 271–86.

Ortner, Sherry. "On Key Symbols," *American Anthropologist*, Vol. 75, No. 5, October 1973: 1338–1346.

Padwick, Constance E. *Muslim Devotions: A Study of Prayer Manuals in Common Use*, S.P.C.K., London, 1961.

Paine, Robert. "Israel and Totemic Time," *Royal Anthropological Institute Newsletter*, 1984.

Parkin, David. "The Rhetoric of Responsibility: Bureaucratic Communications in a Kenya Farming Area." In *Political Language and Oratory in Traditional Society*, Maurice Bloch, editor, Academic Press, New York, 1975: 113–40.

Peacock, James. *Rites of Modernization: Symbolic and Social Aspects of Indonesian Proletarian Drama*, University of Chicago Press, Chicago, 1968.

Peake, Frederick G. *The History of East Jordan*, Jerusalem, 1935.

Peake, Frederick G. *A History of Jordan and its Tribes*, University of Miami Press, Coral Gables, Fla., 1958.

Pedersen, Johannes. "The Islamic Preacher *wāiz, mudhakkir, qāss*," *Ignace Goldziher Memorial Volume*, Part 1, Budapest, 1948.

———. "The Criticism of the Islamic Preacher," *Die Welt des Islams*, Vol. 2, 1949–1950: 215–23.

———. Article, *masdjid*. In *Shorter Encyclopaedia of Islam*, 330–53, Cornell University Press, Ithaca, 1953.

———. Article, *khaṭīb*. In *The Encyclopaedia of Islam*, rev. ed., Vol. 4, E. J. Brill, Leiden, 1978: 1109–1111.

Pickthall, Mohammed M. *The Meaning of the Glorious Koran*, Mentor Books, New York, 1959.

Pipes, Daniel. "Islam in Iraq's Public Life." In *Islam in the Contemporary World*, Cyriac K. Pullapilly, editor, Crossroads Books, Notre Dame, Indiana, 1980: 306–15.

Qur'an Karīm, Mashaykhat al-Azhar, Cairo, 1926.

Radcliffe-Brown, Alfred R. *The Andaman Islanders*, Cambridge University Press, Cambridge, 1922.

Rahman, Fazlur. *Islam*, Doubleday, New York, 1966.

———. "Islamic Modernism: Its Scope, Method and Alternatives," *International Journal of Middle East Studies*, Vol. 1, No. 4, October 1970: 317–33

———. "Pre-Foundations of the Muslim Community in Mecca," *Studia Islamica*, June 1976: 1–24.

———. *Major Themes of the Quran*, Bibliotheca Islamica, Chicago, 1980.

———. "A Survey of Modernization of Muslim Family Law," *International Journal of Middle East Studies*, Vol. 11, No. 4, July 1980: 451–65.

———. "Roots of Islamic Neo-Fundamentalism." In *Change in the Muslim World*, P. H. Stoddard, editor, Syracuse University Press, Syracuse, 1981.

Redfield, Robert. *The Folk Culture of Yucatan*, University of Chicago Press, Chicago, 1941.

———. *The Primitive World and Its Transformations*, Cornell University Press, Ithaca, 1953.

———. *The Little Community Viewpoints for the Study of a Human Whole*, University of Chicago Press, Chicago, 1955.

———. *Peasant Society and Culture*, University of Chicago Press, Chicago, 1956.

Redfield, Robert, and Milton Singer. "The Cultural Role of Cities," *Economic Development and Cultural Change*, Vol. 3, October 1954: 53–73.

Rodwell, J. M. *The Koran*, E. P. Dutton, New York, 1957.

Roff, William. "Pilgrimage in the History of Religions: Theoretical Approaches to Hajj." In *Approaches to Islam in Religious Studies*, Richard C. Martin, editor, University of Arizona Press, Tucson, 1985: 78–86.

Rosenberg, Bruce A. *The Art of the American Folk Preacher*, Oxford University Press, New York, 1970.

Said, Edward W. *Orientalism*, Vintage Books, New York, 1979.

Sale, George. *The Koran*, Frederick Warne, London, 1888.

Sax, W. "The Ram Naga Ram Lila: A Theatre of Pilgrimage," unpublished mimeograph, 1981.

Schacht, J. Article, *fikh*. In *The Encyclopaedia of Islam*, rev. ed., Vol. 2, 886–91, Luzac & Co., London, 1965.

Sermon on Work, Kufr al-Ma, January 15, 1960.

Sermon on Palestine, Kufr al-Ma, January 22, 1960

Sermon on Pilgrimage, Kufr al-Ma, April 15, 1960

Sermon on Education, Kufr al-Ma, April 22, 1960.

Sermon on Pilgrimage, Kufr al-Ma, Jordan, April 29, 1960.

Sermon on Justice, Kufr al-Ma, Jordan, July 8, 1960.

Sermon on Magic, Kufr al-Ma, April 23, 1965.

Sermon on Reconciliation, Kufr al-Ma, Jordan, August 19, 1966.

Sermon on rahm (Kinship, Womb, Compassion), Kufr al-Ma, September 2, 1966.

Sermon Radio Broadcast, Amman, July 8, 1977.

Sermon Radio Broadcast, Jerusalem, July 8, 1977

Sermon Radio Broadcast, Acre, July 15, 1977

Sermon Radio Broadcast, Amman, July 15, 1977

Shariati, Ali. *On the Sociology of Islam*, Hamid Algar, translator, Mizan Press, Berkeley, 1979.

———. *Marxism and Other Western Fallacies, An Islamic Critique*, R. Campbell, translator, Mizan Press, Berkeley, 1980.

———. *Hajj*, Ala A. Behzadnia and Najla Denny, translators, Free Islamic Literatures, Houston, 1980.

Shepard, William E. "Islam and Ideology: Towards a Typology," *International Journal of Middle East Studies*, Vol. 19, No. 3, August 1987: 307–36.

Shweder, Richard A., and Edmund J. Bourne. "Does the Concept of the Person Vary Cross-Culturally?" In *Cultural Conceptions of Mental Health and Therapy*, Anthony J. Marsella and Gregory M. White, editors, D. Reidel, Boston, 1982: 97–137.

Singer, Milton. *When a Great Tradition Modernizes: An Anthropological Approach to Indian Civilization*. Praeger, New York, 1972.

———. "Robert Redfield's Development of a Social Anthropology of

Civilizations." In *American Anthropology, The Early Years,* John V. Murra, editor, West Publishing, Boston, 1976: 187–260.

Smelser, N. E. "Essays in Sociological Explanation." In *Industrialization and Society,* W. E. Moore and B. F. Hoselitz, editors, UNESCO, Paris, 1963.

Smith, Donald Eugene. *Religion and Political Development,* Little, Brown, Boston, 1970.

Smith, Wilfred Cantwell. *Islam in Modern History,* Princeton University Press, Princeton, 1957.

———. "The True Meaning of Scripture: An Empirical Historian's Non-reductionist Interpretation of the Quran," *International Journal of Middle East Studies,* Vol. 11, No. 4, July 1980: 487–505.

Smith, William R. *Kinship and Marriage in Early Arabia,* Beacon Press, Boston, 1962.

Spicer, Edward. "Spanish-Indian Acculturation in the Southwest," *American Anthropologist,* Vol. 56, 1954: 663–84.

Srinivas, M. N. *Religion and Society Among the Coorgs of South India,* Clarendon Press, Oxford, 1952.

Swartz, Merlin L., translator. *Ibn al-Jawzi's Kitāb al-Quṣṣāṣ wa'l-Mudhakkirīn,* Dar el-Mashreq, Beirut, 1971.

Teilhet-Waldorf, Saral. "A Clutch of English Clergy, A Study of Religious Leaders in a London Suburb," unpublished manuscript, n.d.

The Encyclopaedia of Islam, rev. ed., Vol. 4, Leiden, E. J. Brill, 1978.

The Evening Press, November 8, 1984.

The New York Times, May 5, 1974, October 14, 1974, August 28, 1976, November 15, 1976, May 27, 1979, December 30, 1979, March 22, 1980, April 28, 1981, June 8, 1981, June 9, 1981, June 16, 1981, June 22, 1981, November 20, 1983, March 4, 1984, July 3, 1984, August 18, 1984, September 8, 1984, September 13, 1984.

The Proceedings of the Conference on Middle East Agricultural Development, Agricultural Report No. 6, Middle East Supply Center, Cairo, 1944.

Turner, Victor. *Chihamba the White Spirit: A Ritual Drama of the Ndembu,* Manchester University Press, Manchester, 1962.

———. "Three Symbols of Passage in Ndembu Circumcision Ritual." In *Essays on the Ritual of Social Relations,* Max Gluckman, editor, Manchester University Press, Manchester, 1962: 124–74.

———. *The Forest of Symbols,* Cornell University Press, Ithaca, 1967.

———. *The Ritual Process: Structure and Anti-Structure,* Cornell University Press, Ithaca, 1969.

———. "The Center Out There: Pilgrim's Goal," *History of Religions,* Vol. 12, 1973: 191–230.

Voll, John. "Hadith Scholars and Tariqas: An Ulama Group in the 18th

Century Haramayn and Their Impact in the Islamic World," *Journal of Asian and African Studies*, Vol. 15, Nos. 3–4, July–October 1980: 264–72.

———. "Islamic Renewal and the Failure of the West." In *Religious Resurgence: Contemporary Cases in Islam, Christianity and Judaism*, Richard T. Antoun and Mary E. Hegland, editors, Syracuse University Press, Syracuse, 1987.

von der Mehden, Fred. *Religion and Modernization in Southeast Asia*, Syracuse University Press, Syracuse, 1986.

Weber, Max. *The Theory of Social and Economic Organization*, Talcott Parsons, editor, and A. M. Henderson and Talcott Parsons, translators, Glencoe, Ill., Free Press, 1947.

Wehr, Hans. *A Dictionary of Modern Written Arabic*, J. M. Cowan, translator, Cornell University Press, Ithaca, 1961.

Wenner, Manfred W. "The Arabian Peninsula and the Islamic 'Revival'." In *Islam in the Contemporary World*, Cyriac K. Pullapilly, editor, Crossroads Books, South Bend, 1980: 143–57.

Wensinck, A. J. Article, *khuṭba*. In *The Encyclopaedia of Islam*, rev. ed., Vol. 5, E. J. Brill, Leiden, 74–75.

Weulersse, Jacque. *Paysans de Syrie et du Proche-Orient*, Gallimard, Paris, 1946.

Whymany, Robert. *Binghamton Evening Press*, January 22, 1974.

Wright, Robin. *Sacred Rage: The Wrath of Militant Islam*, Simon & Schuster, New York, 1986.

Yusuf, Ahmed B. "A Preliminary Survey of the Islamic Hadj: Its Overall Meaning and Sociological Implications with Reference to Africa," mimeographed, n.d.

Yusuf Ali, Abdullah, translator and commentator. *The Glorious Kur'an*, Call of Islam Society, Libyan Arab Republic, 1973.

Index

Abdur Rahman, Amir, 189, 212; and Islamization, 241
Abraham (Ibrahim), 115, 172, 222–24; and Ka'bah, 177–78, 181, 230; as rebel, 216–17
Abu Hurayra, 108
Abu-Lughod, Lila, 8
Ahmed, Mumtaz, 251
Ajami, Fouad, 213
Amish, 18–20, 23
Audience, sermon's: and classical Arabic, 9, 103, 115–16; the impact of, 101–5, 257–67; and occupational differentiation, 103; and sermon's meaning, 103
Avicenna, 258
Ayoob, Mohammed, 235, 245
Ayubi, Nazih, 235

Banna, Hasan al-, 237
Baydawi, Nasr al-Din al, 99, 193
Bellah, Robert, 134
Bennett, John, 15, 40
Bharati, Agehananda, 163, 166
Binder, Leonard, 254
Bloch, Maurice, 10, 106, 115–17, 125; and argument about formalized speech, 230–32
Borthwick, Bruce, 10, 127–28, 196, 207–8, 244, 256
Bourdieu, Pierre, 8, 257
Braswell, George, 212
Bujra, Abdullah, 42
Bukhari, al-, 24, 95–96, 99
Bulliet, Richard, 98
bureaucrats: and bureaucratization, 187, 189, 241–42; co-optation of, 186, 213–15; dress of, 39, 121; office as symbolic arena for, 106, 120–22; views of, 196–97, 199–202
Burke, Kenneth, 106

capitalism, 199–201
change: administrative, 53–54; economic, 45–54, 85, 123, 141, 189; educational,

103; and elections, 104–5; in intellectual technology, 257, 266; in international migration, 141; of land tenure, 48–49; in mode of cultural transmission, 261–62, 266–67; occupational, 45, 50–54, 85, 103, 189; of pilgrimage incidence, 168; in population, 50, 85; in religious norms, 126; social, 45, 123; and tribalism, 104–5; in village religious institutions, 85–86, 168
Christianity, 10, 17, 35, 38, 192, 195, 237, 252; in England, 65; and historical image of Islam, 246; in Latin American, 26, 187; and proof-text for political obedience, 254; among slave preachers, 216; and the two-swords doctrine, 227; in the U.S. armed forces, 65–66
Cohen, Abner, 34, 186
colonialism, 94, 104, 131, 188, 196, 204, 210, 228, 237–38, 245, 261
communism, 197, 199, 201, 204; and communists, 160; and Islam, 201–2
compartmentalization, process of: 5, 31, 33–35, 121, 125
compassion, xiv, 74, 87, 106–25, 159, 224. See also *rahm*
courts: civil, 33, 39, 54, 188; in Jordan, 34, 63, 138; and judges, 26, 34, 36–37, 83, 96, 188–89, 205–6, 210, 240; religious, 26, 33–34, 37, 54, 62–63, 69, 79, 83, 123–24, 205–6; supreme, 183–84
Crapanzano, Vincent, 4, 42
Crecelius, Daniel, 212, 241
culture: articulation of, 257; brokers, 4, 9, 11, 13, 15–17, 19, 22–23, 26–31, 44, 65–66, 202, 257, 264; core elements of, 35; Islamic, 99; its mode of reproduction, 257, 260–62, 266; political, 188, 190, 196; structure of, 15; transvaluation of, 188, 190, 212
Cuomo, Mario, 184

Daniel, Norman, 246
Danner, Victor, 245

283